Hebrew and the
Bible in America

BRANDEIS SERIES IN AMERICAN JEWISH HISTORY, CULTURE, AND LIFE   *Jonathan D. Sarna, Editor*

Leon A. Jick, 1992
The Americanization of the Synagogue, 1820–1870

Sylvia Barack Fishman, editor, 1992
Follow My Footprints: Changing Images of Women in American Jewish Fiction

Gerald Tulchinsky, 1993
Taking Root: The Origins of the Canadian Jewish Community

Shalom Goldman, editor, 1993
Hebrew and the Bible in America: The First Two Centuries

Marshall Sklare, 1993
Observing America's Jews

Shalom Goldman, Editor

HEBREW and the Bible in America

The First Two Centuries

Brandeis University Press and Dartmouth College

Published by University Press of New England

Hanover and London

Brandeis University Press and Dartmouth College
Published by University Press of New England, Hanover, NH 03755
© 1993 by Trustees of Brandeis University and
Trustees of Dartmouth College
Printed in the United States of America   5 4 3 2 1
CIP data appear at the end of the book

The research and writing of this book were supported by the American Jewish
Archives, the William Barnet II 1934 Fund, the National Endowment for the
Humanities, the Nelson A. Rockefeller Center for the Social Sciences at
Dartmouth College, and the Touro National Heritage Trust.

To Deborah Erdman of UCLA and Gail Vernazza of Dartmouth College many thanks
for their long-term encouragement and assistance. To my colleagues Kevin Reinhart
and Alan Tansman of Dartmouth, and to Thomas Siegel of Harvard, many thanks for
support both intellectual and social. And to Jeanne West of University Press of New
England I owe a debt of gratitude for being there at the beginning and seeing it
through to the end.

Acknowledgments for previous publication:
"Ezra Stiles and the Jews: A Study in Ambivalence" by Arthur A. Chiel in *A Bicentennial
Festschrift for Jacob Rader Marcus*, edited by B. W. Korn. American Jewish Historical Society,
Waltham, Mass., 1976. Reprinted with permission.

"Biblical Hebrew in Colonial America" by Shalom Goldman in *American Jewish History* 79:2
(Winter 1989–90). Reprinted with permission.

"The New England Puritans and the Jews" by Arthur Hertzberg in *Israel and the Nations: Essays Presented in Honor of Shmuel Ettinger*. The Historical Society of Israel and the Zalman
Shazar Center for Jewish History, Jerusalem, 1987. Reprinted with permission.

"The Rise and Fall of the Jewish Indian Theory" by Richard H. Popkin in *Menasseh Ben Israel
and His World*, edited by Yosef Kaplan, Henry Mechoulan, and Richard H. Popkin. Brill's Studies
in Intellectual History, copyright 1989 by E. J. Brill, The Netherlands. Reprinted with permission.

For Liora and Daniel

Contents

Isa. 32. 5

א לֹא־יִקָּרֵא עוֹד לְנָבָל נָדִיב וּלְכִילַי

לֹא יֹאמֶר שׁוֹעַ

a nigardly-foole shall no more be called
liberall, nor the Churle said to be boun-
tifull.

לֹא ־יֵאָמֵר לָךְ עוֹד עֲזוּבָה וּלְאַרְצֵךְ

לֹא ־יֵאָמֵר שְׁמָמָה כִּי לָךְ יִקָּרֵא חֶפְצִי

בָהּ וּלְאַרְצֵךְ בְּעוּלָה

Isa: 62. 4

It shall no more be said vnto the for
saken; neither shall it be said any more
to thy land desolate; but thou shall be
caled Hephzi-bah, and thy Land Beulah

וְיִשְׁתַּחֲווּ לוֹ לַעֲבוּרָת כֶּסֶף וְכִכַּר לָחֶם

shall bow-downe to him, for a peece of
siluer, and a morsel of bread. 1. sam

וְהָיָה לְרֹאשׁ וְאַתָּה תִּהְיֶה לְזָנָב

He shall be the head, & thou shall be ye t

A page from the exercise book of Governor William Bradford of the Massachusetts Bay Colony (1652). Reproduced from Isidore S. Meyer, The Hebrew Exercises of Governor William Bradford *(Plymouth, Mass., 1973).*

Introduction

A romance with the Hebrew language runs through the fabric of American religious and cultural life. It began with the Pilgrims and the founders of Harvard College, and it deeply influenced the founders of other of this nation's educational institutions. American notions about Hebrew affected the growth and development of indigenous American religious forms: the study of Hebrew and its influence as a language of study, prayer, and scholarly discourse played a pivotal role in the development of American Jewish life. As the Republic grew and America entered its second century, Hebraism helped to shape American ideas about the Holy Land, ideas that would profoundly affect the American relationship to the Middle East, and, in the mid-twentieth century, would influence American thinking about the State of Israel.

This book is an exploration of early American Hebraism: the study of the Hebrew language and the classical Hebrew texts by American scholars of the seventeenth and eighteenth centuries. More precisely, the beginning of these "first two centuries" may be dated to 1638, when instruction in Hebrew and other subjects began at Harvard. Eighteen thirty-eight offers us an elegant closing date, for it was then that Isaac Nordheimer, the first Jewish scholar of Hebrew to teach at an American university, was appointed "instructor in sacred literature" at Union Theological Seminary. The contributors to this volume are from a number of disciplines (including history, religion, the classics, and literary criticism) and their essays constitute a significant first step in the exploration of a topic that has long been neglected in the scholarly literature.

Colonial Hebraism had an impact on American life in the early years of the republic. Thus the historical reach of this introduction to *Hebrew and the Bible in America* extends beyond the colonial era into the period of America's great growth before the Civil War. Throughout this time "Hebraic knowledge" appealed to American elites, and the roster of American Protestant Hebraists includes prominent scholars, political figures, and diplomats.

The contributions to this volume indicate that an interest in the Hebrew language runs through the fabric of American cultural and religious life. In examining the American romance with Hebrew, we must look to its European background. Both American Hebraism and its European antecedents are in need of revaluation. As Frank Manuel noted recently: "'The third culture,' the Hebrew, which alongside the Greek and the Latin was once an ornament of the trilingual gentleman-scholar, deserves a more prominent place in the history of Western thought than has been accorded it."[1] In both Europe and America, Christian Hebraism was an attempt to claim the heritage of Israel for Christianity. Other American claims on that heritage were to follow.

America and European Christian Hebraism

It has long been recognized that the New England Puritans and their intellectual heirs both imagined and described themselves with Hebraic imagery. But it was not only the imagery of the Old Testament that fired the Puritan imagination. It was the Hebrew word itself that served Puritan divines in their search for self-definition. "That most ancient language and sacred tongue" became the "object of desire" of many a New England scholar.

The study of American Christian Hebraism leads us back to the study of Hebrew in Christian Europe. In the opening essay of this volume, Ktziah Spanier points out that European Christian study of the Hebrew language had long been an endeavor fraught with ambivalence and tension, for "apologetic and polemical objectives inspired much of traditional Christian interest in the Hebrew language and Jewish literature." The same ambivalence would manifest itself in America. Christian Hebraism sought to reveal the "original meanings" of Scripture, and, in doing so, to ease the appropriation or incorporation of the Hebrew text into the greater corpus of "the two Testaments"—the Old and the New. This endeavor was as old as the fourth century C.E., when St. Jerome made his pilgrimage to Palestine to study at the feet of the rabbis. In Medieval Europe the intricacies of the Hebrew language were of little interest to scholars. The Catholic church saw itself as the "New Israel," replacing the language and culture of the "Old Israel"; and thus the study of the language of the "Old Israel" held little interest. There were periodic outbursts of interest in the study of Hebrew, most significantly in twelfth- and thirteenth-century England. But it is only with the Renaissance and the Reformation that we find a resurgence of the Christian study of "the sacred language."[2] In the sixteenth century the Church's reformers invoked the concept of *sola scriptura,* by which only the text of the Bible was to be used as a source of religious authority.[3] In this view, the closer we can get to the original meaning of the Bible, the closer we are to God's intentions. In the endeavor of *sola scriptura,* as in the study of Hebrew in the twelfth and thirteenth centuries, England was in the forefront of Christian Hebraism. In 1540, the Regius professorships in Hebrew at Oxford and Cambridge were established by Henry VIII.[4] In England, as on the continent, knowledge of Hebrew was the mark of a truly educated person, one with access to the original texts of "the classics" and the Bible. In Renaissance Europe, one often finds expressions of admiration for "the trilingual man," the scholar who was master of the three great languages of antiquity—Greek, Latin, and Hebrew. For the collection of one such scholar, Albrecht Dürer designed a wonderful bookplate in which the phrase from Psalms "the beginning of wisdom is the fear of God" appears in each of the three scripts (see p. 1).

As interest in Hebrew grew, Protestant scholars compiled dictionaries, grammars, and chrestomathies, and, in the sixteenth and early seventeenth centuries, these books were printed widely and used in colleges in Europe and in the new schools of the American colonies. In Europe, some Christian scholars availed themselves of Jewish informants. In Italy we find a good deal of Jewish-Christian scholarly cooperation. But in Germany and Poland mutual suspicion and wariness precluded any such collaborative efforts. The Jews were afraid of missionary activity; Christians who studied with Jewish scholars were likely to be accused of "Judaising tendencies."[5]

In Christian Europe, Hebrew had long been thought of as "the original language of mankind." In Charles Stinson's essay in this volume, "The Northernmost Israel," we learn that the Venerable Bede, the eighth-century English churchman, was one of a number of early Christian writers who "evince a special fascination with the 'Veritas Hebraica': God's own chosen means of communication with the world, and thus, Bede declares, Hebrew was the 'prima lingua'—the 'prime' or 'first language' of the human race. Later it was disrupted and dispersed at Babel as a punishment for still another sin of pride. And from that disruption there arose the current multiplicity of languages coexisting with Hebrew, Adam's original tongue."[6] Moreover, Stinson notes, "in conceiving of the newly Christianized Anglo-Saxon peoples as a parallel to the people of Israel, Bede strikingly foreshadows the later English Reformed who would identify themselves and their New England refuge with Israel."

The Legend of the Ten Lost Tribes

Another American claim to the heritage of Israel was the identification of the people of the New World with the Ten Lost Tribes. In responding to the great geographic discoveries of the fifteenth and sixteenth centuries, European writers, both Christian and Jewish, often had recourse to biblical explanations. The early sixteenth-century Jewish scholar Yosef Hacohen reported to the readers of his universal history that the European discoverers of America found that "the Indians of the Americas were able to speak a little of the language of Ishmael."[7] This imaginative detail, which may have resulted from reports that Columbus's navigators attempted to speak Arabic to the Indians, was soon to be matched by a more astounding assertion about the languages of the peoples of the New World. In 1632 Antonio Montezinos, a converted Jew, returning to Amsterdam from what is now eastern Colombia, claimed that he had met the remnants of the tribe of Reuben, one of the "Lost Tribes of Israel" and that they had spoken to him in Hebrew. As Montezinos put it, "they greeted me with the Shema Yisrael."[8]

These two forays into speculative linguistics mark an early attempt to link America and the Semitic languages. Both stories are indications of the European need to find the familiar in the New World. For Christians and Jews the discovery of the New World offered a religious challenge: how did the newly found places and peoples fit into their biblical view of the world? If Genesis 10 offered the believing Christian "the table of nations," where did these newly discovered people, who did not seem to be mentioned in that all-inclusive table, fit in? And in what way were the indigenous peoples of the Americas, and the discoveries themselves, part of the divine plan? For many Europeans the notion of a divine plan was used to justify the subjugation of the indigenous populations of the Americas. They saw the "natives" as sons of Canaan, whose fate, as decreed in Genesis, was subjugation. For others, the biblical world view, especially the injunction to care for "the stranger in your midst," dictated a more humane attitude towards these "new" peoples.

The most influential of the books that promoted the Lost Tribes theory was Menasseh ben Israel's 1650 publication, *Hope of Israel*. Menasseh, inspired by Montezinos's reports, used a description of the "Jews in the New World" as the point of departure for his eschatological enthusiasms about Jewish history and the scheme of redemption. Grant Underwood's essay in this volume argues that *Hope of Israel* can only be understood in the context of the tradition of rabbinic writings about the Lost Tribes of Israel, writings which Christian writers enthusiastically adapted for their own purposes. "Most readers saw what they wished to see in *Hope of Israel*, rather than what Menasseh intended. Menasseh's book became popular among Christian readers because it satisfied their speculative needs. *Hope of Israel* was an important piece of Jewish messianism primarily because of the notoriety Gentiles gave it." As Richard Popkin points out in his essay, "The Rise and Fall of the Jewish Indian Theory," the notion that the American Indians were the remnants of the Lost Tribes of Israel had a long life. This idea persisted into the early nineteenth century. The most extensive elaboration of the theory, Lord Kingsborough's nine volume *Antiquities of Mexico*, is a massive and lavishly illustrated work, the publication of which drove Lord Kingsborough to bankruptcy and eventually led to his death in debtor's prison in London.[9]

As Popkin notes, "The Jewish Indian theory fell victim to a scientific movement aimed at getting rid of the scriptural framework of human history and substituting a secular one, of migrating peoples." The theory fell out of favor as "a casualty of the war between science and theology. Therefore, contemporary scholars who posit similar Old World-New World connections are at a distinct disadvantage." In his essay on "The Ten Lost Tribes," Cyrus Gordon presents the evidence for such connections, and, as Popkin remarks, "Gordon has marshalled a fair amount of evidence . . . that there were Mediterranean contacts with America going back to Phoenician and Roman times."

The formal study of the Hebrew language, the Hebrew Bible, and rabbinic texts was undertaken by American Christian scholars. As an imagined link between Hebrew and America, the Jewish Indian theory was soon forgotten. A real link, one of American scholarly interest in the Hebrew language, was being forged. It would flower in New England, where an American Puritan Hebraism took root.

American Puritan Hebraism

On the *Mayflower* there were two Hebraists of competence, William Bradford and William Brewster. Bradford, author of colonial America's first narrative history, *Of Plymouth Plantation*, was governor of the Plymouth Colony. His colleague William Brewster, who was both teacher and preacher at Plymouth, was regarded by many as leader of the

Pilgrims. Both men, busy as they were in the early years of settlement, set time aside each day for the study of the Bible and the sacred tongue. In the original manuscript of *Of Plymouth Plantation*, written in 1650, Bradford included eight pages of Hebrew vocabulary notes. These were his "Hebrew Exercises," a list of over one thousand Hebrew words and phrases and their English equivalents. The exercises are graced by Bradford's charming hymn of praise to the study of the Hebrew language:

> Though I am growne aged, yet I have had a longing
> desire to see with my own eyes, something of that most
> ancient language, and holy tongue, in which the law
> and Oracles of God were write; and in which God
> and angels spake to the holy patriarchs of old
> time; and what names were given to things
> from the creation. And though I cañot
> attaine to much herein, yet I am refresh-
> ed to have seen some glimp̄se hereof
> (as Moyses saw the land of Ca-
> nan a farr of). My aime and
> desire is, to see how the words
> and phrases lye in the
> holy texte: and to
> discerne somewhat
> of the same,
> for my owne
> contente.[10]

As Egal Feldman noted in his recent study of the Jewish encounter with Protestant America,

Bradford was driven to study Hebrew in order to catch a glimpse of Israel's past, a past he wished to re-create in New Plymouth. . . . And this wish influenced the Puritan view of the Jews. . . . The centrality of the Bible in the life of early Puritanism bestowed upon the historical Jew a special place in the mind of Protestant America. New England Puritans patterned their laws upon the Mosaic codes of the Old Testament, and they adopted the experiences of the early Hebrews as a model upon which to shape their own lives. Like the Jews of old they conceived themselves to be chosen by God to perform a special mission in the wilderness of the New World.[11]

Sacvan Bercovitch has noted that

nothing more clearly attests to the power of the American Puritan imagination than [this] mythico-historiography. The emigrants had fled England as from certain destruction. Behind them, they believed, lay the failure of European Protestantism—and before them, as their refuge, what they called "wilderness," "desert." The image speaks for itself of their fear. It also proclaims the means they found to persevere: the daring symbolic pattern which justified their migration by justifying America. The New World, according to that image, was the modern counterpart of the wilderness through which the Israelites reached Canaan, of the desert where Christ overcame the tempter. More than counterpart, it was antitype: the journey then was a foreshadowing of the journey now by a Christian Israel to the long-awaited "new heavens and a new earth."[12]

For all the early English settlers in the colonies the Bible was the central text of religious and political discourse. Though few were familiar with "the sacred writ in its original tongue" all knew the Bible in its various English translations. The King James version, soon to become the standard text, was completed in 1611, only nine years before the establishment of Plymouth. More than twenty Christian Hebraists, many of them familiar with the classical Jewish commentaries, were among the group of scholars that produced the King James Bible. Some of these scholars had studied with Jewish informants.[13]

In 1636, before Bradford wrote his chronicle of the early years of the English settlements in New England, Harvard College was established.[14] Its first two presidents, Dunster and Chauncey, were, in the words of Samuel Eliot Morison, "first and foremost Orientalists, students and teachers of Hebrew and its cognate languages" (Arabic, Syrian, and Aramaic).[15] The spirit of the University of Cambridge in England, stronghold of Puritanism and seat of Hebrew learning, was kept alive at Harvard, the "new American Cambridge." At Harvard, and at the other nine colleges founded before the Revolution, Hebrew was an integral part of the curriculum. Some students objected to its "uselessness," but the faculties stood firm and continued to teach the language.

Despite some resistance from students, the American colonies were soon to produce their own unique brand of Hebraic scholarship. Its most prolific, if not its most precise, practitioner was Cotton Mather. In many of the three hundred books and pamphlets listed in his bibliography, Mather used Hebrew words and phrases. He adopted rabbinic titles in referring to his New England associates, and at times styled himself "rabbi." And, just as an interest in the Hebrew sources and language had occupied the attentions of William Bradford, it also engaged Mather, who drew on Hebraic materials in the composition of *Magnalia Christi Americana*, his history of the church in New England. In his essay in this volume, "The New England Puritans and the Jews," Arthur Hertzberg highlights the centrality in Mather's thought of his lifelong wish for the conversion of the Jews. In the subsequent essay, Louis Feldman demonstrates that Mather's interest in Hebrew extended beyond the Hebrew of the Bible to the Hebrew of rabbinic literature, although, as Feldman notes, "his knowledge of Hebrew was less than perfect."

In the American colonies, as in Europe, a catalyst to the study of Hebrew (and one overlooked by much of modern scholarship), was the interest of Christian occultists in the use of Hebrew for magical purposes. Sources about "magical Hebraism" are elusive; by its nature such mystical speculation was secretive. Texts and sources that might shed light on this "hidden Hebraism" were kept secret for many centuries. In the fifteenth and sixteenth centuries this type of "Hebraic occultism" existed among Christian intellectuals, and we know that both Pico della Mirandola and John Reuchlin studied with rabbis and kabbalists.[16] It was also popular among the common folk of Europe, who used Hebrew writing and Hebraic symbols in amulets, talismans, and magic parchments. An indigenous American Hebraic occultism emerged in seventeenth- and eighteenth-century America, where Hebrew, seen as a divinely inspired and magical language, played an important part in American folk religion. Recent scholarship has shown that this folk Hebraism was an element in the formation of Mormon beliefs in the nineteenth century.[17]

The American Jewish Community

Naturally, the small colonial American Jewish community was proud of its Hebrew heritage, but it had to be reminded of the necessity for Hebrew study. Gershom Mendes Seixas, hazzan of New York's Congregation Shearith Israel, exhorted his congregants to study the language and reminded them that "the Hebrew language was the only true means for ascertaining God's will."[18] Perhaps Seixas was asserting, in his mild way, a Jewish claim on the Hebrew language. But, for the most part, the study of Hebrew in the American colonies, on both the individual and the college level, was a Christian endeavor, undertaken in the conviction that a profound knowledge of Hebrew would lead the student to see the "truth" of Christian doctrine. There was only a handful of Jews in the colonies, and we shall see that the use of Hebrew by the members of that small community of American Jews was quite limited.

There was no real Jewish scholarship until the middle of the nineteenth century. (Abraham Rice, the first ordained rabbi, came to the United States from Germany in 1840, and *Avnei Yehoshua,* Joshua Falk's commentary on the *The Ethics of the Fathers,* the first book-length Hebrew text with literary qualities, was not produced until 1860. A year earlier a short technical treatise on ritual slaughter, *Dine Nikur,* was published.[19]) As America's small Jewish community grew to maturity, and as synagogues and Hebrew schools were established, we may note some early markers of Jewish self-consciousness. One of the first of these was the 1800 Hebrew oration at the Columbia College commencement. Orations in Hebrew, along with speeches in Greek, Latin, and, on occasion, French, were not uncommon at eighteenth-century American college commencements. What was remarkable about this Hebrew oration was that the Hebrew was Rabbinic, and the orator was Jewish. Jacob Rader Marcus has described Sampson Simson's address as "the first evidence of a communal self-consciousness among American Jews."[20] In this oration, Simson cited a mid-seventeenth-century date as the beginning of Jewish settlement in the new world, and noted that he was marking the 150th anniversary of the presence of Jews in America.[21]

Questionable as that date in the mid-seventeenth century might be for the first Jewish *settlement* (as Leo Hershkowitz indicates in his contribution to this volume), it was true that Simson's own family had been in America since 1718. They were members of New York's oldest congregation, Shearith Israel, and the leader of that congregation, Gershom Mendes Seixas, was the author of Sampson Simson's Hebrew oration. Seixas, a close friend of the family, served Columbia as a trustee of the college—the only Jewish trustee—for a period of over twenty years. In this oration, Seixas, through Sampson Simson, speaks proudly of the Jewish contribution to American intellectual life.

Sampson Simson's oration, a speech delivered by a Jew on an American Jewish topic in a Jewish language, was an unusual event, the first of its kind in American history. Use of Hebrew within the small colonial American Jewish community had been limited, for the most part, to the Hebrew of the prayer book. The language was familiar through repetition, though not generally understood. As Nathan Kaganoff notes in his essay, on "Hebrew and Liturgical Exercises in the Colonial Period," "Enough copies of prayer books for every possible religious occasion have survived from colonial American Jews that would indicate that almost everyone had some prayer book in his possession. Presumably they could also read the Hebrew it contained, though in many instances they understood very little of its contents." Against this background it is all the more remarkable that the only Jewish student in Columbia's small graduating class of fifteen students would choose to deliver a speech in Hebrew.

Though Hebrew was not always understood by members of the early American Jewish community, and its use was generally limited to the liturgy, it did find other forms of expression. As Jacob Kabakoff points out in his essay, "The Use of Hebrew by American Jews During the Colonial Period," "Hebrew was used in folk crafts" but "there are but few instances of the use of Hebrew by Jews for secular purposes." One of these was a diary kept by Benjamin Sheftall, who settled in Savannah, Georgia, in 1773. That Sheftall had to translate his diary into English in order to make it comprehensible to his son "is sufficient indication that the family did not continue the chain of Hebrew knowledge."

Christian Hebraism and the American Colleges

The link between Hebraism and the foundation of American colleges is a recurrent theme in the essays in this volume. At Harvard the Hebraic tradition of the first two presidents was maintained for the first century and a half of the college's existence, though not without opposition both from students and from some of the faculty. The founders of Yale were also Hebraists and it was the greatest American Christian Hebraist (or "Hebrician" as he styled himself), Ezra Stiles, who was appointed the president of Yale in 1777. Stiles, formerly the pastor of the Congregational church of Newport, Rhode Island, had befriended the small but influential Jewish community of that city. At the age of forty he began to study the Hebrew language and texts. After a number of years he gained facility in reading rabbinic literature and even tried his hand at the study of the texts of the Zohar, the great kabbalistic compilation of the thirteenth century. The ambivalence inherent in the venture of Christian Hebraism—the attraction to the "Hebraic" coupled with an aversion to or suspicion of individual Jews—was vividly reflected in the career of Stiles, a man thought of as "the Gentle Puritan" and the foremost intellectual of America in the revolutionary period. As Arthur Chiel points out in his essay in this volume, "Ezra Stiles and the Jews: A Study in Ambivalence," "Although there was undoubtedly an ambivalence in his attitude to the Jews, he had not allowed the scales of judgment to tip over into a fixed antipathetic stance on his part."

In the 1750s the founder and first president of Kings College (later Columbia) was Samuel Johnson, a man who saw the study of Hebrew as the most important endeavor of his own intellectual life. Johnson declared in 1759 that "as soon as a lad has learned to speak and to read English well, it is much the best to begin a learned education with Hebrew . . . the mother of all languages." His son, William Samuel Johnson, first president of Columbia College, was taught Hebrew by his father. Another son, Samuel, was said to have "spoken Hebrew at the age of five."[22] In the nineteenth century, as in the seventeenth and eighteenth centuries, the foundation of American colleges was linked to Hebrew scholarship. William Rainey Harper, founder and first president of the

University of Chicago, began his academic career as an instructor in Hebrew at Yale.

Thus the founders of Harvard, Yale, Columbia, and the other early colleges were men for whom the Hebrew language was a source of inspiration and an essential component of a good education. Often, their idea of what a college should be was based on a biblical model. Matthew Wiencke demonstrates in his essay on "Classical and Hebraic Models of Moral Instruction at Dartmouth College" that Dartmouth's founder, Eleazar Wheelock, consciously evoked an Hebraic model when he organized the college in the years immediately preceding the American Revolution. That the modern college should emulate the Israelite "School of the Prophets" was an idea that exercised a strong hold on eighteenth- and nineteenth-century imaginations.

One is tempted to dismiss this "Hebraic connection" as peripheral to the lives of these gentlemen, as it seems unrelated to their main concern, which was the establishment of American centers of learning. A closer look at their biographies, their published works, and the legacies they left their families, indicates that study of Hebrew, the Bible, and the history of the Holy Land, was central to their self-concept as educators and to their notion of an emerging American culture.

Christian scholars dominated Hebrew studies from the time of the first English settlement in America to the mid-nineteenth century. If a Jewish scholar wanted to teach Hebrew in an American college it seems that he had to first become a Christian. Judah Monis, a Sephardic Jew from Italy or North Africa, came to Cambridge, Massachusetts, in 1722. He offered his services as a Hebrew teacher to the overseers of Harvard College. Monis wrote a Hebrew grammar and presented the manuscript to the college as an indication of his competence; while awaiting their decision he worked at a hardware store in Cambridge. (There he fell in love with the Christian owner's daughter and asked her father for her hand in marriage, which was granted.) The college considered Monis's request. It was not until after his public conversion to Christianity (in a ceremony performed at the Cambridge Church in 1723), that Monis was deemed worthy of a Harvard position. He served Harvard for the next forty years, but never received the full recognition of his students or peers. Monis remained a poorly paid instructor, never gaining the rank of professor. He was continually harassed by students; the more sarcastic among them persisted in calling him "Rabbi" Monis.[23] The "decline" of Hebrew at Harvard College is often attributed to Judah Monis's antiquated teaching methods and his unattractive personality. In his contribution to this volume, Thomas Jay Siegel, a historian of Harvard College, corrects this impression. He places what he terms "the transformation of Hebrew at Harvard" in the context of the general changes taking place in the educational philosophy of the college. The conception of the curriculum had changed dramatically in the mid-eighteenth century. With that change came a secularizing influence. Stephen Sewall, Monis's successor and Harvard's first professor of Hebrew presented to the students a more modern and aesthetic approach to a language that he described as "not only easy but delightful." As Siegel puts it, "It was Sewall's intention, therefore, to strip away the medieval schema and rabbinical practices that had prevented the students from seeing the Hebrew language in what he thought was its purest, most natural light."

Hebrew Beyond the Colonial Period

Hebrew was held in such high esteem by the founders of the American Republic that a story emerged at the time of the Revolution that Hebrew was being considered as a possible substitute for English as the American language. In what H. L. Mencken would later describe as "a furious onslaught upon the whole American scheme of things," the English writer Charles Ingersoll claimed that some had "recommended the adoption of Hebrew . . . considering the Americans, no doubt as the 'chosen people' of the New World."[24] While spoken Hebrew did not take root in the emerging Republic, biblical imagery retained its hold on the imagination of the colonial elites. Old Testament concepts of oppression and liberation had great appeal to the founders of the Republic. "American Revolutionaries equated their rebellion against England with the struggle of the Israelites against the Egyptian Pharoah. When the official seal of the United States was being created a design was submitted by Thomas Jefferson, Benjamin Franklin and John Adams depicting the Israelites crossing the Red Sea with Pharoah in pursuit and Moses standing on the other side. This seal had on one side the name of the new Republic—the United States of America, 1776—and on the reverse, surrounding the picture of Egyptians drowning in the Red Sea, the phrase "rebellion to tyrants is obedience to God."[25]

The end of the eighteenth century saw a decline of the Puritan cultural heritage; this was reflected in the decline of Hebrew studies at the American colleges. But at Yale, in the last quarter of the century, there was a considerable revival of interest in Hebrew under the presidency of Ezra Stiles.[26] Upon Stiles's death in 1795 there was a further decline in Hebrew study at Yale and the other New England colleges. This was, in part, the result of a shift in the system of education at American institutions. As American elites became secularized, greater emphasis was placed on studying the new developments in science and technology. The classics and the Bible were no longer at the center of the curriculum. This shift also had a marked effect on the emerging Protestant theological schools, where greater emphasis was placed on the development of pastoral skills and the formation of a more "well-rounded" clergyman. But this was not the end of Hebrew learning in Christian America. In the first half of the nineteenth century, the Reverend Moses Stuart, professor of Sacred Literature at Andover Theological Seminary, revived Hebrew studies at Andover. His primary goals were to educate a new generation of Protestant ministers and to aid in the translation of the Bible into the languages of Asia and Africa. Among the almost fifteen hundred students who studied with Stuart during his forty-year tenure at Andover, were clergymen who would later devote themselves to teaching Hebrew and the Bible in other seminaries and colleges. Thus this Hebrew revival spread throughout the country. For Stuart, a knowledge of Hebrew was essential to the training of the Protestant clergyman. From 1827 to 1837 he was able to institute the "Hebrew Rule" at Andover: all entering candidates for the ministry had to have a reading knowledge of the language.[27]

Stuart's students, among them the illustrious Edward Robinson, were soon to revive the study of the "sacred tongue." By the 1830s and 1840s, hundreds of American Christians were studying the Bible in Hebrew. This new Hebraism was distinct from, but related to, a general American familiarity with the text of the Bible. While most Hebrew students were seminarians, there was interest and activity among the laity as well. The study of Scripture was widespread; the New Testament in Greek was studied at all of the American colleges, and the Bible in the King James translation was familiar to all Americans from the weekly sermons delivered in churches. Historians of American culture have noted that churchgoers of the eighteenth and early nineteenth centuries, especially churchgoers in New England, were more familiar with the Bible than they were with the daily newspapers. The newspapers were read by only a small elite; the weekly sermons were heard, and often read, by all.[28]

Hebrew, America, and the Holy Land

During the first half of the nineteenth century, the Protestant romance with Hebrew and the Bible was expressed in a striking new way. In the earlier periods of the discoveries and the European settlement of the Americas, Christians had used an Hebraic model to interpret their experiences in the New World. In the nineteenth century we find the heirs to this Protestant tradition using their knowledge of Hebrew and the Bible to understand the ancient world, especially the world of ancient Israel and its neighbors.

American scholars, among them Hebraists, archaeologists, and New Testament scholars, flocked to the Holy Land in the mid-nineteenth century. Using the knowledge of Hebrew and the Bible that they had gained in American colleges and seminaries, they went on to explore and uncover the world of biblical antiquity. Many of these "biblical research-ers" were Protestant missionaries to the various peoples of the Near East. Pliny Fisk, an Andover Seminary graduate and member of the first American Palestine Mission (1819), noted in his "sermon preached just before the departure of the Palestine mission" that "There are now a considerable number of Jews at Jerusalem, and in the vicinity. Notwith-standing all that this people have suffered; notwithstanding all their dis-persions; they still continue a distinct people, and retain their ancient language, customs and religion. . . ." It was the culture of this still "dis-tinct people" that fascinated American travellers and scholars. The Jews of their own day were viewed as "the long descendants of the Israelite." The subtext here is a familiar one. Knowledge of the "ancient language, customs and religion" of the Jews would make American missionaries all the more effective in their efforts to convert the Jews at "the scene of almost all that is interesting in sacred story."[29] When, in the 1840s, English missionaries opened a hospital for the Jews of Jerusalem, they placed a Hebrew translation of the New Testament in every room. With the establishment of the English-Prussian church in Jerusalem, under the leadership of Bishop Solomon Alexander (a Jewish apostate), daily prayers in Hebrew were instituted.

The career of Edward Robinson illustrates this change from "Hebrew in America" to "Hebrew in Palestine," from the use of an Hebraic under-standing of the American experience to the use of Hebrew to understand the Holy Land. Trained by Moses Stuart at Andover Theological Semi-nary, Robinson was to become Stuart's successor as Protestant Ameri-ca's most respected scholar of the Bible. Robinson felt that to truly understand the Bible one had to go to Palestine and identify its lost holy sites. The Holy Land was considered "the Third Testament" by Robin-son and his followers. The five volumes that he produced, his *Biblical Researches in Palestine* (published in 1838 and 1852), became a widely read American classic.

Just as American Hebraism had its English antecedents, American interest in Holy Land exploration was preceded by English interest in "The Land of the Book." As Barbara Kreiger points out in her essay on

"Seventeenth-Century English Travellers to Palestine," "For centuries of Christianity, travel to the Holy Land was undertaken primarily by pilgrims, but the age of the pilgrimage had come to a virtual end by the seventeenth century, as the Protestant Reformation took hold. . . . a new breed appeared on the scene at around this time—not pilgrim, but not merchant either, simply, as one Fynes Moryson claims of himself, the traveller." Over the next two centuries English travellers took a lively interest in the study of "sacred geography." Their observations, which filled many a travel volume, were later amplified and corrected by Robinson and his followers.

When Robinson wanted to travel to Palestine in 1838, he requested a leave of absence from his recent appointment as professor of Sacred Literature at Union Theological Seminary. As a replacement he suggested that the trustees employ, on a temporary basis, Professor Isaac Nordheimer of New York University. This caused something of a furor. The appointment of a Jew to the faculty of a major Protestant seminary was unheard of. The trustees, after considerable discussion, approved Nordheimer's appointment. The next time that a Jewish scholar was appointed at Union was in 1961, when Rabbi Abraham Joshua Heschel served as a visiting professor.[30]

The multifaceted strands of Hebraism in American life, its relationship to America's self-image as a new Promised Land, its centrality in the new nation's intellectual life, and its effect on American attitudes toward the fate of the biblical Promised Land, were best expressed by Edward Robinson in 1838:

As in the case of most of my countrymen, especially in New England, the scenes of the Bible had made a deep impression upon my mind from the earliest childhood; and afterwards in riper years this feeling had grown into a strong desire to visit in person the places so remarkable in the history of the human race. Indeed in no country of the world, perhaps, is such a feeling more widely diffused than in New England; in no country are the Scriptures better known, or more highly prized. From his earliest years the child is there accustomed not only to read the Bible for himself; but he also reads or listens to it in the morning and evening devotions of the family, in the daily village-school, in the Sunday-school and Bible-class, and in the weekly ministrations of the sanctuary. Hence, as he grows up, the names of Sinai, Jerusalem, Bethlehem, the Promised Land, become associated with his earliest recollections and holiest feelings.[31]

From the very concrete world of biblical archaeology we move to the more speculative and fanciful one of the place of Hebrew in American eschatology—that is the reckoning of "the last days," of "the end of time." This is an aspect of Hebraism that has not yet been fully discussed in the history of American religion. Seventeenth century American spec-

ulation about the Jews' role in "salvation history" and their restoration
to Zion appeared in the writings of Increase Mather, the illustrious father
of Cotton Mather. In the eighteenth century, Yale's Ezra Stiles, in rereading Increase Mather's *Mystery of Israel's Salvation*, became convinced of Israel's pivotal role in the redemptive process. Stiles found
himself moved to "take pains to gain an idea of the present state of the
Jews in the world." He examined "Daniel's Prophetic Numbers," those
enigmatic references in Daniel 7 and 8, texts which have served as a
source of eschatological speculation for centuries.[32] Similarly, in 1767
Dartmouth's Samson Occom, in calculating the date of "the end of
time," had recourse to the tantalizing mystical numbers of Daniel. Curiously, he arrived at the date of 1843, the date later chosen by Miller
and his adventist followers.

A later manifestation of this "eschatological Hebraism" can be seen
in the career and writings of the Mormon prophet, Joseph Smith. In the
mid-1830s Smith invited Joshua Seixas, son of Gershom Mendes Seixas,
to be the Hebrew teacher at his "temple school" in Kirtland, Ohio. Under Seixas's tutelage, the Mormon Prophet and his disciples labored in-
tensively for a number of months to learn "the language of the Lord in
its original tongue." Though the Mormons thought of him as a "devout
Jew," Seixas had converted to the Unitarian Church a few years earlier
and taken the name James. After seven months with the Mormons,
Seixas certified some of their elders as *teachers* of Hebrew. There is evidence that there was an occult aspect to the Mormon elder's intense
interest in the Hebrew language.[33]

In a pattern familiar to us from other Christian groups, the Mormon
fascination with Hebrew and the Jews developed into an interest in the
Holy Land. In 1841 Joseph Smith sent his apostle Orson Hyde to Jerusalem, and ordered him to bless the city from the Mount of Olives and
pray for the return of the Jews to the Promised Land.[34]

Among American Protestants, support for the restoration of the Jews
to Zion had its origins in Hebraist and millennialist circles. This idea
would soon filter down to the political consciousness of many Americans. Of course, sympathy with "proto-Zionist" ideas was not limited
to those given to eschatological speculation. As Nadav Safran noted in
The United States and Israel:

> The idea of Return was a tenet of faith not only for the Jews, but also for
> some influential groups among the Christian, particularly Protestant, pow-
> ers in modern times. And for them too the idea was not only eschatological.
> During the nineteenth century sympathy for nationalist causes in general
> and unsettled conditions in the Near East and Palestine encouraged the no-
> tion among some enthusiasts of the Jewish Return that the time for the ful-

fillment of the biblical prophecy had come. These enthusiasts, while they were personally moved by religious sentiment, advanced all sorts of political arguments to win the support of their governments for their schemes.[35]

Later Protestant speculation about the millennium was also informed by Hebraism. As did Ezra Stiles, many Americans studied the Hebrew text of the Bible in search of the date of the last days. Eager to point to a precise date for the Second Coming, Christian scholars of the Bible would publish their interpretations of the Book of Daniel and the Book of Revelations, texts long associated with eschatological speculation. Those dates in which such speculation was rife—1843, 1864, 1880— mark the religious history of the second half of the nineteenth century. Both William Miller, the founder of adventism in America, and Clorinda Minor, who was briefly known as the "prophet" of the adventist movement, took a lively interest in Jewish texts and ritual. One charming indication of the belief that one had to go back to the Hebrew source to know when the redemption would occur can be seen in the following episode:

When in 1843 William Miller announced that the world would end 10,000 or more of his followers assembled in a park on the outskirts of Philadelphia to await the Second Coming of Christ. When the Second Coming did not occur and when a terrible storm raged on the outskirts of Philadelphia and destroyed the tent city in which Miller's followers were housed, many were bitterly disappointed and gave up their millenial dream. But a small group of followers who were later to form a core of Seventh Day Adventists, insisted that Miller had erred because he had used a Christian calendar. They said that if he had used the Jewish calendar, and had followed the dates of Rosh Hashanah, his predictions would have been correct.[36]

Hebraism also manifested itself in the careers of a series of American visionary colonists who, armed with "biblical knowledge" and farm implements, went to live in Palestine in the 1850s, 1860s, and 1870s. Among these colonists was the adventist Clorinda Minor. She founded two small colonies in Palestine, one at Artas, near Bethlehem, and the other on the outskirts of Jaffa. This second settlement effort she dubbed Mt. Hope, and to it she attracted a number of Jewish laborers. Four years after coming to Palestine, she died and was buried in Jaffa, far from her native Philadelphia, and the case can be made that her efforts, though short-lived, had a salutary effect on the fledgling Jewish settlement efforts of the pre-Zionist period.[37]

As America moved out of the millennialist fever of the last decades of the nineteenth century there occurred a new flowering of Hebrew studies among Christians. This Hebrew renaissance was an intellectual one, not a visionary one, and it was sparked by the activities of William

Rainey Harper, a Baptist minister from Chicago. Harper had taught Hebrew at Yale but conceived of his new Hebrew program as not being limited to a small group of intellectuals. Rather he hoped to teach Hebrew to the masses throughout America. To this end he established, in the 1880s, a Hebrew Summer School on Lake Michigan. There, hundreds of American Protestant clergymen learned the rudiments of the Hebrew language. They, in turn, were to teach Hebrew to their congregants. We know that Harper's plans to teach Hebrew to Americans did not succeed, but his interest in biblical and "oriental" studies fueled his intellectual energies. When Harper became the first president of the University of Chicago, he placed "oriental studies" at the forefront of his concerns. His friendship with John D. Rockefeller led to the founding of the Oriental Institute and to Rockefeller's lifelong support of archaeological research.

As the nineteenth century drew to a close, Christian hegemony in Hebrew studies was soon to meet a formidable challenge in the person of Jewish scholars from Europe. While a small band of these scholars was able to enter the American Academy as full-fledged members—one thinks of Morris Jastrow at the University of Pennsylvania, and Richard Gottheil at Columbia—their influence was limited. But through their writings, and through their subtle but effective challenge to Christian control over the newly defined field of "Semitics," they enabled Jewish scholars to enter into the American academy. The "long descendants of the Israelite," acculturated to American life, had now entered the academies founded by colonial era Hebraists, Orientalists, and other claimants to the heritage of the "Old Israel."

Notes

1. F. Manuel, *The Broken Staff: Judaism Through Christian Eyes* (Cambridge, Mass., 1992), 11.
2. For a masterful survey of Christian writers on Judaism, and the relationship of their writings to the study of Scripture, see G. F. Moore, "Christian Writers on Judaism," *Harvard Theological Review*, 14 (July 1921): 197–254. For a recent history and interpretation of European Christian Hebraism see Manuel, *The Broken Staff.*
3. On *sola scriptura*, see Moore, 215.
4. See R. Wakefield, *On the Three Languages*, ed. and trans. by G. Lloyd Jones (Binghamton, New York, 1989), 33.
5. J. Friedman, *The Most Ancient Testimony: Sixteenth-Century Christian-Hebraica in the Age of Renaissance Nostalgia* (Columbus, Ohio, 1983).
6. On this view of Hebrew as the "original" language, see Edmund Sutcliffe, S.J., "The Venerable Bede's Knowledge of Hebrew," *Biblica* 16 (1935).
7. Yosef Hakohen, *Divre ha-yamim le-malkhe Tsarefat u-malkhey Beyt*

Ottoman Ha-togar, ed. Z. Benhardt (Jerusalem, 1967). On Hakohen's thought, see Y. H. Yerushalmi, "Messianic Impulses in Joseph ha-Kohen," in B. Cooperman, ed., *Jewish Thought in the Sixteenth Century* (Cambridge, Mass., 1983), 460–87.

8. For a survey of the extensive literature on Montezinos's claims, see R. Popkin, "The Rise and Fall of the Jewish Indian Theory," in Y. Kaplan, H. Méchoulan and R. Popkin, *Menasseh Ben Israel and His World* (Leiden, 1989), reprinted in this volume. For a recent interpretation of the meaning and fate of the Jewish Indian theory, see Andrew Delbanco, *The Puritan Ordeal* (Cambridge, Mass., 1989), 108–12.

9. Edward King, Viscount Kingsborough, *Antiquities of Mexico,* 9 vols. (London, 1830–48).

10. J. Rosenmeier, "With my owne eyes": William Bradford's *Of Plymouth Plantation* in S. Bercovitch, *The American Puritan Imagination: Essays in Revolution* (Cambridge, Mass., 1974). For the full text of the Hebrew exercises see I. Meyer, *The Hebrew Exercises of Governor William Bradford* (Plymouth, Mass., 1973).

11. E. Feldman, *Dual Destinies: The Jewish Encounter with Protestant America* (Chicago, 1990), 15.

12. S. Bercovitch, *The American Puritan Imagination: Essays in Revaluation.*

13. D. Daiches, *The Making of the King James Bible* (London, 1954).

14. For the cultural background see S. E. Morison, *Builders of the Bay Colony* (Boston, 1930), 188.

15. S. E. Morison, *The Puritan Pronaos* (New York, 1936), 36.

13. On Pico's Hebraism, see C. Wirszubski, *Pico della Mirandola's Encounter with Jewish Mysticism.* (Cambridge, Mass., 1989). On Reuchlin, see Friedman, *The Most Ancient Testimony;* and G. Scholem, *Od Davar* (Tel Aviv, 1989), 309–17.

17. M. Quinn, *Early Mormonism and the Magic World View* (Salt Lake City, 1987). On the persistence of occult beliefs in America, see J. Butler, *Awash in A Sea of Faith: Christianizing the American People* (Cambridge, Mass., 1990), 83–84.

18. J. R. Marcus, "The Handsome Young Priest in the Black Gown: The Personal World of Gershom Seixas," *Hebrew Union College Annual* 40 (1969): 413.

19. On A. Rice, see A. Hertzberg, *The Jews in America: Four Centuries of an Uneasy Encounter* (New York, 1989), 126–27. For publication information on the two earliest American Hebrew books, see R. Singerman, *Judaica Americana* (New York, 1990). Avne Yehoshu'a is entry #1653, Dine Nikur is #1575.

20. Marcus's comments on the Simson oration are in his *Studies in American Jewish History* (Cincinnati, 1968), 231.

21. For the most recent publication of the text and translation of the Simson oration, see S. Goldman, "Two American Hebrew Orations, 1799 and 1800," in *Hebrew Annual Review* 13 (1991).

22. On the Johnsons, see I Meyer, "Doctor Samuel Johnson's Grammar and Hebrew Psalter," in J. Blau, ed., *Essays on Jewish Life and Thought* (New York, 1959).

23. An early paper on Monis is that of Lee M. Friedman, "Judah Monis,

First Instructor in Hebrew at Harvard University," *Publications of the American Jewish Historical Society* 22 (1914). For a survey of the literature on Monis see Milton M. Klein, "A Jew at Harvard in the 18th century," *Proceedings of the Massachusetts Historical Society* 97 (1985): 138–40.

24. H. L. Mencken, *The American Language*, 4th ed. (New York, 1936), 79, and Supplement I (New York, 1945), 137.

25. M. Davis, *With Eyes Toward Zion* (New York, 1968). An illustration of the proposed seal appears in the plates following p. 138.

26. In addition to the essay on Stiles in this volume, see G. A. Kohut, *E. Stiles and the Jews* (New York, 1902). The standard biography is E. S. Morgan, *The Gentle Puritan: A Life of Ezra Stiles, 1727–1795* (New Haven, 1962).

27. J. Giltner, *Moses Stuart: The Father of Biblical Science in America* (Atlanta, 1988), 22.

28. On the centrality and wide dissemination in New England of the sermon, see Butler, *Awash in a Sea of Faith*, 57, 172–73.

29. Pliny Fisk, "The Holy Land an Interesting Field of Missionary Enterprise: A Sermon, Preached in the Old South Church, Boston, Sabbath Evening, October 31, 1819, Just Before the Departure of the Palestine Mission," reprinted in *Holy Land Missions and Missionaries* in M. Davis, ed., *America and The Holy Land Series* (New York, 1977).

30. W. Sloane Coffin, *A History of Union Theological Seminary* (New York, 1987). For a recent summary of Robinson's activities in Palestine, see N. Shepherd, *The Zealous Intruders: The Western Rediscovery of Palestine* (New York, 1987), 80–85. On Nordheimer, see S. Goldman, "Isaac Nordheimer (1809–1842)," *American Jewish History* 80 (Winter 1990–91): 213–29.

31. Quoted in R. Handy, *The Holy Land in American Protestant Life* (New York, 1984).

32. A. Chiel, "The Rabbis and Ezra Stiles," *American Jewish Historical Society Quarterly* 61 (June 1972): 296. On J. Seixas, see my forthcoming article "Joshua/James Seixas, 1802–1874," in *Jewish History*.

33. D. Michael Quinn, *Early Mormonism and the Magic World View* (Salt Lake City, 1987).

34. A Voice From Jerusalem (Boston, 1842), iii.

35. N. Safran, *The United States and Israel* (Cambridge, Mass., 1963).

36. On Miller and the religious background of the adventist movement, see E. S. Gaustad, *The Rise of Adventism: Religion and Society in Mid-Nineteenth Century America* (New York, 1974).

37. B. Kreiger and S. Goldman, "Clorinda Minor" (unpublished manuscript). Z. Vilnay, *Minorities in Israel: Moslems, Christians, Druze, Bahais* (Hebrew) (Jerusalem, 1959), 194–202.

One

European Background

Ktziah Spanier

Christian Hebraism and the Jewish Christian Polemic

Apologetic and polemical objectives inspired much of traditional Christian interest in the Hebrew language and Jewish literature. Within the text of the Hebrew Bible early Christians sought confirmation of the divinity of Jesus and the truth of the Christian faith. They studied early Jewish sources in order to enhance their understanding of the social and cultural milieu in which Jesus and his disciples lived.

The early Christians' belief that they were the true heirs of the Hebrew biblical tradition created a dualistic attitude toward the Jews and their writings. They viewed their Jewish contemporaries as the direct descendants of their own spiritual ancestors, having been the first to receive divine revelation. The Jews' steadfast refusal to accept the divinity of Christ and to embrace the Christian faith provided justification for their oppression and punishment. This duality contributed to the emancipation of Christianity from strict adherence to the precepts of Mosaic Law. The Church regarded itself and its adherents to be the true Israel, the people of God, and the sole heirs to all the prerogatives and promises which had once been given to the Jews.

The effort to substantiate these christological claims, together with the need to establish the Church, rather than the text, as the ultimate authority, resulted in the increased use of the allegorical method of interpreting the biblical text. This, coinciding with the appearance of Jerome's authoritative Vulgate version of the Hebrew Bible, caused a decline in the study of Hebrew in the middle of the first millennium.

Following the Arab conquests in Europe, Jews and Christians found themselves on a more or less equal footing under the hegemony of the Muslim rulers. Disputations on the relative merits of Islam, Judaism, and Christianity became a popular form of entertainment in the intellectually stimulating environment of the Abbasid caliphate. This encouraged Jewish scholars to polish their polemical skills in order to respond to Christian attacks. Christian polemicists found themselves hard put to defend themselves against their Jewish opponents who insisted that arguments concerning the biblical text be conducted on the basis of the original Hebrew and Aramaic rather than the Greek or Latin translations.

The Jews had the advantage of traditional knowledge of the Hebrew language and scriptures as well as commentaries that were based on the philological method and often contained historical and critical insights. They were thus well able to separate the literal sense of the text from homiletic interpretations and to refute the Christian disputants' positions on textual grounds.

Christian polemicists soon became convinced that they could not prevail over their opponents unless they mastered the original languages of the text and commentaries. Jewish converts served as tutors to Christians wishing to learn Hebrew and other Semitic languages. These new Christians, who were usually well versed in the Hebrew language and Jewish tradition, also engaged in polemical disputations on behalf of Christianity. They justified their own decision to convert and demonstrated the sincerity of their conversion by using Hebrew and traditional Jewish sources to extol the virtues of their new faith and dispute the validity of the faith they had renounced.

Petrus Alphonsi (1062–1110) was one such convert. He wrote a polemical work in which the disputants were Moses and Petrus, respectively representing the writer's own views before and after his conversion. In this work he demonstrated his knowledge of Hebrew theological and philosophical literature. Eschewing the use of the actual Hebrew scriptures, he chose to base his christological arguments on the folkloric Haggadah, providing ample quotes and arguments that served to ridicule this Jewish source.[1]

David Kimhi, an influential Jewish scholar and polemicist (1160–1235?), represented the prevailing Jewish attitude during the following period. He wrote one of the earliest Hebrew grammars, which was used by Christian Hebraists. His polemical material was easily accessible as it was incorporated in his very popular biblical commentaries.[2] He repeatedly asserted that the biblical text had been corrupted by Christian translators and commentators and that verses were taken out of context in order to adduce the desired christological meaning.[3] Kimhi insisted on textual consistency within each passage, claiming that Christian interpreters evinced a nearly total ignorance of the Hebrew language by failing to do so. He was particularly critical of the allegorical method of interpretation, which he took to be the central characteristic of Christian exegesis.

As Europe became Christianized, mounting pressure was brought to bear upon the Jews to convert, and Christian interest in Hebrew and Jewish literature became more widespread. In the early part of the thirteenth century it was believed that before true salvation could be achieved all Muslims and Jews had to be converted to Christianity. In order to achieve this the Christian converters had to study Hebrew and related Semitic languages and to become thoroughly familiar with the scriptures of the potential converts in their pristine form.

The Franciscan and Dominican orders were established in the early part of the thirteenth century. The Franciscans' interest in Jewish literature was primarily motivated by their identification with the religious experience of Jesus, the Apostles, and the early church. The Dominicans were charged by Pope Gregory IX (1227–41) with the conversion of all nonbelievers to the Christian faith. Raymond de Pennaforte, the master general of the order, believed that the conversions should be accomplished through conviction rather than by force. He therefore established an academy in Barcelona devoted to the study of Semitic languages, the scriptures of the Jews and Muslims, and their philosophical and theological literatures.[4]

In 1263 a disputation on the subject of the Talmud took place before King James I of Aragon.[5] Representing the Christian position was Pablo Christiani, a member of the Dominican order and a convert from Judaism. Rabbi Moses Ben Nachman (Ramban), a great talmudic scholar, represented the Jewish position.[6] There are two extant records of this disputation. Ramban kept a daily log of the discussions in Hebrew; a shorter, Latin, protocol representing the viewpoint of the Church has also survived. Pablo set out to prove that the Messiah had already come; that according to the Prophets he was both human and divine; that he had suffered and died for the salvation of mankind; and that with his arrival all legal and ceremonial provisions of the Old Testament were terminated. As proofs he offered several biblical citations, but relied primarily on haggadic sources. Rabbi Moses refuted his opponent's interpretation of the biblical text and dismissed the haggadic material as nonauthoritative. Pablo was nevertheless declared by the king to have won the disputation.

Following this event and upon the Dominicans' insistence, the king issued a royal edict requiring all Jews to attend sermons given by members of the order. He also empowered the Dominicans to appoint a commission to be charged with confiscating all available Hebrew books and expurgating from them any material that was deemed to be blasphemous.[7] Raymundus Martini (1210–85), who had studied Greek and Semitic languages at Penaforte's academy and later occupied the chair of Hebrew Studies at the University of Barcelona, was a member of this commission. He evidently examined much of the material confiscated by the commission, and later made use of these sources in the preparation of his monumental polemical work, to be used for the purpose of converting Muslims and Jews to Christianity. *Pugio Fidei adversus Mauros et Judaeos* was first issued in 1278. The work was divided into two major sections; the first was addressed to the Arab Aristotelians, and the second was aimed at the Jews. In the latter section Martini provided arguments and proofs for the truth of the Christian faith and discussed the divine rejection of the Jews and the necessity for their ultimate conversion. The work includes extensive citations from the Babylonian and Jerusalem Talmud, the *Midrash Rabbah*, the works of David Kimhi, Rashi, Maimonides, Ibn-Ezra, Ramban, and others. It also cites some Jewish sources which have since been lost and are known only through this work.[8]

Church authorities had thus embarked upon a two-pronged approach aimed at the conversion of the Jews: the encouragement of Christian Hebraica, coupled with expurgating from books held by Jews all material deemed to be anti-Christian. The need to train scholars for this purpose was the chief impetus for the decision made in 1311 at the Council of Vienne to establish chairs for the study of Hebrew, Aramaic, Syriac, Arabic, and Greek at the universities of Oxford, Paris, Bologna, and Salamanca.[9]

Evidence that the conversion of the Jews was the impetus for the systematic study of Hebrew and Jewish sources may be found in the work of Roger Bacon (1210–90?). A Franciscan living in Oxford, he exemplified the new humanistic thinking that was to overtake European intellectuals and provide the underpinnings of the Reformation movement.[10] He stressed the importance of studying Greek, Hebrew, Arabic, and Aramaic, believing that these languages offered a wealth of scientific and philosophical as well as theological knowledge.[11] His primary interest in the study of Hebrew, however, remained the need to convert the Jews:

The power of converting resides in the hand of the Latins, and so among us infinite numbers of Jews perish because no one knows how to preach to them or to interpret the scriptures in their language, nor argue and dispute with them according to the literal meaning ... what an unspeakable loss of souls. ... And it is still worse because from them began the foundation of our faith. ... We ought to consider that they are of the seed of the patriarchs, the prophets, and ... from their stem the Lord was born; and the glorious Virgin, and apostles and saints innumerable have descended.[12]

Bacon's work also provides evidence of a departure from the previous primary motivation for Christian study of Hebrew. In the following passage he provides a reason for the study of Hebrew that is independent of polemical or apologetic motives: "God has revealed philosophy to his saints, to whom also he gave the Law. He did so because philosophy was indispensable for the understanding, promulgation, adoption, and defense of the Law. It was for this reason that it was delivered in all its details in the Hebrew language . . . to the patriarchs and the prophets."[13]

In the fourteenth century Nicolas de Lyra, who was greatly influenced by the writings of Rashi,[14] produced an extensive biblical commentary in which he gave priority to the literal meaning of the text. In his introduction he emphasized that

As a building declining from its foundation is likely to fall, so [any] exposition, which deviates from the literal sense, must be reckoned unbecoming and unsuitable. . . . Those . . . who wish to achieve proficiency in the study of the sacred scriptures, must begin with the literal sense, especially because from it alone can any argument be brought to prove or illucidate that which is doubtful. . . . The literal sense has been much obscured by . . . others . . . who have hedged it around with mystical interpretations so as nearly to choke it. . . .[15]

Lyra stressed that it was necessary to be thoroughly familiar with the languages of the original text and the other available Jewish sources. His own biblical commentary was the first to be printed (Rome 1471–72), and is acknowledged to have greatly influenced the writings of Luther and Wycliffe. In his polemical writings Lyra referred to the Hebrew and Jewish works cited in his commentary as follows: "Although writings of this kind are false in great part, that is, the Talmud and the commentaries of the Hebrew doctors, nevertheless we are able through these [writings] to efficaciously argue against them."[16]

During the fourteenth and fifteenth centuries Christian Hebraism was an integral part of the Renaissance revival of learning that enthusiastically embraced the study of the three classical literatures—Greek, Latin, and Hebrew. The fifteenth-century Florentine, Giovanni Pico della Mirandola (1463–94), was an influential humanist, a pioneer in the study of Semitic languages, and considered by many to be the father of the Christian Kabbalah. He had been a student of the Jewish scholar Yochanan Allemanno, who was thoroughly familiar with the Greek and Arabic philosophers and the author of a kabbalistic commentary on the Pentateuch. It was under his guidance that Pico collected an extensive library of Hebrew manuscripts, mostly on kabbalistic topics. Pico later translated some of the works in this genre into Latin, notably Recanati's *Homath ha-Nefesh.*

Pico chose the foundations of the Jewish Kabbalah as proofs for his argument in support of the truth of the Christian faith.[17] In his *Oratorio de dignitate Hominis* he wrote:

Among the Hebrews of the present day these books are cherished with such devotion that it is permitted no man to touch them unless he be forty years of age. When I had purchased these books, at no small cost to myself; when I had read them through with great diligence and with unwavering toil; I saw in them . . . not so much the Mosaic religion as the Christian faith. There is the mystery of the Trinity . . . the incarnation of the Word . . . the divinity of the Messiah. There I read about original sin, its expiation through Christ, the Heavenly Jerusalem, the fall of the devils. . . . The same things we read daily in Paul, Jerome and Augustine.[18]

In his defense against accusations of Judaizing he responded: "There is hardly a point of controversy between us and the Jews on which they cannot be refuted out of the books of the Kabbalists. [So much so] that there will not be a corner left for them to hide in."[19] He thus used his thorough knowledge of Jewish mystical writings to support his arguments against Judaism and provide an intellectual as well as mystical underpinning for the need to convert the Jews.

The German humanist Johannes Reuchlin met Pico in 1490 and was greatly influenced by his work. Reuchlin himself believed that both the speculative and practical aspects of the Kabbalah centered on the doctrine of the Messiah. George Foot Moore has suggested that Reuchlin brought the Kabbalah into prominence in Christian apologetic and polemical literature, placing it alongside the Targum, Talmud, and Midrash.[20]

Born in 1455, Reuchlin is considered to have been the moving force behind the German Reformation movement.[21] In the course of his career he functioned as a judge, ambassador, and professor of Greek and Hebrew. He maintained an extensive correspondence with Erasmus, Luther, and other leading scholars, humanists, and Reformers. He had studied with eminent Jewish scholars, first with Jacob Loans, the court physician for Emperor Fredric III, and later with Obadiah Sforno, another distinguished scholar. It was under these teachers' influence that Reuchlin authored his *Linguae Hebraicae Rudimenta.* In a letter to his friend Arnold von Tungarn, he discussed the purpose of this work: ". . . I have composed a Hebrew grammar and dictionary, a work hitherto unheard of, which has cost me the greatest trouble and a large portion of my fortune, induced to do it by the great worth of the sacred writings . . . for the advantage of students from them." He also published a number of kabbalistic treatises in which he posited that ancient culture was the repository of all wisdom and that the Hebrew language was the gateway to this great source of knowledge. He went so far as to claim that he shook with terror when he read Hebrew because he could feel God's presence in every letter of the alphabet.[22]

Reuchlin's reverence for the Hebrew language and the ancient culture it represented appears to be in stark contrast to his attitude toward the Jews who were his contemporaries. In 1505 he was commissioned to investigate the condition of the Jews, and produced a work titled *Dr. Johann Reuchlin's tutsch missive, warum die Juden so lang ellend sind*.[23] In this work he expressed the view that the persecution of the Jews was justified. "The misery of the Jews," he said, "is the consequence of so great a sin, that its equal has never been committed . . . the punishment for this sin has already continued for 1300 years. It is also a transgression which they slight and do not consider as such. This can be none other than the crime they committed toward Christ, as the prophets had foretold. . . . The punishment [for it] was so severe and so long lasting on account of the obstinacy of the Jews, who continually blaspheme afresh. This punishment will only cease whenever they acknowledge Jesus as the Messiah."

In the first decade of the sixteenth century Reuchlin became involved in a controversy with the convert Pfefferkorn. The latter was associated with the Dominicans at Cologne and produced a work which he called *Judenspiegel*. In it he described the beliefs and customs of the Jews and proposed a number of measures that would bring about their conversion. All Jews were to be compelled to listen to the preaching of the Gospels, thus exposing them to the truth of the Christian faith. Hebrew and Jewish works would be destroyed on the ground that they were blasphemous to Jesus and Christianity. As a further incentive for the conversion, Pfefferkorn proposed a number of economic sanctions against the Jews that would limit their means of livelihood. He reasoned that these sanctions would induce many of the leaders of the Jewish community to convert, and that the rest of their coreligionists would soon follow.

The emperor Maximilian agreed to enact at least one of Pfefferkorn's suggestions and issued an edict requiring the confiscation and destruction of all Hebrew and Jewish works deemed to be injurious or insulting to Christianity.

The Jews appealed this order on legal grounds and gained the support of many prominent humanists and scholars. Reuchlin was appointed by the emperor to examine the confiscated books.[24] In his report, he separated Hebrew and Judaic literature into seven categories, and determined that the works that comprised six of these categories should not be destroyed because they were valuable to Christians in the study of theology and science. The works within these categories included the Talmud, the Zohar, the works of Rashi, the Kimhis, Ibn Ezra, and Geshonides, among others. Reuchlin called for the destruction of the works comprising the seventh category, indicating that they contained blasphemous material and had no other redeeming value.[25]

His apparent lack of zeal in the destruction of Hebrew and Jewish literature heated the controversy between Reuchlin and Pfefferkorn and made it a cause célèbre. It continued for many years, with much invective published by both sides that was polemical and acrimonious in nature. This dispute constituted a turning point in the conflict between the authority of the Church and that of the Scriptures, and became an important feature in the development of the Reformation movement. The battle to preserve Hebrew literature was now waged on behalf of Christian Hebraica and was no longer directly connected with the conversion of the Jews. The primary motive was that it held the key to a better understanding of the foundations of Christianity and provided confirmation of its truth.

Reuchlin's attitude represented a new development in the Christian Jewish polemic. While Pfefferkorn followed the traditional Catholic belief that the Jews had to be converted before the ultimate redemption, Reuchlin regarded the conversion of the Jews to be irrelevant to the Second Coming. He believed that the original ideal state that the Jews had represented could now be achieved through the command of the ancient Hebrew sources by pious, learned Christians.

Erasmus supported Reuchlin in his struggle against Pfefferkorn and the Dominicans. His role in the Christian Jewish polemic was significant because of his great popularity and the great respect he commanded among the humanists. Erasmus understood that the controversy was not an isolated incident but an integral part of a larger struggle between the humanists and church orthodoxy.[26] His attitude toward the biblical text serves to illustrate the new humanistic approach to learning. Like Lyra, he believed that it was necessary to penetrate through the mystic and allegorical sense of the text in order to achieve understanding of its original, literal meaning: ". . . it is impossible," he wrote, "to understand the message of Moses without knowledge of the language in which he transmitted it, or having access to the Hebrew commentaries which had been referred to by Origen, Jerome, and other diligent Christian scholars."[27]

The rise of Christian Hebraism in Europe from the early medieval period through the sixteenth century was based on the belief that the religion of the Hebrew Bible formed the foundation of the Christian faith and had a profound influence on the New Testament. Early Jewish extrabiblical writings were of interest to Christians because they shed light on the milieu in which Jesus and the Apostles had lived.

The proselytizing impulse was one of the basic tenets of Christianity, and the conversion of the Jews was considered particularly important because of their close connection to the roots of Christianity. Polemical disputations were considered to be an important tool in the efforts to convert the Jews. The disagreement between Jews and Christians centered on their different methods of interpreting the biblical text. The christological approach most often relied on the allegorical and symbolic sense, while the Jewish usually adhered to the literal and historical meaning of the text. The rise in prominence of the latter approach among Christian exegetes may be attributed to their increased familiarity with Hebrew and access to the original texts.

An element common to all polemical arguments between Christians and Jews was the question of who of the disputants represented the true Israel, the people of God. Since Christianity grew out of the old Israelite belief, the legitimacy of the Christian faith could better be argued after the elimination of its predecessor. Judaism had to be disposed of in order for Christianity to be the sole receptor of divine revelation. Jews, for their part, sought to refute the christological interpretation of Scripture and the polemical pronouncement of the Church by demonstrating the eternal and irrevocable nature of the covenant between God and his people, the original Israelites and their descendants, the Jews. This could be accomplished by proving the truth of the original covenant against Christian interpretations. The Jews regarded Christianity as a form of usurpation, while the Christians viewed Judaism as a relic of a defunct order that was superseded by the advent of Jesus and the birth of Christianity. As long as Jews were not willing to convert to the new covenant, Christianity could not take its rightful place as the only true religion.

Christian Hebraism was an important element in this struggle. Knowledge of the Hebrew text provided an important tool for the conversion effort. Old Testament verses could be cited as proof of the coming of Christ, his divinity, and of the replacement of the old covenant by the new Christian faith. Knowledge of the language enabled the Christian disputants to refute the Jewish arguments through the use of Hebraic literature.

Having despaired of the mass conversion of the Jews to Christianity, the Reformers of the fifteenth and sixteenth centuries made use of Christian Hebraism in their struggle against the Catholic church and, through the use of the Hebrew text and commentaries, to bolster their argument for the authority of the text over that of the church. It was through the knowledgeable reading of the biblical text that they would realize their aspiration of becoming the true Israel.

Notes

1. See G. F. Moore, "Christian Writers on Judaism," *Harvard Theological Review* 14 (1921): 203 and n.5.

2. See F. E. Talmadge, "R. David Kimhi as Polemicist," *Hebrew Union College Annual* 38 (1967).

3. See his commentaries on the Psalms (22:17, 110:1,3; 2:6); Isaiah (2:22, etc.); Ezekiel (44:1,2), for example.

4. See L. Newman, *Jewish Influence on Christian Reform Movements* (New York, 1925), 61

5. This followed a similar event in Paris, which culminated in the seizure and burning of all available copies of the Talmud on the ground that they contained great blasphemies against Christ and the Church. See S. Grayzel, *The Church and the Jews in the XIIIth Century* (Philadelphia, 1933), 9ff.

6. See Cecil Roth, "The Disputation of Barcelona (1263)," *Harvard Theological Review* 43 (1950): 117–40.

7. See J. Cohen, *The Friars and the Jews* (Ithaca, 1982), 108–22.

8. Some of the Jewish sources have since been lost, and are now known only through this work. See G. F. Moore, 203, P. E. Lapide, *Hebrew in the Church* (Grand Rapids, 1984), 13.

9. See L. Newman, 25.

10. For further discussion of the topic see E. Bevan and C. Singer, *Legacy of Israel* (Oxford, 1965), 299ff.

11. He wrote grammars for Greek and Hebrew. See G. Lloyd Jones, *The Discovery of Hebrew in Tudor England* (Manchester, 1983), 11–12.

12. See *Opus Majus* 3, no. 13, *Studies in English Franciscan History*, trans. A. G. Little (Manchester, England, 1917).

13. See *Opus Tertium* 10:32 and 24:79, trans. A. G. Little, in *Roger Bacon Commemorative Essays* (Oxford, 1914), Bevan and Singer, 300.

14. See H. Hailperin, *Rashi and the Christian Scholars* (Pittsburgh, 1963).

15. *Postillae Perpetuae*, written 1322–1330.

16. Hailperin, 140.

17. See *Conclusiones cabalisticae secundum opinioneum propriam.*

18. E. Cassirer, ed., *The Renaissance Philosophy of Man* (Chicago, 1948), 252.

19. G. F. Moore, 210.

20. See G. F. Moore, 208.

21. See F. Barham, *The Life and Times of Johann Reuchlin* (London, 1843).

22. See Bevan and Singer, 322–23; J. Friedman, *The Most Ancient Testimony*, 20. Reuchlin's treatises are *De Verbo mirifico* (1494) and *De Arte Cabalistica* (1517).

23. The title may be translated as "Dr. Johannes Reuchlin's German Missive on Why the Jews Have Been in Misery for So Long."

24. Note the parallel between Reuchlin and Raymundus Martini in the court of King James I.

25. This category included the polemical treatise *Toledoth Yeshuah*, which had originated in the medieval period and was a purported account

of the life of Jesus. It had been cited in Martini's *Pugio Fidei* and in the thirteenth century disputation that led to the burning of the Talmud. Another work was *Sepher Hanizahon*, which had been written at the beginning of the fifteenth century and, according to Reuchlin, included material against the Virgin Mary and Christ (see his *Tutch Missive* and Newman, 300, 567).

26. See Bevan and Singer, 317f.

27. *The Collected Works of Erasmus* (Toronto, 1974), 4:267, Letter 541. For a discussion of Erasmus's short-lived attempt at mastering Hebrew see G. Lloyd Jones, 31–32.

Charles Stinson

"Northernmost Israel": England, the Old Testament, and the Hebraic "Veritas" as Seen by Bede and Roger Bacon

This essay, like those of Professor Spanier on Christian Hebraism and Professor Kreiger on English travelers in the seventeenth century, will attempt to sketch in a sort of "European prologue" or general background to the Anglo-American colonial data on Christian Hebraism and interest in the Hebrew Bible and language as "Old Testament."

For the earliest Christian reflective writers, such as Justin Martyr and Origen in the Greek East and Tertullian and Cyprian in the Latin West, as for all Christians, the Hebrew Bible is, in Gen. 1–3, the source of cosmic and anthropological truth, and, from Noah, Abraham, and Moses onward, prophetic preparation for the New Testament and the Church. The Hebrew Bible is not, however, used as a source of analogues or models for a Christian *society*. This is quite understandable, given the Christian movement's illegality in the Roman Empire. The Church had no public structural expressions at all parallel to those of Israel until the fourth century when the Church's situation changed radically with Constantine's adoption of Christianity as the religion of the empire. Thus, Eusebius, called "the father of church history," can begin drawing parallels between Constantine's victory at the Tiber and Moses's victory at the Red Sea—as crucial instances of Divine Providence.[1] On the whole, though, Eusebius prefers to draw parallels between the earthly emperor and the heavenly Pantokrator (the Ruler of All Things),[2] and this will be the dominant theme among Greek Christian writers from that time forward. The same theme will be continued by Russian Christian writers. These authors will employ the Old Testament fairly extensively, but they will do so chiefly for royal, liturgical, iconic, and mystical purposes—in short, for eternal "Platonic" purposes central to Eastern Christian thought. Eastern writers show little interest in the sort of this-worldly, linear-historical, social parallels that certain Western Latin Christian writers will finally begin to develop, a process that will reach its fullest stage in Protestant writings about the "New Israel" in the New World.

The stress here is on the phrases "certain . . . writers" and "finally . . . develop." De facto, some of the leading Latin Christian Fathers do not move very far, if at all, in this direction. Jerome is too much the philologist—and conceptually too scatter-brained—to have much sense for larger patterns of history. Ambrose's focus is almost exclusively on the inward life of the Church: liturgy, ministry, asceticism. So his use of the *Vetus Testamentum* is, with few exceptions, intraecclesial only. In this regard he hardly differs from his pre-Constantinian fellow bishop Cyprian, who uses the rebellion against Moses by Korah, Dathan, and Abiram in the desert and the punishment of the three rebels as a cautionary analogue for presbyters insubordinate to their bishop.[3] In an empire still pre-Christian there is no external social resonance here. And even in a Christianized Empire Ambrose has moved only a little beyond this. These writers use the Old Testament spiritually, allegorically.

Augustine might, a priori, be thought to be the great, even the majestic exception to this narrowness of perspective. Certainly, one would think, in his enormous *De Civitate Dei* he must put the *Vetus Testamentum* to maximum use. So one would guess. But one would be wrong. In fact, Augustine surprises the reader here. He does nothing of the sort with the *Vetus Testamentum*. To be sure, he gives the longest-and-amplest-yet chronicle of Old Testament history: from Adam and Noah through Abraham, Moses, David, and Solomon, down through the Prophets and the Exilic Period and Ezra and Nehemiah, and on to the era of Christ.[4] And he sets it alongside an equally lengthy and dense account of extrabiblical history. He is very much fuller than Lactantius[5] before him and Orosius[6] after him, who are sketchers and dabblers next to Augustine. But, like them, he seems quite uninterested in finding structural parallels between ancient Israel as a society and the structures of the church and of Christian society in his own day. This "lack" makes full sense, however, when we remember Augustine's general mindset: his Neoplatonic preference for inner over outer, and soul over body; and his strong residual sourness toward any external social structure or power structure. Even when Christianized, such structures are understood by Augustine to be "mixed" phenomena of good and evil. They are parts of the often ugly and struggling "Civitas hominis," not the pure and beautiful and peaceful "Civitas Dei." Hence, Augustine can find significant analogues only between the inner spiritual life of Israel and the inner spiritual life of the Church on earth, and above all in "the tranquility" of eternal life, where "all of Israel" finally shall be gathered.[7] But, then, while Eusebius wrote as the Christian empire was new and blooming, Augustine wrote as he contemplated it daily falling apart, at least in the West, under barbarian assaults.

Similarly, Gregory the Great uses the Old Testament spiritually, that is, allegorically, to describe states of individual souls and of the inner life of the church community: troubles and triumphs, sorrows and joys.[8] But he does not apply much of this to the externalities of Christian society. Why do so? It would be superfluous since this world, Gregory is sure, is approaching its last days: "The termination of the present world is already near," he assures Ethelbert, King of the Anglo-Saxons, "and the Reign of the Saints is to come which will never have any termination."[9] Isidore treats the *Vetus Testamentum* and Israel as a subsection in his *Etymologies* or encyclopedia where they are twinned with the *Novum Testamentum* and the Church.[10] But the discussion is always, as it is for Augustine and Gregory the Great, intraecclesial. Isidore does not, in that section, discuss *natio* or *populus*, nor even the Hispanic church in particular.

Neither does Gildas in his fiercely gloomy little tract of church history, *The Complaining Book about the Cutting Down of Britain*, which deals with the rise, the affluence, the worldliness and sins, and then the punishing decline and fall of British Christianity.[11] The Old Testament is used here—and with a literal vengeance—in almost numbing abundance. There are unbelievably long *catenae*, indeed, cascades of vehement "increpatio" or "reproaches" for British Christian leaders taken straight from the Hebrew Prophets. Huge swatches from Isaiah, Jeremiah, Amos, Joel, Ezekiel, and others are simply inserted, undigested, uncommented-on, into Gildas's text. He concedes that he is writing "in vili stylo"—"in a low style." But he does not care. His goal is not to charm or please but to cause "pain," "sorrow," and "astonishment" in his British readers. Yet for all his Hebrew-style prophetic furor, Gildas does not present Christian Britain as an explicit parallel to Israel. British Christians are just another collection of sinners to be chastened by the Scriptures. But for Gildas the Church of Britain is no more another Israel than is the Church of Gallia for Irenaeus, or the Church of North Africa for Augustine, or the Church of Hispania for Isidore.

Something different begins to appear, modestly enough, in later Gallia. Salvian of Marseilles, a representative of the old Roman-Latin populace, admires the Levitical Laws of Israel on slavery and on crimes and punishments. And he thinks that they should be incorporated into the secular legislation of Christian Gallia.[12] Yet Salvian draws no wider parallels that could lead to the concept of the Gallic church and society as an Israel. Later on in Gallia, to the north, Gregory of Tours imitates Eusebius's ten-volume *Church History* and produces a ten-volume *History of the Franks* in which he chronicles the conversion and progress and problems of the Frankish Christians. Gregory, like Gildas, uses the *Vetus Testamentum* in abundance, both to record the highlights of Israel's history and as solemn and fearful warnings against vice.[13] Alongside this, however, a new development is evident: an increasing use of Old Testament figures and/or events as typological guidance or warning for individuals in very personal contexts and situations. To be sure, earlier Latin writers like Cyprian and Ambrose—and Greeks like Eusebius, too—had pointed to parallels between Old Testament persons, scenes, and crises, and the lives of Christian kings, nobles, and clergy. But in Gregory of Tours this process seems to increase both in intensity and mundane intimacy of application. Where Ambrose, functioning as "Nathan to David," rebuked the Emperor Theodosius in grave but measured language for "massacring" some thousands of people to punish a rebellion in Greece,[14] Gregory of Tours uses Isaiah 5:8 and Proverbs 3:17 to terrify King Guntchramnus with heavy-handed maledictions and prophecies of death for seizing church property and other relatively petty matters.[15] The whole scale and tone of Old Testament parallelings are being reduced here to fit a much smaller and less majestic context.

The reason for this development is obviously sociocultural. Christianity had entered the old western provinces of the empire—Italia, Gallia, Africa, Hispania, Britannia—by missionary osmosis. There it had encountered old, established populaces and fixed social structures. So Christian writers have no "new people," no "new nation" or "new tribe" to analogize freshly with the ancient newness of Israel moving out of Egypt through the Sinai and into the Canaan of Promise. With Gregory of Tours we find a middle situation: Gregory is a writer confronted by a new people—his own tribe, and Franks—entering, however, into a long Christianized and stable Gallic Christian populace. So the *novitas* is rather blurred by pre-existing Christian realities.

But what would happen to Christian images of Israel and of Church and People if a Christian writer were to examine a new, non-Christian *populus* entering into a previously Christianized society but destabilizing and displacing it—not relatively smoothly converting into it, but remaining for a considerable length of time pagan and hostile to its defeated neighboring Christians? In such a case—in fact, the first of its exact kind in Western Christianity—the *novitas* would be far clearer, far more striking. This is the situation with the Venerable Bede, who described the pagan Anglo-Saxons—his own tribe—invading and chasing off Gildas's Christian people in Roman Britain. (Patrick, in confrontation with Druidic Ireland—Celts untouched till then by Christianity—might have preceded Bede here with an earlier *novitas*. But Patrick, while he can quote prophetically from the Old as well as the New Testament,[16] is a practical missionary, not a historian and not a close student of the *Vetus Testamentum*.)

In comparison with his near predecessors as church historians—Gildas and Gregory of Tours—Bede seems at first reading rather restrained in his use of the Old Testament, at least in his best-known work, *The Ecclesiastical History of the Anglo-Saxon Peoples*. Gregory, imitating Eusebius, begins with a panorama of Israel's history before he reaches the New Testament era and Greco-Roman Christian history. Only then does he proceed to the beginnings of the new Frankish Christianity. And while Gildas does not give the same resumé of Israel's history, his account of the British Christian church, its growth, its sins and faults, and its decline and final "cutting down" is, as noted, in parts almost overwhelmed by astonishingly long extracts, chiefly of a moral and minatory sort, from the Hebrew prophets. By contrast, Bede's use of the Old Testament is in sheer quantity of citations, very much less. Everything is much more subsurface, on a plane deeper than mere chronological recounting or even moral warning.

Bede begins, modestly enough, with the physical geography of the British Isles. He follows this with an account of the conquest of the island by Roman troops and the development of "Britannia" as a prosperous "colonia" of the Empire. This is followed by the rise of the British Christian church in the second and third centuries C.E., the arrival of Germanic peoples—Angles, Saxons, Jutes, and others—on British Christian territory in the fifth and sixth centuries, and the process of their Christianizing. As Bede notes with grim, purse-lipped disapproval, the British Christians had little to do with this conversion. The British, naturally enough, much resented their displacement by Germanic invaders, and hardly cared to expend much effort evangelizing them. In any case, Bede adds, Divine Providence intended the conversion to be effected not by lazy and uncharitable Britons but by "worthier heralds" of the gospel from papal Rome:[17] the Benedictine monk Augustine and his confreres, who arrived in 597 in the kingdom of Kent to set up a Christian bishop in the small trading town of Canterbury, and from there to push northward and westward over the largely Germanized island.

Although Old Testament citations and echoes are not overwhelming in quantity in the *Ecclesiastical History*, they are striking when we do encounter them. Bede found special Hebraic references to the new Anglo-Saxon peoples in the archival material at Canterbury available to

him by correspondence. He then wove it into his narrative and made it his own. At the very start there was, of course, Pope Gregory the Great's letter to the Abbot Melitus, who was heading for Britain around 601 C.E. Gregory there explicitly compares the task of evangelizing the Anglo-Saxons with the divine pedagogy that weaned the people of Israel from Egyptian and Canaanite paganism. "We wish you," Gregory tells Melitus,

to inform [Augustine of Canterbury] that we have been giving careful thought to the affairs of the Angles, and have come to the conclusion that the temples of the idols among that people should on no account be destroyed. The idols are to be destroyed, but the temples themselves are to be sprinkled with holy water, altars set up in them and relics deposited there. For if these temples are well built they must be purified from the worship of demons and dedicated to the service of the true God. In this way we hope that the people, seeing that their temples are not destroyed, may abandon their error and, flocking more readily to their accustomed resorts, may come to know and adore the true God. . . .

For the pagan Germanic "sacrifice of oxen," let "some other solemnity be substituted" for it: a "dedication" or some "festivals for holy martyrs" with the honoring of their "relics." Instead of "sacrificing beasts to the Devil," the Anglo-Saxons as Christians "may kill" the beasts "for food to the praise of God. . . . For certainly it is impossible to eradicate all errors from obstinate minds at one stroke, and whoever wishes to climb to the mountain top climbs gradually step by step and not in one leap." The history of Israel shows the divine wisdom here. "It was," Gregory reminds Melitus,

in this way that the Lord revealed Himself to the Israelite people in Egypt, permitting the sacrifices formerly offered to the Devil to be offered thenceforward to Himself instead. So He bade them sacrifice beasts to Him, so that, once they became enlightened, they might abandon one element of sacrifice and retain another. For, while they were to offer the same beasts as before, they were to offer them to God instead of to idols, so that they would no longer be offering the same sacrifices. You are kindly to inform our brother Augustine of this policy so that he may consider how he may best implement it on the spot. . . .[18]

Carrying on in this missionary tradition, Pope Boniface V addressed a personal letter to the (future model Christian) king, Edwin of Northumbria, urging him to convert to Christ and bring his people and kingdom with him into Christianity. The pope commands Edwin to break with the local northerly equivalents of the fleshpots of idolatry of Mesopotamia and Egypt: "The profound guilt of those who perversely cling to pernicious superstitions and idolatrous worship," the pontiff inveighs in prophetic tones, "is clearly seen by the damnable example of those whom they adore. Of such the Psalmist says [Psalm 96:5]: 'All the gods

of the nations are idols. But the Lord made the heavens.' And again [115]: 'Eyes have they, but they see not; they have hands, but they handle not; feet have they, but they walk not. They that make them are like unto them; so is everyone that trusts in them.'"

The pope applies Hebrew monotheistic logic to Edwin's pagan mind: "How," he asks,

can such objects have power to help you, when they are made for you from perishable materials by the labor of your own subjects and servants? Even their inanimate resemblance to living shapes is due solely to man's craftsmanship. Unless you move them they cannot move, but are like a stone fixed in its place: they are manufactured, but have no intelligence, being utterly insensible and having no power to hurt or to help. We cannot understand how people can be deluded as to worship as gods objects to which they themselves have given the likeness of a body.

Conversion to biblical faith is the only solution to the absurdity problem here. "Accept, therefore," the Pontiff commands,

the Sign of the Holy Cross by which the entire human race has been redeemed, and exorcise from your heart the damnable crafts and devices of the Devil who jealously opposes all the workings of God's goodness. Overthrow and destroy these artificial gods of your own making; and the very destruction of these things, which never drew the breath of life and could never receive understanding from their makers, will itself afford you clear evidence of the nothingness of these objects of your former worship. Consider, you yourselves, to whom God has given the breath of life, are nobler than these man-made things; for Almighty God has ordered your descent through countless generations from the first man He created. . . . [19]

A generation later the same high prophetic note is struck by Pope Vitalian in a letter carried up from Rome to King Oswy or Oswiu of Northumbria, another converted Anglo-Saxon ruler. "To our son," Vitalian writes,

the most excellent Lord Oswy, King of the Saxons, from Bishop Vitalian, Servant of the Servants of God: We have read Your Excellency's welcome letter in which We recognize your very sincere devotion and fervent desire for eternal life. And We know how you have been converted to the true and apostolic faith by the guiding hand of God, and We trust that, as you now reign over your own nation, so you will one day reign with Christ. Your nation is fortunate to have a king so wise and devoted to the worship of God, who not only adores God Himself, but labors day and night to lead all his people to the Catholic Apostolic Faith, and to save his own soul. Who can help being glad to hear such encouraging news? And who will not be delighted at such works of devotion?

The pope then draws the king's attention to some interesting scriptural details: how especially have the Divine Scriptures prophesied, and

with such unusually pointed clarity, the conversion of an *insular* people. "For your nation," Vitalian continues,

has come to believe in Christ our mighty God in fulfillment of the words of God's prophets, as Isaiah says [Chs. 11, 42, 49] 'In that day there shall be a root of Jesse, which shall stand as an enseign of the people; to it shall the Gentiles seek.' And again: 'Listen, O Islands, unto Me; and hearken, you people from afar.' And a little later, he says: 'It is a light thing that you should be My servant, to raise up the Tribes of Jacob, and to restore the preserved of Israel. I will also give you for a light to the Gentiles, that you may be My salvation unto the end of the earth.' And again: 'Kings shall see, princes also shall arise and worship.' And later: 'I have given you for a Covenant of the people, to establish the earth and possess the desolate heritages; that you may say to the prisoners: Go forth; to them that are in darkness, show yourselves.' And again: 'I, the Lord, have called you in righteousness, and will hold your hand, and will keep you, and give you for a Covenant of the people, for a light of the Gentiles; to open the blind eyes, to bring out the prisoners from prison, and them that sit in darkness out of the prison house.'

The biblical pre-portrait here—a sort of divine sketch of the future—is so striking with regard to the conversion of the Anglo-Saxons that the pope considers it virtually definitive. "Here you may see, most excellent Son," he says, "how clearly it is prophesied, not only of you but of all nations, that they shall believe in Christ the Maker of all things."[20]

True, prophecy foretells of a plurality of nations—"not only of you but of all nations"—still there *is* that special reference to "islands." And this clearly does not apply to "all nations." But it does fit most beautifully a "Britannia" turned Angle-land. Either Vitalian himself or some curial scribal assistant—perhaps a secretary for biblical citations—knew precisely which texts from Isaiah to pluck for use in a letter to King Oswy. And certainly Bede appreciates their perfect applicability to his own insular Populus Anglo-Saxonus, conscious of being a collection of ragged tribes brought newly "from afar" and made into a Populus Dei in accord with the example and ideal of the Tribes of Israel gathered into the prime Populus Dei in history.

The new people really can be thought of rather in the terms of a newly evangelized part or even extension of Israel. As Georges Tugène comments: for Bede the Anglo-Saxon church is both "a reflection of the primitive community"[21] of the New Testament church, and also, more ultimately, "an echo" of "the election of Israel" in the Old Testament.[22] And this echo can extend through time down to very intimate analogies between internal difficulties and deviations in Israel and those in the Anglo-Saxon church.

Of one monarch of a half-Christianized kingdom Bede speaks with cold reproach, comparing him pejoratively with Edwin of Northumbria, a true Christian king utterly faithful to the gospel. "So great," Bede says, "was Edwin's zeal for the true faith that he persuaded King Earpwald, son of Redwald, King of the East Angles to abandon his superstitious idolatry and accept the faith and sacraments of Christ with his whole province."

But there was unsoundness of faith in the latter king's case:

[Earpwald's] father Redwald had, in fact, long before this [conversion of Earpwald] received Christian baptism in Kent, but to no good purpose; for on his return home his wife and certain perverse advisers persuaded him to apostatize from the true Faith. So his last state was worse than the first: for, like the ancient Samaritans, he tried to serve both Christ and the ancient gods, and he had in the same temple an altar for the Holy Sacrifice of Christ side by side with an altar on which victims were offered to devils. Aldwulf, king of that province, who lived into our own times, testifies that this temple was still standing on his day, and that he had seen it when a boy. This King Redwald was a man of noble descent but ignoble in his action.[23]

Redwald had created an Anglo-Saxon version of the ruins of Hebrew faith in the shards of the vanished Northern Kingdom of Israel where the half-paganized "Samaritans" were found. Dwelling in an Ahab-and-Jezebel-style of impurity, they were all that was left of the unworthy Ten Tribes whose dissolution into paganism was their divine punishment subsequent to the Assyrian invasion of 721 B.C.E.

It has been noted by some that Bede divided his *Ecclesiastical History* into five books. He begins with the geographical foundations of Britain and runs through communal foundings and progress and wonder stories and finally ends with a summary and a sermonic-style conclusion about the religious future of the people in the land. In effect, in a certain subtle way, we can discern a miniature semiversion of the structure of the Pentateuch from Genesis 1 through Deuteronomy 34. While this is not at all demonstrably certain as a consciously intended analogue in Bede's mind, it has a certain degree of possibility. Hence, the late distinguished Bede scholar, Professor J. M. Wallace-Hadrill of Oxford was willing to tolerate it with, perhaps, an indulgent smile. "Five languages in Britain," he comments, "Five books of the *Lex Divina* (the Pentateuch): therefore, five books of the *Ecclesiastical History*. This is a better explanation, if one is required, than to suppose that Bede saw the ten books of Gregory of Tours' *History [of the Franks]* and divided by two."[24]

Given Bede's intense love of the Old Testament, the use of five books was not likely to have been totally accidental. Gregory divided his *History* into ten books. But that was most probably in conscious imitation of his own model Eusebius rather than a mirroring of the Decalogue. Certainly, as Judith McClure writes,

revelational moments, still the basic structural parallel remains. While the "elders of Israel"—the "seventy" of them called by Moses—could not accompany him to the peak of Sinai, still the election of those "seniores" predemonstrates the basic form of the future Church: "Moses chose seventy elders to assist him in governing the people" in its tribes and clans. And that foreshadows the future election of "bishops"[35] to rule various regional portions of the Church. In essence, "the Synagogue" of Israel was "the Church" of that time, while the Church is "the Israel" of this present time. The Jews were "the senior people" of God, "the prior part" of the Church as Israel.[36]

Fittingly, then, the Tabernacle and the Temple and their hierarchy and ministers, especially the later, larger Temple furnish clear prototypes for the hierarchical-pastoral structure of the Church: as the Aaronic high priest stands to his fellow assistant priests, so does the Christian bishop stand to his assistants, the presbyters. "Aaron designates," Bede says, "especially the Highest Priest, that is the Lord and Savior [Christ]." But Aaron "also, indeed, [stands for] the priests of our [present] order" in the Church.[37] "With the Lord ordering it," Bede comments,

through Moses in the Law, the first Pontiff Aaron was constituted, after whose death his son Eleazar received the gift of the Priesthood. And with him dead, his son Phineas became his successor in the Priesthood. And so on down to the time of David. . . . One after another heir of the Pontificate [took office]. . . . But David wanted that, along with the growing cultus and magnificence of the Temple, the beauty of its ministry and ministers should grow also. So convoked a gathering of all the progeny of the sons of Aaron and Eleazar and those also who descended from the stock of Ithamar. And he divided them into 24 parts, electing in each single part individual Pontiffs, and electing others who were in the parts of a lesser Priesthood which is now [in Christian times] called the Presbyterate. . . .

Now, Bede continues commenting, "while all [the priests] were equal in the sacerdotal grade, one, however, among them who was seen to be worthier by a special reverence and pre-eminent by power would have the name of "High Priest'. . . ."[38]

Hence, the operating distinction between the New Testament and the Church parallels that between Christian bishops and lesser priests, between the "episcopi," who had the plenitude of the priesthood, and the mere "presbyteri," who shared it only in part. And all of this was foreshadowed quite discernibly in Israel from Moses's era onward, and then with crystal clarity from David's time onward.[39]

At the very center of the Old Testament cultus is Scripture and preaching—the verbal-didactic work of "the Word." And for Bede it is absolutely superior to any physical ritual, however significant or even divinely commanded, in Israel and in the Church also. This is seen in advance in the Law given at Sinai and its exposition even by *ritual* specialists, the Aaronic priests and the Levites. Even they, Bede thinks, had as their chief duty the interpreting and preaching and application of the Law. Moses's own preaching at the foot of Sinai and in the desert,[40] and Ezra's assembling and preaching to the returned people before the watergate in Jerusalem after the Exile, furnish models and guidelines for Christian preaching to congregations. "The whole people," Bede quotes from the Book of Nehemiah (ch. 8), "wept when it heard the Words of the Law." The same holy teachers," he comments, "who excited the minds of their hearers to tears by sacred readings and devout exhortations, also consoled them when they rightly promised to them eternal joys to come." And then Ezra spoke "and said to the people: 'Go and eat fat and drink sweet wine and send portions to him for whom nothing is prepared. For this day is holy unto the Lord. And do not be sad,'" Ezra is a seasoned and wise pastor and a model pedagogue. "Fat" and "sweet wine" are certainly also symbols of "good action" and the "sweetness of the Word," Bede says, but here the alternation of preaching and feasting is also a quite literal lesson and not just allegorical. "This text," Bede insists, "it is proper for us to imitate even according to the letter. Thus, on feast days after prayer, the reading and the study of the Psalms are completed, we dispose ourselves to take care of the flesh by refeshments, and we remember to give part of it to the poor and to pilgrims,"[41] to travellers. The preached word stands, then, at the center of all—whether in Israel as the Old Church, or in the Church as the New Israel.

Outside the clerical precincts of the Church, the Christian kings of the Anglo-Saxon peoples may find in the Old Testament royal pictures of what they should be and do, and warnings of what will happen to them if they neglect their duties. Even the neighboring pagan rulers of kingdoms surrounding Israel reveal a pattern of helpfulness to the house of God. Bede points out that when "Solomon said to King Hiram of Tyre: 'Order that they [i.e., laborers] cut me cedars from Lebanon, and let my servants [work] with your servants.' This aptly fits the things of the Church."[42] Solomon is the model for the wise Christian monarch, and Hiram and his workers from Tyre typify "the learned teachers of the gentiles" contributing their efforts and gifts to the building up of the Church. Hiram also symbolizes, more specifically, pagan monarchs, "the Lords of things," who often "aid the Church with their wealth" and "nobly augment" her while protecting her "by decrees from heretics, schismatics and pagans."[43]

Great non-Hebrew rulers like Darius, Cyrus, and Artaxerxes aided Nehemiah and Ezra and their successors to rebuild the Jerusalem Temple and reestablish the Land of Israel, albeit as a vassal state of Persia. Nevertheless, they gave crucial assistance to the patterns of divine providence. Thus, they are splendid models for Anglo-Saxon kings who, a fortiori as Christians, should be even more zealous in building up the Church: "In the same order," Bede writes, "now also in the Holy Church things are done by earthly powers who are converted to the Faith and who propose public edicts for the state of the Church." So, "with the Lord aiding, and [the monarchs] putting all [the Church's] enemies under their feet, [the monarchs] desire to have an ever-placid quiet and peace" in their kingdoms and in the Church.[44]

On this theme McClure comments:

[as Bede read] a history of the Acts of Solomon and . . . the Royal Annals of the Kings of Israel and Judah, he could have been in no doubt that the History of the Chosen People, in both spiritual and political terms, depended, under God, on the influence, ability and military strength of its kings. The internal rivalries of the early contenders for power over the Israelites are made very plain in the scriptural text: the dispute between Saul and David, and the attempt to resolve it by marriage alliance; the exile of David in the territories of other kings, and his difficulties there; the final resolution of the conflict in battle, and the subsequent feud between the House of David and the House of Saul. Such material must inevitably have colored Bede's view, and increased his understanding of the struggle [in England] between the royal families of Bernicia and Deira. Bede would also have learned from his scriptural reading the overriding significance of the military strength of kings, and their need to serve as effective warleaders against the encroachments of surrounding tribes with their own hostile and aggressive kings. Indeed, his understanding of this point is explicit in his commentary and in his comparison of [King] Aethilfrith of Northumbria, *rex fortissimus et gloriae cupidissimus,* with Saul. So he would have seen the way in which powerful Kings like Saul and David extended their territories, and multiplied the peoples under their control; how the authority of a great King like Solomon depended upon the acceptance of his rule over a wide area inhabited by diverse peoples under minor rulers.[45]

The Anglo-Saxon parallels to this Bede finds abundantly around him. Of the wise and much admired King Edwin of Northumbria, he writes:

So peaceful was it in those parts of Britain under Edwin's jurisdiction that the proverb still runs that a woman could carry her newborn babe across the Island from sea to sea without any fear of harm. Such was the King's concern for the welfare of his people that in a number of places where he had noticed clear springs adjacent to the highway he ordered posts to be erected with brass bowls hanging from them, so that travelers could drink and refresh themselves. And so great was the people's affection for him, and so great the awe in which he was held, that no one wished or ventured to use those bowls for any other purpose. So royally was the King's dignity maintained throughout his realm that whether in battle or on a peaceful progress on horseback through city, town or countryside in the company of his thanes the royal standard was always borne before him. . . .[46]

Old Testament accounts of pious kings, Israelite and non-Israelite, should not go by as so much ancient history only, or as mere types for the generic moral guidance of anyone in any life situation. On the contrary, they can and should be taken sometimes very literally and personally by royal personages in particular who sit and listen to sermons about the Exile and its aftermath. With the aid of Cyrus and Darius, Ezra and Nehemiah restarted divine worship in the restored Temple: "They ordered Priests to be set up in their orders and Levites in their turns in the works of God in Jerusalem. As it is written in the Book of Moses." Bede then makes the contemporary point here: "The order of devotion demands that after the building and dedicating of the House of the Lord, soon Priests and Levites be ordained to minister in it, lest the House should have been built, and should shine for no purpose, if there were absent anyone inwardly who served God there." This is not ancient news and ancient rules. It is news and rules for the eighth century. "Very often," Bede adds, "it is to be inculcated into those who build monasteries with a magnificent work but do not set up in them [any] teachers who might exhort the people to the works of God, but rather [they allow persons living] there to serve [their own] pleasures and desires,"[47] as Bede complains elsewhere in his celebrated and caustic letter to Archbishop Egbert of York.[48]

Certain Christian writers evince a special fascination with the "Veritas Hebraica": God's own chosen means of communication with the world, and thus, Bede declares, the "prima lingua"—the "prime" or "first language" of the human race.[49] Later it was disrupted and dispersed at Babel as a punishment for still another sin of pride. And from that disruption there arose the current multiplicity of languages coexisting with Hebrew, Adam's original tongue.

On this matter Bede is pleased to concur with his teachers, Augustine[50] and Isidore,[51] who, in turn, were preceded by Origen,[52] though, oddly, not by Jerome,[53] who, for all his special expertise in the language, expresses some degree of skepticism about the identity of Hebrew with the "one language" spoken before the catastrophe at Babel. But Bede follows Augustine here. "It is obvious," he remarks "that Adam spoke in that language by which the whole of mankind spoke until the construction of the tower at which [time] the languages were divided. . . . But it seems that the first language for human kind was Hebrew, since all the names that we read in Genesis until the division of languages [are in Hebrew] speech. . . .[54] This is not only a deduction which Origen, Augustine, and Isidore have quite logically made from the biblical data, it also fits perfectly into Bede's own special veneration for the "Veritas Hebraica" in his exegetical writings.

In fact, after Bede's time a story grew up that he was himself a "Hebrew scholar," handling that tongue as fluently as he did Latin, Greek, and his childhood Anglo-Saxon. There are, to be sure, some at least quasi-reasonable reasons to support this notion—as medieval Christians saw it. The Hebraism story is thus distinguishable from other tales, utterly gratuitous, that Bede had journeyed to Rome at papal invitation to give the Curia expert counsel, and had even stopped off en route just long enough to found universities at Cambridge and Paris.[55]

Unlike those amusing stories—which reveal the medieval essence of Bede—the Hebraist story is relatively sober and serious. In the first place, there is Bede's image as "incredibly learned in the Scriptures."[56] And certainly by the standards of his time and place he is unbelievably erudite as an exegete and in other fields as well. Further, there are his not infrequent references to Hebrew terms and his discussions of them and their Greek and Latin translations: "'Azotus,'" he says, "which is said in Hebrew 'Asdod' and refers even today to a not ignoble municipality in Palestine."[57] And "'Avoth' Iair which is interpreted as 'Epaulic' in Greek—this is 'Basan' in which sixty towns on Mount Galaad fell in the lot of half the Tribe of Manasseh."[58] There is "'Tyre' which is called 'Sor' in Hebrew, a Phoenician metropolis . . ." and "'efratha' and 'Betleem,' the city of David whose double name is under a similar interpretation. . . ."[59] And "the Name 'Jesu' [which] begins among the Hebrews with the letter 'ioth', and among the Greeks with an 'iota'. . . ."[60] In Hebrew "'Adam' like 'Enos' is interpreted as 'homo'. But 'Enos' is taken to mean 'homo' so that it fits men alone." By contrast, "Adam" is such that it can be adapted to either sex. Wherefore, it is rightly said that [God] called their [man and woman's] names "Adam," that is, "homo." As "homo" in Latin has its name-etymology from "humo" because from the "humo"—the earth—man took his origin, so among the Hebrews "Adam" is named from the "earth" because from the slime of the earth "homo" was formed. Wherefore, "Adam" can even be interpreted as "earthy" or "red earth." . . .[61] [and Eve] will be called "woman" because she was taken from "man." In that way [also] the Latin etymology flows together in these names, since from "vir" is called "virago." And this thus fits also Hebrew in which language "vir" is called "his" and "femina" derived from this name is called "hissa." . . .[62]

Reading this, one might easily tend to picture Bede as having the Hebrew text of Genesis right there on his work desk side by side with the Vulgate and the Vetus Itala and perhaps the LXX as well. And certainly when we read him discussing literary forms in the Bible in his treatise

On the Schemata and Tropes of Sacred Scriptures, it is hard to avoid forming just such a picture. While most of his original examples are from the Koine Greek New Testament, a fair number of them are from the Old Testament, and a few are cited in the original. Bede is discussing "paronomasia" in Hebrew prose: a "nearly similar saying with diverse meanings" obtained by altering "a syllable or a letter according to the Hebrew Verity." He cites a Latin echo of this in Psalm 22:6 "In Thee, [O Lord], they confided and were not confounded"—"In Te confisi sunt, et non sunt confusi." Then, turning to Isaiah 5:7, Bede comments: "The Prophet does this most elegantly in his language: 'I expected that you would do judgment, and behold iniquity, justice and behold clamor.'" Only "in Hebrew" does the perfect "paronomasia" show up: "For in Hebrew 'Judgment' is called 'mispat' [and] 'iniquity' is called 'mispah'; 'Justice' is 'sedaqah' and 'clamor' is 'se'aqah'. Thus, beautifully, with one letter either added or changed, [the Prophet] tempers the likeness of words so that for 'mispat' he might say 'mispah', and for 'sedaqah' he might posit 'se'aqah.'"[63]

Bede's confidence as he discusses Hebrew vocabulary or notes subtle word plays, as he translates or transliterates Hebrew names and nouns, is undoubtedly impressive in his time and place. It fairly amazed and dazzled early medieval churchmen and students of Scripture, for whom Bede seemed to be opening up the deep secrets of the "Prima Lingua."

Thus, the idea fixed itself that he was, in addition to being an expert on Greek, also a "Hebraist." This notion continues on through the later medieval era and down through the Renaissance, the Reformation, and into very modern times. In the 1880s Karl Werner thought it plausible enough,[64] and S. Hirsch accepted it in his 1905 study *A Book of Essays.*[65] It survived even into the 1928 Oxford symposium, *The Legacy of Israel,* one of whose contributors, Charles Singer, writes: "For centuries during the Dark Ages the Hebrew alphabet and language stood for something odd, strange and difficult. They were often invested with a magical quality. Thus, St. Isidore of Seville (560–636) exhibits a naive curiosity concerning Hebrew, but betrays no trace of Hebrew knowledge save what he derived from Jerome. . . ." In "the British Isles," Singer continues, a number of writers who authored the "Hisperic Literature"—Aldhelm and others—exhibit "a vocabulary drawn from the most out-of-the-way sources. A few words artificially derived from Hebrew are included. These words may have been obtained from wandering Syrian or Byzantine travellers." By contrast, Singer thinks, "on a higher plane than such magical incantation is the little Hebrew knowledge displayed by the Venerable Bede (673–735). His acquaintance with the language, although exceedingly elementary, was real. In this he was superior to Alcuin (735–804) . . . who had no knowledge of Hebrew. . . .[66]

There are problems, however, with this picture of Bede having a "real" if "elementary knowledge" of Hebrew, when we look at it up close. First, Bede nowhere claims to know Hebrew. He nowhere does any independent textual criticism, no emendations with the Old Testament parallel to his careful working over of the Koine Greek New Testament text of the Book of Acts. It is difficult to picture Bede having the scrolls of any Hebrew biblical book on his work desk as he discusses Isaiah 5:7. He shows no knowledge of the Hebrew verb system, nor does he reproduce any letters of the Hebrew alphabet. Without a knowledge of letters and verbal forms one cannot write—or read—sentences in a language. No knowledge of verb forms is tantamount to no "real knowledge" of the language. Finally, in the absence of a Jewish community in England much earlier than the Norman Conquest—as is established fairly definitively by Salo Baron and others[67]—there would have been, a fortiori, no rabbinical scholars or other Hebraists there for Bede to learn from as Jerome reports himself to have learned from rabbis in Palestine.

These and other reasons led Jesuit Fr. Edmund Sutcliffe, the distinguished English Old Testament scholar, to conclude in his 1935 essay "The Venerable Bede's Knowledge of Hebrew," that Bede "had no knowledge of Hebrew beyond the scraps of information he was able to glean from the writings of St. Jerome."[68] He was not a "Hebraist" even in the most elementary sense of that term, not even a beginning student of the language itself qua language.

Impressive as are Bede's references to Hebrew terms, to nouns and names of persons and places, Fr. Sutcliffe found not a single text reference there that is independent of the material in his sources, in Jerome or in Josephus or in both. Bede falls fully as much under Singer's strictures as does Isidore, though he shows greater shrewdness in how he uses what he finds in his sources. One of his chief "Hebrew" works, *The Names of Places*, even bears the subtitle—at least in later MS tradition—*Collected Out of Jerome the Presbyter and Flavius Josephus.*[69] Bede hands on, then, only what he discovers in those two authors. With his linguistic gifts, as Fr. Sutcliffe says, he would certainly have been able "to acquire Hebrew" with ease—had he had a teacher, or even a rudimentary grammar book. But neither was available in seventh- or eighth-century England. Nor would such be available for any other medieval Latin Christian. Assuredly, in the high medieval period there are a few superior individuals here and there who, like Bede, know how to reach out and contact a bit of the sacred tongue. In the twelfth century Hugh, the distinguished abbot of the monastery of St. Victor in Paris, shows an acquaintance with Hebrew terms and phrases quite similar to Bede's. As a start he corrects the ordinary Christian ignorance and arrogance about sacred languages. Some actually claim, Hugh reports, that "the Septuagint translation is to be more approved than the Hebrew 'Veritas' because Greek copies are truer than Hebrew copies, and the Latin copies are truer than the Greek." But this is absurd; it reverses the historical order of things. With such a silly notion, "nihil proficis," Hugh declares, "You make no progress since, to the contrary, the Greek copies are truer than the Latin, and the Hebrew copies truer than the Greek."

In his *Elucidating Annotationlets* on the Pentateuch, Judges, and I Kings, in several places full Romanized Hebrew sentences are given by Hugh: "Diviso contra se Ruben, magnanimorum reperta est contentio," "With Ruben divided against himself there was a great contention of minds" or "a great hotness of heart." This is "in Hebrew: 'biflagoth Ruben gotholib helchiche lem.'" And the Latin sentence in I Kings 15 "Porro Triumphator in Israel non parcet, nec paenitudine flectetur," "And the Triumpher in Israel will not spare, nor will he be deflected by repentance," is "in Hebrew: 'Vagham, Nez alzrahelloe Zachir.'"

This, like Bede's "Hebraism," is striking for its era, though Hugh, with a typical modesty, confides that he is dependent on his biblical "teacher" for these bits of information: As "Jerome—who instructed us in the Scriptures"—says: "We have learned from the Hebrew. . . ." So, then, "these things Jerome [takes] from the Hebrew; [and] indeed, the Hebrew [is received] from Jerome."[70] Still, Hugh, like Bede, knows how to put these scraps to maximum possible use in exegesis.

By the mid-thirteenth century things had developed apace and the famously immodest English Franciscan Friar Roger Bacon of Oxford boasted that he had "studied Hebrew," unlike most of his less competent scholastic confrères. There is some (though not coercively strong) evidence to support this claim. For one thing, Bacon reproduces not just Romanic transliterations and translations of Hebrew, or a few Hebrew letters, but the entire Hebrew alphabet itself, and even some sentences in Hebrew—and "Chaldean" (or Aramaic) as well.

He complains in Part 3, ch. 2 of his *Opus Maius* that one of "the causes of error," indeed of "wretched error" among Christian theologians is their "ignorance of these [ancient scriptural] languages"— Hebrew as well as Greek. He and his distinguished patron, Robert Grosseteste, bishop of Lincoln, and a few others in England form an elite, he implies, a select circle of superior scholars who take "grammatica" seriously. Friar Roger intends, in fact, to write a "Hebrew Grammar." But for the nonce he settles for a few sample pages in the *Opus Maius* in which he reproduces for the edification of readers all the letters of the Hebrew alphabet with their Latin equivalents (and not all of these are correct):

z	v	e	d	g	b	a	m
zain	vaf	he	dalet	gimel	bet	aleph	mem uverte
ן	ו	ה	ד	ג	ב	א	מ

l	ch	ch	i	t	h	s
lamet	chaf˙	chaf	iot	teis	heis	sazake dreite
ל	ך	כ	י	ט	ה	ע

s	a	s	n	n
sazake torte	ain	samech	nun dreite	nun torte
צ	ע	ס	ן	נ

m	t	s	r	k	p	p
mem close	taf	sin	ris	kof	pe	pe
ם	ת	ש	ר	ק	ף	פ

Friar Roger goes on to give the vocalics as well:

ba	be	bi	bo	bu
בַּ	בֶּ	בִּ	בֹ	בֻּ

And even some sentences, in which he compares Latin with not only Hebrew but "Chaldean," too:

dii	eis	dicetis	sic	
elohim	lahem	tomeru	co	) Hebrew letters
אֱלֹאִים	לָהֶם	תֹּאמְרוּ	בֹּה	) Hebrew tongue

dii	eis	dicetis	sic	
elaa	lehom	temerun	chidena	) Hebrew letters
אֲלִהיָא	לְהֹם	תֵּאמְרוּן	בְּדֵנָה	) Chaldean tongue

This is, of course, vastly more impressive a display than we find in Hugh or Bede, though Friar Roger, with a rather uncharacteristic generosity, attributes to his English predecessor a full knowledge of both

Hebrew and Greek. Bede was, he says, "most literate"—"literatissimus"[71]—in both tongues.

Bacon scholars like S. Hirsch (who, as noted, writes favorably about Bede also) think Bacon's knowledge of Hebrew was extensive. Hirsch theorizes that Bacon may have learned from rabbis in thirteenth-century England and/or via contacts with Arabists fluent in Hebrew as well.[72] Thus, J. A. Weisheipl includes the traditional reference to Hebraism in his *New Catholic Encyclopedia* article on "Roger Bacon."[73] But the Jesuit Hebraist Fr. Mitchell Dahood passes over in complete silence both Bede and Hugh, and Bacon also, and proceeds directly from Jerome to the High Renaissance in his *NCE* article on "Hebrew Studies (in the Christian Church)."[74] For all his bluster, the Oxford Franciscan's "Hebraism" may well have come ultimately from the usual suspect, Jerome, whom Bacon cites at all the crucial junctures, even though pointing out Jerome's own admissions of his noninfallibility as a translator. It is significant also that the only verb forms Bacon gives are in preset sentences. He does not "conjugate" or inflect any Hebrew verbs on his own, at least not in what appears in the *Opus Maius*, whatever may have been the case with the intended "grammar" book of which Hirsch reports that a possible fragment has been found.[75]

The matter remains unresolved. And whatever the true extent of Friar Roger's "Hebraism," Western Latin Christianity would have to wait until the High Renaissance—until the late fifteenth and early sixteenth centuries—when scholars like Johann Reuchlin in Germany and several others elsewhere really laid the foundations for Christian "Old Testament" study of Hebrew as it has been understood ever since. Bede could only have marveled at that breakthrough from afar.

In sum, it is standard for all Christian writers, East and West, to use Genesis 1–3 for speculative purposes. But it is Western Christians who show a vastly greater penetration into the historical-communal aspects of the Pentateuch. Of this group of Western Christians only a very few go beyond the Pentateuch to take in the later history of Israel for doctrinal or practical purposes. And the documentary data reveal that of all patristic and early medieval Western Christian writers, Bede is unique in his sensitivity for Hebraic history and language. And it is he alone who applies it all most deeply to a branch of the Christian church and to daily life within that branch.

Why is this so? Why does an Anglo-Saxon, a proto-Englishman reveal this mindset—and, in doing so, present striking parallels to later English and then "New England" Reformed Christians living a millennium after him? Is there some "English temperamental" factor at work here? Is it because England is a psychological isolate, easily demarcatable as an island-nation and a separate entity? Do such things engender a special-ness? These are, of course, blatantly unempirical hypotheses. And even historians who are not professed Ockhamists or Nominalists would have difficulty hypostatizing such invisible causal links making up a supposed "English mentality." (After all, the very different Anglican tra-dition, which appeals back to Bede's liturgical and hierarchical and mo-nastic sides, is also English, and indeed, the central strand of religion in England.)

Is the English specialness simply a contingency, an accident of his-tory? Is it because the Anglo-Saxons were the first new people to be brought into the postimperial Western church? It was Rome—in the let-ters of Gregory and his papal successors—that created the rhetoric of missionary specialness. Bede just happened to be on the scene to record that rhetoric and incorporate it into the foundational history and scrip-tural scholarship of the land. Or was it that the Anglo-Saxons could, *objectively*, be talked about and written to in ways that those pontiffs could not talk of and write to Gauls, Hispanics, Italians, North Africans? Or even to the new Franks? Only after the Anglo-Saxon conversion by Mediterranean missionaries would there be conversions of the Germans, the Poles, and the Scandinavians—and not by papal missionaries but by Anglo-Saxon missionaries like Boniface sent to the Germans, and then by German missionaries going in turn to Poland and Scandinavia. Thus, in the "North" the Anglo-Saxon conversion is, curiously, both a first and a median activity. These data are all "objective," and fixed in the records. Can they explain the "specialness" of English Christianity here: that after Bede and Hugh the next leading theological enthusiast for He-brew—and the most extensive disquisitor yet on the topic—in the Latin church is another Englishman, Bacon? Or that the popular fantasy-theory of "the Ten Lost Tribes" has produced "British Israelites" but not German or French claimants to that title?

Even as the sheerest contingency, even as mere happenstance, it re-mains striking that a thousand years later on the island one would see, after the Reformation had reached speed, a very strong preaching-and-Hebraicizing movement reborn among a major group of English Chris-tians—as if "seeds" deeply planted by Bede had in some manner ger-minated and borne fruit. As if—since post hoc is never necessarily propter hoc. Certainly, Bede's own "quasi-Protestant" emphasis on Scripture, on the Word and preaching, and on Israel as the great model for church and kingdom was hardly typical of later medieval Catholic piety and thought. Like most of popular Christianity in Western (and Eastern) European lands, English Catholicism was centered largely on physical ritual. In fact, Bede's elite outlook on religion tended to be marginal to the popular piety of his own day—judging by his repeated complaints about "the neglect of preaching" and reliance on "sacraments alone."[76]

To be sure, many of the Old Testament themes and the Israel/Church parallels continue to be cited and are added to by medieval writers, who tend to continue on well-trod paths either marked out or widened by Bede as northern heir of the Fathers. With the thirteenth and fourteenth centuries, however, challenges to papal central government, wealth, and power start to break out into the open. And a new, strongly "negative" use of the Old Testament as prophetic parallel or paradigm develops. Then, with the "High Reformation" of the sixteenth century, the negative polemic turns into a prophetic-declamatory use of the Old Testament. Luther, Zwingli, and Calvin open fire on the papal monarchy with its "human" traditions, laws and rituals which Luther, in his famous title phrase, calls "the Babylonian Captivity of the Church."[77] Zwingli and Calvin go past Luther to attack the Roman use of iconic art in the church. Zwingli lists all the Old Testament texts condemning "idols." He "notes them by book and chapter" for the convenience of his readers.[78] And Calvin continues the argument at even greater length in his *Institutes.*[79]

This new prophetic mode turns traumatic when the papal church threatens retaliation against its new "Protestant" critics. Calvin, in making the antipapal case for the Reformed churches to King François I of France, compares himself and his persecuted disciples to the bold prophets Micah and Jeremiah, Daniel and Elijah, while the Roman church is Ahab and Jezebel.[80] Knox, extending Calvin's ecclesial crusade to the British Isles, "blasts" his "Trumpet" against the "monstrous" travesty which is "regiment" or government "by women."[81] And Knox means both Mary Stuart, that shameless popish hussy and, later on, Elizabeth Tudor also, that cleverer pretend-Protestant. Knox stands right up to them just as Elijah and others stood up to King Jereboam and Queen Jezebel.

Thus, we see growing up a new tradition, more intense than its predecessors, in which the Reformed Protestant cleric becomes in his self-imaging an Old Testament figure via a sort of sacred psychodrama. He *is* spiritually whom he cites. When Anglican England stubbornly refuses "to reform" itself "without tarrying," as one Reformed cleric demands that it do, then many Reformed writers, men like Thomas Hooker of Cambridge—a future father of the Hartford, Connecticut, colony—call down maledictions on the land. Hooker considers himself and his flock to be "saints of the Lord" evilly persecuted and not listened to by a semi-pagan Anglicanism. They are all "Noahs" ready to flee the "deluge" of divine punishment coming soon upon corrupt "Olde England." There are, Hooker announces, "five Arks"—five ships—at the docks set to sail for the godly safety of a "Newe Englande" beyond the seas.[82]

Hence, William Bradford could compare his Plymouth group's "Covenant" with God to Moses's Covenant statement in Deuteronomy 26 with echoes in Psalm 107.[83] And John Winthrop in Massachusetts Bay could do the same with his group, proclaiming Moses's final charge to Israel in Deuteronomy 30 in order to fix the New Massachusetts "Covenant" with "the Lord."[84] And then Cotton Mather, coming after those and other worthies, could "magnify" them all as parts of "Christ's Great American Deeds." Governor Bradford is a new "Moses . . . in the Wilderness"[85] and Governor Winthrop is "our New English Nehemiah,"[86] the rebuilder of "Jerusalem" alive again, "the City on the Hill" in God's newest Israel. And let the corrupt Olde Worlde take notice! This is but a later and posttraumatic version of Bede's pictures of Anglo-Saxon kings as "Solomon" and "Nehemiah," and the "aged" Abbot Ceolfrid of Jarrow and his "young" successor Huetbert as a "Moses" followed by a "Joshua" in Northumbria.[87]

It is possible but not very likely that Dr. Mather ever read anything by Bede directly. He makes no mention of him in his preface on "Church Historians" in the *Magnalia Christi Americana*,[88] nor in the historical section of his almost comically lengthy bibliographical guide for the ideally well-read young pastor, the *Manuductio ad Ministerium*.[89] (A parish cleric would have little time for anything else were he to take even half of Dr. Mather's advice ad litteram.) However, Professor Louis Feldman reports having found several references to Bede in the vast intellectual lumber room of Mather's six-volume *Biblia Sacra*, still unedited, though these may be mere secondary citations or excerpts from florilegia.[90] Yet Mather's Old Testament views of the primacy of Scripture, of the centrality of Word and preaching, and on church and state and secular Christian leadership are, in effect, transplantations, bypassing much of later English Catholic thought, of Bede's views on those same things. Mather himself seems to have recognized a peculiar "Englishness" in his and his confrères' Christian mindset. "As the English nation," he writes, "has been honoured above most of the Protestant and Reformed world, with clearer discoveries of several most considerable points in our Christian Religion—particularly the points of true Evangelical Church-Order—so the New-English part of this Nation hath had a singular share in receiving and imparting the illuminations which the Light shining in a dark place hath given thereabout. . . ."[91]

Had the Harvard polymath pressed back further into "the English nation" he would have encountered Bede at its start. Mather and Thomas

Hooker, the Cambridge-and-Connecticut Deutero-Noah are separated from Bede the monk-exegete and historian of Jarrow by ten centuries of time. But they are at times astonishingly close in the scope and tone of their ecclesial use of the *Vetus Testamentum*, and in their common veneration of the Hebrew "Veritas" which Mather emphasizes that Bradford "most of all studied."[92]

Incidentally, by the high middle ages the old notion of Origen, Augustine, Isidore, and Bede that Hebrew is the "prima lingua" of mankind has largely faded away from learned theological discourse. Hugh[93] and Aquinas[94] appear to make no mention of it, and Roger Bacon only hints at it—perhaps.[95] Among the nonprofessional laity, however, the notion is not lost at all. Salimbene, the Franciscan historian, reports that the "Amazement of the World," the Emperor Frederick II, as one of his "seven" imperial "idiosyncrasies," once tried to test the "prima lingua" theory scientifically. He had "some infants" cared for but isolated from adult talk to see if, left alone without human sound around them, they would begin to "speak Hebrew" as the "prime" or natural language of humankind. Or whether they would speak "in Greek, Latin, Arabic or the language of their parents." The ingenious experiment failed, however, when the infants, alas, all died of unrelated causes![96] In the Reformation era Luther[97] and Calvin[98] seem to be silent about the matter, as are, apparently, later Lutheran and Reformed writers. Perhaps the Church's leading divines in these later ages lost, somewhere along the way, the courageous imagination of their ancient predecessors who were not afraid to fill in the information gaps which the Spirit had mysteriously left in Genesis. Fortunately the concept of Hebrew as the "prima lingua" continues to flourish among less technically learned thinkers at least here and there in Reformed North America during the eighteenth and nineteenth centuries. But, then, we should expect that. A really interesting idea can never fully die even after the Academy has abandoned it.

Notes

1. Eusebius, *Ecclesiastical History* (henceforth *EH*), bk. 9, ch. 9, in *Loeb Classical Editions*, 2 vols. (Cambridge, Mass.: Harvard University Press, 1926, 1959), 2:361f on Moses; for parallels on Solomon, cf. bk. 10, ch. 4, vol. 2, 399–403. (Hereafter, book and chapter are cited as 10.4, volume and page as 2:399–403.)

2. Eusebius, 10.4, 2:399–421.

3. Cyprian, *On the Unity of the Church*, sec. 18, in series *Ancient Christian Writers* (Westminster, Md.: Newman, 1957), 60f.

4. Augustine, *On the City of God*, bks. 15–18, in *Post-Nicene Fathers*, Series 1 (reprint, Grand Rapids, Mich.: Eerdmans, 1956), 2:284–396.

5. Lactantius, *The Divine Institutes*, 2.14ff and 4.5–30, in *Ante-Nicene Fathers*, 7:61ff and 104–34.

6. Orosius, *Books of History Against the Pagans*, 1.3–16 and 7.27, in series *Fathers of the Church* (Washington, D.C.: Catholic University of American Press, 1947), 20–37 and 325–28.

7. Augustine, *On the City of God*, 17.4ff and 18.48, 2:339ff and 390ff.

8. Gregory, *Pastoral Rule*, 3.24, for example, *Ancient Christian Writers*, 11:171ff.

9. Gregory, *Letter to King Ethelbert, Patrologia Latina* (hereafter *PL*) (Paris, 1844–55), vol. 77, column 1205.

10. Isidore, *Etymologies* (Oxford, 1911), 1971), vol. 1 (unpaginated; divided only by bk and ch.), 6.1–4, 7.7, and 8.1.

11. Gildas, *A Complaining Book on the Cutting Down of Britain*, parts 2 and 3 in *PL* 69:347ff, 367ff.

12. Salvian of Marseilles, *On the Governance of God*, 4.7ff, in series *Fathers of the Church*, 1947, 101ff.

13. Gregory of Tours, *The History of the Franks*, 1.1–16; 2.34; 4.11, 16, and 25; 5.14, 19, 35, 43, 50, et al. loc. *Patrologia Latina* (hereafter *PL*) (Paris, 1844–1864), vol. 71.63–170, 230f, 270, 281, 288, 327ff, 333f, 349f, 358f, 365f.

14. Ambrose, *Letter 51 to Theodosius*, in *Post-Nicene Fathers*, Series 2, 10:45off and *PL* 16:116off.

15. Gregory of Tours, 4.24 and 5.14, *PL* 71:288 and 273f.

16. Patrick, *Confessions*, sections 1–3, 5, 29, 34, 40, and 48 in series *Ancient Christian Writers*, 17:21f, 30f, 33, and 36.

17. Bede, *The Ecclesiastical History of the English Peoples* (hereafter *EH*), 1.22, in *Bede's Ecclesiastical History*, ed. Bertram Colgrave and R. A. B. Mynors (Oxford, 1969, 1981), 66ff.

18. Ibid., 1.30, 106ff.

19. Ibid., 2.10, 166ff.

20. Ibid., 3.29, 318ff.

21. Georges Tugène, "L'Historie écclésiastique du peuple anglais: Réflexions sur le particularisme et l'universalisme chez Bède," *Études augustiniennes* 17 (1982): 129–72; 159.

22. Ibid., 152ff.

23. Bede, *EH* 2.15, 188ff.

24. J. M. Wallace-Hadrill, *Bede's Ecclesiastical History of the English People: A Historical Commentary* (Oxford, 1988), 7.

25. Judith McClure, "Bede's Old Testament Kings," in *Ideal and Reality in Frankish and Anglo-Saxon Societies* (Oxford: Blackwell's, 1983), 76.

26. Ibid., 82.

27. Bede, *EH* 5.24, 536ff.

28. Charles W. Jones, Preface to *Libri IV, In Principium Genesis usque ad Nativitatem Isaac et Ejectionem Ismahelis Adnotationum* (hereafter *In Gen.*), in *Corpus Christianorum Series Latina* (Turnholti: Brepols, 1967), 118A:x (hereafter given as *CC* with number of volume and page, e.g., *CC* 118A:x).

29. Bede, *EH* 5.23; *In Gen., CC* 118A:201; *In Samuel, CC* 119:231.

30. *In Gen., CC* 118A:55ff, 92f.

31. Ibid., 118A:114ff; in *I Peter*, *CC* 121:249.

32. *In Gen.*, *CC* 118A:138.

33. Ibid., 118A:169f.

34. *De Tabernaculo*, *CC* 119A:6f.

35. *Epistula ad Ecbertum*, sec. 9, in Charles Plummer, *Baedae Opera Historica*, 2 vols. (Oxford, 1895), 1:412.

36. *In Gen.*, *CC* 118A:138, 239f; *In Parabolis Salomonis*, *CC* 119B:190, 344.

37. *De Tabernaculo*, *CC* 119A:130.

38. *Homiliae*, *CC* 122:318ff.

39. *Ep. ad Ecbertum*, sec. 9.

40. *In Lucam*, *CC* 120:23, and *In Marcum*, *CC* 120:543.

41. *In Ezram et Neemiam*, *CC* 119A:368.

42. *De Templo*, *CC* 119A:149.

43. Ibid., 119A:148f.

44. Ibid., 119A:296.

45. McClure, 87.

46. Bede, *EH* 2.16, 190ff.

47. *De Templo*, *CC* 119A:302f.

48. *Ep. ad Ecbertum*, secs. 9–12.

49. *In Gen.*, *CC* 118A:55f.

50. Augustine, *City of God* 11:11.

51. Isidore, *Etymologies* 9.1.

52. Origen, *Commentary on Genesis*, *Patrologia Graeca* (hereafter *PG*) (Paris, 1857–1866), 12:110f, and *Commentary on Numbers*, *PG* 12:649.

53. Jerome, *Commentary on Zephaniah*, *PL* 25:1414.

54. Cf. n. 49.

55. Cf. the "Rome voyage" story—as treated with some skepticism—by William of Malmesbury, *History of the Kings of England* 1:3; and also *PL* 90:16. For the academic legends, cf. Karl Werner, *Beda der Ehrwürdiger und seine Zeit* (Vienna, 1881), 85, and R. W. Chambers, *Bede: Annual Lecture on a Mastermind: Proceedings of the British Academy* (London, 1936), 24f. For the Paris and Cambridge stories Chambers cites, respectively, *Historia Universitatis Parisiensis* (Paris, 1655), 1:113 and T. Fuller's *Church History* (London, 1655), 98.

56. *Vita Venerabilis Baedae*, *PL* 90:46 (author anon.).

57. *Nomina Locorum*, *CC* 119:273.

58. Ibid., 119:274.

59. Ibid., 119:286.

60. *De Tabernaculo*, *CC* 119A:135.

61. *In Gen.*, *CC* 118A:92f.

62. Ibid., 118A:57.

63. *De Schematis et Tropis Sacrae Scripturae* 1, *PL* 90:175ff. Critical text in *CC* 123A:142ff.

64. Werner, 100f.

65. S. Hirsch, *A Book of Essays* (London, 1905), 7.

66. Charles Singer, in *The Legacy of Israel* (Oxford, 1928), 287.

67. Salo Baron, *A Social and Religious History of the Jews* (New York, 1952–85), 2:235, 303, 306; 3:136. Cf. also Cecil Roth, *Encyclopedia Judaica* 6:747.

68. Edmund Sutcliffe, S.J., "The Venerable Bede's Knowledge of Hebrew," *Biblica* 16 (1935): 300–306.

69. *Nomina Locorum, CC* 119:273.

70. Hugh of St. Victor, *Adnotatiunculae Elucidatoriae in Exodum, Leviticum, Librum Judicum et I Regum, PL* 175:72, 78, 87, 91, 94, 99, 102. I am indebted to Professor Louis Feldman of Yeshiva University for drawing these passages to my attention. He judges that, despite Hugh's modest ascription of his knowledge of Hebrew to "Jerome" (*PL* 175:398), some of it may be independent of Jerome.

71. Bacon, *Opera Quaedam Hactenus Inedita*, vols. 1 and 15, ed. by J. S. Brewer *Rolls Series*, vol. 15, 1859): 332.

72. S. Hirsch, in *Roger Bacon: Commemorative Essays* (Oxford, 1914), 138–45.

73. J. A. Weisheipl, "Roger Bacon," in *New Catholic Encyclopedia* (hereafter *NCE*), 12:522.

74. Mitchell Dahood, S.J., "Hebrew Studies (in the Christian Church)," *NCE* 6:977.

75. Hirsch, in *Roger Bacon*, 139, 142. Bacon's Hebrew letterings, unlike those in the *Patrologia Latina* texts of Jerome and Bede, survive into twentieth-century critical editions. The Hebrew letterings following the Romanizatins of Jerome and Bede would appear to have been inserted by later copyists, and hence have vanished from the *CC* edition. And the same may prove to be the case with Hugh if and when a critical edition of his *Annotationlets* is done.

76. Bede, *In Ezram et Neemiam, CC* 119A:366.

77. Martin Luther, *On the Babylonian Captivity of the Church*, trans. A. T. W. Steinhaeuser, et al., in *Three Treatises* (Philadelphia, 1947), 115ff.

78. Huldreich Zwingli, *Commentary on True and False Religion* 29:2, trans. S. M. Jackson, et al. (American Society of Church History, 1929; reprinted Durham, N.C.: Labyrinth Press, 1981), 334.

79. John Calvin, *Institutes of the Christian Religion*, 2 vols. (Philadelphia: Westminster, 1960), 1:11, 3:9, 4:9.

80. Calvin, Preface to *Institutes*, secs. 6 and 7, 1:24ff.

81. John Knox, *The First Blast of the Trumpet against the Monstrous Regiment of Women* (Geneva, 1558; reprinted Amsterdam, 1972), 2–6.

82. Thomas Hooker's sermon on *The Danger of Desertion, Harvard Theological Studies* 38 (Cambridge, Mass., 1975), 244ff.

83. William Bradford, *Of Plymouth Plantation* and *The Mayflower Compact*, in *The American Puritans*, ed. Perry Miller (New York, 1956), 18.

84. John Winthrop, *A Model of Christian Charity*, in ibid., 84.

85. Cotton Mather, *"Magnalia Christi Americana" and Other Works*, ed. Kenneth B. Murdock, in *Cotton Mather: Selections* (New York, 1926; reprinted 1960), 49.

86. Ibid., 58, 64.

87. Bede, *In Samuel, CC* 119:212.

88. Mather, *Magnalia*, in Murdock, 18f.

89. Mather, *Manducatio ad Ministerium* (Boston, 1726; reprinted New York: Columbia, 1938), 60ff, 64ff.

90. Communication from Professor Feldman at conference session, Monday, May 21, 1990.

91. Cotton Mather, *Magnalia Christi Americana*, 2 vols. (Hartford, Conn., 1853), 2:276.

92. Mather, *Magnalia*, in Murdock, 50.

93. Hugh of St. Victor, *Adnotatiunculae in Gen. 11*, PL 175:50.

94. Aquinas, *S. Th.* I, Q. 94, art. 3.

95. Roger Bacon, *Opus Majus*, 3 vols. (Oxford, 1891, 1900), 3:96ff. Bacon comes fairly close, but only obliquely so, when he says that "God has revealed philosophy to His saints"; and it "was delivered, complete in all its details, in the Hebrew language." It was "delivered to the Patriarchs and the Prophets . . . before the infidel [Greek] sages obtained it." And those "saints" include "Adam" as well as "Solomon and the others" in Israel's history. So, by implication, Hebrew must have preexisted Babel as the language of "Adam." *Opus Tertium* 10:32 and 24:79, in Brewer ed., cited by Hirsch, *Bacon*, 137. But Bacon appears to content himself with insinuation rather than making a direct statement here. On the primality of Hebrew, other similar hints are found in *Opus Majus* 2:9 about "Noah and his sons."

96. Salimbene de Adam, *Chronicle*, trans. J. L. Baird, et al. (Binghamton, N.Y., 1986), 357. I am indebted to Professor Charles Wood of Dartmouth College for drawing to my attention this amusing instance of what might be termed "empirical theological research" by nonprofessional laics.

97. Luther, *Lectures on Genesis 11*, *Luther's Works* (St. Louis, 1960), 2:226ff.

98. Calvin, *Commentary on Genesis 11* (1847; reprint, Grand Rapids: Eerdman's, 1948), 226ff, 329ff.

Barbara Kreiger

Seventeenth-Century English Travellers to Palestine

It may seem that the topic of English travellers to Palestine in the seventeenth century is far removed from the subject of Hebrew and the Bible in colonial America. Geographically speaking, this is obviously so. But I am reluctant to allow topographical obstacles to isolate what may be some interesting material; so I shall ask the reader to bear with me as I try to make at least a tentative connection between travellers to Palestine and Hebrew in America.

The seventeenth century, generally considered to be a low point for the non-Muslim population of Palestine, also seems to represent a gap in modern scholarship. There are studies of the sixteenth and eighteenth centuries, but one is hard-pressed to discover in-depth studies of the seventeenth. Complicating matters is the fact that this century seems also to sit between two great ages of travel, that of the medieval pilgrim, throughout and following the Crusader years, and that of the enlightened traveller, beginning in the eighteenth century. In the first seventy years of the 1600s, as Barbara Tuchman has pointed out, we find only 160 or so English travellers signing a visitors' register in Jerusalem,[1] or fewer than three per year.

We do find a number of English business travellers in Constantinople, trying from the early days of the Ottoman Empire to establish trade with the Turks. In 1599, for example, with trade already well under way in the form of the Levant Company, an organ-maker named Thomas Dallam accompanied to Constantinople a magnificent instrument of his design to be presented in the name of the Queen to the Sultan, who was apparently delighted by the chiming of bells striking each hour, and the singing birds whose wings fluttered. But though Dallam spent a long period of time in the East, he does not seem to have visited the Holy

Land, and if this strikes us as odd, it was the case for others as well, for whom Palestine was by then a mere decrepit waystation. The country was in very bad shape, largely because of oppressive Ottoman taxation and banditry that went unchallenged by Constantinople. If we put this together with the facts that religious pilgrimage was frowned mightily upon by the Reformation, and that English trade sights were being increasingly shifted toward India,[2] we can conclude that there was little reason for travellers to risk their lives with such an imprudent choice of destination.

Still, there is fascinating material, for the hold of the Holy Land on the English imagination was never entirely loosened, and travellers, even in small numbers, did not cease to be propelled there. They had different motivations—a desire to see the holy sites, mere curiosity, and potential business interests—but in all they represented a new breed: the traveller, a species that had not been much seen before their time, but one which would become of incalculable importance for the literary records they bequeathed us. Indeed, it is our good fortune that most of these travellers wrote about their journeys, as narratives, diaries, or letters, and though one has to be cautious at times about accepting fully what they describe, it would be a mistake to dismiss their accounts as quaint, primitive, or biased, the last of which they often were. Travellers' accounts offer a wealth of information, and it is in part for their very prejudices that we value them. For one thing, their unself-consciousness is refreshing. For another, with no self-censorship at work, these texts enlighten us not only about the observed, but also about the observers, whose attitudes were at times idiosyncratic, but were as often reflective of their home environment.

The questions which serve this essay as a kind of umbrella, if a somewhat porous one, have to do with Hebraism and Palestine. Did Christian travellers to Palestine know Hebrew? Did they have any special connection with the Jews—with the issue of the Jews' reentry into England or with the debate about their physical restoration to Palestine? Were their travels in any way relevant to the journeys of their contemporaries to America? Without meaning to oversimplify, I think these questions can all be answered in the negative. Yet despite the discouragement this suggests, the information yielded by an examination of this literature does, I believe, shed at least an oblique light on the subject under discussion here. For the subject of Hebrew, in America as elsewhere, is unavoidably linked to the Jews, and though the Puritans' identification was with the ancient Jewish people, the spiritual hopes of Protestants in the seventeenth century were linked to the fate of the then modern Jewish people.

I am not an historian; I come to this material with an interest in travel narratives, particularly those relating journeys to Palestine, and my approach is more exploratory than argumentative. What this essay offers is a description, mostly through the eyes of English travellers, of life in Palestine in the seventeenth century, focusing on the Jewish community. Who were these travellers, and why did they risk the journey to this part of the world? What were their attitudes toward the small Jewish population they encountered? What was the emotional climate in England concerning the Jews, and what place did Palestine occupy in the lives of Englishmen? The answers to these questions may reflect back across continents and oceans to the New World, and help illuminate the general questions that guide this volume.

The Holy Land had been known intimately, its geography felt viscerally, during the centuries of the Crusades, but in later years, familiarity and passion had been replaced by ignorance and indifference, and Palestine, like the Jews, was judged to be truly Godforsaken. If we look at a geography text published in 1670, we read that "there is now scarce any place of Mark in all the Holy Land; whereas under the Cananites, under the Hebrews, under the Jews, there were so many People, so many Kings, so many Cities, so rich, and so powerful, that throughout the whole Continent of the Earth, there was no Country that might compare with it."[3] This impression of desolation was shared by most travellers, with only rare dissension. In a small volume containing the accounts of English travellers from 1667, travellers are advised not to believe those pilgrims who out of fear hastened from Jaffa to Jerusalem and back again; for others, more adventurous and having the courage to depart from this desolate route, reported that "though the face of the land be somewhat deformed for want of cultivation, by the barbarous infidels," still some features of its former glory are yet to be found, particularly in the Galilee. We read that the "salubrity of the air is excellent," and that the "inner part of the country is diversified with beautiful mountains and hills, advantageous for vines, fruit-trees, and small cattle, and the delightful valleys are watered with a great number of torrents, beside the river Jordan."[4]

Nevertheless, the picture of desolation is the predominant one, local wars and an untenable system of tax collection having led to the ruin of the country, as the historian James Parkes observes:

The penalty for non-payment was often the destruction of the means by which future payments might be made. Trees were cut down, villages destroyed until whole areas passed out of cultivation. . . . The decline of the population and the increase of waste land in its turn brought in the bedouin, accustomed to pasturing their destructive goats on any unoccupied area.

Whole tracts passed back to a state in which they could only support the desert nomad instead of the rich agriculture of earlier centuries; and the tragic process of soil erosion, and the turning of rivers and streams into stagnant marshes, continued unchecked while the Turks looked on indifferent."[5]

Thus it is that travellers repeatedly told of decaying land, the striking disappearance of the peasant population, and the takeover by the Bedouin, to whom tribute had to be paid.

The vicissitudes of the Jewish community of Palestine had for a period of time reflected the military fortunes of the Crusaders and the Muslims. The Crusaders had slaughtered Jew and Muslim alike when they took Jerusalem in 1099, and no Jew or Muslim was allowed to live in the city. The ban was relaxed somewhat in the twelfth century, at which time Maimonides visited, and a few prominent Jewish families lived in the city, where they were dyers, as the famous Jewish traveller Benjamin of Tudela observed then. With the defeat of the Crusaders by Saladin, Christians, whom he spared, were allowed access to their holy places, and Jews were officially granted permission to settle in Jerusalem, where a small Jewish community developed. A demographic study of Jerusalem in the sixteenth century shows that the city's population, Jews included, tripled in the second quarter, there being roughly 2,000 Jews and Christians out of a total population of 16,000.[6] Numbers declined for all groups for the rest of the century, so that there were fewer than 1,000 Jews at the beginning of the 1600s,[7] but under a benign Muslim governorship from 1620 to 1625, Jews were living there freely, coming to visit, bringing money to care for their brethren, and praying at the Western Wall, a happy condition that moved a Jerusalem Jew to comment, perhaps with exaggeration, that more Jews were then living in Jerusalem than at any other time since their banishment.[8] In the next years, corruption and natural disasters would take their toll, and the population would go into a decline.

The condition of the Jewish community elsewhere in Palestine was also determined by events in Europe. The fourteenth, fifteenth, and sixteenth centuries were a period of expulsions and persecutions for the Jews, and many had fled from Spain and Portugal, Germany and Italy, to Palestine. Until the death of Suleiman the Magnificent in the middle of the 1500s, Jews from Europe were willing to endure the dangers of travel there, where Turkish rule offered some protection, and where Jews, like Christians, were allowed a degree of self-rule in exchange for paying a non-Muslim tax. Palestine became for a time the center of world Jewry, with most of the immigrants settling in Safad and Tiberias.[9]

It is worth taking a brief look at those two towns, for astonishing things were happening there. As we know, Safad was the center of Jewish mysticism, but it was also an important commercial center for weaving, Parkes commenting that there were 3,000 looms, as well as several times that many mystics. It was also the place where, at this time, rabbinic law was codified by Joseph Caro. By the middle of the sixteenth century Safad had a population of 15,000 Jews,[10] and by early in the seventeenth century there were at least 20,000, and perhaps closer to 30,000.[11]

Tiberias was in squalor when an ambitious plan to restore it was proposed by a wealthy Spanish Jewess named Dona Gracia.[12] In the middle of the sixteenth century, with Suleiman's permission, she established a settlement and a college and obtained a charter to rebuild the city walls, and to settle immigrant and native Jews on the land. With the aid of her son-in-law/nephew, Don Joseph Nasi, she offered transportation to Italian Jews, who were then suffering under the reigns of Popes Paul IV and Pius V. They planted mulberry trees to begin a silk industry, imported Spanish wool for weaving, and intended to begin a fishing trade. But their plan for a semiautonomous Jewish community was never realized; indeed, so many factors mitigated against its success that it is perhaps remarkable that the settlement was ever begun. Few Italian Jews could make the arduous and dangerous trip; some who did were taken by pirates and sold into slavery. This Dona Gracia died in 1569, after living in Tiberias only a year; Don Joseph Nasi was kept in Constantinople by various intrigues. The fledgling community was opposed by the Franciscans and threatened by local Arab tribes, and with Don Joseph Nasi's death in 1579, the plan was abandoned. It was taken up later in modified form, but for scholarship, not commerce, and in 1603 the Jews of Safad had to come to the rescue of their starving brethren in Tiberias. At the beginning of the seventeenth century, Safad and Tiberias were sacked by Bedouin, then by Druze; Tiberias would not be rebuilt for decades, and Safad would not regain its modest splendor.[13]

The Jewish community of Palestine was demoralized on several counts: Unlike Christian sects, the Jews had no parent nation to protect them, and they were completely at the mercy of local tyrants, for the Turks were indifferent to raids and persecutions. Then there was the crushing disappointment at the apostasy of their supposed messiah, Sabbatai Zevi. His choice of Islam over death, in 1666, meant a loss of hope for the Palestine Jewish community; the oppression and taxation they had lived with overwhelmed them, and they experienced a decline that continued through the nineteenth century.[14] Thus was the prosperity of the sixteenth century largely vanished by the time our seventeenth-century travellers came onto the scene. This is no doubt one of the reasons for the dearth of references to the Jewish inhabitants of Palestine, though one notices a striking lack of references to the sedentary Arab population as well.

For centuries of Christianity, travel to the Holy Land was undertaken primarily by pilgrims, but the age of the pilgrimage had come to a virtual end by the seventeenth century, as the Protestant Reformation took hold. No longer would droves of pilgrims flock to the sites that were linked to the life of Jesus, buying indulgences, picking up trinkets, worshipping saints and relics, and in this way working their way into heaven. The Protestants, encouraging a spiritual journey instead, scoffed at superstitious practices, and in the accounts of travellers to Palestine we see a crystallization of this anti-Catholic sentiment.

As I mentioned, a new breed appeared on the scene at around this time—not pilgrim, but not merchant either, simply, as one Fynes Moryson claims of himself, the traveller. As he explained, he had no thought of going to Jerusalem "to expiate any least sinne," but having begun to travel, was envious of anyone who saw more than he. During his short stay in Jerusalem in 1596, he was guided by Franciscan friars, one of nine Christian sects represented in the city and squabbling over the Church of the Holy Sepulchre. He ridicules them for the tales of wonder they attach to religious monuments. In Bethlehem, for example, they explained that a hole in the roof of the small church was made by the star which guided the wise men, and fell to earth there. To which Moryson asks, "Can he forbeare laughter who considers the bigness of the starres"? On his departure, he noted that many Christians and Jews tried to sell him "divers toies," but he calls these beads and crosses "far fetcht," and of no use. In fact, he condemns the friars for greed, and denounces the papists as superstitious.[15]

With a similar attitude, the Scotsman William Lithgow arrived in Jerusalem on Palm Sunday nearly twenty years later, and described what he called a "ridiculous Ceremony," an "Apish imitation of Christ," whereby someone, mounted on a donkey, rode to Jerusalem, while along the way people cried "Hosanna, the Son of David, blessed is he that cometh in the name of the Lord." Lithgow and the other Protestants laughed "in their sleeves," as he put it, as they watched the rider pass by, and he was moved to irreverence, commenting that the "greater Asse [was] riding upon the lesser." One can be sure that in demeanor as well as in print Lithgow was not very discreet, for that night he was approached by the rider himself, who beseeched Lithgow and the others that, if they didn't participate in these rites and customs, at least to refrain from mockery.[16]

This Lithgow was an interesting character. His reasons for travelling are unclear, but it has been suggested he was escaping the humiliation of having had his ears cut off by the outraged brothers of a young woman whom they had found in his company. Anyway, he was surely an adventurer, spending nineteen years walking throughout the Middle East. In 1609 he set off on the first of three journeys, and it might be interesting to take a brief look at the kind of trip a traveller was likely to have in those days. The year 1612 finds him on the threshold of the Holy Land. Crossing the Jordan River in the Galilee, he proceeded south, a six days' journey to Jerusalem. Canaan, he remarks, was once "the most fruitfull Land in the World," but is now quite the contrary, "God cursing the Land together with the Jewes." Reading travellers' accounts, one has at times to be suspicious that the desire for a conceit does not distort the picture offered. In obvious contradiction of himself, Lithgow then describes the Galilee as offering a twice yearly grain harvest, an abundance of silk, cotton-wool, wines, honey, oil, and fruits of all kinds, "never a whit more decayed now, than at any time when the glory of Israel was at the highest."

Lithgow was plagued by demands for tribute, and paid "more than he ever paid in Asia for a day's journey, demanded by the awful king." As he explains, there were two kings in Arabia, as he refers to the region, and they were mortal enemies. One lived on the Euphrates, in Mesopotamia, and in some parts of Arabia Felix and southern Syria; and this one wandered with his tribes in Arabia Petrea and Deserta, and sometimes in the Holy Land, wherever he found good pasturage and fresh water.

The next day the Armenian pilgrims with whom he was travelling were attacked by about three hundred Arabs shooting arrows; they fought them off with guns, but lost nine women and five men, with thirty others badly wounded. They entered the hilly country of Judea, and he noted that the whole of Canaan was populated with Moors, looking like sunburnt Egyptians, some Turks, so-called "civil" Arabs, a few Christians, and scattered Jews. The Arabians, he says, were mostly thieves and robbers, the Moors cruel and uncivil, hating the Christians to the death; the Turks were the best of the lot, yet all were sworn enemies of Christ.

They continued on their mountainous way, pushing on in order to reach Jerusalem before the gates were shut for the night. Lithgow and two Armenians rode on ahead, but were waylaid and robbed, a knife held to his throat when he resisted. On spotting Jerusalem, he burst into tears, and the Armenians into song, but ceased for fear of the Turks. Having left his caravan, Lithgow was joyously taken by a group of friars who sang and washed and kissed his feet, overjoyed that a Christian would come all the way from Scotland to Jerusalem. But when they later discovered he was "no Popish Catholicke, it sore repented them of their Labour." The brash Lithgow got his come-uppance, one could say, when the group travelled to the Jordan River and was attacked while he, stark naked after a dip, was up in a tree appreciating the view. Jumping down, he left his clothes behind and ran. He must have cut quite a figure, rod in hand, cloth on his head, as he dashed among the thickets; a friar in his company spotted him and threw him a gray habit to hide "the secrets of nature."[17] Thus was he aided by the cloth he despised.

At the turn of the century, in 1600, we find William Biddulph, the chaplain at Aleppo, travelling to Palestine, asserting that his journey was not undertaken "with any superstitious devotion to see Relikes, or worship such places as they account holy"; not, in other words, as a pilgrim, but as an interested traveller.[18] Where Lithgow's account is of interest for its description of the countryside and its narrative liveliness, Biddulph's is of interest chiefly for his comments about the Jews. In discussing their customs, he comments that they observe all the ceremonies as in ancient days, except for sacrificing; that most can read Hebrew, but that only in Salonika and Safad, which he calls universities of the Jews, do they speak it. In Safad the Jews have a synagogue, and live with more freedom than elsewhere in the Holy Land.

Not to offer too rosy a picture, he remarks also that they can be identified throughout the Turkish empire by their red hats, but that lately the color had been changed to blue, red seeming too princely for them. The Turks despise them much more than Christians, he claims, and if a Jew wishes to become a Muslim, he must first convert to Christianity, an observation made also by other travellers. As an indication of the contempt Muslims had for Jews, Biddulph observes that when a Turk is wrongly accused of a crime, he protests: "If this be true, may I die a Jew." Christians dwelling in these lands also hate the Jews "uncharitably and irreligiously," even stoning those who dare to go out on Good Friday. In fact, Biddulph learns when in Safad that no Jew dares to travel to Jerusalem at all, for fear of being stoned.

This was probably not an exaggeration, for another traveller, in 1612, confirmed the observation. Thomas Coryat, known to seventeenth century scholars for his unabashedly titled book, *Coryat's Crudities*, went later on to the Holy Land, an account of which journey appears in his more tamely titled volume, *Coryat's Maturities*. About the Jews, he comments: "No Jew may appeare neere the Sepulcher, for any Christian may stone him, or bring him to the Officer to be executed."[19]

George Sandys's account, like that of Biddulph, offers a fascinating description of the Jews in the Turkish empire, particularly in Palestine.

Travelling in 1610, he observed that the Jews "in their owne Countrey doe live as Aliens; a people scattered throughout the whole world, and hated by those amongst whom they live."[20] Sandys offers a lengthy account of the Jews, ranging from a detailed description of their clothes, to the color of their complexions. It might be of interest to include his comments about the Jews at prayer, in this passage describing an Italian synagogue. It seems to me that his bias is not a cruel one, but rather his language reflects the attitudes of his day, and suggests the utter foreignness of the Jews to an English audience: "They reade in savage Tones, and sing in Tunes that have no affinitie with Musicke: joyning voyces at the severall closes. But their fantasticall gestures exceed all Barbarisme, continually weaving their bodies, and often jumping up-right. . . . They pray silently, with ridiculous and continuall noddings of their heads, not to bee seene, and not laught at."[21]

Another half century did nothing to enlighten an English readership. Our 1670 geography text author also felt obligated to describe the Jews, long absent in any real numbers from England. In discussing Palestine, he observed: "The People which antiently possest this Countrey, were the Jews, being of a middle stature, strong of body, of a Black complexion, goggle-ey'd, a subtile and ingenious people."[22]

Our next traveller of interest is John Sanderson, who as early as 1584, as an apprentice merchant, was becoming familiar with the East, as England began trading with the Ottoman Empire. In 1601, while waiting for the ship that would take him home, he decided to make an excursion to Jerusalem, and set out from Damascus.[23] His account is very scanty, and made up largely of geographical details, but the makeup of his party is alone cause for interest, for he travelled with a group of Jews from Constantinople, one of whom, Abraham Coen, was taking a substantial amount of money to Palestine for charity and to buy books. This Sanderson was an ill-mannered fellow who had more than once to be bailed out of trouble by his companions for his insolence with both Catholics and Turks, but he seems to have respected Coen, for later on, in Jerusalem, he speaks of temporarily leaving the company of "my great companion Jewe," whom he describes as kindly and charitable. In Safad, where Sanderson noted there were six Jewish schools of learning, his companions bought so many books as to require two or three mules to carry them. They also gave charity, served food to the poor, and donated their annual stipend to support the colleges.[24] In all the time they were together, Sanderson was respectful of his companions, and they of him, he says, never being unpleasant or offensive about his belief in Christ.

One small but very important detail must not be overlooked. Sanderson relates the following incident that took place in Constantinople, two years before his journey to Palestine: From "one of the Coens, an ancient and very learned Jew priest, I did with much intreatie and my money get a very old booke. It was the five bookes of Moses in foure Languages. I presented it to my brother, Doctor Sanderson. He lent it Doctor Barlow, hee to Doctor Andrewes. They used it in their translation at Cambridge."[25] An editorial footnote in this reprint of Sanderson's text informs us that the book he bought was the edition of the Pentateuch, in four languages, printed at Constantinople in 1546, two copies of which are now in the Bodleian Library. Of particular interest is that this Doctor Andrewes was no doubt Lancelot Andrewes, Dean of West-minster, who knew Hebrew, Chaldee, Syriac, Greek, Latin, and probably ten other languages. So proficient in ancient Near Eastern languages was he, that Thomas Fuller, whom we shall come to momentarily, was moved to remark that Andrewes, if living in ancient days, "might ... almost have served as an interpreter-general at the confusion of tongues."[26] Andrewes's reputation as a Hebrew scholar resulted in his appointment as chairman of the Westminster Group, which translated Genesis through Kings II in the new Authorized Version.[27] The trans-lation for the King James Bible was begun in 1604, just two years after Sanderson's return to England.

We turn now to a nontraveller whose travel book was as popular as any, and which remains a most instructive and delightful episode in lit-erary travel history. I am speaking of the much-admired churchman Thomas Fuller, and his 1650 book, *A Pisgah-Sight of Palestine.* Fuller is known in part for the political highwire act he performed throughout the years of England's civil disturbances, when, as a royalist, he preached moderation and conciliation.[28] He is best known for his *Church History* and his *History of the Worthies of England,* as well as for his history of the Crusades.

Fuller, whose wit could be acerbic, was a nontraveller by intellectual design, not by accident. In a 1631 sermon on the Book of Ruth, he holds forth on travel abroad, which, he asserts, is justifiable only for mer-chants, ambassadors, and individuals wishing to better themselves to serve king and country. "But unlawfull it is for such to travell, which *Dinah* like, go only to see the Customes of severall Countries, and make themselves the Lackies to their own humorous curiosity." He goes on to say that on their return they will have learned "Jealousie from the *Italian,* Pride from the *Spaniard,* Lasciviousnesse from the *French,* Drunkennesse from the *Dutch;* and yet what need they go so farre to learn so bad a lesson, when (God knows) we have so many Schooles where it is taught here at home."[29]

There is an interesting aside to be made at this point, and that is in regard to the Pilgrim Fathers. By this time, around 1630, as one of Fuller's biographers points out, much of the excitement about their journey to America had died down, and the stories in current circulation were about the hardship and deprivation they were suffering.[30] Fuller's opinion concerning them is that he could find no "just warrant" for their going, and he advises those who have not yet gone, with the words King Joash spoke to Amaziah: "Tarry at home." But for those who have already gone, he asks, "let us pitty them, and pray for them; for sure they have no need of our mocks, which I am affraid have too much of their own miseries."[31]

Fuller is not easily definable, for this conservatism did not characterize all his views, particularly his attitude toward the Jews. Devoted to the study of English history, he chastised those travellers who, "sharp-sighted abroad, are little better than blinded at home: know the way from Paris to Lyons better than the way from London to York." But not satisfied with aiming his barbs at Englishmen who are ignorant of history, he let fly his sharpest arrows toward historians who are biased: "What by greatest errors is falsely told of the Jews that they are always *crook-backed,* will be found most true of the authors of this age."[32] In short, he was a man of intellectual independence and courage, and was not taken in by fashion or favor.

Fuller's book, *A Pisgah-Sight of Palestine,* is a geographical description of the Holy Land, replete with maps, and intended to illustrate the Bible. Our attention will be focused only on the last small chapter, and that is where Fuller offers his opinion concerning the Jews. To put his views in their proper context, we might take a moment to consider the status of the Jews, who had been expelled from England in 1290.

As Cecil Roth explains in *A History of the Jews of England,* the return to the Hebrew Bible which accompanied the rise of the Puritans was responsible for a new philo-Semitism which, along with what he calls "an incipient movement in favour of religious toleration,"[33] raised the question of the Jews' readmission. But such idealism, or humanism, was not sufficient, and the question of toleration of the Jews moved to the commercial arena, where it could be argued with hard facts concerning the prominence of Jews in Dutch mercantile life.[34]

The year 1650 is a notable date in book publishing history not only for Fuller's *A Pisgah-Sight,* but also for *The Hope of Israel,* by Menasseh ben Israel, a Portuguese Jew of Amsterdam who was a friend of Rembrandt and the subject of some of his engravings. Motivated by a messianic hope, Menasseh was also oppressed by the continuing persecution of Jews in Spain and Portugal, and by the slaughter of Polish Jews,[35] 200,000 of whom were victims of the 1648 Cossack massacres.

Menasseh's book was occasioned in part by the report of one Antonio

Montezinos, a Portuguese traveller from a converted Jewish family, who claimed to have discovered the Ten Lost Tribes in Colombia. Using that speculation as a starting point, Menasseh argues for the readmission of the Jews to England as a necessary step preceding the coming of the Messiah, whose advent would be delayed until the Jews' complete dispersion was a fact. A year later, he formally petitioned Cromwell, but war broke out between England and Holland, preventing a decision. Three years later a further petition was offered, but, though in fact a small number of Jews had already resettled in England, Cromwell rejoined that toleration could not be "stretched so far as to countenance those who denie the divinity of our Saviour."[36] Still, Menasseh persisted, and Cromwell brought the matter in 1655 to a high level of government consideration, in a public atmosphere of considerable xenophobia. War with Spain ensued, and the petition was never formally acted upon; and though readmission was tacitly granted, Menasseh died brokenhearted that a full vindication of Jewish life and presence in England had not been granted. The death of Cromwell and the restoration of the monarchy might have reversed even the small gains that Menasseh had been responsible for initiating, but actually Charles II looked with some favor on the Jews, and formally, if casually, legitimized their presence in England in 1664.[37]

Thus things turned out for the Jews, but it is now necessary to return to Thomas Fuller, because the question of the Jews' readmission to England was closely connected to their destiny, as it was perceived, in Palestine. Fuller maintained that the Jews had a threefold claim to Palestine; it was given them by God, they conquered it from the Canaanites, and they possessed it for seven hundred years.[38] But the connection was broken "with the weight of their sins," and they were dispersed as a fulfillment of God's curse that they would be scattered. Scattered, but not extinguished, maintains Fuller, as he considers various opinions of the day. He examines the then current hypothesis that they may be found to be the Indians of North America, a suggestion he takes seriously, but for which the circumspect Fuller needs more proof. As we know, this was a widely held opinion, put forth, among others, by William Penn, who, as cited by an editor of a seventeenth-century narrative to Palestine, asserted that the native Americans look a good deal like Jews, practice similar rites and ceremonies, use a lunar calendar, have a kind of feast of tabernacles, mourn a year, and have a very lofty language, much like Hebrew. All of this was more than idle speculation, for there were those who believed that the Lost Tribes had to be located and restored to Palestine in expectation of the millennium.

Fuller, however, was not among those who espoused the importance of the Jews' temporal restoration. In fact he was quite clear in asserting that if the Jews expected to be restored "to an illustrious condition in their own country," they should be disabused of this hope, for the return from Babylon marked that fulfillment, and if they expect anything further, it can only be in the spiritual realm—that is, with their embrace of Christ. The Jews will not come back to their land, he asserts, but the various lands in which they reside shall become comfortable to them on their conversion. Temporal repossession is a mere dream.

Fuller goes on to argue for the readmission of the Jews to England, but though his view is humanitarian in effect, it is based on what we today might call a not so hidden agenda. Addressing the question of the Jews' convertibility, he asks, in essence, how can we convert them if we don't know any? Conversing must precede converting, he acknowledges pragmatically. Meanwhile, Christians should stop fighting with one another and begin to show a pious example. With his heart turned to God, Fuller asks, how long will You be angry with them? "Remember Abraham, Isaac, and Jacob, not for any merit in their persons, which was none, but for the mercy in Thy promises, which is infinite."

There is one additional traveller we should take note of, so peculiar was his destination, so odd his account. In 1650, one Samuel Beert, or Brett, wrote a paper describing his attendance at the so-called Great Council of the Jews in the plains of Hungary.[39] As he describes it, this was a gathering of 300 rabbis, in addition to which there were 3,000 observers, meeting with the purpose of examining the scriptures concerning Christ. Had he come? Or could they expect him? They searched the Hebrew Bible for evidence, amid much dispute, but at the end of the first day, they agreed he had not yet arrived. Some disagreed, and were moved to think he had come, "by the consideration of the great judgments that have been upon them these 1600 years." We are not idolaters, they reasoned, so why should we be so afflicted, if not because we spilled the blood of God's prophet?

The Council went on for a full week, and on the last day, six Roman clergy sent by the pope began to instruct them in the doctrine of the Roman church. At this, Brett says, the Jews were so troubled that they called out against them, "No Christ, no virgin Mary, no women Gods, no intercession of the saints, no holy crosses, no worshipping of images, &c. Their grief and trouble was so great, that it would have troubled an hard heart to have seen and heard it: for, they rent their clothes and tore their hair, and cast dust upon their heads, and cried out Blasphemy . . . and in this great confusion and perplexity the council brake up."

The next day, according to Brett, an eminent rabbi explained to him that he might have known that the representatives from Rome would cause trouble, and that the Jews regarded the Roman church as idolatrous. This, claims Brett, is the major obstacle to their conversion. Furthermore, many Jews did not know another Christian religion existed, but some had heard that Protestants love them better and pray for their conversion. The rabbi hoped that some Protestant divines would be present at their next convocation, in Syria three years later.

What should we make of this strange report? Is it to be believed, so contrary to Jewish ways does it sound? Any insight I have I owe to the scholar Richard Popkin, who put forth the following ideas about it: A meeting of Jewish leaders was held in Lublin in 1650 to discuss ways of aiding the Jewish community, which had so recently been decimated by the Cossacks. This Samuel Brett, who heard about it later, claimed to have been present, and gave the convocation an altogether different meaning. Millenarian expectations were widespread among Christians, and he took the moment to persuade his countrymen that the Jews were ripe for conversion, if only the Catholics would keep out. Now apparently Menasseh ben Israel rejected this story when it was first printed in 1655, but it was nonetheless taken as fact for two centuries.[40] As for the identity of Samuel Brett, Popkin suggests that the story is a dramatized version of an account by one Paul Isaiah, England's major convert from Judaism, who wrote a pamphlet in which he described a similar gathering, where, he claimed, the Jews agreed to relinquish their stubborn denial of Christ.[41]

Thus we return to our original question: Was English Hebraism related to Palestine? I don't want to force an affirmative answer for the sake of integration, at the expense of material that is rich in its own right. It does seem that the subjects of Hebrew, the Jewish people in the seventeenth century, and conditions in Palestine are all delicately but inextricably interwoven. If seventeenth-century travellers did not know Hebrew, it still figured in their travel accounts, for wherever they met Jews or observed them at their customs, their ears had to become tuned to the language of the Bible. And if they were not concerned with such questions as readmission or restoration of the Jews, still those questions hover over these texts as a modern reader approaches them.

Then perhaps it is from our contemporary vantage point that the question becomes clarified. The story of what these travellers saw as they passed through the ancient land of the Hebrew language may be peripheral to the saga of Hebrew in America. But language and a people are bound together and invigorate one another; and if their fortunes diverge, still the vitality of one can be conserved, and passed to the other when history offers a more benign moment. In this way, it could be that our stories are as one.

Notes

1. Barbara Tuchman, *Bible and Sword* (New York, 1961), 153–54.

2. Ibid., 119–20.

3. Richard Blome, *A Geographical Description of the Four Parts of the World* (London: printed by T.N., 1670), 22.

4. R. Burton, alias Nathaniel Crouch, *A Journey to Jerusalem* (Hartford: J. Babcock, 1796), 3–6.

5. James Parkes, *A History of Palestine from 135 A.D. to Modern Times* (New York: Oxford University Press, 1949), 156–57.

6. Amnon Cohen, *Jewish Life under Islam* (Cambridge: Harvard University Press, 1984), 16.

7. Ibid., 34.

8. Abraham Yaari, *The Goodly Heritage,* trans. Israel Schen (Jerusalem: Youth and Hechalutz Department of the Zionist Organization, 1958), 11.

9. Parkes, 167.

10. Ibid., 168.

11. H. H. Ben-Sasson, ed., *A History of the Jewish People* (Cambridge: Harvard University Press, 1976), 635.

12. Cecil Roth, *The House of Nasi: The Duke of Naxos* (Philadelphia: The Jewish Publication Society of America, 1948), 97–135.

13. Parkes, 168–70.

14. Ibid., 178–79.

15. Fynes Moryson, *An Itinerary Containing His Ten Yeares Travell* (1566), ed., reprint, J. MacLehose (Glasgow: J. MacLehose & Sons., 1907), 2:1–46.

16. William Lithgow, *The Totall Discourse of the Rare Adventures & Painefull Peregrinations* (1632), ed., reprint, J. MacLehose (Glasgow: James MacLehose & Sons, 1906), 218–19.

17. Ibid., 191–231.

18. William Biddulph, "Letters," *Hakluytus Posthumus or Purchas His Pilgrimes,* ed., reprint, J. MacLehose (Glasgow: J. MacLehose & Sons., 1905), 8:279.

19. Thomas Coryat, "Master Thomas Coryate's Travels to, and Observations in Constantinople . . . and his Journey Thence toward Jerusalem," in MacLehose, *Hakluytus Posthumus* 10:447.

20. George Sandys, "A Relation of a Journey begunne, Anno Dom. 1610," in MacLehose, *Hakluytus Posthumus* 8:171–72.

21. Ibid., 172.

22. Blome, 20.

23. John Sanderson, *The Travels of John Sanderson in the Levant, 1584–1602,* ed., reprint, W. Foster (London: The Hakluyt Society, 1931), 2d ser., no. 67, 95–120.

24. Ibid., 116.

25. Ibid., 84–85.

26. G. Lloyd Jones, *The Discovery of Hebrew in Tudor England* (Manchester, 1983), 147.

27. Ibid., 149.

28. Morris Fuller, *The Life, Times, and Writings of Thomas Fuller* (London: J. Hodges, 1884), 2:69–70.

29. Thomas Fuller, *The Collected Sermons of Thomas Fuller*, ed. J. Bailey and W. Axon (London: The Gresham Press, 1891), 1:13–14.

30. William Addison, *Worthy Dr. Fuller* (New York: Macmillan, 1951), 50–51.

31. T. Fuller, 14.

32. M. Fuller, 2:70–71.

33. Cecil Roth, *A History of the Jews in England* (Oxford: Oxford University Press, 1964), 150.

34. Ibid., 154–58.

35. Henry Mechoulan and Gerard Nahon, ed., *The Hope of Israel*, by Menasseh ben Israel (Oxford: Oxford University Press, 1987), 47.

36. Roth, *History*, 157.

37. Ibid., 171.

38. Thomas Fuller, *A Pisgah-Sight of Palestine* (London, 1650), 622–39.

39. In Burton, 98–110.

40. Richard H. Popkin, "Jewish Messianism and Christian Millenarianism," *Culture and Politics from Puritanism to the Enlightenment*, ed., P. Zagorin (Berkeley, Calif.: 1980), 78–79.

41. Richard H. Popkin, "The First College for Jewish Studies," *Revue des études juives*, 143:157.

Two

The Legend of the
Ten Lost Tribes

Rembrandt's portrait of Menasseh ben Israel, author of Hope of Israel *(1636).*

Cyrus Gordon

The Ten Lost Tribes

Until the eighteenth century, it is fair to say that the people of what was to become the United States belonged, for the most part, to a believing world. There were, as always, some skeptics but, by and large, solid citizens accepted the biblical account of ancient history.

In both Testaments, the restoration of all Twelve Tribes in Jerusalem and the Promised Land is assured as an integral part of the divine plan before the inception of the Messianic Age (e.g., Matthew 19:28). Only then could our tormented world become a fit place for God's creatures to live in peace and harmony in accordance with the divine blueprint for history.

Such neat schemes have to be adjusted to the facts of history. The Twelve Tribes were envisaged as the respective descendants of the twelve sons of Jacob. However, the tribe of Levi was scattered among the other tribes to serve them as hereditary priests. The remaining eleven tribes had to be restructured into twelve because ideally there had to be twelve secular tribes corresponding to the twelve months of the year, so that the twelve could take turns in shouldering federal service to the nation.[1] Accordingly the tribe of Joseph was split into two tribes bearing the names of Joseph's two sons, Ephraim and Manasseh. Ancient Israel was eventually split (schematically) into two kingdoms which consisted respectively of (1) ten northern tribes (descended ideally from Joseph and Benjamin, the sons of Rachel) and (2) one large southern tribe, Judah (a son of Leah).

The Ten Tribes of the north were vanquished by Assyria in 722 B.C.[2] In accordance with Assyrian policy the Northern Kingdom of Israel was not only exiled to distant provinces of the Assyrian Empire, but an alien population was settled on Israelite soil to prevent any return of the con-

quered Israelites to their native land. The Babylonians, who subsequently conquered Judah and destroyed Jerusalem and the Temple that
Solomon had built there, had a different policy. When Nebuchadnezzar
of Babylon conquered Judah (starting in 597) and destroyed the Temple
in 586 B.C., he exiled the nobility, the craftsmen, and in general the
uppercrust to Babylonia, leaving the poor, common people behind; but
he did not introduce an alien population. Accordingly it was possible for
the Judeans, but not for the Ten Tribes of northern Israel, to return. Some
members of the Ten Tribes managed to join the Judeans but most were
dispersed in the alien lands of their exile.

The myth of the Ten Lost Tribes is a result of the breakdown of contacts between Western Europe and the Islamic Near East, and of the
emergence of Western Europe as the center stage of active and creative
Christendom since the time of the Crusades. Asia and Africa had, in fact,
large communities of Jews, many of which claimed descent from northern tribes. During 1944 when I was in Isfahan, Iran, local Jews told me
that they were descendants of the tribe of Naphtali whose emblematic
animal (Genesis 49:21) is a gazelle "sent forth" (at large). Their "proof"
of this was that they had for generations sighted in the environs of Isfahan a gazelle of wondrous beauty that could only be the totem of their
tribe.

There is a long succession of travellers who explored exotic parts of
Asia and Africa to find the northern tribesmen and report on them, to
inform the persecuted Jews of Europe that they had numerous long-lost
brethren, many of whom were strong, well-off, and even warlike: ready
and able to reconquer their Promised Land. One of the earlier travellers
was Eldad the Danite,[3] who claimed to be a native of East Africa and a
member of the northern tribe of Dan. He flourished in the ninth century
A.D. and, though he is scarcely a reliable historian, a critical scholar can
extract kernels of truth from his writings. In any case, he made an
impression on the Jews of Europe and stimulated the quest for the Ten
Lost Tribes. He claimed that in the vicinity of Ethiopia, the Danites
along with tribesmen of Naphtali, Gad and Asher had established a warlike independent kingdom.

A far better source is Benjamin of Tudela, in northern Spain. He was
a merchant, scholar, and traveller. Much of his data is reliable for he was
a keen observer and visited many of the places he describes. He was im-
pressed with Rome, but more so with Constantinople and even more
with Baghdad, which was the cultural and intellectual center of the
world. During the thirteen years of his travels (1160–73), he went
through and beyond southwestern Asia. He was the first European since

antiquity to report on the western fringes of the Chinese Empire. He returned to Spain via North Africa and Sicily. Everywhere he went, he took a special interest in the Jewish communities and noted their size and the number of scholars in them. The intellectual life of the Jews of Europe, Asia, and Africa was remarkable, even in the smaller settlements. Benjamin of Tudela's purpose was to count and describe the Jewish communities on the world scene to pave the way for the restoration of Israel in its entirety ("all twelve tribes") in the Holy Land.

We must limit ourselves to only one more document bearing on the "not-so-lost" tribes. The scholar and geographer Abraham ben Mordecai Farissol was born in Avignon in 1451 and died sometime during the first half of the sixteenth century. While still young he settled in Italy. He reports on an exotic Jew (identified as David Reubeni) who claimed to belong to one of the tribes, and bore the august title "The General of the Army of Israel." He had come from the Holy Land on a Venetian ship to Venice whence he proceeded to Rome. He reported on the presence, great numbers, and military prowess of Hebrew tribesmen in Arabia. However, the powerful segments of those Arabian Jews could not unite because the Muslims constituted wedges between them. The presence of Christian ships in the Red Sea acquainted the Arabian Jews with the military technology of Roman Catholic Europe. The Christians had the firepower to assault and demolish fortresses. The strange Jew was sent to Pope Clement VII (1523–34) with the endorsement of the king of Portugal, whose ships visited the Red Sea on their way to India. The story goes that Pope Clement agreed to provide the Jew with a ship loaded with military supplies, along with European Jewish and Christian technicians, via Portugal, to enable the Jews to fight the Muslims and reconquer the Holy Land. The victorious Jews in Palestine would repay their debt to the Pope by extending special privileges in Palestine to the Holy Roman Church.

The above suffices to show the interest in the "Ten Lost Tribes" down to the Age of Discovery culminating in the voyages of Columbus to the New World, starting in 1492. It is not surprising that Columbus took along with him an interpreter who knew Hebrew. Although the Age of Discovery was characterized by widening intellectual as well as geographical horizons, we must not forget that until the eighteenth century our planet was a believing world and all "right-thinking" people, including scientists, accepted Scripture as revealed truth. Since it was widely held that the Ten Tribes were lost, they had to be found somewhere because the Bible assures us that all twelve tribes must be reestablished in the Holy Land to fulfill God's plan for his Kingdom of

Heaven on Earth (the Messianic Age). This is why there had to be a myth of the Ten Lost Tribes including the Amerindian population in the New World when Columbus crossed the Atlantic in 1492.

It was in the early 1950s that I first became interested in the question of pre-Columbian transoceanic navigation. At that time the academic consensus ruled out all such crossings as technically impossible. The prevailing opinion had it that America had been populated by primitive Asiatics who walked across the Bering Strait during the coldest part of the year when it was iced over. Those primitive hunters followed the game and gradually pushed southward until they peopled all of North and South America. Yet, there is such diversity racially, linguistically, and culturally among the so-called Indian tribes that this never made any sense. But consensus does not require sense; authority followed by acceptance is all that is needed. Gradually Pacific crossings came to be accepted, but a reluctance (though gradually diminishing) has persisted down to the present, as regards Atlantic crossings.[4]

There is no doubt whatever that crossings of both the Atlantic and the Pacific took place since remote pre-Christian times. Jews, though by no means the first to sail from the Mediterranean to the Western Hemisphere, were among the visitors and immigrants to the New World. The clearest evidence for this comes from the first and second centuries A.D., when imperial Rome reached its maximum extent and strength.

Inasmuch as our conclusions run counter to professional academic consensus, we should establish an incontrovertible starting point, because the opposition insisted that until we have one inscription in an Old World script and/or language, professionally excavated in America in a pre-Columbian context, no claim for transoceanic contacts between the Old and New Worlds before Columbus should be made. Specifically, such an inscription should be authenticated before any pre-Columbian Old World presence in America is posited. As we shall soon see, there is such an inscription and it happens to be Judean.

Before presenting the inscriptional evidence for a Jewish presence in pre-Columbian (and pre-Viking) America, it will be helpful to show that there is an archaeological context for such evidence in America. We shall start with the Roman head of the second century A.D. excavated in situ by professional archaeologists in a pyramid at Calixtlahuaca near Toluca, west of Mexico City. The respected Austrian expert Robert Heine-Geldern declared that it was made about 200 A.D. in Rome and imported to Central America, or at least made by a Roman sculptor who had migrated to what is now Mexico.[5]

From the same general period is a Mayan monument with Jewish connections, direct or indirect. It is the "Phylactery Stele" from Tepatlaxco,

Veracruz, now on permanent display in the National Anthropological Museum in Mexico City. Specialists in Mayan art date it between A.D. 100 and 300. The wrapping of the thong (securing the phylactery) seven times around the forearm, followed by winding it around the hand and fingers, is perpetuated by observant orthodox Jews to this day.[6]

In 1775, James Adair, after living with the Indians in what is now the southeastern part of the United States for nearly forty years, published *The History of the American Indians*,[7] in which he gave twenty-three "arguments" to support his view that those Indians (Cherokees, Creeks and Chickasaws) were descended from Jews. He knew the Indians well and, for a pioneer, his judgment was excellent and his errors excusable. His "Argument I" includes the comparison between the tribal systems of the Indians and biblical Hebrews. The segments of each tribe had official symbols, often animal's names.[8] The loyalty to one's own tribe provided a social support system; yet, at the same time, hospitality to strangers was a sacred duty. "Argument II" contains something far more specific: The Indians call God "Yohewah," which strikingly resembles what scholars now agree to pronounce as God's name "Yahwe(h)." Through a technical misunderstanding, the latter has been garbled to "Jehovah" in a widespread European tradition. I can personally attest that when I attended in 1969 the Green Corn Festival of the Yuchi Indians (which strikingly resembles the Jewish Feast of Tabernacles) I distinctly heard the tribesmen invoking "Yawe, Yawe" as they circumambulated the sacred fire. Adair also stresses that, like the ancient Hebrews and their Jewish descendants, the Indians shun idolatry of any kind. Anyone interested in this subject should read Adair's *History* carefully, and especially his twenty-three arguments.

In 1823 Justice John Haywood of Tennessee published his *Natural and Aboriginal History of Tennessee*[9] recording the antiquities of his state, including Roman coins of the Antonines and Commodus from the second century A.D. Those finds are chance discoveries such as those turned up by farmers while plowing their fields. By themselves they cannot be used as proof of contacts between ancient Rome and America. But the date of their discovery (eighteenth and early nineteenth centuries) and the frontier character of Tennessee at that time, render it unlikely that such coins were imported by colonial settlers.

At this juncture, we must consider the surfacing of three Hebrew coins of the Bar Kokhba Rebellion against Rome (A.D. 132–135) in the neighboring state of Kentucky. One surfaced in Louisville in 1932, another in Clay City in 1952, and the third in Hopkinsville in 1967.[10] It is improbable that a prankster orchestrated the finds, found so far apart in time and place.

The Bar Kokhba Rebellion, which ended disastrously for the Jews, had caused considerable trouble for the Romans. As a result, the deterioration of life for the Jews in the Mediterranean impelled many to get as far away as possible from Roman reprisals and persecution. Many Jews had naval experience and the vessels for escaping by sea. The most likely scenario is that some reached the Western Hemisphere and of them some had to penetrate westward in quest of a place to live.

We are now ready to turn to hard inscriptional evidence that meets all the requirements of scientific method. In 1889 the Smithsonian Institution in Washington, D.C., was conducting excavations on mounds in the southeastern states under the direction of Dr. Cyrus Thomas. One of the sites was Mound #3 at Bat Creek, Loudon County, Tennessee. As Cyrus Thomas correctly reported in 1894, the mound was an intact burial. Thomas was not present at the time of the excavation. However, the handwritten field notes of the person in charge of the dig, John Emmert, confirm that the soil of the mound had not been disturbed between the time of the burial and the excavation in 1889.

The tomb contained nine undisturbed skeletons. All of the artifacts found in the tomb were with one particular skeleton who was evidently the chief or head man. The most interesting artifact was an inscribed stone. The premise of Cyrus Thomas was that the mound Indians were ethnographically the same as the native population found in the southeast by the first white colonial settlers. Accordingly, since Bat Creek was in Cherokee country, the inscription a priori "had to be" Cherokee. Thomas published the inscription upside down and called it Cherokee. The fact that Sequoiah invented the Cherokee system of writing in 1821 did not disturb Dr. Thomas. He cheerfully concluded that Bat Creek's Mound #3 was considerably less than a century old. A few persons (W. W. Strong in 1950, J. C. Ayoob in 1964, and also H. Mertz in 1964) identified two or three letters as Phoenician but none of them were trained Semitists and therefore could not interpret the inscription. It was Dr. J. B. Mahan who, around 1969, acquainted me with the Bat Creek Stone and asked me, as a Semitist, to study it. The sequence of letters, in the script used on Hebrew inscriptions of the First (A.D. 66–70) and Second (132–135) Rebellions against Rome—to wit, LYHWD[ ] "for Judah"—left no doubt as to the meaning, date, and ultimate source. It was Judean from about A.D. 100. As far as the letter-forms go, the inscription could hark back to either Rebellion, but the Second (Bar Kokhba) Rebellion is more likely historically and in the light of the Kentucky coins.[11]

As long as the Establishment reckoned with the inscription as Cherokee, no insinuation of fraud or modern forgery was made, but as soon as I identified the script and language as ancient Hebrew, Amerindian specialists became uneasy. There was absolutely no reason for questioning the antiquity of the tomb or the authenticity of the inscription. Nevertheless in 1970 I requested the Smithsonian to run a Carbon-14 test on some of the wooden fragments and bones found in the tomb. I was told that the excavators had covered the wood and bones found in the tomb with shellac for preservation and that the application of shellac had rendered any C-14 test unreliable. I did not pursue the matter further.

Two brass bracelets found in the tomb were considered modern, but I pointed out that the Romans knew of, and used, brass as well as bronze. As far as I was concerned, the matter was settled factually, though I knew perfectly well that the facts were not welcome. As a scholar, it is my task to ferret out the truth and to teach and publish it with proper documentation. I am not a salesman and it is not my duty to spend my time trying to persuade reluctant customers to buy the factual truth.

Around 1979, unbeknownst to me, Professor J. Huston McCulloch of the Economics Department of Ohio State University became interested in the Bat Creek Stone. He knew neither Hebrew nor Cherokee, but was interested in the Indians and specifically the Cherokees. Upon delving into the literature on the Bat Creek Stone, McCulloch was led to the conclusion that the inscription was Hebrew and not Cherokee. He persisted in requesting the Smithsonian to send wooden fragments from the burial to a laboratory for a C-14 test to settle the date. His efforts met with success when on May 2, 1988, laboratory scientists reported that the earliest possible date was A.D. 32 and the latest possible date was 769.[12] Accordingly the imperial Roman date is possible and in any case all the contents of the tomb were interred and sealed centuries before the Vikings, to say nothing of before Columbus. The inscribed stone may have been kept as an heirloom and cherished for many generations before it was buried, but it harks back to a trans-Atlantic crossing ca. A.D. 100. It cannot be a modern forgery nor any kind of intrusion (i.e., inserted into the grave during the last 1,200 years).

McCulloch did a lot of good "homework" on Bat Creek Mound #3. I had not gone farther with the problem of the brass bracelets than to state that brass (that is, copper alloyed with zinc, as distinct from bronze, which is copper alloyed with tin) was known to the Romans. McCulloch ascertained that Roman brass, like the alloy of the Bat Creek bracelets contained about 3.3 percent lead and was used by the Romans only from about 45 B.C. to about A.D. 200. Such brass with about 3.3 percent lead has been used in modern times only since around 1400. Therefore the C-14 dating favors the Roman date and rules out any modern manufacturing of the Bat Creek bracelets.

The Bat Creek inscription is definitely Judean. It has no demonstrable, or even likely, connection with "The Ten Lost Tribes." The importance of the Bat Creek Stone is that it constitutes incontrovertible proof of contact between the Mediterranean and the Atlantic coast of North America. Consequently it should no longer be asserted that no pre-Columbian text in an Old World script or language has ever been found in the Western Hemisphere. We shall have to reexamine the other inscriptions and artifacts found in America that are possibly of Old World origin. Some are doubtless fakes but others will turn out to be genuine. Each case will have to be judged on its own merits. Jews, though not the earliest visitors or settlers to come across the oceans to America, did come and contribute to the makeup of the native American populations and cultures before Columbus. At this time, I can offer no proof that segments of the "Ten Lost Tribes" migrated to these shores. My guess is that some of them probably did. But that some Judeans landed here and penetrated inland is established. A lesson we learn from all of the above is: Factual truth and consensus are not necessarily the same.

Notes

1. Solomon reorganized Israel into twelve administrative districts, so that each could render federal/royal service for one month per year (I Kings 4:7).

2. For the history of the world of the Old Testament, see C. H. Gordon, *The Ancient Near East* (New York: W. W. Norton, 1965). For the fall of Samaria, see p. 233.

3. Excerpts (with notes and basic bibliography of the sources) from our three travellers (Eldad, Benjamin, and Farissol) are in B. Halper's *Post-Biblical Hebrew Literature: An Anthology*, with text, notes and glossary. (Philadelphia: Jewish Publication Society, 1946).

4. For the extensive literature on the subject, see the comprehensive, annotated bibliography by J. L. Sorenson and M. H. Raish, *Transoceanic Culture Contacts Between the Old and New Worlds in Pre-Columbian Times: A Comprehensive Annotated Bibliography* (Provo, Utah: Foundation for Ancient Research and Mormon Studies, 1988).

5. R. Heine-Geldern, "Ein römischer Fund aus dem vorkolumbischer Mexico," *Arzeiger der Österreichischen Akademie der Wissenschaften, Philosophische-historische Klasse* 98 (1961): 117–19.

6. C. H. Gordon, *Riddles in History* (New York: Crown Publishers, 1974), 49, 151–52.

7. Reissued with notes by S. C. Williams, Johnson City, Tennessee, 1930.

8. See Genesis 49 for the lion of Judah (v. 9), the ass of Issachar (v. 14),

the serpent of Dan (v. 17), the gazelle of Naphtali (v. 21) and the wolf of Benjamin (v. 27).

9. Republished by M. U. Rothrock (Jackson, Tennessee: McCowat Mercer Press, 1959).

10. See C. H. Gordon, *Before Columbus* (New York, 1971), 175–79.

11. The fullest treatment is C. H. Gordon, "The Bat Creek Inscription," in his *Book of the Descendants . . ."* (Ventnor, N.J.: Ventnor Publishers, 1972), 5–18.

12. See J. H. McCulloch, "The Bat Creek Inscription: Cherokee or Hebrew?" *Tennessee Anthropologist* 13 (Fall 1988): 79–123.

Richard H. Popkin

The Rise and Fall of the Jewish
Indian Theory

Though Menasseh ben Israel was far from an advocate of
the Jewish Indian theory, his discussion in *The Hope of Israel* became
crucial at the time, and was revived and revived until well into the nineteenth century. The history of the theory provides an insight into the
changing ways Europeans and European Americans saw their place in
the world, and the changing ways they perceived the world.

This essay deals with the crisis about interpreting the American Indians around 1650, with Menasseh's resolution of this crisis, with the
impact his resolution had on millenarian thinking and politics in the
second half of the seventeenth century, with the revival of Menasseh's
theory in colonial America, with the struggle over the Jewish Indian theory in early United States history until it was rejected by President Jefferson, with the lingering aspects of the view in other nineteenth-
century theories, and, finally, with its demise with the rise of racist anthropology and American nationalism.

Whenever I tell students in America that there was a serious theory
years ago that the Indians were Jews, and that some of the Lost Tribes
were located in America, they look blankly at me as if it's my nonsense,
or they laugh embarrassedly to be in a room where such things are said.
However, I quickly try to calm their fears by pointing out that, after
Columbus met the Indians in 1492, there was a problem of accounting
for who they were and where they came from. If everyone on the surface
of the earth was a descendant of Adam and Eve and the seven survivors
of the Flood, then the Indians had to be connected to the biblical world.
Columbus himself had no problem. He thought they were Asians, since
he was sure that he had reached Cathay. Amerigo Vespucci was a bit
more baffled. He knew that the Indians were not Stoics or Epicureans,

but was not sure who they might be. The pope, in 1537, declared the Indians to be fully human.[1] Various explorers and missionaries offered theories tracing the Indians back to migrations from the Middle East—from Phoenicia, Arabia, or maybe from Solomon's Ophir. To deny a biblical origin for the Indians was to see them, and their history, as outside of Scripture, and Scripture as incomplete and inadequate.[2] Only a few hardy souls in the sixteenth century dared suggest this—Paracelsus, Giordano Bruno, Christopher Marlowe, and maybe Sir Walter Raleigh. Bruno had read about the Aztec calendar stone (which, once discovered and deciphered, was promptly buried for more than two centuries). It led him to embellish Paracelsus's theory that there were multiple origins of mankind. Marlowe had heard of the findings of Raleigh's trip to Virginia, and had probably met Bruno. Marlowe is supposed to have given a lecture in which he claimed that Indian history was 16,000 years old, hence much older than the world according to the Jewish calendar, or according to the revised dating system of Archbishop Ussher.[3]

In the early seventeenth century various Spanish explorers and theologians debated the origins of the Indians, always indicating that the solution had to involve tracing them back to their biblical roots. More and more refined theories developed, some just simple migration views to the effect that the Indians, like the Europeans, Asiatics, and Africans, all got to where they are now living by migration after Noah's Flood and the dispersion after the Tower of Babel episode. Detailed histories of European, Asian, and African travels already existed, and ones suitable to account for the Indians were added. Most of these were not intended to glorify or extol the virtues of the Indians, who were being horribly exploited by the Conquistadors.[4] Only the theory of Bartolomé de las Casas, the defender of the Indians, involved first making them co-equal descendants of Adam and Eve, better people than the Europeans because they had not been corrupted, and some even the very best people: the "elect" described by St. Paul, who are to be preserved until the end of time to rejoin Jesus in his Kingdom on Earth. Las Casas and his followers, who tried to create a millennial state in Guatemala without Spanish Conquistadors, introduced a supernatural element into theories about the Indians, namely that some of them had special properties that were crucial in providential times to come.[5] This view may have interacted with a Marrano millenarianism that developed in the late sixteenth and seventeenth centuries in New Spain to the effect that God would save the faithful, the hidden Jews in America.[6]

At the same time, from around 1640 to 1650, a difficulty emerged in accounting for the Indians and in relating them to religious developments in European history. On the one hand, the French Marrano millenarian, Isaac La Peyrère, offered his theory that the Indians, like the South Sea Islanders, the Chinese, and lots of other groups, were not descendants of Adam. La Peyrère wrote his statement of this around 1642, but only published it in 1655. As secretary to the prince of Condée, he showed his theory to people in various parts of Europe, and gathered new evidence for it from his discussions with scholars. His case, briefly, was that mankind existed for an indefinitely long period of time. Because the human race was such a mess, a war of all against all, God created Adam, the first Jew, as a means of saving everyone. The Adamites were called, then were rejected when Jesus came, and were now about to be recalled. Their recall, with the arrival of the Jewish Messiah, would lead to the rebuilding of Jerusalem, and the messianic world in which everyone—pre-Adamites, Adamites, and post-Adamites—would flourish in peace and happiness. But only Jews were Adamites. La Peyrère insisted that his theory would better explain what we know of ancient pagan history, of other cultures found through the voyages of discovery, and also the anomalies in the text of the Bible.[7]

La Peyrère's theory was answered long before it was published, by the great Dutch scholar Hugo Grotius, who saw the work in manuscript. In 1643 he wrote a pamphlet on the origins of the American people, and claimed they were descendants of the Viking explorations.[8] (La Peyrère became Europe's leading expert on the Eskimos in order to answer Grotius, and pointed out that if Grotius could solve the Indian problem by appeal to the Vikings, then what about the Eskimos, who were in Greenland when the Vikings got there?)[9]

Grotius's solution was just a new version of connecting the Indians to the European-biblical world. La Peyrère sought to sunder the worlds entirely and restrict divine history to Jewish history. This might easily account for the many kinds of peoples in the world, but it also required a radical rereading and rewriting of the accepted scriptural picture. All this La Peyrère's many critics, including Menasseh, were not ready to do.

As the English began colonizing New England, the Scots Nova Scotia, the Swedes New Sweden (Delaware), these Protestant missionaries and settlers sought to understand whom they were dealing with, and where these people came from. Two of the leading English millenarians of the seventeenth century, the very pious and highly learned Joseph Mede of Cambridge, who had deciphered the chronologies of Daniel and Revelation, and his student, the Cambridge Platonist Henry More, offered a most negative theological interpretation of the American Indians. As Europe was, according to them, reaching its millenarian climax, which would occur between 1650 and 1680 with the conversion of the Jews,

God was revealing aspects of the world hitherto unknown, through allowing for the increase of human knowledge, partly through the extension of navigation and commerce. The Indians, so discovered, were the children of Satan, who had been driven out of the Old World when Jesus arrived, and now were to be destroyed by his Second Coming. The Indians were purely malevolent beings whose total defeat was to be their only contribution to the course of divine history. Henry More delighted in retelling the goriest Spanish tales about the Indians to show how demonic they were.[10]

Although Mede carried great weight with the English Puritans, they realized that even he could be wrong. He claimed that various events in the Book of Revelation would occur in 1642, and they did not. Besides, the settler-missionaries found matters in Massachusetts Bay Colony quite different than Mede had described. They found docile, friendly Indians, some of whom wanted to become Christians. They established schools for them, and they tried to get the great Jan Comenius to use Harvard as the center of universal enlightenment for Indians and Europeans.[11] They translated the Scriptures for the Indians. The missionaries began to suspect something radically different was going on in the environs in Boston, namely that pure English Christians were baptizing and converting Indians who were Jews. And, if the Indians were Jews, an enormous missionary effort would be needed. So, on behalf of the New England missionary society, a volume was written by a Norfolk preacher, one Thomas Thorowgood, called *Jewes in America, or the Probability that the Indians are Jewes.*[12] This was to be dedicated to Charles I, but his overthrow delayed the publication of the book. The job of writing a preface to it was given to John Dury, perhaps the most active millenarian theoretician in the Puritan revolution. Dury, 1596–1680, a Scot, was born in Holland, studied at the Walloon Seminary in Leiden, and became a pastor in Germany. He then began a lifelong campaign to reunite all of the evangelical churches in Europe, and to this end travelled all over, from Sweden to Poland, Germany, Holland, Switzerland, France, and England. He lived for a while in Amsterdam and was one of Cromwell's chief agents on the Continent.[13]

Dury was in England when he encountered Thorowgood's text. He immediately put it in the context of some providential data he had learned from Jews in Holland, especially from Menasseh ben Israel. The Lost Tribes of Israel would reappear just before the millennium (which Dury was sure would occur in 1655).[14] He had heard from a Jewish jeweler in The Hague that some of the Lost Tribes had been located east of the Holy Land, in Persia or in Afghanistan.[15] He had heard from the most learned Jewish writer of the time, his friend and coworker Menasseh ben

Israel, that a Portuguese Marrano explorer, Antonio de Montezinos, had encountered a Jewish tribe in the Andes Mountains. He knew that Menasseh had had Montezinos, who came to Amsterdam in 1644, give his account before a notary. So Dury (who was at the time planning to set up a college of Jewish studies in London, with Menasseh as one of its three professors)[16] wrote Menasseh for a copy of the Montezinos report, which he was duly sent.[17] Then Dury and his fellow millenarian Nathaniel Homes wrote Menasseh to see if he made out of this what they did, namely that the Indians were the Lost Tribes. The correspondence, printed in the preface to Thorowgood's book, shows Menasseh being most cautious, unconvinced; until he was finally willing to say that the group encountered by Montezinos could be part of a Lost Tribe, while the rest of the inhabitants of the Americas were migrants from Asia. Homes immediately pointed out that this meant that the climax of world history was at hand, because the Lost Tribes were beginning to reappear. Menasseh was asked what was the Jewish view about the Lost Tribes and their reappearance.[18] Rather than write another letter, Menasseh wrote his most famous work, *The Hope of Israel*, which appeared in 1650 in Spanish, Latin, Hebrew, and English, and in Dutch a few years later. The English edition, dedicated to the revolutionary parliament of England, was translated by a friend of John Milton's, the wild-eyed millenarian Moses Wall. This translation appeared in editions in 1650, 1651, and 1652. The last two editions included an appendix in which Wall exchanged views with a reader, and emphasized the millenarian importance of his work, *and* that it should help bring about the conversion of the Jews.[19]

Even prior to Wall's translation, and Menasseh's own publication in Spanish, Hebrew, and Latin, his text of the Montezinos report and his views about it were having reverberations on both sides of the Atlantic Ocean. One Edward Winslow, in 1649, published a work entitled *The Glorious Progress of the Gospel among the Indians in New England. Manifested by three Letters under the hand of the famous Instrument of the Lord, John Eliot.* The work was dedicated to Parliament and the Council of State. In his preface, Winslow said that there are two great questions which have troubled ancient and modern writers, and men of the greatest depth and ability. They have tried to resolve (1) what became of the Ten Tribes of Israel? and (2) where did the American Indians come from? "A godly Minister of this city (no doubt, John Dury) wrote to Rabbi ben-Israel, a great Dr. of the Jewes, now living at Amsterdam" to find out if he knew what became of the Ten Tribes. According to Winslow, Menasseh's answer was that they were certainly transported to America. For Winslow it was wondrous that God had opened the hearts of the

Indians to the gospel just when so many eminent divines expect the conversion of the Jews.[20]

Dury wrote an appendix to the work in which he stressed that the gospel being revealed to the Indians led many judicious and godly theologians to believe that the conversion of the Jews is at hand. In fact Dury reported that "It is the expectation of some of the wisest Jews now living that about the year 1650, *Either we Christians shall be Mosaick, or else that they themselves Jews shall be Christians.*" No indication was given of who these wisest Jews were.[21] We know Dury was a close friend of Menasseh's, and he probably knew Rabbi Judah Leon Templo. Dury added "that those sometimes poor, now precious Indians . . . may be as the first fruits of the glorious harvest of *Israel's* Redemption."[22] Thus Dury connected the missionary activities of the Reverend John Eliot in Massachusetts with the imminently expected conversion of the Jews. Both the English translator Moses Wall and the anonymous author of a letter written in 1650 *To the Learned Jew: Menasseh ben Israel of Amsterdam and to all of his Brethren there and elsewhere, Grace, Mercy and Truth from the Most high God be granted and given,* saw the news in the Montezinos report as evidence that the Jews should convert right away. In the anonymous letter Menasseh was urged over and over again to convert and to convince his brethren to do so, because of the discovery that the Indians were Jews, the Lost Tribes.[23]

Henry Méchoulan and Gérard Nahon have shown in their preface to the recent French translation of Menasseh's work that Menasseh did not become a believer in the Jewish Indian theory, but held to the view that just part of a Lost Tribe had been discovered.[24] Menasseh, after printing Montezinos' statement, carefully delineated the problem—there are so many opinions about the origins of the Indians that it is very hard to tell which is true. There is no scriptural statement on the matter. Menasseh said that he had only written about solid and infallible things ("as those things are which concern our Law").[25] But his friends asked for his view about where the Lost Tribes were. One has to have faith, Menasseh claimed, that all people are descended from Adam and Eve and the survivors of the Flood. So the Indians must be part of the human dispersion after the Flood and the Tower of Babel. Second, the Ten Tribes, as described in 2 Esdras were scattered, not all at once, nor to one place. Then it is reasonable to expect some possibility of dispersion throughout the world—the Chinese Jews, the Jews of South India, of Ethiopia, all seem to be remnants of the Lost Tribes. So, Menasseh argued, the people encountered by Montezinos are probably also a part of a Lost Tribe that was driven from Tartary across some land bridge in the Pacific to America. The reemergence of the Lost Tribes fits with other evidence that the fulfillment of God's Promise is at hand, the Redemption of Israel. The Ten Tribes will emerge and return to join the other two in Israel in the near future.[26]

Menasseh said he saw no reason to doubt Montezinos's story, but, as it was a human account, it could not be proven. However, it fitted with a lot of other data, and helped explain the peopling of America, with part of a Lost Tribe, plus other branches of humanity descended from our biblical parents.[27]

Nonetheless, in all of the excitement that followed in England, with the publication of Thorowgood, Menasseh, and the Montezinos narration, the Jewish Indian theory was truly launched. Menasseh was invited to England to confer with Cromwell about fulfilling the final prophecies before the Redemption of Israel.[28] Dury envisaged the Jews, the Lost Tribes, including the Indians, and the Caraites marching into the Holy Land.[29] In 1660, after the Restoration, a new edition of Thorowgood was issued, in which the missionaries to the Indians in Massachusetts wanted to distance themselves a little from Menasseh's non-Calvinist theology. But they were also filled with more and more data about Indian customs, practices, and languages that indicated that the Indians were Jews, albeit a bit degenerate in their behavior. Dury wrote a new preface reporting that a Dutch student had had a vision that Charles II would be restored, and that he would bring about the conversion of the Jews.[30]

Later English colonists, like the Quaker William Penn, found it easy to discover signs of Judaism amongst the Indians. Penn wrote back after his first winter in Pennsylvania that it was like being in Duke Street in London, surrounded by Jews.[31] Bishop George Berkeley apparently started with a similar view until he met drunken Indians in Newport, Rhode Island.[32]

The Jewish Indian theory had its virtues. It explained where the red-men came from, and obviated the need for revising our historical framework by adopting some kind of polygenetic theory about the origins of mankind. Some scholars, however, showed that the evidence of Menasseh and Montezinos left much to be desired. In the eighteenth century, when "scientific" anthropology developed, one of its main tasks was to explain the varieties of mankind. Most of the workers in this new science were monogenesists, insisting on a single source of human beings, but then explaining the differences as due to their being several species of men. Linnaeus, Buffon, Blumenbach, to name a few, divided mankind into four or five species. The Indians were one species, but a rather dismal one, ranking far below the Caucasians and the Asiatics in intelligence and moral character. The biblical aspect was toned down to the mere assertion that all mankind came from a common source. The differences amongst men were due to climate, education, environment, diet, etc. Presumably the defects of Negroes and Indians could be remedied by bringing them up to the level of Europeans.[33] (Some of the same people recommended that this course also be followed for Jews, if they could be brought out of the ghettos, secularized, and made to behave like others in their locales.)[34] In contrast, some forms of polygenesis were also being propounded. Hume offered a pretty drastic version that left the blacks inferior forever.[35] His cousin, Lord Kames, expressed a more modest view: that some peoples were created after Adam and Eve, including the inhabitants of the Americas, who, in view of their later origin, did not have to be connected to the biblical world.[36]

Against Kames a new form of the Jewish Indian theory was offered that took on providential significance in the millenarian excitement surrounding the American and French revolutions. In 1775, just the publication in New York of a pretty detailed debunking of the Jewish Indian theory by a Captain Bernard Romans, who suggested the possibility of divine multiple creations,[37] an English trader, James Adair, published his *History of the American Indians* in London.[38] Adair had been trading with the Indians in the southern English colonies of America for forty years. In this work he offered detailed linguistic, cultural, social, and historical evidence that the Indians were Jews, based on his close observation of their speech and practices. He assured his readers that "The public may depend on the finality of the author, and his descriptions are genuine."[39] Lord Kames, on the contrary, was offering reasonings contrary "both to revelation and facts."[40] Adair contended that, from his most exact observations made over forty years, the Indians "lineally descended from the Israelites."[41] His evidence of the Jewish characteristics of the Indians went on for hundreds of pages. At the time, Adair's evidence was taken most seriously by American historians like Hannah Adams, who wrote an important *History of the Jews* and appended some of Adair's text.[42] Menasseh's *Hope of Israel* was reissued.[43] Some of the religious thinkers involved in the American Revolution saw Adair's findings as justification for a providential interpretation of what was happening in the colonies. Charles Crawford, an English nobleman who had moved to America, and who became an important abolitionist and millenarian, saw America's role as that of bringing about the final providential events before the millennium, the freeing of slaves, the finding of the Lost Tribes, and the conversion of the Jews. More significant, Crawford indicated, was that a rabbi who converted to Christianity came to Philadelphia to live with the Lost Tribe Indians, to prepare to lead them to Jerusalem. Apparently the converted rabbi gave up, however, and became a Catholic official instead.[44]

A more important figure, Elias Boudinot, took up the Jewish Indian cause. Boudinot, a lawyer from New Jersey, was one of the leaders of the American Revolution, and possibly the most important figure in the beginning of American fundamentalism.[45] Adair showed his findings to Boudinot's close ally, Governor Livingston of New Jersey, before the book was published in London. Boudinot heard about this and was very intrigued. He bought a copy of Adair's book right after the Revolutionary War. He wanted to make his own text. A friend who knew Hebrew sought out an Indian tribe that had never encountered Europeans before. He spoke to them in Hebrew, and decided from their responses that they were Jews.[46] Boudinot saw the American revolutionary events as premillennial developments. He served as the head of the Continental Congress during the Revolution, was the head of the revolutionary state at the end of the war. He was the patron of Alexander Hamilton. When the United States was formed he became a congressman, and later director of the Mint (like his millenarian predecessor, Sir Isaac Newton).[47] Boudinot became convinced during the French Revolution that the events predicted in the Book of Revelation were taking place. When Thomas Jefferson was elected president, Boudinot resigned from the government, telling Jefferson that he could not serve in a deist government, and that he had to prepare for the Second Advent. He founded the two most important fundamentalist organizations in the United States, the American Bible Society and the Society for Ameliorating the Condition of the Jews. He checked with a United States congressman who had been a governmental Indian agent, who confirmed Adair's claims.[48] Then Boudinot wrote *The Star in the West*, pointing out that the Indians, the Lost Tribes, would lead the way into the millennium by returning to Jerusalem.[49] Boudinot, Crawford, Jonathan Edwards, and other religious interpreters of the American and French revolutions could see in the Jewish Indian theory an all-important role for the indigenous Americans in developing God's climax to human history, and could see America as central in the drama. Other millenarians, especially British, from Sir William Jones onward, found evidence that the Lost Tribes were in Afghanistan and that the millennial drama involved the true Christians of Europe locating the Afghan Lost Tribes, and so creating the final moments of history without need of any Americans, native or immigrant.[50] Boudinot, Crawford, and others rejected the Afghan theory.[51] Some combined the Afghan and Jewish Indian theory, saying the tribes were scattered. Some came to America, and some moved to the east to Afghanistan.

One reason for the decline of the Jewish Indian theory was the shift of attention to the Middle East after Napoleon's Egyptian campaign, coupled with the excited reports of missionaries who had been in India and Afghanistan. But long before the American focus was pushed aside, some further developments took place, to secularize and minimize the role of the American Indians. (These were, we will see, rejected by the new American religion of the Mormons, and by the leading American Jewish writer of the period, Mordecai Noah.)

Jefferson was concerned about whether there could be anything to Adair's claims. He asked John Adams, the second president of the United States, what he thought about the matter. They agreed that Adair's evidence was superficial and inconclusive.[52] Based on this discussion, a recent scholar has shown that Jefferson decided that the Indians were probably not part of any providential scheme.[53] (Boudinot, on the other hand, was converting Indians to make them leaders in the millennium. A Cherokee who took the name "Elias Boudinot," after his sponsor, became a Christian minister. When he married a white member of his congregation, he was ostracized and left to be the unhappy negotiator who gave away the Cherokee territories and rights.)[54] If the Indians were just people, then they had to find their place or role in a secular world, not in a fanciful voyage to the Holy Land. So, as it has recently been shown, Jefferson indicated that his decision to purchase the Louisiana territories from Napoleon was in part to find adequate space for secular Indians as they became part of the American polity. The Louisiana Purchase was for Jefferson a commitment that the United States would develop as a secular redeemer nation, solving the problems of mankind by reason and science, and not as part of scriptural history.[55]

If Jefferson politically removed the Indians from divine history, American anthropology sought to accomplish this "scientifically." The so-called school of American ethnography, headed by Dr. Samuel Morton of Philadelphia, examined the cranial history of various groups and tried to establish human racial differences in terms of differences in skull capacity. Morton, in his *Crania Americana* and his *Crania Ægyptica*, measured skull capacities by filling skulls with pepper seed and then weighing how much could go into each skull. Morton had the largest skull collection in the world at the time. He found that the Indians and the Negroes had lower cranial capacity than Caucasians and Asiatics. He also found that Indians from Canada in the north to Tierra del Fuego in the south had the same capacity.[56] On the basis of this, his disciples insisted that Indians and Negroes were separate races, which had separate origins. The Bible was not about them, and they had no role to play in the Scriptural world. The Mound Builders of the Ohio Valley and the uncivilized Indians were indigenous to the Western Hemisphere. They were an inferior race compared to the Asiatic or Caucasian ones, and had no special spiritual or intellectual destiny.[57]

Morton's ethnology was adopted primarily as a "scientific proof" of Negro inferiority, and as a justification for continuing the slave system in America. Morton's disciples tried to convince Southerners to adopt the new ethnology over Scripture as a defense of their world. The Swiss biologist Louis Agassiz came to the United States in the 1840s and became the leading scientific advocate of Mortonism, with its blatant racist conclusions about the status of Negroes.[58] Frederick Douglass, the leading black spokesman before the Civil War, and Alexander von Humboldt fought against this polygenetic racism as a *desolante* theory that condemned much of mankind to perpetual slavery and inferiority.[59]

The application of ethnology to the Indians justified taking away their lands, driving them westward, and decimating them. It is interesting that Morton's view, insisting on the indigenous, autochthonous character of the American Indians, rejected the theory advanced by Menasseh ben Israel, in which there was growing interest, that the Indians came from the Orient. From the time of the discovery of the Bering Strait, it was realized that people could have walked from Asia to America. (A Mexican Jesuit, Alexo de Oririo, joyfully announced that this destroyed the pre-Adamite theory.[60]) The Indians could thus be connected with the Chinese or the Mongolians, who in turn had been connected with the descendants of survivors of Noah's Ark. Mortonism disconnected the Indians and Africans from scriptural history and left them to be dominated by the Caucasians and the Asiatics. Morton's followers de-emphasized the scriptural basis of human history, in exchange for so-called scientific factors—the amount of pepper seed that can be held in a cranium—paving the way for a secular-racist account of the Indians and Negroes. (And it has been found that Morton "fudged" his data to get his "scientific" results.)[61]

Before such a view became predominant, at least in America, one more stage of the Jewish Indian view emerged. While Boudinot, Crawford, and other millenarians saw the Indians as the Lost Tribes, new evidence emerged, and two new theories were offered, one being that of the leading Jewish spokesman, Mordecai Noah, the other that of the founder of Mormonism, Joseph Smith.

The new evidence was some artifacts that were discovered: phylacteries in an Indian burial mound in Pittsfield, Massachusetts; a Hebrew inscription outside New Milford, Connecticut; a Hebrew tomb in Ohio. These added weight to the evidence provided by alleged resemblances to ancient Hebrew motifs that Lord Kingsborough thought he had found in the Aztec codices. Lord Kingsborough published nine folio volumes of the codices, magnificently illustrated, with copious notes from Menasseh, Adair, and others, to prove that the Indians, especially those of Central America, were Jews. Although he bankrupted himself in the process of publishing the material, he convinced only the already convinced, and became a laughing-stock to others.[62]

The Hebrew inscription in New Milford was examined by America's greatest Christian Hebraist, Ezra Stiles, president of Yale, who guessed it was somebody's name. No one in the area could be found who was Jewish or who knew Hebrew, so a suggestive mystery remained. The phylacteries were a more exciting find, when it was realized that these are used by a Jew in his morning prayers. The physical object was found around 1820, halfway down a pile of Indian bones in a burial mound. Because of the Hebrew letters contained in the object, Christian scholars from Harvard were consulted, who identified the object for what it was. But how did it get to where it was found? An intensive investigation was carried out to find out if any Jewish traders had been in Pittsfield, if any captured British soldiers held there were Jewish, with negative results. The great Jewish convert, the Reverend Joseph Frey, who gave 30,000 sermons in America, said he had never spoken in Pittsfield, and the phylacteries were not his.[63]

The literature of the period indicates that this discovery was taken to point very seriously to the possibility that the Indians were Jewish. No other explanation could be found for the phylacteries being where they were found. The item was deposited with the Massachusetts Historical Society for further study. By now, when some of us would like to see what was discovered, however, the item has been lost. The late Rabbi Arthur Chiel, who wrote an article on the matter and turned up a lot of literature written by others in the period 1820–1825, some rather incredible, found that the phylacteries had been in the Antiquarian Society of Worcester, Massachusetts, but that they had disappeared.[64]

The tomb is interesting, but also unlocatable. The important American historian Hubert Howe Bancroft, in his history of the native races of America, included a chapter on the origins of the Indians, setting out the prevailing theories. The Jewish Indian theory was taken up and disowned by Bancroft, but it was described as having strong evidence in its favor. The evidence consisted of the phylacteries and the tomb. The latter, Bancroft said, was discovered by his father, a minister in Ohio. It had Hebrew inscriptions indicating that it was from the first or second centuries C.E. Bancroft's father deposited it in the local historical society, from whence it seems to have disappeared.[65]

The news of physical remains reinforced the believers. One major believer was the Jewish politician, publisher, and playwright Mordecai Noah, who has usually been written off as a crank for setting up a Jewish state on Grand Island off Buffalo, New York. To appreciate his role, one has to realize that he was *the* leading public Jew in the America of his time. He spoke out for Judaism in many ways. He was a public official who became the United States consul in Tunis. He received a letter from James Monroe firing him from his position because of his religion.[66] (This is the only such publicly known case in American history.) Noah wrote to Jefferson, Adams, and Madison and got them to write statements that Jews were coequal citizens of the United States and could not be punished or discriminated against officially because of their religion.[67] He also argued publicly with the millenarian Christians who wanted to convert the Jews.

His plan for a Jewish state seems to have grown out of his meeting with the abbé Henri Grégoire in Paris at the end of the Napoleonic era. Elsewhere I have shown that Noah's Jewish state was planned as a continuation of the Paris Sanhedrin.[68] (Noah did not seem to notice Grégoire's millenarianism, or his hopes for the conversion of the Jews, and Grégoire defended Noah against the wrath of the chief rabbi of France, who had been one of the leaders of the Paris Sanhedrin, Grand Rabbi Cologna.)

Relevant to the theme of this essay is that in Noah's Jewish state, whose constitution was carefully worked out to conform to American law, and allowed coequal status to non-Jews, all of the Jewish groups in the world were to be invited to rest and prepare for the messianic Jewish state to come. Included in the invitation were the poor Jews Noah had met in north Africa, the oppressed Jews of Eastern Europe, the fortunate American Jews, the Caraites, and the Jewish Indians. All would be reunited as the Jewish people would come to know each other, to appreciate each other, and to prepare together to go to the ultimate redemptive state in Palestine.[69] I think Noah's passion for the Caraites came from Grégoire, who regarded them as pure Jews, uncorrupted by rabbinical superstitions.[70] The passion for the Indians was Noah's version of the Jewish Indian theory, drawn from Menasseh, Adair, Boudinot, and others. He set forth the theory over and over again in public lectures in the United States. It is sad to report that with all of this good will toward the poor, the oppressed, the benighted Jews everywhere, no Jew, including Noah himself, ever set foot in his Jewish state. It had a rousing inauguration ceremony at Buffalo, with a parade, speeches, and music, and it promptly died. Noah was the most prominent Jewish advocate of the Jewish Indian theory, and seemed oblivious to the growing "scientific" opposition.

Another intriguing case of Jewish interest in the Jewish Indian theory appears in the missionary report by the Scottish missionaries who travelled across Europe to the Holy Land trying to convert Jews. As they started out, they stopped in Boulogne. There they met "a very interesting Jew, a person of education and agreeable manners, who spoke English fluently."[71] The person unfortunately is not named. He had been rich, but had used up his money "in travelling for the sake of his brethren," all over North America, investigating whether the Indians were really descended from the Ten Tribes. He lived with different Indian tribes, learned their languages, adopted their customs. And he came to the negative conclusion, the Indians were not Jews, and now was trying to regain some funds so he could go to Palestine.[72]

A different and more religious version of the Jewish Indian theory, influenced by the "evidence," and either influenced or strengthened by Noah's views, is Mormonism. The Mormon movement has been described as the first really indigenous American religion, building on biblical tradition and the American situation. It claimed new revelatory material showing that some of the ancient Jews went to America instead of to Babylon at the time of the destruction of the First Temple, that Jesus preached to them in America, and that they, the Latter-day Saints, were the bearers of Christianity and would lead it into the millennium. The Mormon claim is not that all Indians are Jews, but that a remnant of the ancient Hebrews exists in America and will join with the followers of Joseph Smith. The Lost Tribes are not the Indians, but are still hidden somewhere in the Arctic and will reappear at the end of time. Although Mormonism is one of the fastest-growing religions, it has not made the Jewish Indian theory more acceptable to "enlightened people" in America or elsewhere.[73]

The anthropologists have moved from Morton's theory of the indigenous Indian to the Mongolian origin theory, with the forebears of the present Indians having crossed over the Bering Strait about 25,000 years ago. With Providence and theology cast aside, the Indians do not have to be connected to the biblical world. Late nineteenth-century anthropology saw the Indians as pretty primitive. American developments made them the most dispossessed group in the country. Nobody would want to relate them to the Bible, or to any other group than the Siberians or the Mongols. As secular anti-Semitism developed, the Europeans and Americans saw no need to be descended from the Jews. So, then, who needs a Jewish Indian? What role could such a double outcast play?

The Jewish Indian theory fell victim to a scientific movement aimed at getting rid of the Scriptural framework of human history and substituting a secular one, of migrating peoples. If there were superior providential people, they could be British Israelites (a late-nineteenth-century claim that the Anglo-Saxons are the Lost Tribes),[74] or Aryans. But the easiest thing to do was to measure people by their technical abilities and their ability to survive in modern industrial society.

The immense change in the evaluation of peoples left the Jewish Indian theory a bad joke, an anachronistic hangover from an unfortunate religious past. If anyone still believed it, he or she was a menace to the scientific understanding of man. The theory, which in Dury and Thorowgood's version, or in Menasseh's, was to intensify the pursuit of the millennium, made no sense anymore.

The collapse of the Jewish Indian theory in the face of nineteenth-century science is a casualty of the war between science and theology. Part of the price that has been paid is that we have lost our ability to understand the force and significance of the theory for at least two hundred years, and to appreciate Menasseh ben Israel's serious contribution in this area. Further, it has made it difficult or impossible to interpret or evaluate evidence that does not fit with the Mongolian origin theory.

In his book *Before Columbus*, Cyrus Gordon has marshalled a fair amount of evidence that there were Mediterranean contacts with America going back to Phoenician and Roman times.[75] Scientists are afraid to take his evidence seriously because they see the Jewish Indian theory looming up again. Gordon has pointed to Phoenician inscriptions in Georgia and Brazil, to Roman and Hebrew coins found in Central and North America, and to other Mediterranean artifacts. He has posed a plausible, nontheological explanation, that early seafarers had crossed the Atlantic Ocean. Nobody finds it implausible that the Hawaiians travelled over nine thousand miles across the Pacific Ocean from their point of origin to their present location. But it is regarded as nonsensical when applied to the Atlantic Ocean (even though Cabral, the accidental discoverer of Brazil, was about two hundred miles off course, rounding the coast of West Africa, when he landed in South America).[76] All sorts of navigational problems are raised that had not been solved until the fifteenth century. Melanesians crossed the Pacific in open boats, but Mediterraneans could not have done a much shorter voyage with large sailing ships. So Gordon's evidence is ignored instead of reviving the possibility that Mediterraneans got to the New World, that Hebrews might have also, and that Jews might have lived somewhere in the Americas before Columbus. (Both the nineteenth-century historian George Bancroft and Cyrus Gordon point out that there was a group in Tennessee of Mediterranean character who were driven into the wilderness by the Indians.)

The rise and fall of the Jewish Indian theory is a measure of the change of the roles of religion and science in accounting for the world. The discovery of America, made in a world which saw its history delineated in Scripture, raised a most serious problem of accounting for the origins of the American Indians. To avoid the polygenetic explanation of La Peyrère limiting scriptural history to Jewish history, theorists tried to link the Indians to some already known group. The Jewish Indian theory was one of many possibilities. The joining of this to the millennial expectations of the mid-seventeenth century led to the excitement over Menasseh's statement in *The Hope of Israel*. Although Menasseh may have been trying to limit the Jewish Indian theory to a small group that could be part of a Lost Tribe, his contemporaries saw amazing implications. The conversion of the Indians was the prelude to the conversion of the European Jews, which was the prelude to the Second Coming and the millennium. Menasseh, in spite of his cautious efforts, became the official spokesman for the millenarian Jewish Indian theory, and it was his account that was debated. The discussion was revived and revitalized by Adair and by those who saw the American Revolution as a great premillennial event. The secular deism of Jefferson and the "scientific" ethnology of Morton sought to put the Indian in his secular place, as inferior inhabitants of North and South America. Later anthropologists made him a descendant of Mongolians rather than the original people of Scripture. Only in Mordecai Noah's version or in Mormonism was there still place for the Indians, or some of them, in providential history. The Jewish Indian theory has become an intellectual pariah to be avoided even if there is evidence in its favor. Even in the present resurgence of millenarian and messianic thought, the American Indians seem to have been left aside, to be accounted for as wanderers from Siberia who have nothing further to contribute. Thus a theory that could have been such a vital explanation and source of hope for two centuries has been discarded as science and American rationalism found other ways of explaining the Indians and their minimal place in history. The displacement of the Jews from national history from the French Revolution until Zionism left no need to relate Jews and Indians. They could both be outcasts in one world or another. The present flowering of Judaism in America and Israel needs no connection with the ancient inhabitants of the New World to account for what is happening. And so, there seems little left for the theory to explain, and little desire to have it explain anything. So perishes the glory of what was an exciting and intriguing theory!

Notes

1. The Papal Bull is dated June 9, 1537. On it see Lewis Hanke, *The Spanish Struggle for Justice in the Conquest of America* (Philadelphia, 1949); and R. H. Popkin, "The Pre-Adamite Theory in the Renaissance," in Edward P. Mahoney, ed., *Philosophy and Humanism, Renaissance Essays in Honor of Paul Oskar Kristeller* (Leiden, 1976), esp. 57ff.

2. Popkin, "Pre-Adamite Theory," 57, 63–64; Lynn Glaser, *Indians or Jews?* (Gilroy, Ca., 1973), chap. 2. Two Spanish writers at the beginning of the seventeenth century, Joseph de Acosta and Gregorio García, insisted that one had to accept that the Indians were somehow descended from Adam and Eve, in order not to contradict Scripture. Citations are given in Popkin, "Pre-Adamite Theory," 63–64.

3. See Popkin, "Pre-Adamite Theory," 57–62.

4. See Lynn Glaser, chap. 2, and the authors quoted there.

5. Bartolomé de las Casas, *A Selection of his Writings,* trans. and ed. George Sanderlin (New York, 1972), Part IV.

6. Luis de Carvajal, *The Enlightened: The Writings of Luis de Carvajal, el Mozo,* trans. and ed. Seymour H. Liebman (Coral Gables, Florida, 1967); and Martin A. Cohen, *The Martyr. The Story of a Secret Jew and the Mexican Inquisition in the Sixteenth Century* (Philadelphia, 1973).

7. On La Peyrère, see Popkin, "The Marrano Theology of Isaac La Peyrère," *Studi internazionali di filosofia* 5 (1973): 97–126; and my book on *Isaac La Peyrère (1596–1676), His Life, His Work and Influence* (Leiden, 1987).

8. Hugo Grotius, *Dissertatio altera de Origine Gentium Americanarum adversus obtrectatorem* (n.p., 1643).

9. Isaac La Peyrère, *Relation de Groenland* (Paris, 1647) and *Relation de l'Islande* (Paris, 1663).

10. Mede's view on the Satanic origin of the American Indians appears in his letter to the Reverend William Twisse, March 23, 1634/5, in *The Works of the Pious and Profoundly Learned Joseph Mede, B.D.* (London, 1664), 980–81. Mede said, "So the Devil, when he saw the world apostazing from him, laid the foundations of a new Kingdom, by deducting this Colony from the North into *America,* where they have increased into an inumerable multitude." Henry More, in *An Explanation of the Grand Mystery of Godliness* (London, 1660), book 3, chaps. 3, 13, and 14, dealt with the horrendous practices of the demonic savages.

11. Cf. G. H. Turnbull, *Hartlib, Dury and Comenius* (London, 1947), 59–70; and Popkin, "The Third Force in 17th Century Philosophy: Scepticism, Science and Biblical Prophecy," *Nouvelles de la république des lettres* 1 (1983): 52.

12. Thomas Thorowgood, *Jewes in America, or Probability that the Indians are Jewes . . .* (London, 1650).

13. On Dury, see J. Minto Batten, *John Dury: Advocate of Christian Reunion* (Chicago, 1944); Charles Webster, *The Great Instauration* (London, 1975).

14. So Dury indicated in his preface to Abraham von Frankenburg's *Clavis Apocalyptics,* published in London in 1651 by Samuel Hartlib.

15. John Dury, *An Epistolicall Discourse of Mr. John Dury to Mr. Thorowgood, Concerning his Conjecture that the Americans are descended from the Israelites*, Jan. 27, 1649, prefaced to Thorowgood, *Jewes in America*.

16. R. H. Popkin, "The First College for Jewish Studies," *Révue des études juives* 142 (1984), 351–64.

17. The notarized copy was published by Dury as an appendix to Thorowgood, *Jewes in America*. It also appears in the forematter of Menasseh's *Hope of Israel*.

18. Dury, "An Epistolicall Discourse," at the end.

19. See David S. Katz, *Philo-Semitism and the Readmission of the Jews to England 1603–1655* (Oxford, 1982), 186–89. Glaser has published a photo-reproduction of the 1652 edition appended to *Indians or Jews?* Henry Méchoulan is publishing a critical edition of the English text to which I have added a note on Moses Wall. Ernestine van der Wall has found that Dury decided to whom to dedicate the work. Cf. her "Three Letters by Menasseh ben Israel to John Durie," *Nederlands Archief voor Kerkgeschiiedenis* 65 (1985): 46–62; see especially 57 and 61.

20. Edward Winslow, *The Glorious Progress of the Gospel among the Indians in New England. Manifested by Three Letters under the Hand of the Famous Instrument of the Lord, John Eliot* (London, 1649), 73.

21. John Dury, "An Appendix," in ibid., 93.

22. Ibid., 95.

23. The anonymous author is Sir Edmund Spencer, who wrote both *A Briefe Epistle to the Learned Menasseh ben Israel* (London, 1650) and a letter "To the Translator of Menasseh ben Israel's Spes Israelis," published in the 1651 and 1652 editions of *The Hope of Israel* after Moses Wall's "Considerations upon the Point of the Conversion of the Jewes." On Spencer, see Katz, 148, 184, 210.

24. Henri Méchoulan and Gérard Nahon, Introduction to Menasseh ben Israel, *Espérance d'Israel* (Paris, 1979).

25. Menasseh ben Israel, *The Hope of Israel* (London, 1650), 17.

26. Ibid., 7, preface: "To the Courteous Reader."

27. Ibid., 17.

28. Katz, 182–99.

29. Dury, "An Epistolicall Discourse," 4; and R. H. Popkin, "The Lost Tribes, the Caraites and the English Millenarians," *Journal of Jewish Studies* 37 (1986): 213–23.

30. Dury, dedicatory preface to T. Thorowgood, *Jewes in America* (London, 1660), 6–7.

31. William Penn, *The Selected Works of William Penn*, 4th ed., 3 vols. (London, 1825), 3:232–33, see XXVI.

32. See Harry M. Bracken, "Bishop Berkeley's Messianism," in R. H. Popkin, ed., *Messianism and Millenarianism in English Literature and Thought*, William Andrew Clark Lectures 1981–82 (Leiden, 1988).

33. R. H. Popkin, "The Philosophical Basis of Eighteenth-Century Racism," in *Studies in Eighteenth Century Culture*, 3 (1973), esp. 248–51.

34. See, for example, Henri Grégoire, *Essai sur la regeneration physique, morale et politique des juifs* (Metz, 1789).

35. David Hume, "Of National Characters," in *The Philosophical Works*, ed. T. H. Green and T. H. Grose (London, 1882), 3:252n. See R. H. Popkin, "Hume's Racism."

36. Henry Home, Lord Kames, *Six Sketches on the History of Man, Containing the Progress of Men as Individuals* (Philadelphia, 1776), 13–14, 29–30, 41–47.

37. Bernard Romans, *Natural History of East and West Florida* (New York, 1775), 54–55.

38. James Adair, *The History of the American Indians . . . Containing an Account of their Origin, Language, Manners, Religious and Civil Customs* (London, 1775).

39. Ibid., 2.

40. Ibid., 3.

41. Ibid., 15.

42. Hannah Adams, *The History of the Jews from the Destruction of Jerusalem to the Present Time* (London, 1818), 556–61.

43. Robert Ingram, *Accounts of the Ten Tribes of Israel being in America, originally published by R. Menasseh ben Israel. With Observations Thereon* (Colchester, 1792).

44. Charles Crawford, *An Essay on the Propagation of the Gospel, in which there are numerous Facts and Arguments adduced to prove that many of the Indians in America are descended from the Ten Tribes* (Philadelphia, 1799), quoted in Glaser, 52–53. Crawford stated that late accounts mention that the rabbi "proved to be an Imposter and that he is now in an elevated Station in the Church of Rome."

45. See the article on him by Walter Lincoln Whittlesley in the *Dictionary of American Biography*, 2:477–78.

46. Cf. Elias Boudinot, *A Star in the West, or A Humble Attempt to discover the long Lost Tribe of Israel, preparatory to their return to their beloved city, Jerusalem* (Trenton, New Jersey, 1816), 27–28.

47. Boudinot wrote a friend on May 11, 1796 that he now had "the same berth the famous Sir Isaac Newton enjoyed many years." See George Adams Boyd, *Elias Boudinot, Patriot and Statesmen, 1740–1821* (Princeton, 1952).

48. Boudinot, *Star in the West*, at end of book.

49. Ibid., 279–80.

50. Sir William Jones, "Note to Mr. Vansittart's Paper on the Afgans being descended from the Jews," in *Works* (London, 1807), 4:70; and George Stanley Faber, *A General and Connected View of the Prophecies, relative to the Conversion, Restoration, Union and Future Glory of the Houses of Judah and Israel* (London, 1809), 1:69–81.

51. Boudinot, 30–31; and Charles Crawford, *An Essay on the Propagation of the Gospel, in which there are Numerous Facts and Arguments adduced to prove that many of the Indians in America are descended from the Ten Tribes*, 2d ed. (Philadelphia, 1801), 4–25. Crawford was willing to consider that other groups than American Indians might be part of the Lost Tribes, and this could include some Afghans.

52. Harold Hellenbrand, "Not 'to Destroy But to Fulfil': Jefferson Indians, and Republican Dispensation," *Eighteenth Century Studies*, 18 (1985): 523–25, where the references in Adams and Jefferson on the matter are given.

53. Hellenbrand, 527–40.

54. Ralph Henry Gabriel, *Elias Boudinot & His America* (Norman, Oklahoma, 1941).

55. Hellenbrand, 540–49.

56. Samuel Morton, *Crania Americana* (Philadelphia and London, 1839). On Morton, see William Stanton, *The Leopard's Spots* (Chicago, 1960), 25–44; and R. H. Popkin, "Pre-Adamism in 19th Century American Thought: 'Speculative Biology' and Racism," *Philosophia*, 8 (1978): 218–21.

57. Josiah C. Nott, *Two Lectures on the Connection between the Biblical and Physical History of Man* (New York, 1849); and Nott and George A. Gliddon, *Types of Mankind* (Philadelphia, 1854).

58. See Louis Agassiz's two articles in the *Christian Examiner and Religious Miscellany* 48 (1850), "Geographical Distribution of Animals," and 49 (1850), "The Diversity of Origin of the Human Races."

59. Frederick Douglass, "The Claims of the Negro Ethnologically Considered," reprinted in Louis Ruchames, ed., *Racial Thought in America* (New York, 1979), 1:478–92; and Alexander von Humboldt, *Cosmos*, trans. E. C. Otte (London, 1888), 368.

60. Alexo de Orrio, Father Francisco Xavier, *Solution to the Great Problem of the Population of the Americas, in which on the Basis of the Holy Book There is Discovered an Easy Path for the Transmigration of Men from One Continent to the Other; and How There Could Pass to the New World, not only Beasts of Service, but Also the Wild and Harmful Animals and by This Occasion One Completely Settles The Ravings of the Pre-Adamites, which Relied on the Difficult Objection until Now Not Properly Solved* (Mexico, 1763).

61. Steven Jay Gould, "Morton's Ranking of Races by Cranial Capacity. Unconscious manipulation of data may be a scientific norm," *Science* 200 (1978): 503–509.

62. Edward King, Viscount Kingsborough, *Antiquities of Mexico*, 9 vols. (London, 1830–48).

63. See Ethan Smith, *View of the Hebrews or the Tribes of Israel in America*, 2nd ed. (Poultney, Vermont, 1825), 217–25.

64. Arthur Chiel, "Strange Tales of the Tefillin," *Jewish Digest*, 80:56–58. See also Lee M. Friedman, "The Phylacteries found at Pittsfield, Mass.," *Publications of the American Jewish Historical Society*, 25 (1917): 81–85.

65. Hubert Howe Bancroft, *The Native Races of America, Primitive History, Works of Hubert Howe Bancroft* (San Francisco, 1883), 5:9ff., reviews the literature on the Jewish Indian theory; 77–97 go over the evidence. The phylacteries are discussed on 92 and the tombstone on 96–97. For a critical evaluation of the evidence of the tombstone, see David Philipson, "Are there Traces of the Ten Lost Tribes in Ohio?" *Proceedings of the American Jewish Historical Society*, 13 (1905): 37–46.

66. The letter is published in Mordecai Noah, *Travels in England, France, Spain and the Barbary States in the Years 1813, 1814 and 1815* (New York, 1819), 241.

67. These letters are published in Noah, *Travels*, Appendix 6 xxv–xxvi.

68. Cf. R. H. Popkin, "Mordecai Noah, the Abbé Grégoire and the Paris Sanhedrin," *Modern Judaism* 11 (1982): 131–48. In Noah's speech opening the Jewish state, he paid tribute to "my venerable and pious friend the Bishop Grégoire, to whom the Jews owe an incalculable debt of gratitude."

69. Mordecai Noah, "Proclamation to the Jews," in Max J. Köhler, "Some Early American Zionist Projects," *Publications of the American Jewish Historical Society* 8 (1900), Appendix 2, 106–13.

70. Henry Grégoire, *Histoire des sectes religieuses* (Paris, 1528–1845), 3:306ff.; and R. H. Popkin, "Les Caraïtes et l'émancipation des Juifs," *Dix-huitième siècle* 13 (1981): 137–39, and "Mordecai Noah, the Abbé Grégoire and the Paris Sanhedrin," 138.

71. A. A. Bonar and R. M. McCheyne, *Narrative of a Mission of Inquiry to the Jews from the church of Scotland in 1839* (Edinburgh, 1842), 6. I wish to thank Ms. Sara Katchav for calling this to my attention.

72. Ibid., 6–7.

73. See H. H. Bancroft's account of Mormonism, in *The Native Races*, 96–102; and Glaser, "*Indians or Jews?* American Eschatology and the Mormons," 60–73.

74. "British Israelites," *Encyclopedia Judaica*, 4:381.

75. C. Gordon, *Before Columbus: Links between the Old World and Ancient America* (New York, 1971).

76. Gordon, *Before Columbus.* In his *Riddles in History* (New York, 1974), 145–46, Gordon discussed a Hebrew inscription, ca. 100 A.D., for a grave in Tennessee. See also G. Bancroft, *A History of the United States of America* (New York, 1898), 2:131; he refers to the Lost Tribes of Israel who "have been discovered in the back cabins of North America, now in the valleys of Tennessee. . . ." Bancroft had his doubts and felt that "the pious curiosity of Christendom . . . has created a special disposition to discover a connection between them [the aborigines of America] and the Hebrews."

Grant Underwood

The *Hope of Israel* in Early Modern Ethnography and Eschatology

Seventeenth-century Amsterdam has been called the capital of the Sephardic diaspora, the "Jerusalem of the North," and one of its leading citizens was the rabbi Menasseh ben Israel. Already renowned within the Jewish community for his earlier publications and his ministry to Marrano refugees, with the publication in 1650 of *Esperanza de Israel* Menasseh stepped permanently into the pages of Gentile history as well. For a time, the English translation, *Hope of Israel*, excited minds on both sides of the Atlantic, with its most enduring legacy being its influence on early American ethnography and eschatology. It spoke to the long-standing debate over the origin of the Indians, and its messianic convictions served as further stimulus to the eschatological enthusiasm already at fever pitch in certain sectors of Dutch and English society. Not surprisingly, however, most readers saw what they wished to see in *Hope of Israel*, rather than what Menasseh intended. The objective of this paper, therefore, will be to carefully reexamine the text and compare it with the uses to which it was subsequently put.[1]

Hope of Israel was actually the result of correspondence between Menasseh and English millenarian John Dury. Dury had written to ask Menasseh's opinion about the legitimacy of a report Menasseh had received several years earlier from a Portuguese Marrano named Antonio Montezinos, or Aaron Levi. Dury thought the Montezinos account supported the idea that the American Indians were descendants of the Lost Ten Tribes, and he wished to append it as corroborating evidence to a tract by his friend Thomas Thorowgood entitled *Jewes in America, or probabilities that the Americans are of that race.*[2] Menasseh authenticated the story, but promised a more comprehensive analysis of it later. The result was *Hope of Israel.*

The work begins, naturally enough, with the intriguing tale of Antonio Montezinos and his experiences in Spanish New Granada—in that part now known as Colombia, not far from Medellin.[3] While crossing the Cordilleras with some Indians, Montezinos heard a curious remark about a "hidden people," but at first paid no attention to it. Later, while imprisoned under the Inquisition at Cartagena, he pondered the comment. "These Indians are Hebrews," he exclaimed to himself, and vowed to return and investigate. After his release, he was able to find his old companion Francisco, who agreed to take him to this people. As in medieval Jewish legends involving the Ten Tribes, the two travellers piously maintained ritual purity and kept the Sabbath during their journey. Finally they arrived at the Rio Cauca, which, reminiscent of the legendary Sambatyon, Montezinos was not allowed to cross.[4] Here he was met by representatives of the mysterious people who greeted him with Shema Israel. Numerous communications took place over several days, and Montezinos learned that he was dealing with part of the tribe of Reuben. As they returned home, Francisco explained to Montezinos: "Your brethren are the sons of Israel, and were brought thither by the providence of God, who for their sake wrought many miracles. We Indians made war upon them in that place" but were defeated. In time we learned that "about the end of the world they shall go forth out of their country and shall subdue the whole world to them, as it was subject to them formerly."[5]

After relating the Montezinos account, Menasseh spends the rest of *Hope of Israel* analyzing its plausibility and significance. Ultimately, he is persuaded "that the Western Indies were anciently inhabited by a part of the Ten Tribes, which passed thither out of Tartary, by the strait of Anian" and was eventually forced into "the mountains and the inland countries by other Asian emigrants of Tartar extraction much like the Britons were driven into Wales by the Saxons."[6]

His defense of this idea rests on four arguments. First is the famous passage taken from the apocryphal book 4 Ezra (2 Esdras in the Christian Apocrypha), where "it is said that the Ten Tribes which Shalmaneser carried captive beyond the Euphrates, determined to go into [a country] far remote, in which none dwelt, whereby they might better observe their Law . . . and that country is called Arsareth. From which," Menasseh reasons, "we may gather that the Ten Tribes went to New Spain and Peru, and possessed those two kingdoms, till then without inhabitants."[7] Second, he cites archaeological evidence, including a sepulchral inscription from the Azores, purportedly in Hebrew, and a massive structure in Peru (allegedly a synagogue) built by an ancient people *unlike* the Indians.[8] Third, Menasseh provides parallels or similarities between cultures. "He that will compare the laws and customs of the Indians and Hebrews together, shall find them agree in many things." As examples, he cites circumcision, ritualistic rending of garments, perpetual altar fires, purificatory rites, strict moral codes, levitate marriage, and similar burial procedures.[9] His fourth and final point is that there are tales of hidden and unconquered peoples in the New World who do not resemble the Indians. In contrast to the Indians, who "are of brown colour and without beards," these remnants of "the first inhabitants of that place were the Israelites of the Ten Tribes, because they were white and bearded."[10]

Within a short time Dury, Winslow, Thorowgood, and a variety of English divines, as well as Americans for two centuries, ranging from John Eliot and Increase Mather to Elias Boudinot and Ethan Smith, enthusiastically pointed to *Hope of Israel* as placing a much-desired rabbinical imprimatur on the "Jewish Indian theory."[11] Yet, an agenda-free reading of the text shows that it has been made to say more than it actually claims. Contrary to popular belief, Menasseh denied that the American Indians descended from the Ten Tribes. Though his comparisons link him to numerous explorers, theologians, and travellers before and after him who noted similar parallels, what he inferred from his observations was different. Given the cultural parallels, he remarked, "you may easily gather that the Indians borrowed those of the Hebrews (who lived among them) before or after they went to the unknown mountains." The key word here is "borrow." The acknowledged similarities proved only that the Indians had been associated with, rather than descended from lost Israel. "May you not judge from these things that the Jews lived in those places and that the Gentiles learned such things of them? . . . the knowledge which the Indians had of the creation of the world and of the universal flood, they borrowed from the Israelites."[12]

Strange as it may have seemed to Christian readers, Menasseh approached the question as a devout Jew. It would be "false," he wrote, to claim "that they are Israelites, who have forgotten circumcision and their rites." On the other hand, the Montezinos account reports a bonafide group of Israelites because to "this day they keep the Jewish religion" in all its particulars. The same held true for the Hebrew language. Faint linguistic resemblances to Indian tongues were a far cry from being greeted with a perfectly rendered Shema Israel. "We have abundantly shown," declared Menasseh, "how with great study and zeal the Israelites have kept their language and religion out[side] of their country."[13]

This view of a culturally and spiritually vibrant Israel stands in sharp contrast to the degenerationist assumption undergirding so much of the early American analysis. Given their wayward-child reading of biblical history, it was easy for Christians to imagine millions of lapsed Israelites populating the Americas. But Rabbi Menasseh felt otherwise. To fully appreciate this distinction and to properly understand the Montezinos account and Menasseh's analysis of it, both must be placed in the context of Jewish legends about the Ten Tribes.

The myth of the Ten Tribes has been so popular with Protestant eschatologists that its Jewish provenance and perpetuity is often overlooked. Extant from the days of Josephus, by the Middle Ages stories locating them in distant lands abounded.[14] No less a figure than Maimonides, or Rambam, himself remarked in a responsum, "as to your question concerning the Ten Tribes, know ye, that their existence is quite certain, and we expect daily their arrival from the dark mountains, the river of Gozan, and the river Sambatyon, places where now they are hidden away."[15]

Medieval Jewish travel literature such as the account of Benjamin of Tudela kept the legend alive by relating actual encounters with their lost kinsmen in far-flung areas of the Middle East. In each case, the tribes were described as a mighty and ritually pure people awaiting the Lord's latter-day command to return and aid in the redemption of their beleaguered Judahite brethren. The connection with messianism was pronounced. In fact, their fabled faithfulness was used by rabbis to both shame and inspire their congregations. Only because they were faithful to their religion could God use them to assist in the Redemption of Israel in the marvelous ways described. In the early 1500s, David Reubeni arrived as an emissary to the pope, claiming to be the actual brother of King Joseph, ruler of over 300,000 members of the Lost Tribes of Gad, Reuben, and Menasseh. And in the very decade in which Montezinos told his story, Baruch Gad brought to rabbis in Jerusalem a letter from the Lost Tribes mourning the plight of contemporary Jewry but indicating that Israel's return was impossible until the time of the end.

Hope of Israel, then, is quite consistent with this earlier lore. Montezinos's Reubenites were hidden and inaccessible, ritually scrupulous, powerful, and prepared to act out their conquering role in the coming eschatological drama. Still, these people represented only part of one of the Lost Ten Tribes, so in the second portion of his treatise, Menasseh moved beyond the Montezinos account to show how dispersed the Lost Tribes really were. He quoted from an abundant Jewish literature to locate portions of the tribes in Tartary, Central Asia, Media, Persia, China, Abyssinia, and "beyond the Sambatyon."[16] "The Ten Tribes being conquered at several times," concluded Menasseh, "we must think they were carried into several places."[17] Not surprisingly, this section was generally overlooked by Anglocentric Christians bent on locating potential Jewish converts in the Americas.

Where readers did not mistake Menasseh, however, was in his eschatological enthusiasm. As to the precise timing of the Return, he cautioned, "it is given to none to know the time thereof." He cited various rabbis over the centuries whose predictions had proven false, including the *Zohar*, whose annus mirabulus of 1648 had only recently come to naught. Nonetheless, Menasseh felt confident to declare, "I can affirm, that it shall be about the end of this age," and "though we cannot exactly show the time of our redemption, yet we judge it to be near for we see many prophecies fulfilled."[18]

The particular prophecies he had in mind pertained to the dispersion and restoration of Israel, and his analysis of them constitutes the third and final component of the treatise.[19] Isaiah 43:5–6, for instance, promises, "I will bring thy seed from the East and will gather thee from the West. I will say to the North, give up; and to the South, keep not back; bring my sons from afar, and my daughters from the ends of the earth." Menasseh saw reflected in this passage the numerous locations of the Ten Tribes he had previously discussed. "From the Holy Land," he explained, "Media, Persia and China lie on the East; Tartary and Scythia on the North; the kingdom of the Abyssinians on the South; Europe on the West. But when he says, 'bring ye my sons from afar,' he understands America; [and] so in those verses he understands all those places in which the Tribes are detained."[20]

It is also apparent that Menasseh is concerned to find scriptural hints of an American hiding place for a portion of lost Israel. In the famous Restoration passage found in Isaiah 11:12, the prophet specified that a remnant would be recovered from "the isles of the sea." But for Menasseh this was a mistranslation. "I think," he declared, "it is to be rendered the islands of the West, for *Yam* in holy scripture signifies the west, as in Genesis 28:14 and many other places; and upon this account those Israelites are implied, who are westward from the Holy land, among whom [are] the Americans."[21] Once identified, the gathering remained to be accomplished. "From all coasts of the world [Israelites] shall meet in those two places, Assyria and Egypt (Isaiah 27:13)" and "thence they shall fly to Jerusalem as birds to their nests (Isaiah 60:8)." This done, "their kingdom shall be no more divided and all Twelve Tribes shall be joined under one prince, Messiah the son of David; and they shall never be driven out of their land."[22]

Portents abounded that these great events were nigh, but Menasseh saw an opportunity to influence British sentiment toward readmission of the Jews by drawing attention to a part of prophecy that remained to be fulfilled. Addressing the "commonwealth of England," he remarked:

the opinion of many Christians and mine do concur herein, that we both believe that the restoring time of our Nation into their Native country, is very near at hand; I believing more particularly, that this restoration cannot be, before these words of Daniel, Ch. 12 ver 7 be first accomplished, when he saith, and when the dispersion of the Holy people shall be completed in all places, then shall all these things be completed: signifying therewith, that before all be fulfilled, the People of God must be first dispersed into all places and countries of the world. Now we know, how our Nation at the present is spread all about, and hath its seat and dwelling in the most flourishing parts of all the Kingdoms, and countries of the world, as well in America, as in the other three parts thereof; except only in this considerable and mighty island. And therefore this remains only in my judgment, before the Messiah come and restore our nation, that first we must have our seat here likewise.[23]

From all of this, it is clear that an eschatological orientation is a hallmark of *Hope of Israel*, and that millenarians were not mistaken in finding it congenial to their enthusiasms. We have already stressed the important but neglected point that *Hope of Israel* fits squarely within Jewish traditions of the Lost Ten Tribes and that Menasseh stands at the center of Marrano messianism in mid-century Amsterdam, but it was anxious Protestant millenarians (several generations worth in America), who kept the message of the tract alive. To understand why this was so, a brief review of Protestant eschatology as it pertained to the Jews is necessary.[24]

For a thousand years prior to the Reformation, the Augustinian formulation prevailed wherein the Christian church was seen allegorically as spiritual Israel and the fulfiller of all Old Testament prophecies. This interpretation obviated the need for any special work among the Jews. During the Reformation, however, efforts to restore a literal hermeneutic to prophetic interpretation surfaced and occasionally gained center stage. Particularly among some of Calvin's followers, prophecies and statements dealing with Israel and Zion came to be understood at face value. Thus, the apostle Paul's promise that one day "all Israel shall be saved" was taken literally as referring to scattered Jews and the Lost Tribes.[25] Combined with a renewed interest in the prophecies and prophetic numbers of Daniel and Revelation, such approaches led unprecedented numbers of people to expect a national conversion of the Jewish people before the Second Coming. Some even began following rabbinic exegesis of Old Testament prophecies and postulated a territorial restoration for Israel. This significant shift occurred in the later 1500s and early 1600s and became especially strong in Holland and England. Serjeant Henry Finch, the London lawyer, for instance, found himself in jail for several weeks because he described the future political supremacy of the restored Jewish kingdom a little too enthusiastically for the king's tastes.[26] By the time Increase Mather delivered his famous sermon "The Mystery of Israel's Salvation," the idea of a "temporal" restoration was commonplace,[27] and *Hope of Israel's* arguments for the Return to the Promised Land were often invoked as the idea became more popular with Protestants.

Other developments also heightened the relevance of Menasseh's work. Reformed Protestantism in England prospered in the late sixteenth century and again during the 1640s and 50s. Throughout Christian history, religious reform movements such as Puritanism have often generated anticipation that this time the work of renewal would be carried through to its glorious conclusion. Such sentiments made the ideas of Thomas Brightman, Joseph Mede, John Cotton and others seem plausible and imminent when they argued that there would be a final flourishing of Spirit-revitalized Christianity associated with the Second Coming of Christ.[28] Since this dramatic outpouring of the Spirit upon gathered Saints and unbelieving Gentiles, in turn, was linked to the "calling" or conversion of the Jews,[29] it is hardly surprising, given the climate of opinion, that Menasseh's pronounced messianism encouraged Protestant readers to think that God's Spirit was stirring the Jews to psychological readiness for the Second Coming. The only difference was the minor matter of the Messiah's identity. Menasseh himself explicitly fueled this false hope, when he later wrote that the two groups could stand together on this issue since it was the "same Massias"; "the Iewes believe that that coming is the *first* and not the second," but "by that faith they shall be saved; for the difference consists only in the circumstance of the time."[30]

All of this was strengthened by the Jewish Indian theory, which *Hope of Israel* was understood to endorse. Given the vital link between the conversion of the Jews and the coming of Christ, if the Indians were of Israel, then missionary work among the native Americans could have a direct impact on the Second Advent. Some end-time sequences placed the calling of the Jews before the final reinvigoration of Christianity and conversion of the Gentiles. If these were correct, then John Eliot and other New England missionaries could expect a rich harvest of converts on the horizon. If, however, the sequence was reversed, the Indians could only be prepared to receive grace at some future time.[31] In either case, having the bulk of future Jewish converts in their own backyard would, when the time came, make it convenient to play midwife to the millennium.

Thus, whether it was the anticipated conversion of European Jews, or their territorial restoration to the land of Israel, or hope for the conversion of Jewish Indians, all aroused eschatological excitement among Protestants certain they were living in the shadow of the millennium, and all seemed to be supported by *Hope of Israel.* That Menasseh did not actually say what many readers claimed he did was of little consequence. He was close, and they would be happy to help him the rest of the way. Like the story of George Washington and the cherry tree, the fit overwhelmed the facts. *Hope of Israel* was an important piece of Jewish messianism primarily because of the notoriety Gentiles gave it. Other rabbinical writings before and after were more significant, but less well known. Menasseh, however, through his association with Protestant eschatology generally and the Jewish Indian theory specifically, lent legitimacy to the theory.[32] That theory always sought legitimation, and who better to provide it than the distinguished Jewish rabbi from the Dutch Jerusalem?

Notes

1. Two recent publications greatly advance our knowledge of Menasseh and his world: Joseph Kaplan, et al., eds., *Menasseh ben Israel and His World* (Leiden: Brill, 1989); and the 95-page introduction to Henry Méchoulan and Gérard Nahon, eds., *Menasseh ben Israel, The Hope of Israel: The English Translation by Moses Wall, 1652* (Oxford: Oxford University Press, 1987).

Earlier studies still worth consulting include Lucien Wolf, *Menasseh ben Israel's Mission to Oliver Cromwell* (London, 1901); and Cecil Roth, *A Life of Menasseh ben Israel, Rabbi, Printer and Diplomat* (Philadelphia: Jewish Publication Society of America, 1934).

Unless otherwise noted, the Méchoulan and Nahon edition of *Hope of Israel* will be used throughout this paper when quoting from that text.

2. Dury's letter is *An epistolicall discourse of Mr John Dury to Mr Thorowgood concerning his conjecture that the Americans are descended from the Israelites. With the history of a Portugall Iew Antonio Monterinos [sic] attested by Menasseh ben Israel to the same effect,* Saint James, 27 Jan. 1649, unpaginated, in Thomas Thorowgood, *Iewes in America, or probabilities that the Americans are of that race, with the removall of some contrary reasonings and earnest desires for effectuall endeavours to make them christians* (London, 1650).

3. "The Relation of Antonio Montezinos," *Hope of Israel,* 105–11. Because geopolitical arrangements in Latin America have changed significantly since the seventeenth century, the location of Montezinos's encounter has been erroneously described as Peru, Ecuador, or even Brazil. Méchoulan and Nahon, "Introduction," 70.

4. According to Jewish legend, the Sambatyon served as a sacred barrier between lost Israel and the outside world. It was also called the Sabbatical River because it stopped flowing on the Sabbath.

5. *Hope of Israel,* 109–10.

6. Ibid., 159, 115.

7. Ibid., 116.

8. Ibid., 116–18.

9. Ibid., 118–19.

10. Ibid., 119, 161.

11. Richard H. Popkin, "The Jewish Indian Theory," in *Menasseh ben Israel and His World*; and Walter Hart Blumenthal, "The 'Lost Ten Tribes': Prehistoric Peopling of America: a Bibliographical Survey of the Early Theory of Israelitish Derivation, and the Origin of the American Indians" (manuscript, Hebrew Union College, Cincinnati, 1930).

Of related value are Lee E. Huddleston, *Origins of the American Indians: European Concepts, 1492–1729* (Austin: University of Texas, 1967); Margaret T. Hogden, *Early Anthropology in the Sixteenth and Seventeenth Centuries* (Philadelphia: University of Pennsylvania Press, 1964); Robert Wauchope, *Lost Tribes and Sunken Continents: Myth and Method in the Study of American Indians* (Chicago: University of Chicago Press, 1962); Robert F. Berkhofer, Jr., *The White Man's Indian: Images of the American Indian from Columbus to the Present* (New York: Vintage, 1979).

12. *Hope of Israel*, 119.

13. Ibid., 159, 161.

14. Information in this and subsequent paragraphs is drawn from Moses Edrehi, *An Historical Account of the Ten Tribes Settled Beyond the River Sambatyon in the East* (London, 1836); Joshua Trachetenberg, *The Lost Ten Tribes in Medieval Jewish Literature* (Rabbinic Thesis, Hebrew Union College, Cincinnati, 1930); Joseph Sarachek, *The Doctrine of the Messiah in Medieval Jewish Literature* (New York: Jewish Theological Seminary of America, 1932); George Wesley Buchanan, ed., *Revelation and Redemption: Jewish Documents of Deliverance from the Fall of Jerusalem to the Death of Nahmanides* (Dillsboro: Western North Carolina Press, 1978); Abba Hillel Silver, *A History of Messianic Speculation in Israel: from Nahmanides* (Dillsboro: Western North Carolina Press, 1978); Abba Hillel Silver, *A History of Messianic Speculation in Israel: From the First through the Seventeenth Centuries* (New York: Macmillan, 1927); Allen Howard Godbey, *The Lost Tribes: A Myth; Suggestions Towards Rewriting Hebrew History* (Durham: Duke University Press, 1930, reprint. New York: Ktav, 1974).

15. Cited in Trachetenberg, *The Lost Ten Tribes in Medieval Jewish Literature*, 25.

16. *Hope of Israel*, 126–40.

17. Ibid., 126.

18. Ibid., 147, 148.

19. Ibid., 140–48.

20. Ibid., 143.

21. Ibid., 141.

22. Ibid., 159.

23. Menasseh ben Israel, *To His Highnesse the Lord Protector of the Common-Wealth of England, Scotland, and Ireland. The Humble Addresses of Menasseh ben Israel, a Divine, and Doctor of Physick, in behalfe of the Jewish Nation* (London, 1655; reprint. London: Lucien Wolf, 1901), 79.

24. Information found in the following paragraphs relies on Peter Toon,

ed., *Puritans, the Millennium and the Future of Israel* (Cambridge: Clark, 1970); David S. Katz, *Philo-Semitism and the Readmission of the Jews to England, 1603–1655* (Oxford: Clarendon Press, 1982); *Sabbath and Sectarianism in Seventeenth-Century England* (Leiden: Brill, 1988); Richard H. Popkin, "Jewish Messianism and Christian Millenarianism," in *Culture and Politics from Puritanism to the Enlightenment*, ed. Perez Zagorin (Berkeley: University of California Press, 1980), 79–83; Popkin, "Millenarianism in England, Holland and America: Jewish-Christian Relations in Amsterdam, London and Newport, Rhode Island," in *Philosophy, History and Social Action*, ed. S. Hook, W. L. O'Neill, and R. O'Toole (Kluwer Academic Publishers, 1988), 349–71; and Popkin, "The Lost Tribes, the Caraites and the English Millenarians," *Journal of Jewish Studies* 37 (Autumn 1986): 213–27.

25. Romans 11:25–26. Mayr Verete in his 1981–82 Clark Lecture, "The Idea of the Restoration of Israel in English Thought," argued that when Calvinist theologians reinterpreted the phrase "all Israel" in verses 25–26 to mean the historical Jews rather than taking it to be a symbolic reference to the church, Christian Zionism was born. See Richard A. Popkin, ed., *Millenarianism and Messianism in English Literature and Thought, 1650–1800* (Leiden: Brill, 1988), 10–11.

26. [Henry Finch], *The Calling of the Iewes* (London, 1621). See Franz Kobler, "Sir Henry Finch (1558–1625) and the First English Advocates of the Restoration of the Jews to Palestine," *Transactions of the Jewish Historical Society of England* 16 (1952): 101–20.

27. Increase Mather, *The Mystery of Israel's Salvation, Explained and Applied: or, a Discourse Concerning the General Conversion of the Israelitish Nation. Wherein is shewed, 1. That the twelve tribes shall be saved. 2. When this is to be expected. 3. Why this must be. 4. What kind of salvation the Tribes of Israel shall partake of, Viz., A Glorious, Wonderful, Spiritual, Temporal Salvation* (London, 1669).

Regina S. Sharif, *Non-Jewish Zionism: Its Roots in Western History* (London: Zed Press, 1983); and Mayr Verete, "The Restoration of the Jews in English Protestant Thought," *Middle Eastern Studies* 8 (1972): 3–50 provide excellent surveys of Christian Zionism.

28. Bryan W. Ball, *A Great Expectation: Eschatological Thought in English Protestantism to 1660* (Leiden: Brill, 1975); Richard Bauckham, *Tudor Apocalypse: Sixteenth Century Apocalypticism, Millenarianism, and the English Reformation* (Appleford: Courtenay Press, 1978); Paul Christianson, *Reformers and Babylon: English Apocalyptic Visions from the Reformation to the Eve of the Civil War* (Toronto: University of Toronto Press, 1978); Katharine R. Firth, *The Apocalyptic Tradition in Reformation Britain, 1530–1645* (Oxford: Oxford University Press, 1979); and George Kroeze, "The Variety of Millennial Hopes in the English Reformation, 1560–1600" (Ph.D. diss., Fuller Theological Seminary, 1985); Richard W. Cogley, "Seventeenth-Century English Millenarianism," *Religion* 17 (Oct. 1987): 379–96.

29. Christopher Hill, "'Till the Conversion of the Jews'," in *Millenarianism and Messianism*, 12–36, demonstrates how widespread in seventeenth-century England was the idea that the conversion and restoration of the Jews was the crucial antecedent to the millennium. Mel Scult, *Millen-*

nial Expectations and the Jewish Liberties: A Study of the Efforts to Convert Jews in Britain up to the Mid-Nineteenth Century (Leiden: Brill, 1978), illustrates the persisting marriage of missionism and millennialism.

In Reformed Protestant soteriology, conversion was not simply cognitive acceptance of theological propositions, it was a work of divine grace from start to finish. Therefore, contemporary writers spoke of "the calling of the Jews" when referring to their conversion.

30. Menasseh ben Israel, *Vindicae Judaeorum* (London, 1656), 18, cited in Popkin, "Millenarianism in England, Holland and America," 354.

31. Richard W. Cogley, "John Eliot and the Origins of the American Indians," *Early American Literature* 21 (1986–87): 210–25.

32. As recently as 1973, an American reprint of *Hope of Israel* carried a lengthy introduction entitled "Indians or Jews?" See Lynn Glaser, *Indians or Jews? An Introduction to Menasseh ben Israel's "Hope of Israel"* (Gilroy, California: Roy Boswell, 1973).

Three

American Puritan
Hebraism

College seals of Yale, Dartmouth, and Columbia. All three seals were designed in the eighteenth century.

Arthur Hertzberg

The New England Puritans
and the Jews

The Puritans of New England were obsessed by the Jewish Bible, but they were not hospitable to Jews, or to Judaism. The Puritans had left Europe, which was their "Egypt," the place of their enslavement, and they had gone out into the American wilderness on a final messianic journey to found the New Jerusalem. In their own mind, they were the Jews, the ultimate and total heirs of the promises that God had made in the Hebrew Bible.

In the late 1690s the greatest of all the Puritan scholars, Cotton Mather, the climactic figure of three generations of Puritan divines, took to wearing a skullcap in his study and to calling himself a rabbi. Mather was no eccentric on the fringes of New England. True, he was moody and imperious. He was twice denied the post which he sought all his life, the presidency of Harvard College, but even his enemies acknowledged that Mather was the moral leader of Boston, and the greatest scholar in North America. He also bore the right names. His grandfathers, John Cotton and Richard Mather, had been leading figures among the Puritan divines who had put their stamp on the Massachusetts Bay Colony at its very beginnings. At the moment at which Mather donned the skullcap, probably in 1696, and took to calling himself "rabbi," he was completing his most important work, the *Magnalia Christi*, a voluminous account of the founding of the Massachusetts Bay Colony. In this book Mather defined and summed up the meaning of the Puritan venture into the American wilderness.

Mather retold Puritan history in biblical, mythic accents. The essential significance of the enterprise was to establish the new Zion. Some thought that the "City on the Hill" was a refuge for a saving remnant, which would remain as God's kingdom on earth after Europe was destroyed, along with the rest of the sinful world, in the conflagration of Armageddon. Others held that the Puritan theocracy was redemptive, that those who were creating it were saving the world by their example of godly living. All agreed that the journey to the New world was the reenactment of the wandering of Moses and the children of Israel for forty years in the desert, on their way to the Promised Land. The Puritans had no doubt that they, and not the Jews, were the Chosen People.

Essays without number have been written to argue that the Puritan theocracy, which was so self-consciously modelled on biblical Judaism, created a pro-Jewish core to the American intellectual and political tradition. This reading is wrong. Because the Puritans knew that they possessed the truth, they were, of course, intolerant of all other Christians. One of the founders of New England, Nathaniel Ward, wrote in 1645 that anyone who "is willing to tolerate any religion . . . besides his own . . . either doubts his own or is not sincere in it."[1] A generation later, in 1681, another divine, Samuel Willard, looked back on the Puritan beginnings of Massachusetts and flatly asserted that the first to come were "professed enemies of toleration."[2] It was, therefore, possible to hang Quakers in Boston and burn witches in Salem as deviants from Christian truth.

Jews had never been Christian and, therefore, even at the height of Puritan power in New England, they were never in danger of their lives— but they were not wanted. The first test case came in 1649. Solomon Franco arrived, in charge of goods consigned to the military. He may have jumped ship or he may have been left behind. It is not known whether he wanted to remain in Boston, but the local authorities gave him no choice. On May 3, 1649, they decreed to "allow the said Solomon Franco six shillings per week out of the Treasury for ten weeks, for subsistence, till he can get his passage into Holland," and they commanded him to leave before the ten weeks of grace ran out.[3] He left. A family of Jewish extraction had come even earlier to North American shores, to join the Pilgrims. Moses Simonson landed in Plymouth Harbor in 1621, two years after the *Mayflower*; he and his family were reputed to be "from the Jewish settlement in Amsterdam." The Simonsons had probably already turned Christian in Holland before joining the Pilgrims, or, at the very least, they converted in Plymouth. One of their daughters is known to have married a grandson of Miles Standish and John Alden.[4]

At the beginning of their settlement in New England, the Pilgrims in Plymouth had, thus, allowed a convert to remain in their colony, while the Puritans had chased a professing Jew out of Boston. Three generations later, Samuel Willard summarized these Puritan attitudes in a sermon that he preached in 1700; the Jews were a "scorn and reproach to the world"; it was best to keep them out, for only "the happy day of their conversion could improve their condition."[5] This was standard Christian doctrine, but there was a particular twist—and a unique intensity— to the attitude toward Jews expressed by the more doctrinaire Puritans. The conversion of the Jews was necessary, and not primarily for their own good, or to avoid the infection of society through their presence as Jews. Every Jew who adopted the Puritan faith assured the Puritans that they were right: they were the true Israel. There was an even more pressing reason for converting the Jews: the end of days was coming, and one could not wait patiently for the Jews to see the light; had it not been foretold that Jesus would appear again, but only if the obdurate Jews acknowledged him as Savior?

In the late 1690s when Cotton Mather was finishing the *Magnalia Christi,* his heroic saga about the Puritans, he was also writing a textbook for the conversion of the Jews. It was a set of "proofs" from their own Bible, using verses from the Old Testament alone to establish the incontrovertible truth of Christianity.[6] Mather hoped that this book would, in the first instance, convert the Frazon brothers, who were then trading in Boston. He was disappointed, for the Frazons remained Jews. When one of them died a few years later, his body was transported to the Jewish cemetery in Newport, Rhode Island. On the other hand, Mather was encouraged by the news that his book had fallen into the hands of a Jew in South Carolina who had been brought by it to conversion to Christianity.[7] Mather must have patted his skullcap with approval—and in renewed hope—when the news came from South Carolina, but there were no more such encouraging stories. The Jews ignored Mather's textbook.

The question of the Jews had occupied Mather from the very beginning of his spiritual journey. At the age of twenty-one, he went through the crisis that all Puritans were supposed to experience, that of struggle with his "lusts" in order to become spiritually reborn, and thus to offer "proof" of having joined the "elect," that is, those who had been chosen by God to be His people. Mather wrote about this wrestling with himself in his diary. The rhetoric is biblical: he had resolved to "circumcise all lusts of the flesh." Following St. Paul and the early Church Fathers, Mather had found a place in his spiritual world for the biblical commandment of circumcision, but it no longer meant, as the "literalist Jews would have it," something mundane and even vile, to circumcise the male organ. He had found a way of giving the commandment a Puritan interpretation: he would be "active in the execution of all these evil inclinations as the Jews were in the execution of my dearest Redeemer."[8] Thirteen years later, as he was completing the *Magnalia*

Christi, Mather had another intense experience of inner illumination. This divine light assured him of his own central role in the world. He wrote in his diary that he would not be the one who bears witness "unto the Lord for no less than all the nations and kingdoms." He was now both a rabbi and a prophet; he was donning the skullcap to define a program by which the kingdom of Christ would be realized. At the top of the list, Mather assigned himself the task of the "conversion of the Jewish nation." He then turned to such minor matters as the fate of France and of the British dominions, and the well-being of his own province, all of which needed to be fitted into the divine scheme.[9]

Mather kept hoping for the ultimate triumph of Puritanism, but it did not come. He had to live with his disappointments, and not only about the Jews. His father, Increase Mather, had already been troubled half a century earlier, while some of the founding fathers of Puritanism were still alive, by the growing tendency of men and affairs to put their own interests first, so that what dominated in "New England had now changed from a religious to a worldly interest." When Increase Mather spoke, New England had already grown, around 1650, to a population of perhaps thirty thousand, and most of those who had come were not, like the earliest founders, godly people. Nonetheless, the elect, those few who were admitted to membership in the Puritan congregation, continued to govern the Massachusetts Bay Colony as a theocracy until 1684. In that year, the old charter was revoked by Charles II. One clause of the new charter flatly forbade discrimination on the ground of religion. The world in which Cotton Mather had been born had ceased to exist; politics and religion were now separate realms.

The response in New England to this fundamental change was a religious revival called the New Piety. Men turned inward, away from public affairs, which the Puritans could no longer dominate, toward inner light. Cotton Mather became a leading exponent of this New Piety. He even began to believe, in the last decade of his life, that prophecy had begun again. He gave up on the notion that there would be large-scale conversion of the Jews, or that this was a necessary part of the drama of the end of days. He consoled himself by holding all the harder to the hope that the end of days was at hand, that Christ would soon rise again—and the elect, the chosen, would be given the glory they deserved.[10]

Despite this change of mind, Cotton Mather rejoiced in any convert. There was a very famous case in Boston in his last years. Judah Monis, a Jew from Italy who was, probably, originally from Morocco, had arrived in Boston from New York in 1720. Two years later Monis converted to Christianity before a large crowd in Cambridge, Massachusetts. He was soon appointed to teach Hebrew there, and he was the author of the first grammar of that language to be published in America. Mather was not the clergyman who officiated at Monis's conversion, but he was deeply moved by this event. In 1724 he observed in his diary that he ought to go and talk to Monis about passages in the Old Testament which were unclear to him, but which Monis might understand better, for "a Jew rarely comes over to us but that he brings treasures with him." Monis had indeed brought "treasures" for Puritan believers. At his public baptism, he published "three discourses written by Mr. Monis himself, the Truth, the Whole Truth and, Nothing but the Truth." He even delivered one of these "discourses" as a speech at this great occasion.[11] What he had to say uplifted the elite of Boston. This learned Jew defended Christianity, and especially the doctrine of the Trinity, on the basis of "the Old Testament with the Authority of the Cabalistical Rabbis, Ancient and Modern." Christianity thus stood confirmed in Boston, out of the mouth of a Jew who even sometimes claimed to have been a rabbi. What a joy this was for Mather. He remembered that he had written a book more than twenty years before to prove Christianity from the Jewish Bible, the Old Testament.[12] Mather left College Hall that day in the sure and certain faith that the Second Coming was near.

Mather had grieved when he failed to convert the Frazon brothers: he had rejoiced in Monis's declaration of faith—but these were individuals. The Jews in their hundreds of thousands remained unexposed to Christian truth. How was one to reach them? Even if one followed the unwelcome advice of radicals such as Roger Williams and allowed some Jews freely to come to New England in order to persuade them of Christianity, only a few would come. The bulk of this obdurate people would remain in Europe, unavailable to the light of Puritan truth. The Second Coming could not happen unless most Jews were converted, but the Indians were the only population of many thousands that was available on American shore. Therefore, some of the founding fathers of New England, the contemporaries of Cotton Mather's grandfather, Richard Mather, wanted the Indians to be Jews. Almost inevitably, therefore, it was "proved" that they were Jews—and this "discovery" was made by a rabbi (what greater expert!), thus setting the seal on its supposed authenticity. The man who provided this solution was Menasseh ben Israel of Amsterdam. Menasseh was a man of parts: he was an able, though not outstanding, scholar of the Talmud and a kabbalist who wanted to help effect the end of days. He was unusual even in Amsterdam, the most open society of the day, for this rabbi was a Latinist and a friend of Rembrandt, who painted a memorable portrait of Menasseh. Menasseh was famous in the middle of the seventeenth century, and when he suggested that the Indians of the Western Hemisphere were descendants of the Lost Ten Tribes of Israel, this "finding" speedily reached New England.

Menasseh ben Israel did not, of course, invent the idea that the Indians showed signs of Jewish origin. This myth had begun a century earlier in South America, when the Spanish and Portuguese were conquering the continent. Menasseh revived the story in 1649 for a very clear purpose of his own. During the convulsions of the late 1640s in England, as Charles I was being tried and beheaded, and Oliver Cromwell was coming to power, Menasseh thought that he could persuade the new rulers of the British Isles that the time had come to allow the Jews to return to the land from which they had been banished in the Middle Ages. His first line of argument was to appeal to the Puritan hope for the "end of days." In a pamphlet entitled *The Hope of Israel*, Menasseh maintained that the Messianic Era was about to begin. The Jews would, first, have to spread out to the four corners of the earth; therefore, they had to be allowed into England immediately. As for the Americas, the farthest corner of the world, Menasseh asserted that the Indians were Jews. He told a strange story: Antonio de Montezinos, who was also known as Aaron Levi, had come to Amsterdam in September 1644 and had testified before its rabbinic court that he had met Indians in Equador who were Jews. Montezinos said that he had taken a long and adventurous journey to a river bank, on the other side of which a goodly throng of Indians assembled in his honor (they would not let him cross over). They gave ample evidence of being Jewish by reciting the "Hear O Israel" in Hebrew.[13]

I doubt that Menasseh, and his colleagues in Amsterdam, believed this story. If they did, it makes no sense that they kept such good tidings secret for five whole years. Menasseh ben Israel seems to have put the tale told by Montezinos out of his mind, until the sight—in London, where Charles I was beheaded in 1649—of the world turned totally upside down made it seem more likely that strange tales might be true. In any event, Menasseh found this story useful in his effort to persuade Christian believers in England to readmit the Jews. Several of them did accept this tale with great enthusiasm; they spread it abroad, even before Menasseh's pamphlet was printed in 1650. It was through these enthusiasts that the story travelled almost immediately to New England, where it had an interesting life of its own.

Menasseh seems to have first told the story in Amsterdam to an English Puritan, John Dury, who was chaplain to Mary, Princess of Orange. Dury repeated it to a friend in London, Thomas Thorowgood, who was involved in supporting John Eliot, the first and most famous Puritan missionary. Thorowgood instantly imagined that the Indians whom Eliot was trying to convert were the same as those whom Montezinos had encountered, and so he published a pamphlet under the sensational title of *Jews in America*.[14] A few months later Dury published a pamphlet of his own in which he fully supported Thorowgood's views on the Indians in North America. In order to make his point totally convincing, he told the Montezinos story as he had received it from Menasseh ben Israel.[15]

The only person who seems to have kept his head, at least for a while, was John Eliot, the missionary and apostle to the Indians in New England. He had begun his mission in 1646; he wrote the first printed account of it a year later, in 1647. This was a sober production in which Eliot guessed that the Indians of North America were most probably "Tartars passing out of Asia into America." There was not the slightest suggestion of any possible Jewish origin. Eliot even included a down-to-earth forecast that not many Indians were likely to convert in the near future, for mass conversion of those who had not yet accepted Christianity was likely to happen only when "the Jews came in."[16] It was only after Thorowgood, his chief supporter in England, had made the suggestion that these Indians were Jews, that Eliot turned in that direction; he allowed himself to be half-persuaded that some of these Indians might be Jews. He then argued, without much conviction, that he "saw some ground to conceive that some of the Ten Tribes might be scattered even thus far." It followed that the Puritans, the "true Jews," had the task of reuniting this lost body of Israel with the ultimate "Jews," the Puritan Christians.[17] It is nearly certain that Eliot said this to humor Thorowgood. Eliot was always broke; he needed the money that Thorowgood was collecting in England.

These endeavors among the Indians were marginal in New England. The radical Roger Williams seems to have believed the notion that the Indians were of Jewish origin, and so did a number of more orthodox Puritan divines, but the idea was soon abandoned, as the Puritans became better acquainted with the Indians.[18]

What did remain at the center of Puritan concern was messianic speculation. It had been at its height in the 1640s and 1650s, when the myth of the Jewish origin of the Indians had been floated, but messianic furor lasted throughout the century, and beyond. The spiritual leaders of New England remained particularly attentive to any rumor of messianic expectations, and especially when such hopes appeared among the Jews. In the 1660s there was a major convulsion in world Jewry. Shabbetai Zevi, a kabbalist from Smyrna, had proclaimed himself to be the Messiah, through whom the miraculous restoration of the Jews to their land would happen. Most of world Jewry believed him. In many places sober people sold their goods and awaited the new age. These strange events were widely noticed everywhere, even in New England. As early as 1669

Increase Mather had preached sermons in which he had maintained that "some great revolution of affairs" was widely expected, "not only by Protestants but also by Papists, Jews, Turks, Mohammedans and other idolators." Both the Turks and the pope were about to fall, leaving the field clear for the true Christianity of the Protestants; they would lead the way toward the Second Coming. Jews would join with the Gentiles in one universal society. The Jews would return to Judea "to repossess their own land." In a preface to these sermons by Mather, another Puritan divine, John Davenport, wrote that Mather was maintaining something "reasonable," because there were constant reports from various places in the world that "the Israelites were upon their journey towards Jerusalem," and that they were being carried in great multitudes in that direction by miraculous means "to the admiration and astonishment of all who had heard it." Davenport added that the Jews had written to "others of their nation in Europe and America to encourage and invite them to hasten to them."[19] No communications from the followers of Shabbetai Zevi to Jews in America have yet been found, but it is conceivable that such letters were sent. By 1669, the date forecast for the Restoration of the Jews (the year 1666) had passed, and the "Messiah" himself had converted to Islam, but the messianic convulsion had not yet ended.

A more immediate encounter with contemporary Jewish reality by a Puritan leader occurred in 1689, when William Sewell of Boston was in London as a representative of the Massachusetts Bay Company to try to renegotiate the terms of the new royal charter. Sewell took occasion to see the synagogue and cemetery of the Sephardim. His account of his visit to the cemetery was quite fair. Sewell was interested in the Jewish burial practices; as he left, he told the keeper that he wished that they might meet in heaven.[20] This was a most tolerant encounter, but theological ideas about converting the Jews were not foreign even to the worldly William Sewell. Two years earlier he had recorded hearing a sermon by Samuel Lee, a preacher from Bristol, Massachusetts, who was also visiting in London. Lee had asserted that the end of days was near, the conversion of the Jews was imminent, and that "the Jews were called and would inhabit Judea and Old Jerusalem."[21]

In the greatest days of Puritanism in New England a consensus had been reached about Jews. Even the most tolerant Roger Williams remained deeply committed to converting them. He insisted that he "did profess a spiritual war against Judaism and the Turks."[22] What separated him from the rest was his belief that Jews, along with all other dissenting faiths, could best be persuaded of the truth of Puritan Christianity only at close range, if they were allowed into the civil society. In one of the pamphlets written in 1662, Williams denounced the Christian world for persecuting the Jews, "for whose hard measure the nations and England have yet a score to pay."[23] When he was banished to Rhode Island, he established a commonwealth there on the principles of complete civic equality. Nonetheless, no Jews arrived to enjoy this freedom, perhaps because they did not want to be candidates for even gentle persuasion of the truth of Christianity. Jews did not want to be objects of Christian messianic speculation, or be cast for roles in various strategies for effecting the Second Coming.

Mather and Monis made them unhappy in Boston; even Roger Williams seems to have left them cold in Providence. Jews were most comfortable in America in less believing, rowdier towns. In such places these Jewish petty traders (there was not among them even one man of Jewish learning before the middle of the eighteenth century) were not challenged to defend their Judaism by passionate, messianic Protestants. They were left alone. Most Jews who came to America in colonial times were from among the poor and unlearned of Jewish Europe. They could not have defended their faith in religious debate, but most kept acting on the belief that their remaining Jewish was not negotiable.

By the beginning of the eighteenth century, it could no longer be doubted that Jews were in the American colonies to stay. The proof was not in the occasional strays in New England, some of whom, to be sure, were disappearing among the Christians by intermarriage or conversion. By 1700, organized Jewish communities were already functioning in New York and in Philadelphia. Decade by decade a sprinkling of other Jewish communities was being established in the port towns all along the seaboard, as far south as the Carolinas and Georgia. Nearer at hand, in the middle of the century, the Jewish community in Newport, Rhode Island, which had existed in the 1680s and had evaporated by 1700, had been refounded by a group of sea traders and merchants. Newport had become a visible center of Jewish life for all of New England. Even the heirs of the Puritans had to redefine their attitudes to Jews.

Ezra Stiles was the Puritan divine (he later lost much of his orthodoxy) who was most involved with Jews in the second half of the eighteenth century. He had come to Newport in 1755 as a Congregational minister. Stiles remained for twenty-three years, until he became president of Yale College in 1778. There were then some fifteen Jewish families in this port city; several of them were important in maritime trade, and in the civic community. Stiles became very interested in their synagogue. In 1767 he began to study Hebrew under the guidance of Isaac Touro, who was the religious functionary of the congregation. Newport's Jews were the hosts to a succession of rabbinic visitors from abroad, who came to this far-off place to collect alms for the Holy Land. The most striking figure among these emissaries was Isaac Carigal. Stiles went far out of his way to become friends with this rabbi. A portrait of Carigal, painted for Stiles, still exists. Carigal is depicted with piercing eyes and a long, thin, black beard, dressed in Oriental clothing. The relations between them were so friendly that there were exchanges of letters, in Hebrew, after Carigal left Newport for Barbados in 1774.[24]

Stiles admired the public-spiritedness of some of the leading figures in the Newport Jewish community; and yet he recorded in his diary in 1762 that the dispersal of the Jews was a dire punishment which they merited for having rejected the Lord, and that it was inconceivable that a community of Jews would exist permanently in America.[25] Stiles wrote before he began to study Hebrew seriously, or had met Carigal, but, even as he came to know the Jews of Newport, he never changed his mind. On the contrary, in a speech that he gave in the very midst of the American Revolution, in September 1781, to inaugurate a new academic year at Yale, he insisted that the Jews did not understand their own Bible correctly. They were wrong in denying that the Old Testament taught the basic Christian doctrine of a "suffering Messiah." Hillel, the greatest figure of rabbinic Judaism, had misled the Jews. He had willfully corrupted biblical teaching in the years immediately before the appearance of Jesus.[26]

During the American Revolution, Stiles translated the Puritan doctrine of chosenness into secular terms. He asserted that the founding of America was the climax of human history; the new republic was to be the example, and salvation, for all of humanity. America as a whole had now replaced the theocratic Massachusetts Bay Colony founded by the Puritans as "the City on the Hill." Those who would choose to come to the United States would become part of this new glory. Stiles implied, strongly, that the alien who came in any other spirit had better stay home, for what he brought with him was out of keeping with the meaning of America. The Americans were the new Chosen People, and their history was the realization of sacred drama. Any older claims to chosenness, especially the ones harbored by the Jews, were now canceled and superseded.[27]

In his last years Stiles became not only a partisan of the French Revolution but also a defender of regicide, of the execution of kings by revolutionaries. Such acts were necessary in order to terminate the old order and to usher in the new.[28] Stiles died too soon, in May 1795, to have the time to take full account of the French Revolution. His fervent appreciation of the new, republican America, therefore, remained the capstone of his spiritual career. He expressed it in the sermon that he gave in Connecticut on election day in 1783. He foresaw an America that would extend its population all over the continent and would be the center of international trade. Stiles was certain that a representative democracy, where the government was not imposed from above by a monarch, would guarantee the happiness of all its citizens. In such a democracy the people would elect leaders of stature and merit, and they would have the chance, periodically, to reverse any errors they might have made. This glorious new American society would extend liberty of religion to all Protestant denominations. Stiles, the Hebraist and the friend of the Jews of Newport, and of its rabbinic visitors, was defining an Anglo-Saxon, Protestant republic. Jews, and Catholics, would exist largely on sufferance, until they assimilated and disappeared.[29]

A century before, Samuel Wakeman, one of the New England divines at the heyday of Puritanism, had preached an election-day sermon in which he had asserted that "Jerusalem was, New England is; they were, you are God's own, God's covenant people; put but New England's name instead of Jerusalem."[30] Even earlier, in the famous sermon delivered on board the *Arabella,* the ship that had brought the second group of Puritans to Massachusetts Bay in 1629, John Winthrop had compared the passengers both to Noah's Ark and to the dry bones in the vision of Ezekiel. These were to be the ancestors of a new mankind, after Europe was destroyed for its sins.[31] Ezra Stiles continued this trend of self-estimates. He had broadened the meaning of the Church to coincide with all the varieties of Protestantism. All Americans, and not merely the Puritans, were now the elect, the chosen people. Those who were found wanting were to be reeducated. If they clung to their errors, it would not be wrong to send them to the guillotine.

Stiles was a bearer of the American intellectual and moral tradition that had begun in Boston. Such descendants of the early Puritans continued to conceive of themselves as a spiritual aristocracy. These American ideologues sometimes changed their theologies, or transmuted them into secular doctrines, but they continued to think of themselves, quite self-consciously, as the Brahmins of America. Stiles was one such early figure. He had moved from Puritan to revolutionary, without changing his basic outlook. He was very nearly the first in a long line of American believers who saw secular, republican America as the society that would redress the wrongs of Europe. The new republic had been called to the task, and glory, of being the elect of mankind.

There were several implications for Jews in this vision. The most obvious was to express itself in the next century in "nativism," and in the doctrine of the "melting pot." Newcomers to America were welcome only to the degree to which they conformed to the way of life of the older settlers. When Irish Catholics began to arrive in the middle of the nineteenth century, the descendants of the Puritans felt themselves threatened in their own Boston by these papist refugees from the Irish potato famine. A generation later, when Jews began to arrive in large numbers after the pogroms in Russia in 1881, Boston Brahmins such as Henry Adams and Henry Cabot Lodge wanted to keep more Jews from coming to the United States, and they labored to block those who had already arrived from any of the central roles in American society.

And yet, American intellectual anti-Semitism never became as virulent as its counterparts in Europe. It was saved, at least in part, from such excesses by its Puritan origins. The age-old European tradition of Christian anti-Semitism had simply regarded the Jews as the "synagogue of Satan." They were objects of conversion, but one could wait indefinitely for the time to come. American Protestantism was fashioned by Protestant sects who believed that the end of days was near. The Jews were central to such speculation, and so the "Jewish Question" moved, for the first time in a dozen centuries, to center stage. Without the Jews, the living ones of today, the Second Coming could not happen, and so close attention, even if it was negative, had to be paid to the immediate lives and situations of the Jews. The American religious tradition and its secular offshoots have thus been more involved with and more ambivalent about Jews than medieval Christianity.

This Puritan ambivalence was clear in the early years of the twentieth century. The Brahmins of Boston were not totally enchanted with such figures as Bernard Berenson, Louis Dembitz Brandeis, and Felix Frankfurter, but there was a special, sometimes grudging respect for their "Jewish" brilliance. And yet, even these brilliant Jews remained outsiders; they were held at more than arm's length. The Boston Brahmins continued to "know" that they, and not the Jews, were the true Chosen People. There was really no path, not even that of religious conversion, for Jews to be accepted by this elect as "normal" members of their kind.

New England Puritanism never proposed doing away with Jews, or forcing them to convert. It did continue, for generations, to keep them at a distance from the centers of power, for American society "belonged" to the descendants of the most self-righteous immigrants to early America.

Notes

1. Perry Miller and Thomas Johnson, eds., *The Puritans* (New York, 1938), 230.
2. Ibid., 185. This essential intolerance had been stated very early in the

history of New England. The quotation from Nathaniel Ward appeared in a pamphlet he wrote in 1645 (it was published two years later) under the title *The Simple Cobbler of Agawam*.

3. This story is told in *Records of the Governor and Company of the Massachusetts Bay*, ed. Nathanial B. Shurtleff (Boston, 1853), 2:273, as quoted in Leon Hühner, "The Jews of New England (other than Rhode Island) prior to 1800," *Publications of the American Jewish Historical Society* 11 (1903): 78. See also Jacob R. Marcus, *The Colonial American Jew* (Detroit, 1970) 1:300–301.

4. Marcus, 3:1143. Marcus doubts that Simonson was ever a Jew.

5. Samuel Willard, *The Fountain opened; or The great Gospel privilege of having Christ exhibited to sinfull men* (1783); wherein also is proved that there shall be a national calling of the Jews from Zech. 13:1.

6. C. Mather, *The Faith of the Fathers* (1699). In diary entries at the time when this volume was appearing, Mather told that he had sent copies of the book to "infidel Jews in this town" whom he had been trying to convert for "diverse years" (*Diary of Cotton Mather, 1681–1708*, 2 vols. [Massachuetts Historical Society, 1911–1912] 1:299). The letter from South Carolina came six months later, in September 1699 (ibid., 315).

7. *Diary of Samuel Sewall, 1674–1729*, 3 vols., Collection of the Massachusetts Historical Society, 2 (1879): 97.

8. *Diary of Cotton Mather* 1:64–65.

9. Ibid., 199–200.

10. Robert Middlekauff, *The Mathers: Three Generations of Puritan Intellectuals* (New York, 1971), 348. In the summer of 1724 Cotton Mather no longer believed that the conversion of the Jews was a necessary precondition for the "Second Coming" and, indeed, thought this belief to produce a "dead sleep." On the other hand, so Mather asserted, the end of days is near.

11. The sermon at Monis's public conversion was preached by Benjamin Colman. This sermon and Monis's own works were published together in a pamphlet entitled *A Discourse . . . Before the Baptism of R. Judah Monis, to which were added Three Discourses. Written by Mr. Monis himself. The Truth, The Whole Truth, Nothing but the Truth. One of which was delivered by him at his Baptism* (Boston, 1722).

12. Mather, *Diaries* 2:741, July 1724.

13. The first edition of Menasseh ben Israel's *The Hope of Israel* was published in Latin in 1650. The more interesting edition was the second, in 1652, in which the Latin had been translated by Moses Wall, who added an "Epistle Dedicatory" of his own. Wall believed that the Jews, including their lost brethren, the Indians, would soon convert to Christianity. He seems to have accepted Menasseh ben Israel's argument that the scattering of the Jews to the four corners of the earth was necessary to usher in the end of days, but Wall regarded this scattering as merely a preliminary stage, for the "Second Coming" would happen only after their conversion. Menasseh himself had no doubt that the time of the return and reuniting of the Jews was near. Except for England, the Jews were scattered everywhere. This assertion required Menasseh to take mild issue with Montezinos on the subject of the Indians. Menasseh agreed that they were of the Ten Tribes, but the Ten Tribes were not all concentrated in the Americas. They were widely scat-

tered all over Asia and Africa—and thus Menasseh had "Jewes" dispersed to almost all (except England) of the four corners of the earth.

14. Thomas Thorowgood, *Jewes in America or Probabilities that the Americans are of that race* (London, 1650). Thorowgood was convinced, so he wrote in the "Epistle Dedicatory," that "we are fallen into the last and worst times, the old age of the world, full of dangerous sinnefull diseases," and that therefore "these are the last times." He offered a number of reasons for believing that the Indians were of Jewish origin, such as the observations that Roger Williams had written him ten years earlier that the Indians separate menstruating women in a little wigwam (as the Jews separate themselves under such circumstances), and the Indians believe in a God above who made heaven and earth. Thorowgood's most "convincing" proof that the Indians were Jews was the general assertion that "the American calamities are suitable to those plagues threatened unto the Jews" (26). The point of the pamphlet was that England must support the work of conversion of these "Jews" to Christianity. John Elliot's mission to the Indians would now be the center of the Christian mission to the world, as Jerusalem once was at the time of the Apostles (93, 126).

15. Dury had written a preface to Thorowgood's work. In these pages he appeared, even more firmly than Thorowgood, as a believer in the near coming in the end of days. He asserted that the Lost Ten Tribes of Israel, at least some of whom were represented by the North American Indians, were being rediscovered and would soon be restored, after their conversion to Christianity, to the Holy Land. The Montezinos story appeared first in English in the Thorowgood pamphlet (129–38); it was translated into English from an account in French that had been furnished by Menasseh ben Israel.

16. [John Eliot], *The Day-Breaking if not the Sun-Rising of the Gospel with the Indians in New England* (Boston, 1647), 14–15.

17. Eliot's "recantation" on the subject of the supposed Jewish origins of the Indians is to be found in a letter that he wrote to Thorowgood. It was printed in a second pamphlet by Thorowgood entitled *The Jews in America or Probabilities that those Indians are Judaical made more probable by some Additionals to the former Conjectures* (1660). Eliot argued on the basis of the Bible that the children of Eber went East and so, in their turn, did the Ten Tribes: "therefore we may not only with faith but also with demonstrations say that fruitful India are Hebrewes," including China and Japan, and "these naked Americans are Hebrewes, in respect of those that planted first these parts of the world" (17).

18. See n. 14 for Roger Williams's observations around 1640 on the faith and practices of the Indians, as reported by Thorowgood. In Thorowgood's account, Williams is supposed to have suspected that the North American "natives were of Jewish origin." On the other hand, John Cotton had no such illusions about the Indians. In his *The way of Congregationall Churches cleared* (London, 1648), he calls the natives "these Pagan Indians" (81), and he makes it clear that he distinguishes between them and the Jews: "There will be no great hope" of the end of days until the Indians are converted en masse, and so are the Jews (78). The identification of the Indians with the Ten Tribes was totally discredited within a very few years. An immediate answer to Thorowgood's pamphlet was published by a Royalist writer, Herman l'Estrange, under the title *Americans no Jewes or Improbabilities that*

the Americans are of that race (London, 1652). In 1687 Increase Mather gave a full account of the work of John Eliot among the Indians. He had created six churches and eighteen assemblies of believers, but most of the Indians remained, and are likely to remain for a long while, unconverted. In this sober inventory of a generation of Christian effort on the frontier there is not one word about the supposed "Jewish origin" of the Indians (Increase Mather, *A Letter concerning the success of the Gospel amongst the Indians in New England*, dated July 12, 1687, but published in London in 1689).

19. Increase Mather, *The Mystery of Israel's Salvation, explained or applied, or a discourse concerning the general conversion of the Israelitish Nation* (1669). Increase Mather was persuaded that the end of days would be ushered in by his very contemporaries who had come to New England: "God hath led us into a wilderness, and surely it was not because the Lord hated us, but because he loved us, that he brought us hither into this Gehinom. Who knoweth but that he may send his spirit upon us here, if we continue faithful before him?" (164). In the climactic passage of the pamphlet, he asserts that the Jews are not guilty of such crimes as falsifying the text of the Bible, or of poisoning wells, or murdering Christian children to use their blood in the baking of unleavened bread for Passover, but that they remain guilty of both killing and rejecting Christ. Jews are a combination of idolaters, blasphemers, murderers, and unbelievers; yet despite their debasement, Increase Mather was sure that they could be saved and regenerated through conversion to Christianity. He thus had hope for all Christians, that they (who were in his view less sinful than the Jews) could be brought to the true faith that he and his colleagues who had come to the American wilderness represented (175–77). Despite this harsh account of the Jews, Increase Mather was certain that "the salvation of the tribes of Israel" was near, because, "this work must be brought to pass in the last days." And one of the signs of the last days is that "the saints of God," that is, the Puritans, had fled their persecutors (37–38). One of the most interesting remarks in the pamphlet (it was to recur in the writings of Cotton Mather) was made by John Davenport in his introduction. Davenport estimated that the Jews remain the repository to this day of knowledge about the Bible which is available nowhere else: "there is a multitude of places in the New Testament (and in the old too) which no one can clearly understand except he be acquainted with the notions, customs, phrases etc. which were formerly in use among the Jews." As he got older, Increase Mather kept losing confidence in New England as the redemptive society for mankind, and so speculation about the end of days preoccupied him ever more. In 1695 he returned to the theme of the Jews and forecast their conversion en masse and their return to Canaan. See his *A Dissertation Concerning the Future Conversion of the Jewish Nation* (1695), 3–12.

20. *Diary of Samuel Sewall* 1:301. Sewall recorded his visit to the Jewish cemetery at Mile End. The keeper of the cemetery responded to Sewall's hope that they might meet in heaven by suggesting that they might there drink a glass of beer together.

21. Ibid., 1:165. Samuel Lee is recorded in Sewall's diary as preaching on the theme of the restoration of the Jews to Judea at least twice.

22. In his pamphlet, *The Bloody Tenent of Persecution* (London, 1644), Williams demanded civil toleration for all religious opinions, but he asserted that "it is no civil injury" for wrong doctrine to be opposed.

23. Roger Williams, *Hireling Ministry None of Christs* (London, 1652), as quoted in Cecil Roth, *The History of the Jews in England* (Oxford, 1941), 151.

24. The first account of Stiles's unusual involvement with Jews was published by W. Wilner, "Ezra Stiles and the Jews," *Publications of the American Jewish Historical Society* 8 (1900): 119–26. This article is based on a first reading of Stiles' diary in manuscript as Yale, before any of it was published.

25. Stiles added "a book of miscellaneous notes" to his diary and there he told, among other things, of the refusal of the authorities in Rhode Island to naturalize Aaron Lopez and Isaac Elizur, because they were Jews. He saw enough evidence of anti-Jewish sentiment in British North America to be sure that "Providence seems to make everything to work for Mortification to the Jews & to prevent their incorporating into any Nation: that thus they may continue a distinct people." He was sure that the opposition to their naturalization in Rhode Island, which had been preceded by comparable problems in New York and, earlier, by the veto in England by the House of Lords of the Naturalization Act which Parliament had passed in 1753 "forbodes that the Jews will never become incorporated with the pple. of America, any more than in Europe, Asia and Africa."

26. George Alexander Kohut, *Ezra Stiles and the Jews* (New York, 1902), 51; see also Edmund S. Morgan, *The Gentle Puritan, A Life of Ezra Stiles, 1727–1795* (New Haven, 1962), 302. Stiles, speaking in Hebrew at the Yale Commencement in September 1781, asserted that he had come to Yale as Ezra had come to Jerusalem, to reinvigorate divine learning; Stiles's studies had taught him the doctrine of a "suffering Messiah," which was absent from modern Jewish learning because Hillel had corrupted the biblical tradition. Near the end of his days Stiles almost wrote a book on the Hebrew Bible in order to "prove," as Cotton Mather had attempted a century earlier, that Christianity was the true meaning of the Old Testament (ibid., 443).

27. Ibid., 378.

28. Stiles, *A History of Three of the Judges of Charles I* (Hartford, 1795; written in 1793), 282. Stiles enthused that "all Europe is ripening with celerity for a great revolution; the aera is commencing of a general revolution. The amelioration of human society must and will take place." He compared this "war of kings" to the war of Gog and Magog.

29. Ezra Stiles, *The United States elevated to glory and honor. A sermon preached before His excellency Johnathan Trumbull . . . and the Honorable the General assembly of the state of Connecticut convened at Hartford at the anniversary election, May 8, 1783* (1783).

30. Samuel Wakeman, *Sound Repentance* (1685).

31. See the biography of John Winthrop in Cotton Mather's *Magnalia Christi Americana*, ed., K. B. Murdock (Cambridge, Mass., 1977), 214–28. One of the forerunners of this notion about America was Roger Williams, who argued that the only way to achieve the ultimate triumph of Christianity was to create a civil society, most likely in the New World, in which Christianity would be taught but not forced (*The Bloody Tenent*, 37–38). It is true that Williams did not regard any civil polity, including that of New England, even if it offered complete religious toleration, as a "new found land of Canaan," but a tolerant society was, at least, the necessary preamble

to such an achievement. Cotton Mather, at the height of his career, made himself believe that the triumph of Puritanism in New England was near at hand. Mather asserted in 1690 that "an age of miracles is now dawning upon us" (*The Wonderful Works of God*, 40). The estimate of the existing America as the "City on the Hill" appeared in the thinking of Soloman Stoddard, the most important opponent of the Mathers; he viewed the whole people, and not merely the "visible saints," as the heirs to Israel (Middlekauff, *The Mathers*, 135–37). On this theme of the relationship of Puritanism to the later American self-image of a redemptive society, see Sacvan Bercovitch, *The Puritan Origins of the American Self* (New Haven, 1975), and Edmund S. Morgan, *Roger Williams, The Church and the State* (New York, 1967), esp. 113–14.

Louis H. Feldman

The Influence of Josephus on Cotton Mather's *Biblia Americana*: A Study in Ambiguity

The Influence of Josephus in the Seventeenth and Eighteenth Centuries

That Josephus should have been of great interest to Christians and that his works should have been preserved by them in their entirety is due primarily to five factors: (1) he has a notice about Jesus in all extant manuscripts of his *Antiquities* (Book 18.63–64) and that gives evidence, from a Jew no less, corroborating the Gospels—that Jesus lived, that he performed miracles, that he was the Messiah, that Jews played a key role in his condemnation by Pontius Pilate, and that he was resurrected on the third day; (2) he is our chief source for the historical data of the period between the Jewish Scriptures and the New Testament and, in particular, for the historical and religious background of the times in which Jesus lived; (3) he documents, in gruesome detail, the fall of Jerusalem and the destruction of the Temple predicted by Jesus; (4) his *Antiquities* was of value because he there presents an extensive paraphrase of the Bible in which he adds and interprets numerous details; (5) he, in his treatise *Against Apion,* was by far the most systematic and effective source for attacks on and defenses of the Jews.

For such a Church Father as Origen in the third century, Josephus was his most useful source for confirming the Bible, and hence he employed his writings more fully than those of any other historian.[1] Moreover, Origen's treatise *Against Celsus* was largely modelled on Josephus's essay *Against Apion.*[2] In a famous remark, the most scholarly of the Latin Church Fathers, Jerome (340–420), in his *Epistula ad Eustochium* 22.35 (= J. P. Migne, *Patrologia Latina* 22.421), bestows upon Josephus the supreme praise of referring to him as a second Livy. Indeed, most of Jerome's explanations in his *Quaestiones Hebraicae in Genesin* are taken from the first book of Josephus's *Antiquities,* although he avoids mention of Josephus except to criticize him. Moreover, so marked was Jerome's favor for Josephus that during his lifetime it was thought, to be sure without basis, that he had translated Josephus's *Jewish War* into Latin. The fact that as early as the fourth century a free paraphrase of Josephus's *Jewish War* (attributed to a certain Hegesippus) was made into Latin, and that in the sixth century a translation of most of Josephus's works was made into Latin under the direction of the renowned Cassiodorus, are indications of his popularity. The latter, we may note, exists in a large number of manuscripts, 171, a further indication of its wide dissemination. Still further evidence of his popularity may be seen in the fact that his *Jewish War* was paraphrased in Hebrew (the so-called Josippon) in the tenth century and in Slavonic in the eleventh century.

It is not surprising that during the Middle Ages Josephus was regarded as an authority in such diverse fields as biblical exegesis, chronology, genealogy, arithmetic,[3] astronomy, natural history, medicine, military tactics, grammar, etymology, and Jewish theology, particularly in matters pertaining to the priesthood.[4] Moreover, Josephus was the chief guide to the sites of the Holy Land for pilgrims and Crusaders; indeed, it is not surprising that in the catalogues of medieval libraries his works commonly appear with the Church Fathers and that they were permitted to be read even during Lent at the monastery of Cluny, for example.[5] During the Middle Ages Josephus's influence was even greater than it has been in modern times because he was said to have written certain works which we now generally regard as spurious, notably IV Maccabees. Josephus was widely read in the Middle Ages through the *Historia Scholastica* of Peter Comestor, a summary of biblical history which soon became the most popular book in Western Europe.[6] Indeed, Comestor used Josephus to such a degree that often, even where Josephus is not cited, the Latin Josephus is to be used in determining the text of Comestor and vice versa.

A significant guide to the pervading influence of Josephus in the Renaissance period may be seen in the fact that during the period from 1450 to 1700 there were more editions and translations of Josephus (73 of the *Antiquities* and 68 of the *Jewish War*) than of Herodotus or Thucydides or Plutarch or, for that matter, of any other Greek historian.[7] To be sure, there were more editions in the Greek of Xenophon's *Cyropaedia* (38), Herodotus (31), and Plutarch (27) than of the *Antiquities* (14) or of the *Jewish War* (13); but the fact that there were so many more versions in the vernacular of the *Antiquities* (59) and of the *Jewish War* (55) than of

Xenophon (16), Herodotus (13), or Plutarch (35) is surely an indication of greater popularity among the reading public. In particular, we may note that during the latter half of the seventeenth century (1650–1700), Cotton Mather's own lifetime, the *Antiquities* were translated most often (14 times) and that the *Jewish War* tied with Xenophon's *Cyropaedia* for second place (10). We may suggest, however, that a still better key to the popularity of Josephus may be found in the number of printings during the period from 1450 to 1700, namely 142 for the *Antiquities* and 159 for the *Jewish War*.[8] In addition, we should add that there were 61 printings of the Latin translation of both the *Antiquities* and the *Jewish War*. Finally, we should add that the Hebrew paraphrase of the *Jewish War*, Josippon, in the English translation by Peter Morvvyne, first printed in 1558, went through no fewer than 21 editions between that time and the mid-seventeenth century.[9] Indeed, we may note that the translation of Morvvyne, dated 1718 (though not actually published until 1722, in Boston, and hence during Cotton Mather's lifetime), was the first book of Jewish authorship printed in America. Again, significantly, the second book of Jewish authorship published in America was Roger L'Estrange's translation of Josephus, issued in Boston in 1719.

The place of Josephus in the history of the Protestant Reformation remains to be documented, but it is significant that no fewer than four different translations of his works into German were published in the sixteenth century. Josephus served, both for Luther[10] and for other Reformers, the important role of correcting the Church's "perverse" interpretation of history and of the Bible. Indeed, for the Puritans, such as Cotton Mather, who knew the history of the Jews far better than the history of England, since they identified themselves as the true Israel, Josephus was the historian of first note.

Cotton Mather (1663–1728) and the Biblia Americana

Cotton Mather has had a bad press. Peter Gay[11] says of him that if he had never existed no village atheist would have had the wit to invent him. As the son of the distinguished minister and president of Harvard, Increase Mather (1639–1723), and the grandson of two distinguished ministers, John Cotton (1584–1652) and Richard Mather (1596–1669), Cotton Mather was clearly destined not only for the ministry but also for the life of learning. We hear that when he entered Harvard College in 1674 at the age of eleven he knew more Latin and Greek than was required for admission,[12] and that when he completed his studies at the age of fifteen he was Harvard's youngest graduate. Latin was the official language of college life, and students were not permitted to use English in conversation with one another unless called upon to do so in public exercises of oratory or the like. Most of his first two years at the college were spent studying Greek and Hebrew. It was then the practice at Harvard for the students to take turns at morning prayer in translating portions of the Hebrew Scriptures into Greek and at evening prayer in translating portions of the New Testament from English into Greek.[13] His son writes that he mastered Hebrew perfectly,[14] but this may be disputed,[15] and he normally cites Hebrew in Latin or English translation. There can be little doubt that he became the foremost intellectual in Massachusetts and, indeed, in all the colonies. He possessed the largest private library in the colonies;[16] and this, together with the fact that he had access to the excellent library of his father (who ultimately bequeathed half of his library to him) and to the fine library at Harvard College, meant that he had by far the best bibliographical resources in America. Among these books we may readily assume that there were copies of Josephus in Greek, in Latin, and in English.[17]

Mitchell Breitwieser[18] perceptively remarks that since, according to Mather's theology, good works, even when successful, would not signify clearly the quality of his soul, Mather was driven to seek some partial comfort in sheer quantity, in the apparent belief that the greater the number of his works and the greater the amount of energy that entered into them the greater would be his success in the most important goal of his life, namely converting others to a life of piety, and the more probable would be his election. Indeed, in his diary he makes the incredible resolution to write a book a month![19] Though he did not quite achieve that pace, his bibliography lists 388 books (to be sure, many are mere pamphlets or monographs), making him by far the most prolific writer in the colonies. Peter Gay[20] says that he was so anxious to see his productions in print that it might be said of him, with little fear of exaggeration, that he would rather lose his soul than misplace a manuscript. Indeed, he seems never to have had an unpublished thought. His correspondence, moreover, with European theologians and scientists was massive, and his letters are, indeed, to be found today in a number of countries. In addition, he left a large number of diaries, notebooks (in which he recorded memorable quotations from his reading), and other unpublished writings. As Lovelace[21] has remarked, we consequently know more about him, both his inner and outer life and his ideas, than about any other figure in early American history. He was also the most learned, as we can see from the sheer number of authors that he cites (415, for example, in his *The Christian Philosopher*),[22], though, to be sure, as Rivers[23] notes, his knowledge of these authors, at least in the case of rabbinic works, often came from an anthology. Moreover, his boast[24] that he was able "with little study" to write in seven languages seems clearly exaggerated. Surely, as Morison[25] has remarked, his learning was equalled only by his conceit and by the unpopularity which has pursued him ever since.

In 1693 Mather began an extended exegesis of the complete Bible. In his diary he calls it "one of the greatest works that ever I undertook in my life."[26] In 1714 he published an advertisement, "A New Offer to the Lovers of Religion and Learning," giving an account of this work, which he called *Biblia Americana*, and seeking subscriptions.[27] In 1716 he wrote, with undisguised boastfulness, to Antony William Boehm:[28] "I can without vanity assure you that the Church of G-d has never yet had so rich an amassment of the most valuable things together tendered unto it." The work, which still remains unpublished in six folio volumes at the Massachusetts Historical Society, was apparently not published because so many similar works were already in existence and because the author, despite the massive size of the work, seldom provides more than a miscellany of antiquarian lore and of other people's views with little that is original. An examination of the work has led the present writer to the conclusion that Mather constantly kept adding to it and revising it and never really organized it well. Its form, which is question and answer, and which was, indeed, unusual in Reformation biblical scholarship and was well suited for such an amorphous work, served well to bring together contradictory and disparate kinds of information, precisely the type of data in which Josephus abounds.[29] No American writer has been called pedant more often than Cotton Mather; no American writer has deserved that epithet more than he.[30]

Cotton Mather's Positive Use of Josephus

All the numerous biographies of Cotton Mather have totally ignored the influence upon him of Josephus. Yet Mather was well aware of Josephus's great reputation and, indeed, in his *Magnalia Christi Americana*[31] he remarks that Jerome (*Epistula ad Eustochium* 22.35 = *Patrologia Latina* 22.421) not unjustly nor ineptly calls Josephus the Greek Livy.

For one who was so self-conscious and so concerned with soul-searching, we would expect that one of the attractions of Josephus to Mather was the very fact that he had written an autobiography, the first that has come down to us from antiquity, as Mather realized,[32] and the fact that in it, as in the portion of the *Jewish War* dealing with his generalship in Galilee, he reveals himself in such detail. The book is the first extant record of a modern Jew trying to come to terms with his fate by transmuting his guilt and impotence into words, and its author the first Jewish writer to expose himself to his public, often unwittingly, sometimes courageously, never with grace. For Puritans such as Mather spiritual biography, as Bercovitch[33] has remarked, played a crucial role.

In his lengthy introduction to his commentary on the Gospels, Mather, discussing the non-Christian sources about Jesus, focuses in particular upon Josephus's notice in the so-called *Testimonium Flavianum* (*Antiquities* 18.63–64). He notes that Josephus was a contemporary of the apostle Paul and asserts, without evidence to be sure, that Josephus knew Paul and was a fellow-student under Rabban Gamaliel. He furthermore postulates that the Epaphroditus who was Josephus's friend and patron (*Antiquities* 1.8; *Life* 430; *Against Apion* 1.1, 2.1, 2.296) is the same Epaphroditus who is mentioned in Paul's epistles (*Philippians* 2:25–30, 4:18). Josephus, he contends, was one of the most zealous advocates of the Jewish religion. "Examine his conduct," he asserts, "and you'll find that he sided with no party." He proceeds to note that from his youth the historian halted before joining any one of the various sects that were the most prominent and, indeed, tried them all; and when none satisfied him he joined the hermit Bannus, who, according to Mather, was a disciple of John the Baptist and from whom he might have imbibed a better opinion of Jesus. An examination of Josephus's *Life*, however, we may remark, clearly reveals two errors here, since Josephus states that he eventually did join the Pharisees (*Life* 12) and since there is no indication that Bannus (*Life* 11–12) was a disciple of John, let alone that Bannus had any knowledge of or connection with Jesus.

The fact that Josephus pauses from time to time in order to give appraisals of the biblical heroes should have been attractive to Mather, for whom, as for Carlyle, history would appear to be the biography of great men. But in his published works he cites Josephus only twice in summarizing the character of his heroes. In one case, in his history of the church in New England, *Magnalia Christi Americana* (p. 90), he seeks to establish the point that from the very beginning of the Reformation there has always been a generation of godly men desirous to pursue the reformation of religion according to the word of G-d. As a parallel he cites in Greek Josephus's paraphrase of Samuel's words to Saul (*Antiquities* 6.147), which he then proceeds to translate thus: "They think they do nothing right in the service of G-d, but what they do according to the command of G-d."[34]

In a second instance, in the same work (p. 228), in his encomium of Governor John Winthrop, he cites in Greek Josephus's encomium of

Nehemiah (*Antiquities* 11.183), the governor of Israel, substituting, in his Latin translation, "New England" for "Jerusalem": "He was a man of kind and just nature, and most anxious to serve his countrymen; and he left the walls of New England as his eternal monument."

For Mather Josephus was important not only for content but also for form. Indeed, Josephus's *Jewish War* was the model for colonial New England history, teaching the Puritans how to write military history and supplying the narrative structure. This influence is particularly to be seen in such a narrative as the account of King Philip's War by Cotton Mather's father, Increase Mather, which relies instinctively on Josephus's account of the *Jewish War* and often cites parallels from it.

Otherwise, Mather restricts his use of Josephus almost completely to historical data and antiquarian lore.[35] This is a high compliment, inasmuch as Mather is by any standard a major historian, whose *Magnalia Christi Americana*, the ecclesiastical history of New England published in 1702, is a major work of American historiography, deserving of rank, as Levin[36] remarks, beside the best histories of George Bancroft, William H. Prescott, Francis Parkman, and Henry Adams. His rank as a historian is especially noteworthy in view of the fact that history was much neglected in the curriculum while he was a student at Harvard College, being unmentioned in the college laws of 1655 and in the program of 1723 and being restricted, when taught by President Dunster (1640–54), to a mere single session on Saturday afternoons in the winter semester (where it alternated with a course in botany). Indeed, it was apparently regarded as a kind of recreation and as a means of acquiring worldly wit and wisdom.[37] On the other hand, in the emphasis Mather places upon history in the curriculum he recommends for the training of ministers, the *Manuductio ad Ministerium*, he departs most markedly from the curriculum at Harvard.[38] In fact, he devotes some thirteen pages to listing the historical works with which a minister ought to be acquainted and lists seventy-nine authors or works, the majority, to be sure, dealing with the history of the Church. A knowledge of history, he says,[39] is "one of the most needful and useful accomplishments for a man that would serve G-d"; and, indeed, Mather himself says that he was "entertained with all kinds of histories, ancient and modern."[40] For Mather, as is readily evident from a perusal of the *Biblia Americana*, the speculative abstractions of classical logic and metaphysics are much less important than history, geography, and the natural sciences. By nature, as Woody[41] remarks, Mather reacted against the Aristotelian position (*Poetics*, ch. 9, 1451b1–11) that history, being concerned with what is particular and individual, is less philosophical and of less serious import than poetry. The fact that he does use Josephus repeatedly for historical data is a great compliment to Josephus, inasmuch as Mather is, as Levin states,[42] a more sophisticated thinker about historical objectivity than his reputation would lead us to expect and one whose paraphrases and summaries are remarkably free of distortion. Josephus was particularly appealing to Mather because he, like Josephus, sought not an allegorical or mystical commentary of the sort that was popular during the Middle Ages but rather a rational explication of the text such as the great commentators of the Renaissance aimed at. It is this new attitude that led to an unsurpassed interest in philology, translation, and ancient history,[43] precisely areas where Josephus excelled.

Indeed, in seeking subscribers for his *magnum opus*, the *Biblia Americana*, Mather made a point of stressing that his work contained "an elaborate and entertaining history of what has befallen the Israelitisch Nation, in every place, from the birth of our Great Redeemer to the very day."[44] In fact, as Friedman[45] notes, this was the earliest attempt by an American author to write postbiblical Jewish history.

The present writer, who is the first to evaluate the influence of Josephus upon Cotton Mather,[46] has examined all six volumes of the *Biblia Americana* and has found evidence that Mather knew versions of Josephus in Greek, in Latin, and in English, as well as the Latin translation of the paraphrase in Hebrew of the *Jewish War* known as Josippon, and that he knew all four of Josephus's works—the *Jewish War*, the *Antiquities*, the *Life*, and the essay *Against Apion*. Not only are there numerous citations of individual passages in Josephus (though he never tells the reader exactly where in Josephus these passages are to be found) but there is also a long history of Jerusalem, which is appended to his commentary on the Book of Lamentations, as well as two long histories of the Jews from the period subsequent to the Babylonian captivity to his own day, one of which is appended to his commentary on the minor prophets and the other of which is appended to his commentary on the Book of Acts. In all of these he is dependent primarily upon Josephus. Indeed, for Mather, as for most Christians of the period, one of Josephus's chief values is in filling in the period between the end of the Jewish Scriptures and the birth of Jesus. So great is his dependence upon Josephus for factual information that on one of the few occasions where Josephus is silent, Mather, defensively, says that such silence is not necessarily decisive, inasmuch as even Josephus says nothing about the Herodians at that point.

It may be useful here to cite the kinds of historical data taken by Mather from Josephus. He is particularly indebted to Josephus for additional details pertaining to the Pentateuch. Thus he tells us, in his commentary on Isaiah 17:1, which mentions the city of Damascus, that no city in Syria was more famous than Damascus in its antiquity, and as evidence cites the statement in Josephus that it was built by the sons of Aram (*Antiquities* 1:145) and that it was extant in the days of Abraham (*Antiquities* 1:159). He adds, again citing Josephus (*Antiquities* 1:160), that the name of Abraham was still celebrated in a village near Damascus in Josephus's own day. Mather cites Josephus (*Antiquities* 1.146), together with Philo[47] and the Targum, in asserting that Shelah was the son of Arpachshad and in challenging the text of the Septuagint (Genesis 10:24) which asserts that Shelah was the grandson of Arpachshad through Cainan. In elaborating on the plagues (Genesis 12:17) that came upon the Egyptian Pharaoh because of Sarai, he cites Josephus (*Antiquities* 1.164) that the plagues consisted of pestilence and sedition. He then asks how Pharaoh came to understand that it was Sarai that was the cause of his affliction, and he answers, citing Josephus (*Antiquities* 1.164) again, that the Egyptian priests had so informed him. Likewise, he cites Josephus (*Antiquities* 1.167), whom he calls "the Jewish antiquary," as his source for the tradition that Abraham not only was well skilled in astronomy but also was a public professor of that science, which, we may add, Mather, who was particularly interested in the latest scientific developments, well appreciated. As evidence that the Ishmaelites practice circumcision Mather cites Herodotus and Josephus (*Antiquities* 1.214) and adds the information, found there in Josephus, that the Arabs wait until a son is thirteen before circumcising him. He tells us that the Jews generally say that Isaac was twenty-five years old at the time when he was brought by Abraham as a sacrifice; but it is clear that Mather derived this statement from Josephus (*Antiquities* 1.227), who is the only source who gives this age for Isaac.[48] Here, too, we see Mather's hesitancy to rely upon Josephus alone for such additional data and his instinctive tendency to ascribe them to other sources as well or to the Jews generally. Indeed, elsewhere in the *Biblia Americana*, apparently forgetting that he had dealt with the matter previously, Mather states that some of the Jews (he is probably thinking of the Targum Pseudo-Jonathan of Genesis 22:1, with which he elsewhere shows considerable acquaintance) assert him to have been 37. Again, when citing the new name, "Discoverer of Secrets," given to Joseph in Egypt, he cites as his authority not only Josephus (*Antiquities* 2.91) but also Philo, the Targum, and the Syriac and Arabic versions. For the statement that the Israelites built pyramids in Egypt he is dependent upon Josephus (*Antiquities* 2.203). It is to Josephus (*Antiquities* 2.206–7), whom Mather here calls "the learned Jewish historian and antiquary," that Mather is indebted for the information that the midwives in Egypt were not Hebrews, as the Hebrew text (Exodus 1:15) indicates, but rather were Egyptians. Again, it is Josephus (*Against Apion* 1.286, 2.228) whom he cites for the etymology (from the Egyptian word, *mou*, for water) of the name of Moses. Mather also follows Josephus by silently omitting the admittedly embarrassing episode of Moses's slaying of the Egyptian overseer (Exodus 2:11–12). As to the quails that visited the Israelite camp (Exodus 16:13), Mather notes that there is a dispute as to the meaning of the word *selav*, but he asserts that in this matter he follows Josephus (*Antiquities* 3.25) in translating the word as "quail." He then cites Josephus (*Antiquities* 3.25) that they were such as flew out of Egypt over the Red Sea; but again he is not content to rely upon Josephus and cites Diodorus as well. One notable exception to his preference for rabbinic tradition when it is opposed to Josephus is found in his statement, following Josephus (*Antiquities* 3.54), that Miriam, the sister of Moses, was married to Hur, whereas rabbinic tradition (*Midrash Exodus Rabbah* 48:3) represents that he was not the husband but the son of Miriam. Mather does find Josephus useful in adding to the awesomeness of the scene of revelation at Mount Sinai, citing, as he does, Josephus's addition (*Antiquities* 3.80) that there was a dreadful storm of lightning and thunder from a cloud. Mather also refers to Josephus's assertion (*Antiquities* 4.27), in his address to the Israelite assembly in response to Korah's calumnies, that he was not guilty of nepotism and that he had, indeed, neglected his own family. It is also Josephus (*Antiquities* 4.76, 6.129, etc.) who is his source for the information that the Edomites were a warlike, boisterous, and troublesome sort of people.

For the period after the Pentateuch, in his commentary on the Books of Joshua, Judges, Samuel, and Kings, Mather turns to Josephus considerably less often than he does for the Pentateuch. He does, however, cite Josephus (*Antiquities* 7.110) for the identification of the Cherethites and Pelethites (2 Samuel 8:18, 1 Chronicles 18:17), who served as bodyguards under Benaiah during the reigns of David and Solomon. Mather also notes Josephus's considerable amplification (*Antiquities* 7.316–17) of the biblical account (2 Samuel 23:20) of the slaying of a lion by Benaiah, but here, too, he corroborates Josephus's addition by citing a similar amplification in Rabbi Levi of Barcelona. It is Josephus (*Antiquities* 8.157) who is his source for the statement that the name "Pharaoh" began with the Pharaoh Minaias (i.e. Menes), the builder of Memphis in Egypt. He also cites Josephus (*Antiquities* 8.185) for the colorful detail that the guards who attended King Solomon sprinkled their hair with gold dust so that their heads sparkled. In seeking to resolve the apparent contradiction between 1 Kings 16:8, according to which Baasha reigned for two years, and 1 Kings 15:33, according to which he reigned for twenty-four years, Mather cites Josephus's solution (*Antiquities* 8.307), that the transcriber from the original copy of the annals of the kings made a mistake here, but he expresses a preference for the more common solution, as adopted by his much-admired source, Dr. Simon Patrick. He cites Spinoza's quotation of Josephus (*Antiquities* 10.106–7) that the prophet Ezekiel (12:13) had foretold that Zedekiah would not see Babylon, whereas he actually was carried captive there. Mather then cites Josephus's confirmation (*Antiquities* 10.141) of the truth of Ezekiel's prophecy in that he did not see Babylon inasmuch as he had previously been blinded. He reports, in the name of Josephus (*Antiquities* 10.265), that the palace of Ecbatana in Persia, which was built by Daniel, was in the custody of a Jewish priest even in Josephus's day. His statement that none but the tribe of Judah and Benjamin regained possession of the Holy Land after the Babylonian captivity rests on Josephus (*Antiquities* 11.69), as does his information there as to the number of them above the age of twelve, namely 4,500,000.[49] It seems probable, says Mather, from some words of Josephus (*Antiquities* 11.174ff.), that many of the Samaritan captives who had been exiled by the Assyrians, did in the process of time return to their beloved homeland, where other Syrians joined with them in anniversary celebrations of their mighty friendship.

Throughout his commentary Mather is eager to find support for the biblical narrative from non-Jewish sources as well, since he realized that they were more likely to be viewed as impartial. Thus he notes the fact that Josephus (*Antiquities* 1.93–95) cites a number of non-Jewish sources which make mention of Noah's flood and the ark, and he mentions, in particular, Josephus's citations of Berosus and Nicolaus of Damascus. Likewise, to support the historicity of the longevity of the antediluvian patriarchs he cites parallels in a number of pagan authors—Manetho, Berosus the Babylonian, Moschus, Hestiaeus, Hieronymus the Egyptian, Hesiod, Hecataeus, Hellanicus, Acusilaus, Ephorus, and Nicolaus of Damascus—mentioned by Josephus (*Antiquities* 1.104–8), though he declares that the text of Josephus is given to us more completely and with less corruption by Eusebius (*Praeparatio Evangelica* 9.13). Again, to support the historicity of Abraham he notes that he is mentioned by Berosus, as cited by Josephus (*Antiquities* 1.158), and he likewise notes that Josephus quotes Cleodemus's mention of Abraham's children by Keturah (*Antiquities* 1.240–41). With the same purpose in mind he likewise cites Nicolaus of Damascus's mention that Abram slept in Damascus and became a king there (*Antiquities* 1.159), though Mather admits that it is a very unlikely story. Likewise, he turns to Josephus (*Against Apion* 2.145) for pagan evidence, namely from Lysimachus and Apollonius Molon, of the historicity of Moses.

In a lengthy appendix to his commentary on the Book of Lamentations, Mather summarizes at length not only the history of Jerusalem but also the history of the Jewish people generally from the fall of the First Temple to the destruction of the Second Temple. Here his chief source is Josephus, the only writer who systematically covers this period. Josephus, often through the medium of Jacques Basnage's *History of the Jews*,[50] is Mather's chief source for the postbiblical period, so important to him since this is for him the period between the Testaments. Thus, as evidence that the Egyptian king Ptolemy Philadelphus, at the time when he commissioned the translation of the Torah into Greek, gave notable presents to the Temple in Jerusalem he again cites Josephus (*Antiquities* 12.58). He tells us that it is in the twelfth book of the *Antiquities* (12.186–89) that we find the "very odd story" of how Joseph the Tobiad came to marry the daughter of his brother Solymius, who substituted her for the non-Jewish dancing-girl with whom Joseph had fallen in love. His confidence in Josephus as a source may be seen in the fact that, important as the martyrdom of the seven brothers at the hands of Antiochus Epiphanes is to Christianity, he refuses to accept the historicity of their speeches because, though they are recorded in the Second Book of Maccabees, they are not to be found in Josephus. Again, Josephus (*Antiquities* 13.257) is his source for the statement that the Idumaeans were circumcised under John Hyrcanus. Likewise, Josephus (*Antiquities* 13.282) is Mather's source for the account, twice repeated in his commentary, of the voice from heaven which came to John Hyrcanus at the very moment when his sons were engaged in a battle against Antiochus Cyzicenus two days' journey away and which assured him of their victory. Again, at one point, without even mentioning Josephus by name, he quotes extensively the passage (*Antiquities* 13.316–17) in which King Aristobulus I, who, he notes, was called "philhellene" (*Antiquities* 13.318), after murdering his brother Antigonus, expresses profound remorse. Furthermore, Mather finds Josephus useful for technical terminology; thus he follows Josephus (*Antiquities* 14.93) in interpreting the position held by Peitholaus, who deserted to Aristobulus, as deputy governor (Greek ὑποστράτηγος).

Mather is particularly full, because of its importance for Christianity, for the period when Jesus lived and for the events which followed, down to the destruction of the Temple in 70, an event which, he believed, in accordance with the Gospel (John 2:19), had been predicted by Jesus. Here Mather was in a difficult position, inasmuch as, on the one hand, Josephus was his main source for the whole period and certainly had a great deal of Jewish pride, and yet he was eager to show that, despite what he calls Josephus's flourishes, Jews were in a degraded state in need of the Messiah whom Christianity claims Jesus to have been. Indeed,

Mather concludes that it will be impossible to find a time under the Second Temple when the Jews in their confidence advanced above their fathers and beyond what they were in the days of Kings David and Solomon. There is much about Herod in Mather because of Herod's connection with the Massacre of the Innocents (Matthew 2:16). It is Josephus's witness (*Antiquities* 16.146–49, etc.) that Mather cites for the fact that Herod sought to ingratiate himself with Augustus and the other Romans by building temples and erecting images. For his account of the circumstances of Herod's death he likewise cites Josephus (*Antiquities* 17.190–91). It is again Josephus (*Jewish War* 1.665) whom Mather cites for the information that Herod's death happened not many months before Passover, that (*Jewish War* 2.111) Archelaus, his successor, reigned about nine years before his banishment, and that (*Antiquities* 18.106) Archelaus's half-brother, Philip, who obtained the tetrarchy of Galilee upon Herod's death, was thirty-seven when he died.

Josephus (*Antiquities* 18.120–25) is also his source for his account of the abortive expedition of the Roman governor Vitellius sent by the Emperor Tiberius to attack the Arab king Aretas. He cites Josephus (*Antiquities* 19.343–50) for the correct understanding of the statement (Acts 12:19) that "he went down from Judaea to Caesarea and there abode." The "he," says Mather, refers not to Peter, who had been mentioned in the previous verse, but to Agrippa I, as we learn from Josephus, who gives a full account of the journey and of the occasion. He notes, furthermore, that Josephus (*Antiquities* 19.350) does not say that Agrippa was eaten up by worms but rather that he died after five days of pains in his bowels.

Mather is particularly extensive, because of its importance for the fledgling Christian Church, in his account of the background of the Jewish War against the Romans. He quotes the account, which he says comes from *Antiquities*, Book 20, chapter 6 (actually Book 20, chapter 8, subsection 6, paragraphs 169–72), about the false prophet from Egypt, which parallels the passage in Acts 21:38; significantly, whereas Josephus says that the procurator Felix slew 400 of the prophet's followers and whereas the passage in Acts gives the number as 4,000, Mather implies a preference for the Josephan version, inasmuch as he first gives the Josephan text and then encloses the Acts passage in parentheses, with the words "our text here says 4,000." Elsewhere, he cites the Josephan passage again and says that it is a mistake in Grotius, whom he otherwise much esteems, to say that this episode occurred later, since for Mather the dating in Josephus in the first or second year of Nero is convincing. Even where one would think that he would object, namely where Josephus (*Antiquities* 20.195) refers to Poppaea Sabina, Nero's wife, as a "pious" woman, he cites Josephus without further comment.

Again, it is significant that where scholars of such tremendous reputation as Scaliger and Casaubon disagree with Josephus's statement that Antipater, the father of Herod, was of the Idumaean race (*Jewish War* 1.123), he clearly declares that "we may believe Josephus." Likewise, he makes a point of emphasizing the trustworthiness of Josephus when he declares (*Jewish War* 2.277–79; *Antiquities* 20.252, 254) that the Roman procurator Gessius Florus is "with truth enough" described by Josephus as full of cruelty and avarice. In commenting on the Nazirites, Mather quotes Josephus's Greek phrase (*Jewish War* 2.313) pertaining to the shaving of the hair by Bernice, the sister of Agrippa II. Mather also cites Josephus (*Jewish War* 3.141–339) as his source for the statement that Vespasian came to Jotapata when Josephus was governor and that after a siege of forty days he took it and burnt it. He likewise tells us, basing himself on Josephus though without naming him (*Jewish War* 4.201), that cutthroats used every opportunity to commit the most horrible acts of slaughter not only in all parts of the city of Jerusalem but in the very Temple. To emphasize the degree of the debacle suffered by the Jews during the war against the Romans he cites Josephus (*Jewish War* 6.420) on several occasions for the information that 1,100,000 Jews perished and that 97,000 Jews were taken captive during the uprising, and he also adds, again to stress the tremendous losses of the Jews in the war, basing himself upon Josephus (*Jewish War* 6.424), that the number of paschal lambs slaughtered by the Jews at Passover was 256,000, which would suggest a total population of 3,000,000 if we assume an average of twelve people partaking of each lamb on the average. Indeed, he says that Josephus's history of the Jewish War, particularly his account of the siege of Jerusalem, which, he reminds the reader, had been previously raised by Pompey (*Jewish War* 1.147–49) and by Sosius (*Jewish War* 1.350–51), is the best commentary for the prophecy (Deuteronomy 28:52) that "They shall besiege you in all your towns, until your high and fortified walls, in which you trusted, come down throughout all your land."

In advertising his *Biblia Americana*[51] Mather made a special point of stressing that it surveyed the geography of Palestine and that it gave an account of how the whole earth was peopled. For this information it is clear that his chief source was Josephus. Thus he cites Josephus (*Antiquities* 1.123) as his source for the information that the Gomarites mentioned in the Bible (Genesis 10:2) are the Galatians, that Magog (Genesis 10:2) was the father of the Scythians (*Antiquities* 1.123), that Madai (Genesis 10:2) was the ancestor of the Medes (*Antiquities* 1.124),[52] that Javan (Genesis 10:2) was the founder of Ionia and the ancestor of all the Greeks (*Antiquities* 1.124), that Tubal (Genesis 10:2) was the ancestor of the Theobelians, now called the Iberians (*Antiquities* 1.124), that

Meshech (Genesis 10:2) founded Meschos, now called the Cappadocians (*Antiquities* 1.125), that Tiras (Genesis 10:2) was the progenitor of the Thracians (*Antiquities* 1.125), that Riphath (Genesis 10:3) founded Paphlagonia (*Antiquities* 1.126), that Togarmah (Genesis 10:3) was the ancestor of the Phrygians (*Antiquities* 1.126), that Tarshish (Genesis 10:4) gave his name to Tarsus (*Antiquities* 1.127),[53] that Kittim (Genesis 10:4) gave his name to Cyprus (*Antiquities* 1.128) (though here Mather disagrees with Josephus and instead follows Samuel Bochart [1599–1667] in making him the ancestor of the Italians), that Mizraim (Genesis 10:6) was the founder of Egypt, the old name of which was Mizraim (*Antiquities* 1.132), that Elam (Genesis 10:22) was the progenitor of the Elamites, that is to say the Persians (*Antiquities* 1.143), that Asshur (Genesis 10:22) was the founder of Ninus (that is Nineveh) and of the Assyrians (*Antiquities* 1.143), that Lud (Genesis 10:22) was the ancestor of the Lydians (*Antiquities* 1.144), that Aram (Genesis 10:23) ruled the Aramaeans whom the Greeks call Syrians (*Antiquities* 1.144), that Urus (biblical Hul, Genesis 10:23) founded Armenia (*Antiquities* 1.145), and that the posterity of Arpachshad (Genesis 10:24) occupied Chaldaea (*Antiquities* 1.144).[54] In one of the few instances where Mather disagrees with Josephus on geographical data, he says that it is a mistake on the part of Josephus and others to say that the Chaldaeans were of old called Arphaxadaeans; he prefers the view that they were called Chasdim from their father Chosid, the son of Abraham's brother Nachor. Mather is clearly indebted to Josephus (*Antiquities* 1.146) for the information that Apachshad's son Eber (Genesis 10:24) was the father of the Hebrews, but he is noncommittal on the matter. Mather also cites Josephus (*Antiquities* 8.164) in his effort to locate Ophir (1 Kings 9:28, 10:11, 2 Chronicles 8:18, 9:10), the land to which King Solomon sent his sailors and which Josephus calls Sopheir, and which he, like Josephus, situates in India. Mather says that Josephus and most authors place it in the Aurea Chersonesus, which is now called Malucca, but there is no such information in Josephus; Mather himself prefers to place it in Persia.

Mather is particularly dependent upon Josephus for information about the location of places in Palestine. Thus he reproduces from Josephus (*Jewish War* 4.474) the fact that Jericho is sixty furlongs distant from the Jordan River[55] and that (*Jewish War* 5.70) the Mount of Olives is six furlongs from Jerusalem. He likewise derives his data on the hills of Jerusalem from Josephus (*Jewish War* 5.137). Similarly, his description of the magnificence of Herod's palace in Jerusalem (*Jewish War* 1.402, *Antiquities* 15.318) and of the towers built there by Herod (*Jewish War* 5.161) is taken from Josephus. He also accepts the evidence of Josephus (*Jewish War* 3.420) that there was a rock on the shore of Palestine at Joppa which had excavations on it that contributed to the fiction that the mythical Andromeda had been tied to it.

The era in which Mather lived, as we can see particularly in the writings of Mather's predecessor, Bishop James Ussher,[56] and his contemporary, William Whiston,[57] whom he admired so much, was particularly concerned with establishing the chronology of biblical events. Indeed, in his advertisement for his work[58] Mather makes a special point of noting that in his work he has cleared the chronology of all its difficulties. In fact, Mather begins his *Biblia Americana* with an elaborate discussion of biblical chronology, based largely on Whiston. For this chronology Josephus is his major source, as he was for Whiston. Thus he informs us, basing himself on Josephus, that the length of the period, 532 years, during which the Jews lived under kings from the time of David to the Babylonian captivity (*Antiquities* 11.112), was approximately the same number of years as the period from the captivity to the destruction of the Temple. Mather also follows Josephus (*Antiquities* 14.389)) in declaring that Herod was named king by the Roman Senate a little before the 185th Olympiad about the middle of July 4174 (40 B.C.E. or 3965 and that Jerusalem was taken by Sosius and Herod and that Antigonus was slain (*Antiquities* 14.490) at the end of June 4177 (37 B.C.E. or 3968. This chronology, he says approvingly, affords us three years and three months from the beginning of Antigonus's reign and is consonant with Josephus's testimony.

Furthermore, Mather remarks that Josephus, since he himself was a priest and no ordinary priest at that, inasmuch as he belonged to the first of the twenty-four courses (*Life* 2), is a particularly reliable source for information concerning the priesthood and the Temple. Thus he cites approvingly the statement of his contemporary, Hadrian Reland, in the latter's work, *Antiquitates Sacrae*, published in 1708, that comparing the Scripture with Josephus and Philo will shed light on the difference between the sin-offerings (*Antiquities* 3.230–31), which are nondeliberate, and the trespass-offerings (*Antiquities* 3.232), which are willful. Again, when he is puzzled by the problem as to how there could be two high priests, Annas and Caiaphas (Luke 3:2) at the same time, he turns to Josephus, who, he says, is very accurate in his accounts of such matters but who does not say a word about a joint priesthood. He then suggests that Annas may be here mentioned because he was a man of great eminence and was the father-in-law of Caiaphas. He also proceeds to cite Josephus for the information that the high priests at that time did not observe the Aaronical succession which the Law required but that they obtained the sacerdotal honor by bribes and were displaced by the whim of Roman procurators (e.g. *Antiquities* 18.35).

Mather also takes full advantage of Josephus's expert knowledge, as a priest, of the Temple and its accoutrements. We may recall the statement of Nicolas de Lyra (*Glossa Ordinaria* 1.787 on Exodus 28) that in priestly matters he would rather follow Josephus than the distinguished commentator Rashi, whom he otherwise follows almost slavishly, because Josephus was himself of the priestly order and actually saw the Temple and its cult with his own eyes.[59] Thus it is Josephus (*Antiquities* 15.380) who is his source for the information that when Herod decided to rebuild the Temple he did not pull down Zerubbabel's Temple at once but rather as the renovation proceeded. He describes this Temple in the words of Josephus (*Jewish War* 6.267) as a most admirable structure and for magnificence little inferior to Solomon's, indeed, "the most admirable work we have ever seen or heard of." He then cites the Hebrew paraphrase, Josippon, of the *Jewish War*, as likewise affirming that in the entire world there was no temple equal to it. Josephus (*Antiquities* 3.137), whom he terms more modest than any of the other Jews, whose vast imagination leads them astray, is also his source for the description of the cherubim in the Temple. He is likewise indebted to Josephus (*Antiquities* 3.291) for a long description of the trumpets that were sounded. He also mentions (*Antiquities* 8.94) a vast number of trumpets ordered to be made for King Solomon. Furthermore, he notes (*Antiquities* 15.395) the golden table in the Temple, presented by King Ptolemy Philadelphus of Egypt and described at length by Josephus, as well as the golden vine which was the marvel of all who beheld it.

In addition, Josephus is a major source of Mather's information about religious movements in Judaism. In his appendix to his commentary on the Book of Acts he has a long essay on the Samaritans and on the Sadducees. Thus it is Josephus (*Antiquities* 12.258–61) who is his source for the account of the letter which the Samaritans sent to King Antiochus Epiphanes of Syria in which they not only disclaimed the religion of the Jews but even offered that their temple be dedicated to the Greek Jupiter. However, he notes Josephus's remark (*Antiquities* 9.281) that when the Jews were prosperous, the Samaritans claimed that they were their kindred. Such a statement, obviously derogatory to the Samaritans, is all the more remarkable in view of the favorable attitude toward them in the famous parable of the Good Samaritan (Luke 10:30–37).

As to the Sadducees, Mather notes that Josephus (*Jewish War* 2.166) does not draw a favorable picture of them but rather represents them as people whose morals were savage, with whom strangers could have no correspondence, and who were often divided among themselves. He also cites Josephus's statement (*Antiquities* 18.17) that the common people could not endure to be under them. He likewise draws upon Josephus

(*Antiquities* 20.200–1) for the fact that when the Sanhedrin headed by the Sadducean high priest Ananus condemned James the brother of Jesus, none of the learned Jews remonstrated against it. Here Mather seems to show a bias against the Jews, inasmuch as Josephus (*Antiquities* 20.201) does say that those of the inhabitants of Jerusalem who were considered the most fair-minded and who were strict in observance of the law were offended by the condemnation of James. He likewise seems to show a bias when he declares, citing Josephus's *Life*, that it made no difference among the learned Jews which of the sects they fell in with. Mather is here presumably referring to the passage (*Life* 10–11) in which Josephus refers to his own trial of the three sects; but there is surely no indication that it made no difference to Josephus, or to the learned Jews in general, which of the sects they fell in with.

When it came to a description of the Temple and of the various sacrifices, which he sets forth in great detail, he prefers the Mishnaic tractate *Middoth* to Josephus, despite the fact that Josephus himself was a priest.

Josephus is also extremely useful for Mather in giving other kinds of antiquarian lore in seeking to elucidate the biblical text. Thus he cites Josephus's claim (*Antiquities* 7.305) that Hebrew poetry, such as the Psalms, conforms to a system of meters. It is often Josephus whom he calls upon to fill in details omitted in the Bible. Thus, whereas the Bible (1 Kings 11:2, 2 Chronicles 22:11) says that Jehoash was hidden in a bedchamber, Mather adopts Josephus's view (*Antiquities* 9.168) that he was hidden in that portion of the temple which is called "the first holy place." Likewise, the Bible (2 Chronicles 24:25) does not identify the servants of Jehoash who smote him, but Mather follows Josephus (*Antiquities* 2.171) in identifying them as the friends of Jehoiada, the high priest, who killed Jehoash in revenge for the death of Zechariah (*Antiquities* 9.168), the son of Jehoiada.[60] Again, as to the biblical statement (Esther 6:1) that King Ahasuerus ordered that the book of memorable deeds, the chronicles, should be read before him, Mather, following Josephus (*Antiquities* 11.248), remarks that it is not improbable that the history of some of Ahasuerus's ancestors was included.

Finally, throughout his commentary, we may note, Mather seeks to find external evidence, whether from pagans for the Jewish Scriptures or from pagans and Jews for the Christian Scriptures. Hence, as we might expect, he vehemently attacks those who would impugn the authenticity of the *Testimonium Flavianum*, the Jesus passage in Josephus (*Antiquities* 18.63–64). He refers to Tanaquil Faber,[61] who had published his treatise eight years before Mather's birth, as "the fickle weathercock" who had first argued against its being genuine. Mather set his son Samuel to work to find arguments to refute Faber, and he lists them as follows: (1) Eusebius, who is the first to cite the passage and who lived at a time, in the fourth century, when there were both Jews and pagans to challenge him and who had numerous enemies, would have had to be a madman to insert such a passage; (2) the fact that Josephus has such favorable notices of John the Baptist (*Antiquities* 18.116–19) and James the brother of Jesus (*Antiquities* 20.200–3) shows that he was favorably disposed toward the movement; (3) Josephus was too good an historian to omit events of such importance as those connected with John, Jesus, and James; (4) Origen in the third century says no more than that Josephus did not accept Jesus as the Messiah, but he does indicate that Josephus wrote about him; (5) "Even such a wretch as Isaac Vossius himself" assumed that it was genuine.

Mather and the Jews

Like most Puritans of his era Cotton Mather held ambiguous views with regard to the Jews. That he was, however, less anti-Jewish than many of his day may be gleaned from the fact that in his translation of Josephus's *Testimonium Flavianum*, whereas the Greek (*Antiquities* 18.64) states that Jesus was accused by "the foremost men among us" (τῶν πρώτων ἀνδρῶν παρ' ἡμῖν), Mather softens this accusation, which is the basis of the charge of deicide, and renders that he was accused "by the instigation of some of the chief of our nation." On the one hand, he spoke, for example in his diary for March 14, 1712, of the Jewish infidelity and of Jewish blindness to the truth of Christianity; and, in his long excursus after his commentary on *Lamentations* giving the history of Jerusalem, he makes a point of remarking, citing Josephus as his evidence, on the increasing wickedness of the Jews prior to the outbreak of the war against the Romans. On the other hand, we must note that his ambition to be the means of converting a Jew to Christianity was very nearly an obsession for him;[62] and, indeed, his constant prayers and dreams, especially as he became older, in 1699, 1710, and 1712–16, were to have an opportunity to convert a Jew to Christianity. Thus, in his diary for January 16, 1712,[63] he writes that he has renewed his petition "for the poor Jew, for whom I have been heretofore so much concerned." Later in the same year, in his diary for December 1, 1712, he writes[64] that he has been supplied with a precious opportunity to write "some very pungent things for the conviction both of the Jews and of the Arians, which I desire with much application to Heaven, for assistance, to lay hold upon." In 1716, in a letter to John Winthrop, he writes[65] with great excitement that he had just received a letter from a German divine telling of the miraculous conversions, despite strong parental opposition, of young Jewish children in Berlin to Christianity. Mather concludes: "This German divine sees happy auspices in this rare occurrence." Indeed, Mather looked upon Israel's salvation, though spiritually fulfilled in the Christ, as foreshadowing the conversion of the Jews, an event, as he put it in his *Nehemiah*, "more eminent and wonderful, for the type must needs come short of the antitype."[66] In a work dealing with the Second Coming entitled *Triparadisus*, which he wrote a few years before he died but which he never published, Mather included a long chapter entitled "A National Conversion of the Jews: Whether to be Hoped for."[67] In fact, in the course of his *Biblia Americana* he digresses at one point to mention the story of the conversion in Florence to Christianity of a Jewish physician named Levi, who took the name of Theodore.

Because he regarded Christianity as the *verus Israel*, the true successor to the Jewish people, Mather found Josephus's treatise *Against Apion*, the most extensive apologetic treatise for the Jews which has come down to us, of special value, though he was in somewhat of a quandary, inasmuch as he regarded the Jews of Josephus's day and of the period that followed, as we have noted, as blind to the true interpretation of Scripture. Thus, on a positive note toward the Jews, on two separate occasions in his commentary he refers to the passage, cited by Josephus (*Against Apion* 1.176–83), in which Aristotle is quoted by Clearchus of Soli as complimenting a Jew whom he had met in Asia Minor for the wisdom which the Jew had imparted to him. Realizing that his readers might be suspicious of such third-hand information, Mather notes that Clearchus was himself a follower of Aristotle and that he personally knew this Jew, though if we read the passage carefully in Josephus, there is no such statement. Moreover, he cites, in obvious agreement, the story told by Josephus (*Against Apion* 1.201–4), who is quoting Hecataeus of Abdera, about the Jew named Mosollamus in the army of Ptolemy who shot with an arrow a bird that was being observed by soothsayers and who, in response to their indignation, declared that no sound information could come from a bird which was unable to provide for its own safety. Furthermore, he notes approvingly (*Against Apion* 2.282) Josephus's remark that there is no city anywhere in the world where the Jewish practice of abstaining from work on the Sabbath has not spread.

Inasmuch as some of the charges made against the Jews are likewise made against the Christians, Mather feels impelled to cite and to refute them. Thus he notes Apion's charge (*Against Apion* 2.80–88) that the Jews worshipped an ass in the Temple, a charge that was also made against the Christians.[68] He suggests that the origin of this canard is the attempted wit of the Alexandrian Greeks in connecting the Greek word for ass, *onos*, with the high priest Onias, who had built a temple in Egypt at Leontopolis (*Antiquities* 13.62–73). Mather immediately responds to this by remarking that such an attempted connection is "a strain, and it confounds a man with an ass, without the other circumstances of the story."

Mather also cites (*Against Apion* 1.76) Manetho's charge that the Israelites (Manetho actually speaks of them as Hyksos, and it is Josephus who identifies them with the Israelites) had brought pestilence and sedition upon the Egyptians. Here, interestingly enough, Manetho's actual charge, as cited by Josephus, whom Mather names as his authority, is that the Israelites had brought "troubles" upon the Egyptians, without mentioning pestilence and sedition. Mather undoubtedly confused this charge with the statement by Josephus (*Antiquities* 1.164) that pestilence and sedition were brought upon Pharaoh when he was on the point of laying hands upon Abraham's wife, Sarai.

One of the charges made by Manetho against the Jews was that, far from their leaving Egypt, it was the Egyptians who drove them out because of their leprosy, and that, indeed, Moses himself was one of the Egyptian priests expelled because of leprosy (*Against Apion* 1.279). Here Mather shows his ambiguity in dealing with the Jews, since he cites his favorite authority, his contemporary, Dr. Simon Patrick (1626–1707),[69] who tries to defend Manetho against the charge of maliciousness by suggesting that the statement about Moses's leprosy did not arise out of his own head but rather that it derived from the biblical statement (Exodus 4:6) that Moses's hand suddenly turned leprous before it was returned to its normal appearance as a sign that he had been sent by G-d. Mather himself adds that the simplicity and integrity of those historians who make the charge make one hesitate to think that they forged this fable out of pure malice and suggests rather that they relied upon Egyptian traditions, prejudiced though they were.

An indication of Mather's ambiguity with regard to the Jews may be seen in his comment on the charge that the Jews are guilty of misanthropy. On the one hand, Mather sympathized with the idea of separating oneself from idolaters, as did the Jews, but on the other hand he took note of the fact that the patriarchs had from time to time entered into covenants with idolaters. He explains that this was due to necessity; and he quotes King Solomon's remarks in Josephus (*Antiquities* 8.117) that the Jews "are not inhumane by nature nor unfriendly to those who are not of our country." He remarks, furthermore, that he himself did not like to make sport of anyone else's religion; and, indeed, as we shall see, there are very few blatantly anti-Jewish remarks in his huge work, the

Biblia Americana. As support for his stand Mather cites the precept, which is found in the Septuagint translation (Exodus 22:27), in Josephus (*Antiquities* 4.207 and *Against Apion* 2.237), and in Philo (*De Speciali-bus Legibus* 1.9.53), that one should not speak evil of the gods of other people. But he then explains, perhaps half cynically, that when the Jews went into a strange community they used such a tolerant approach in order to gain proselytes.

One of the most vicious of the Jew-baiters cited by Josephus is Chaeremon (*Against Apion* 1.288–303). Mather obviously sympathizes with Josephus in declaring that others besides Josephus had taxed him as a vain, proud, and ignorant writer. In particular, he cites the much-respected Augustan historian Strabo as saying that Chaeremon had made himself a laughing-stock of this world by his ignorance and arrogance.

Another of the notorious enemies of the Jews cited and refuted by Josephus was Lysimachus. Mather, in the appendix to his commentary on Lamentations, clearly agrees with Josephus in his refutation, since he states that he will take no notice of the ridiculous etymology assigned by Lysimachus (in *Against Apion* 1.311, 318) for the name of Jerusalem, namely that it came from the Greek word for "temple robbery" (ἱεροσυλία).

But regardless of his theological views concerning the Jews, whereas a medieval figure, Peter Comestor, writing a similar commentary on the Bible, the *Historia Scholastica*, had relied heavily on Jerome,[70] Mather follows the Reformation practice[71] in basing himself primarily on Jewish exegetical works. He is well aware, as we can see from the advertisement in which he described his *Biblia Americana*,[72] that many of his readers would raise their eyebrows at the thought that he would prefer Jewish to non-Jewish sources, but he justifies this in his advertisement by declaring that they are "golden treasures, fetched out of those most unlikely helps, the Talmuds and other Jewish writers," and by stating that these citations will actually serve to demonstrate the truth of Christianity. In particular, he draws upon the aggadic passages in the Babylonian and Jerusalem Talmudim, various midrashim, the Mekhilta, Pirqe de-Rabbi Eliezer, the Zohar, the Targum of Onkelos, the Seder Olam Rabbah, and the commentaries of Saadia Gaon, Rashi, Abraham Ibn Ezra, David Kimḥi, Nachmanides, Moses ben Jacob of Coucy, Levi ben Gerson (Gersonides), Bahya ben Asher ben Ḥlava, Yom Tov Lipmann Muelhausen, Solomon ibn Verga, Don Isaac Abarbanel, Abraham Zacuto, Obadiah Bertinoro, Elijah Levita, and Obadiah Sforno. Thus, for example, he prefers to cite the passage in the Babylonian Talmud (*Sanhedrin* 91a) about the lawsuit brought by the Egyptians against the Jews before Alexander the Great to recover what the Israelites had borrowed from them when they left Egypt. As he says, for example, commenting on the apparent discrepancy in the Book of Numbers (3:39) between the number of Levites as given, 22,000, and the number which one arrives at when one adds up the figures, 22,300, it is "those learned rabbins," as he describes them, Rabbi Solomon (that is, Rashi) and Aben Ezra (that is, Ibn Ezra), who saw and solved the difficulty.[73] He then adds: "And the writings of the rabbins are often very helpful to us."

Though his debt to Josephus is large, like Comestor he confines this debt largely to specific data, and less commonly to aggadic details, and still less often to halachic matters. In halachic matters his favorite sources are the Babylonian and Jerusalem Talmudim, Jacob ben Asher (Baal Ha-Turim), Rabbi Levi of Barcelona (i.e., the *Sefer Ha-ḥinukh* ascribed to Aaron Ha-Levi of Barcelona), and especially Maimonides. Thus, in commenting on the "fruit of a goodly tree" (Leviticus 23:40), he does not mention Josephus's identification (*Antiquities* 3:245) as the persea, a fleshy one-seeded fruit of the laurel family, but rather cites Maimonides, who, in accordance with tradition, identifies it as the citron. If he does cite Josephus on points of halachah it is generally to corroborate rabbinic sources. Thus he notes that, according to Josephus (*Antiquities* 18.121), the Jews objected to allowing Vitellius, the Roman governor of Syria, to lead his army through Judaea because the army had banners with images on them. Mather then proceeds to ask why the Jews should have found the Roman eagles on the army banners offensive since neither Scripture nor Josephus nor Philo nor any place in the Talmudim mentions such a tradition. One of the very few places where he cites Josephus on a matter of Jewish law is his statement (*Jewish War* 3.377), in connection with the fact that Saul, though a suicide, was accorded proper burial (*Antiquities* 6.377), that it is a law that the body of a suicide should be exposed unburied until sunset. He realizes Josephus's shortcomings on technical questions of halachah and, indeed, specifically criticizes Josephus's lack of precision in referring (*Antiquities* 1.334) to the hollow of the thigh where Jacob had been wounded and which is consequently the portion of animals which may not be eaten by Israelites as (τὸ νεῦρον τὸ πλατύ) ("the broad tendon"). Mather implies that Josephus is competent in describing the manners and customs of the Jews but presumably not their halachah. Thus, in explaining the law that one should not round the corners of one's beard, Mather notes that Josephus (*Against Apion* 1.173) indicates that the poet Choerilus, in mentioning a people who had such a tonsure and who lived near the Dead Sea, was referring to the Jews.[74] Mather is noncommittal and says merely that whether Josephus expounded the poet correctly or incorrectly "he may be credited as a competent relater of that people's manners and customs." In only one instance, namely in connection with the regulations concerning inheritance (Numbers 36:3–9) does he cite Josephus (*Antiquities* 4.175) on a halachic matter, notably that if daughters were married into another tribe the inheritance was to be left in their father's tribe. Again, though he cites Philo often, he comments that Philo was but indifferently versed in the requirements of the religion of his ancestors, that is, in halachic matters.

Similarly, Mather, who is very much interested in the reasons for the commandments in the Pentateuch, rarely cites Josephus as his authority in such matters; and when he does it is usually in corroboration of rabbinic sources, notably Rabbi Levi of Barcelona and, above all, Maimonides. Thus, in commenting on the reason for circumcision, he asserts that the Jews themselves call it a mystery, and cites as his authorities "Philo and Josephus [*Antiquities* 1.192] and Maimonides and Rabbi Levi of Barcelona and others" for the explanation that it was instituted in order to distinguish the Jews from non-Jews. Again, when he accepts Josephus's explanation (*Antiquities* 4.301) that the reason for the prohibition of transvestism (Deuteronomy 22:5) is to prevent women from entering into battle, he does so on the authority not only of Josephus but also of "many learned men of the moderns, as well as of the ancients." Furthermore, in commenting on the reason for the commandment forbidding the sowing of a field with mingled seed (Leviticus 19:19, Deuteronomy 22:9), he cites Josephus's explanation (*Antiquities* 4.228) that it was instituted in order to avoid the cruelty of exacting from the earth too rich a tribute, for it suffices that the earth rear one plant and be exempt from the labors of the plough. He then proceeds to reduce this to absurdity by remarking that every husbandman will be able to show the insufficiency of this account. Significantly, Mather then expresses a preference for the explanation given by Maimonides, that such mixtures were forbidden as a reaction against their being practiced by the Canaanites as part of their idolatry.

Mather's Criticism of Josephus

Despite his great regard for Josephus's learning, Mather declares that he is aware that Josephus's historical works were not held in esteem among the Jews; and this, we may suggest, may be a major reason why he prefers the talmudic rabbis and the medieval Jewish commentators to him when it comes to matters of Jewish law and lore. Moreover, he is critical of Josephus for his boastfulness. Josephus, he says, declares himself to be the wisest of all the Jews,[75] whereas actually, according to Mather, Josephus could not read the Holy Scriptures in the Hebrew original—a point in which Mather seems to be in the wrong.[76] Furthermore, he criticizes Josephus for boasting that he was admired by the Romans for his virtue and that Titus marveled at his fortitude under affliction (*Jewish War* 3.396). Indeed, he contrasts this trait in Josephus with the modesty of Moses, whom the Bible declares to be the meekest of all men (Numbers 12:3).

Mather is critical of Josephus's errors of commission; but no less, we may suggest, in view of his great dependence upon Josephus, we may note Mather's omission of data added by Josephus. As examples of Mather's omissions of major additions in Josephus we may cite Josephus's elaboration of the episode of Joseph and Potiphar's wife (*Antiquities* 2.41–59) and Moses's march into Ethiopia and his romance with the Ethiopian princess (*Antiquities* 2.238–53). Moreover, it is not surprising, in view of Mather's attack upon the study of logic in his *Manuductio* as a waste of time,[77] that he omits Josephus's original proof for the existence of G-d which Josephus ascribes to Abraham (*Antiquities* 1.156) from the exceptions in celestial phenomena.

On the other hand, Mather[78] is critical of Josephus for omitting the account of the Golden Calf (Exodus 32), a sin which, we may add, Christian Church Fathers, from the time of Justin Martyr, had emphasized as justifying the punishment of the Jews. Moreover, Mather registers agreement with Daniel Chamier, André Rivet, and others, who had lived earlier in the seventeenth century, in taxing Josephus for his partiality toward his countrymen, whereas Mather claims that he, on the contrary, has not omitted some censurable occurrences in the history of the colonies.

There are a number of specific details in which Mather disagrees with Josephus. Thus he disagrees with Josephus (*Antiquities* 1.73), who is in accordance here with the Septuagint (Alexandrinus manuscript) and Philo, that the sons of G-d (Genesis 6:2) who went in unto the daughters of men were angels or devils.[79] As to the date when idolatry was introduced, Mather apparently disagrees with Josephus's view (*Antiquities* 1.72)[80] that it was established long before the Flood, and prefers the rabbinic view, as adopted by Maimonides and John Selden, that it began not long before the Flood. He is likewise critical of Josephus's explanation (*Antiquities* 1.114) that the reason why the Tower of Babel was built was that the people of that generation feared that they would be engulfed by another flood. But, retorts Mather, if so, why would they build this edifice in a valley (*Antiquities* 1.110)—and that between two rivers that had frequent floods—rather than on a mountain, and why would they use brick, which is less able than stone to resist a flood? Moreover, he criticizes Josephus for asserting (*Antiquities* 1.248) that Bethuel, the father of Rebekah, was dead at the time when Eliezer arrives (presumably because we are told, according to Genesis 24:28, that Rebekah ran and told her mother's household about Eliezer's visit), whereas the biblical text, shortly thereafter (Genesis 24:50) expressly states that Laban and Bethuel replied to Eliezer. Mather, to be sure, expresses wonderment at such an apparently flagrant error and declares, in Josephus's behalf, that he is "one of the most faithful guides that can be followed in this study of the Holy Scriptures." Josephus has, nevertheless, he adds, altered a great number of circumstances in his version, and he suggests three possibilities—blind ignorance, partiality, and the fact that human beings are subject to error. Again, though, as we have seen, he turns to Josephus for etymologies, he is critical of Josephus's etymology of the name "Jerusalem" (*Antiquities* 1.180, 7.67; *Jewish War* 6.438) as being a combination of the Greek word for "temple" (ἱερόν) and the Hebrew name of Salem (i.e., "security"), since such a hybrid is most unlikely and since, most likely, it consists of two Hebrew words, *yir'u shalom* ("they shall see peace"). He is particularly critical of Josephus's flagrant error (in which Josephus is joined by Philo and by Jerome) in stating that Moses composed his song at the Red Sea and at the end of his life in hexameters (*Antiquities* 2.346 and 4.303). Again, much as he admires Josephus for geographical information, he is critical of Josephus's statement (*Antiquities* 8.165) that the Queen of Sheba was the ruler of Egypt and Ethiopia, and prefers to locate her in Arabia; he then proceeds to express his preference for the view of Bochart, that Josephus's account of this queen is full of fables. Still another detail in which he declines to follow Josephus is the remark (*Antiquities* 8.236) that the old prophet (1 Kings 13:11) of Bethel was a false prophet; in this matter he prefers to follow his contemporary Hermann Witsius.

Mather's chief criticism of Josephus is that he is guilty of rationalizing the miraculous works of G-d. Indeed, in his handbook for the training of ministers, *Manuductio ad Ministerium*, his last important work, published in 1726, two years before his death, he is sharply critical of Josephus[81] for his ambition to have his work find acceptance among the heathen so that they will find nothing incredible to them. Indeed, he adds that it would be too long a digression to relate his "vile prevarications." All honest men, he adds, are scandalized at the pains that he took to court Roman princes with his "heathen" Judaism. What Mather has in mind, it would seem, is not his surrender to Vespasian but rather his attempts to gloss over miracles or to leave the judgment to the reader.

Thus, in commenting on the longevity of the original patriarchs, Josephus (1.105–6) gives four reasons, namely that they were beloved of G-d and were, indeed, the creatures of G-d Himself; that they followed a special diet; that they had extraordinary merits; and that G-d had to allow them to live long lives in order that they might promote the utility of their discoveries in astronomy and geometry, since it would take 600 years, the period of a great year, to verify their predictions. Mather boldly declares that the causes assigned by Josephus will be found, upon examination, to have no substance to them. Instead, Mather expresses his clear preference for the reason that their long lives were due to the special delight which Divine Providence took in them. As for Josephus's statement about the great year, he contends that among the Egyptians a great year was no more than 365 years. Here again, he shows his preference for the rabbinic commentators, in this case the *Sefer Ha-ḥinukh* ascribed to Rabbi Levi of Barcelona, who explains it as simply the work of Providence, not of Nature, except that Mather, with his great regard for Newton and for the science of his day, adds that we may allow both Providence and Nature as the causes.

Mather is most strongly critical of Josephus's account of the miracle of the crossing of the Red Sea (*Antiquities* 2.247–48), which he quotes at some length, and, in particular, of two details, namely his comparison of this miracle with Alexander the Great's crossing of the Pamphylian Sea and his statement at the very end, leaving it to the reader to judge the miracle as he sees fit. At this point Mather uses his strongest language in attacking Josephus. This is a scandalous passage, he says, and is chargeable with folly and falsehood. Josephus, he emphasizes, was inexorably wicked in saying that Moses waited until the ocean would dry, inasmuch as it is well known that the ocean is never dry. Moreover, Mather retorts, Alexander's crossing of the Pamphylian Sea had nothing to do with a miracle, inasmuch as there is a place there, as noted by Strabo, affording a narrow passage when the sea is at low ebb, so that it may be forded on foot. Mather himself, as Middlekauff[82] has remarked, saw miracles in much the same way that pious Newtonians of his era did,[83] namely as rare interruptions of a nature that ordinarily conformed to reason.[84] His explanation of this miracle is that an angel of G-d was exhibiting himself in the camp of Israel and that an earthquake is not an unusual accoutrement of the descent of an angel. Such an earthquake will quickly make dry land appear where water had previously been deep for ages. In answer to the objection that the text in Exodus (14:10–31) does not mention an earthquake, Mather replies that it may be inferred from Psalm 77:18–20. He then cites the rabbinic work, *Pirqe de-Rabbi Eliezer*, to support his claim that the Shekhinah ("Divine Presence") was there. In their self-righteous tendency to measure everything by human standards, Mather writes in his *Biblia Americana,* men forget that all things are easy for G-d.

Mather gives a similar explanation of the miracle associated with the fall of Jericho, which, he says, was due not to the shout of the people but rather to the work of G-d and of his angels. Here, too, he notes that the miracle was accompanied by an earthquake, similar to the earthquake which caused cities to be sunk into the Dead Sea. Undoubtedly, a basic reason for this very strong language on the part of Mather in attacking Josephus is that miracles are so crucial for the claims of Christianity; and, indeed, he makes a point of expressing wonderment that neither Josephus nor the Talmudim, who, as he puts it, are not sparing in proclaiming the wonders of their own nation, make no mention of the miraculous proof of the pool of Bethesda (Bethzatha [John 5:2–9]), where Jesus is said to have healed a man who had been sick for thirty-eight years. We may further note the importance of miracles for Mather in that in his translation of the *Testimonium Flavianum* (*Antiquities* 18.63–64) he has Josephus declare that Jesus wrought "most wonderful" works, whereas the Greek says merely that his deeds were surprising (παραδόξων).

Mather is likewise unhappy with the way in which Josephus cites pagan authors in support of biblical events. These citations, he remarks, leave the reader with uncertainty and incongruity. As an example he notes that when Josephus (*Antiquities* 1.93) cites such a pagan author as the Babylonian Berosus to support the historicity of the Flood, he does so with the word λέγεται, "so it is said," clearly in a noncommittal mood. Likewise, Berosus does not really support the biblical statement that the ark rested on Mount Ararat, inasmuch as he states that the ark rested πρὸς τῷ ὄρει, that is, "near the mountain." Similarly, Mather complains, the account which Josephus cites from Nicolaus of Damascus (*Antiquities* 1.94–95) is inconsistent with itself. Mather then expresses preference for the account of "the incomparable Newton," namely that the flood can be best accounted for by supposing that, presumably through divine intervention, the force of gravitation was removed for a time from the middle of the inhabited part of the world.

Summary

During the Renaissance and the Reformation the influence of Josephus, as judged by the number of editions and translations that appeared, was at its height. Like so many other writers of the seventeenth and eighteenth centuries, Cotton Mather, in his massive, unpublished commentary on the Bible, *Biblia Americana*, which he conceived as his *magnum opus*, found Josephus to be of enormous value in supplying historical, geographical, genealogical, chronological, linguistic, etymological, religious, and other antiquarian details so dear to him, particularly for the Pentateuch. He found him especially useful in filling the gap of time between the Jewish Scriptures and the New Testament. In particular, Josephus proved invaluable as a source of external evidence, in a passage (the *Testimonium Flavianum*) whose authenticity Mather vigorously defends, for the historicity of Jesus. Like Jerome, whose commendation of Josephus he cites, he praises Josephus in the highest terms as a learned historian and antiquarian. With his elevation of the importance of history and with his denigration of logic, allegory, and mysticism, Josephus proved a natural ally for Mather.

Mather seems to have found in Josephus, the author of the first extant autobiography, a kindred personality, full of soul-searching and very defensive about his actions, very similar to Paul, whose friend, Mather claims, interestingly without evidence, Josephus was. He seems to have taken an extraordinary interest in Josephus, consulting him in the Greek original, in the Latin and English translations, and in the Latin translation of the Hebrew paraphrase of the *Jewish War*, known as Josippon. He found Josephus particularly useful for his citations of pagan confirmation of biblical details.

As to the Jews, Mather, like other leading Puritans of his day, maintained a remarkable ambiguity. On the one hand, he speaks about the increasing wickedness of the Jews prior to the outbreak of the war against the Romans and about the Jewish infidelity and blindness; but, on the other hand, especially when we consider the sheer length of his commentary, the negative remarks about the Jews are few indeed, perhaps because he admired the great learning of the talmudic rabbis and medieval commentators, whom he clearly preferred, certainly in halachic matters, even to that of Josephus himself, perhaps because, more than almost anything else in the world, he hoped to be able to convert even one Jew to his view of Christian salvation.

Clues that Mather looked less unfavorably or even favorably upon the Jews may be seen in his version of the *Testimonium Flavianum*, where he speaks of the role not of the leaders but of some of the leaders of the Jews in the condemnation of Jesus, and in his version of the favorable impression made upon Aristotle by a Jew whom Clearchus, the author of the passage, knew personally, according to Mather, though there is no evidence of this in the text itself.

Mather is aware, however, that Josephus's historical works were not held in esteem by his fellow Jews. Moreover, he is critical of Josephus for his boastfulness—a trait not unknown to Mather himself—which he condemns in the strongest terms by comparing him with the most modest of men, Moses. He is critical of Josephus's omission of such episodes as the sin of the golden calf. Above all, he condemns in the strongest terms Josephus's rationalization of miracles, particularly the central miracle connected with the Exodus, namely the crossing of the Red Sea. Leaving to the reader the decision as to whether to believe this miracle or not is for Mather the height of folly, falsehood, scandal, and wickedness. Pious Newtonian that he was, he insisted that there was here an interruption in nature programmed by a providential G-d. Like Josephus himself, Cotton Mather thus emerges as a study in contrasts.

Notes

1. See Robert M. Grant, *The Earliest Lives of Jesus* (New York: Harper, 1961), 115.
2. See my essay, "Origen's *Contra Celsum* and Josephus's *Contra Apionem*: The Issue of Jewish Origins," *Vigiliae Christianae* 44 (1990): 104–35.
3. The so-called Josephus-spiel, which has had such a long history, attempted to calculate how Josephus managed to save himself and a companion out of a total of forty-one men when the majority had resolved on self-destruction (*War* 3.387–89). See Feldman, *Josephus and Modern Scholarship (1937–1980)* (Berlin: de Gryter, 1984), 868–69.
4. Heinz Schreckenberg, *Die Flavius-Josephus-Tradition in Antike und Mittelalter* (Leiden: Brill, 1972), 68–171, presents a list of citations in ancient and medieval authors, from the first through the sixteenth centuries, who translated, excerpted, cited, or alluded to Josephus; but, valuable as this work is, there are numerous omissions, particularly for the Renaissance period.
5. Andé Wilmart, "Le Convent et la bibliothèque de Cluny vers le milieu du XIᵉ siècle," *Revue Mabillon* 11 (1921): 92–94.
6. See my forthcoming "The Jewish Sources of Peter Comestor's Commentary on Genesis in his *Historia Scholastica*," in Hermann Lichtenberger, ed., *Festschrift Heinz Schreckenberg*.
7. See Peter Burke, "A Survey of the Popularity of Ancient Historians, 1450–1700," *History and Theory* 5 (1966): 135–52.
8. These data are based primarily on Heinz Schreckenberg, *Bibliographie zu Flavius Josephus* (Leiden: Brill, 1968), 161–200.
9. See Moses Marx, "Joseph Ben Gorion Editions," *Studies in Bibliography and Booklore* 6 (1962–64): 38–42.
10. See Betsy H. Amaru, "Martin Luther and Flavius Josephus," in Louis H. Feldman and Gobei Hata, eds., *Josephus, Judaism, and Christianity* (Detroit: Wayne State University, 1987), 411–26.
11. Peter Gay, *A Loss of Mastery: Puritan Historians in Colonial America* (Berkeley: University of California, 1966), 58.
12. See Winton H. Solberg, "Cotton Mather, the Christian Philosopher,

and the Classics," *Proceedings of the American Antiquarian Society* 96, pt. 2 (1987): 325.

13. Ibid., 327.

14. Samuel Mather, *Life of the Very Reverend and Learned Cotton Mather, D.D., F.R.S.* (Boston, 1728), 4.

15. We may note, as an obvious deficiency in his knowledge, the fact that he cites, without challenge, Ultringa's comment on the name of *Rebekah*, which he incorrectly spells *Rivkhah* rather than Rivqah, as a transposition of the word *berakhah*, "blessing"; the fact that he gives the inscription on the cross as *Yeshua Notzri* rather than *Yeshu Ha-Notzri*; and the fact that he translates πᾶσαν τὴν οἰκουμένην as *khol 'eretz* rather than *khol ha-aretz*. These instances would seem to indicate that his knowledge of Hebrew was less than perfect.

16. Mather himself, in his diary dated October 28, 1683, states that he had a library "exceeding any man's in all this land." John Dunton remarks that his library was the "glory of New England, if not all America" (cited by Cheryl Rivers, *Cotton Mather's Biblia Americana Psalms and the Nature of Puritan Scholarship* [Ph.D. diss., Columbia University, 1977], 31) . Charles Chauncy states that "there were scarcely any books written but he had somehow or other got the sight of them. His own library was the largest by far of any private one on the continent" (cited by Julius H. Tuttle, "The Libraries of the Mathers," *Proceedings of the American Antiquarian Society* [1910], 294). By the year 1700, when he began to write his *Biblia Americana*, Mather records that he had between two and three thousand volumes in his library.

17. The catalogue of books belonging to Increase Mather, dated 1664, lists "Josephus, His Works." See Tuttle, 280. This must be the translation of Josephus by Thomas Lodge, titled *The Famous and Memorable Works of Josephus, a Man of Much Honour and Learning Among the Jewes. Faithfully translated out of Latin and French* (London: Peter Short, 1602 and reprinted in 1609, 1620, 1632, 1640, and 1655). This was the only translation of Joseph into English available before 1676.

18. Mitchell Breitwieser, *Cotton Mather and Benjamin Franklin: The Price of Representative Personality* (Cambridge: University Press, 1984), 49.

19. Ibid., 49.

20. Gay, 59.

21. Richard F. Lovelace, *The American Pietism of Cotton Mather: Origins of American Evangelicism* (Grand Rapids: Christian University, 1979), 2.

22. Solberg, 325.

23. Rivers, 160–66.

24. H. E. Mather, *Lineage of Rev. Richard Mather*, 81–82, cited by Tuttle, 294.

25. Samuel E. Morison, *The Intellectual Life of Colonial New England* (New York: New York University, 1956), 195.

26. Cotton Mather, *Diary of Cotton Mather*, ed. Worthington C. Ford (Boston, 1911) 1:169.

27. For the advertisement see Thomas J. Holmes, *Bibliography of the Works of Cotton Mather* (Cambridge, 1940), 734–35.

28. Mather, *Diary*, 2:413.

29. See Rivers, 213.

30. Gay, 60.

31. Edited by Kenneth B. Murdock (Cambridge, Mass.: Harvard University, 1977), 99.

32. See Mather's *Paterna*, ed. Ronald A. Bosco (Delmar, New York: Scholars' Facsimiles and Reprints, 1976), 5: "I will not here mention, for my vindication in this action, the names of those gentlemen who since Josephus have written their own lives."

33. Sacvan Bercovitch, *The Puritan Origins of the American Self* (New Haven: Yale University, 1975), 23–24.

34. The phrase "in the service of G-d," so redolent of Puritanism, is not in the Greek, which reads literally: "Deeming that no act of theirs will have been done rightly save what they do at G-d's bidding."

35. Solberg, 365, remarks that Mather borrows a large proportion of his classical references from intermediate sources, and that he borrows heavily, in accordance with the practice which was common at that time, without attribution. In the case of Josephus, however, he generally does mention Josephus's name when he borrows from him, except when, in his appendices, he presents systematic surveys of Jewish history which are, quite obviously, chiefly indebted to Josephus.

36. David Levin, *Cotton Mather: The Young Life of the L-rd's Remembrancer, 1663–1703* (Cambridge, Mass.: Harvard University, 1978), 251.

37. Samuel E. Morison, *Harvard College in the Seventeenth Century* (Cambridge, Mass.: Harvard University, 1936), 1:264–66.

38. See Kennerly M. Woody, "Cotton Mather's Manuductio ad Theologicam: The 'More Quiet and Hopeful Way,'" *Early American Literature* 4 (1969): 13–14.

39. Cotton Mather, *Munuductio ad Ministerium* (Boston: Hancock, 1726), 58.

40. See H. E. Mather, 81–82.

41. Woody, 36, n. 60.

42. Levin, 255.

43. See Rivers, 7.

44. See the prospectus reproduced by Holmes 2:732.

45. Lee M. Friedman, *Jewish Pioneers and Patriots* (Philadelphia: Jewish Publication Society, 1943), 96.

46. Not only has there been no study of the influence of Josephus upon Cotton Mather, but a perusal of my *Josephus and Modern Scholarship* (1937–1980), 859–63, 894–95, 972–73, where I evaluate work which has been done on Josephus's influence on Renaissance figures and on English literature, and where I discuss desiderata in the field, will indicate that the whole subject of Josephus's influence on American literature remains to be cultivated.

47. Mather is actually referring to Pseudo-Philo's *Biblical Antiquities* 4.9. Here, as elsewhere, he fails to distinguish between Philo and Pseudo-Philo.

48. See my discussion in "Josephus as a Biblical Interpreter: the 'Aqedah,'" *Jewish Quarterly Review* 75 (1984–85): 234–35.

49. Here the manuscripts read 4,628,000; but Marcus, in the Loeb Library edition, emends to 48,462, noting that Ezra and 1 Esdras give the number as 42,360.

50. Jacques Basnage, *L'histoire et la religion des juifs, depuis Jesus-Christ jusqu'à present. Pour servir de suplément et de continuation à l'histoire de Joseph*, 5 vols. (Rotterdam: Reiner Leers, 1707). Basnage's source for volume 1, which covers the Herodian period, is primarily Josephus. Mather apparently knew this work in the English translation by Thomas Taylor, *The History of the Jews* (London: Beaver, 1708). He himself admits in his manuscript that for the postbiblical period his historical data are taken primarily from Basnage.

51. See the advertisement reproduced in Levin, 162.

52. Here, though Mather does not explicitly cite Josephus as his source, it is clear that it is from him that the information has been taken.

53. Here, too, Mather does not cite Josephus explicitly as his source, but it is quite clear that he derived his information from him.

54. Mather does not explicitly cite Josephus as his source for the information on Elam, Asshur, Lud, Aram, and Arpachshad, but it is clear that his data came from him.

55. Mather cites Josephus as his source for the information that the camp of Gilgal was fifty furlongs from the Jordan River, but this is not to be found in Josephus.

56. James Ussher, *Annales Veteris et Novi Testamenti*, 2 vols. (London: Flesher, 1650–54).

57. See, for example, William Whiston, "The Particular Periods of Josephus's Chronology Stated," in his *Essays Towards Restoring the Greek Text of the Old Testament* (London, 1722), 203–19.

58. See Levin, 162.

59. See Herman Hailperin, *Rashi and the Christian Scholars* (Pittsburgh: University of Pittsburgh, 1963), 211–12, 340.

60. In this instance Mather has misread Josephus, who states (*Antiquities* 9.171) that Jehoash was attacked by some of his friends (or, according to another reading, the friends of Zechariah), whereas, according to Mather, he was attacked by the friends of Jehoiada.

61. Tanaquil Faber (Tanneguy LeFèbvre), *Flavii Josephi de Jesu Domino testimonium suppositum esse diatriba* (Saumur, 1655). Actually, it was not Faber but Lucas Osiander, *Epitomes historiae ecclesiasticae centuria I, II, III* (Tübingen: Gruppenbachius, 1592–1604), cent. I, lib. II, cap. 7, 17, who first questioned the authenticity of this passage. Mather states that there is reason to think that the Jews have struck it out from those copies of Josephus that want it, but examination of all the manuscripts and of all printed versions of the *Antiquities* indicates its universal presence.

62. See Friedman, "Cotton Mather's Ambition," in *Jewish Pioneers and Patriots*, 98. In his autobiography, *Paterna*, ed. Ronald A. Bosco, 223, unpublished during his lifetime, after noting his efforts to convert Negroes and Indians, Mather remarks: "Nor has ye Jewish nation been left unconsidered."

63. In William R. Manierre II, *The Diary of Cotton Mather D.D., F.R.S.* (Charlottesville, Virginia: University Press of Virginia, 1964), 18.

64. Ibid., 123.

65. Cited by Kenneth Silverman, ed., *Selected Letters of Cotton Mather* (Baton Rouge, Louisiana: Louisiana State University, 1971), 219–20.

66. See Bercovitch, 61.

67. See Mel Scult, *Millennial Expectations and Jewish Liberties: A Study of the Efforts to Convert the Jews in Britain up to the Nineteenth Century* (Leiden: Brill, 1978), 49. Mather (ibid., 50) argues that the expected conversion has already taken place and that the destruction of the Temple in the year 70 led many Jews to convert.

68. See Tertullian, *Apologeticus* 16.1–3, *Ad Nationes* 1.14; Minucius Felix, *Octavius* 9.3.

69. See Rivers, 138–39.

70. See my "The Jewish Sources of Peter Comestor's Commentary."

71. See Rivers, 154.

72. See Levin, 159.

73. The 300 men, he explains, were the first-born of the Levites and, "being the L-rd's already, they were left out of account."

74. The round tonsure here described by Herodotus was practiced by the neighboring Arabs (Herodotus 3.8) but was expressly forbidden to Jews (Leviticus 19:27).

75. Actually, Josephus does not quite say this. What he does say (*Antiquities* 20.263) is that his compatriots admit that in Jewish learning he far excels them.

76. See my "Use, Authority and Exegesis of Mikra in the Writings of Josephus," in Jan Mulder and Harry Sysling, eds., *Mikra: Text, Translation, Reading and Interpretation of the Hebrew Bible in Ancient Judaism and Early Christianity (Compendia Rerum Iudaicarum and Novum Testamentum*, vol. 1, sec. 2) (Assen: van Gorcum, 1988), 460–66.

77. See Woody, 11.

78. In his *Magnalia Christi Americana*, ed. Kenneth B. Murdock, Introduction, 99.

79. See David Levin, "Giants in the Earth: Science and the Occult in Cotton Mather's Letters to the Royal Society," *William and Mary Quarterly* 45 (1988): 762.

80. Josephus does not explicitly indicate that idolatry began at that time. What he says is that men abandoned the customs of their fathers for a life of depravity. Cotton Mather, *Manuductio ad Ministerium*, 61.

81. Cotton Mather, *Manuductio ad Ministerium*, 61.

82. Robert Middlekauff, *The Mathers: Three Generations of Puritan Intellectuals, 1596–1728* (New York: Oxford University, 1971), 292.

83. See Julius H. Tuttle, "William Whiston and Cotton Mather," *Publications of the Colonial Society of Massachusetts* 13 (1910–1911): 197–204, who remarks on the mutual admiration, noted by Cotton Mather's son Samuel, in his biography of his father, which Cotton Mather and William Whiston, Newton's successor as Professor of Mathematics at the University of Cambridge, had for each other. As Bercovitch (97) has noted, Mather's scientific investigations earned him membership in Britain's Royal Society, as well as acclaim, in our time, as the first significant figure in the history of American medicine.

84. We may also note that Mather seeks scientific explanations for the ten plagues in Egypt.

Arthur A. Chiel

Ezra Stiles and the Jews:
A Study in Ambivalence

During the thirteen years Ezra Stiles spent at Yale (1742–55), as student and tutor, he wrestled mightily before he arrived at any theological stance. The Calvinist doctrines of Predestination, Election, and Salvation were serious stumbling blocks to Stiles. "My Deistical Turn," he later recalled, "gave me a very thoro' Disgust against the Authority of Councils and Decretals."[1] But, having rejected the bleak dogmas of his Puritan forefathers, Stiles was not satisfied to let the matter rest there. He persisted in his search for some basic religious principles to which he might remain committed as a believing Christian. In that pursuit he read a variety of religious works. Stiles concentrated, in particular, on the Scripture. Was the Bible truly the revealed Word of God? That was the question uppermost in his consideration.

Having compared the Bible with other ancient historical sources, Stiles was at last convinced that the Scripture of Israel did contain dependable accounts of historical events. Insofar as the New Testament was concerned, he had had greatest difficulty in accepting the resurrection of Christ. This challenge was finally resolved for him, too, by what he perceived to be the inner consistency of the New Testament. "At first," wrote Stiles about his theological quest," I found myself ready to demand too much. I wanted to have displayed before me Demonstration that every Word, or at least every Sentiment in the Scriptures was inspired by God; and was liable to have my Faith overset, if I found one insuperable Difficulty." But here his exposure, at Yale, to Newtonian science proved unexpectedly helpful to him in his religious dilemma: "Newton tho't, whether the power by which a stone falls to the Ground might not retain the Moon her Orbit; and then went on and investigated the law of Gravity demonstrably obtaining in the solar system and probably thro'out the stellar Universe." And Stiles had decided to emulate Newton in resolving his religious problems. "In like manner," concluded Stiles, "some *one principle* may be the basis upon which the whole system of Revelation may be firmly supported. *Such* is the fulfillment of Prophecy respecting the Jews. *Such* is the Fact of the Resurrection of Jesus."[2] The credibility of the resurrection, then, together with the fulfillment of biblical prophecy concerning the dispersion of the Jews,[3] constituted for Stiles the bases on which he could accept Scripture and New Testament as divinely inspired. At last, with a reasonably good conscience he could enter the ministry when he was called to the pulpit of Newport's Second Congregational Church in 1755.

In Newport, Rhode Island, a flourishing, cosmopolitan seaport town, Ezra Stiles would have the opportunity for an encounter with "Jews of the Dispersion," some twenty families of them, whose origins were in Holland, England, Germany, and Portugal.[4] In a sense, Stiles had in Newport an excellent laboratory in which to observe Jews, to learn at first hand about their customs and traditions, and, eventually to develop into an "Hebrician" with extensive knowledge of the Hebrew Bible, the Commentaries, the Talmud, and the Zohar.[5] His scholarship was further enriched by his long and fruitful dialogues with visiting learned rabbis from Palestine and Poland.[6] And if all this were not enough for Stiles, he became, too, a steady visitant at Newport's *Yeshuat Israel* Synagogue, where he enjoyed Hazzan Touro's "grandeur of utterance, and bold lofty *Sonitus Verborum.*"[7]

Yet, while the Jews and Hebrew lore loomed large in Ezra Stiles's theological and historical scheme, it cannot be said that he was an unequivocal Judeophile. The evidence adduced from his extensive writings reveals an anti-Jewish bias at times, certainly during his early years at Newport, somewhat less so in his later years there, and a growing Jewish sympathy in the post-Revolutionary War period, during his presidency of Yale. Perhaps Stiles's attitude toward the Jews might be best characterized as one of ambivalence. Certainly, Stiles's feelings about Aaron Lopez, Newport's outstanding Jewish figure, could be so described.

Aaron Lopez, a Marrano Jew who had fled his native Portugal, settled at Newport in 1752. Nine years later, in 1761, Lopez, together with Isaac Elizer, petitioned the Superior Court of Rhode Island for naturalization. They had the legal right to do so under an act of Parliament of 1740 which enabled Jews who were domiciled for at least seven years in any of the British colonies to receive their naturalization. Provision had been made, too, that exempted Jewish applicants from swearing "on the true faith of a Christian." But the Superior Court gave Lopez and Elizer no satisfaction for their effort. Whereupon the two petitioners turned to the

Rhode Island General Assembly, which body could also grant naturalization to legitimate applicants. In the instance of Lopez and Elizer, however, the General Assembly suddenly decided that naturalization was the legitimate responsibility of the Superior Court! With no alternative available to them, the two hapless applicants once more petitioned the Superior Court for their rightful naturalization. In March of 1762, the petitions of both men were rejected for the second time.[8]

To Ezra Stiles, the Lopez-Elizer case was of the keenest interest, and he recorded fully the court's decision. But Stiles was not satisfied with merely fulfilling the chronicler's role. He proceeded to do some strong theologizing. Begins Stiles: "And on the Eleventh Day of March 1762, Sentence was pronounced upon the Criminals successively bro't to the Bar; first upon Jn°. Sherman a noted Thief & Burglar for Burglary, sentenced to be hanged; secondly upon Fortune an abandoned Negro who set Fire to the Warehouses at End Long Wharf 19th Feb^r. which did Damage £5,000 ster. & endangered the Conflagration of the Town, sentenced to be hanged; thirdly upon—Lawton for Perjury in swearing to an acco^t. which he had falsely forged against another, sentenced to the Pillory. . . ."[9]

Stiles goes on to report of the naturalization matter: "And then the Jews were called to hear their almost equally mortifying sentence and Judgt. which dismissed their Petition of Naturalization. Whether this was designedly or accidental in proceeding upon the Business of Court I dont learn."[10]

Had Ezra Stiles here ended his entry, it would have left future judgment of his attitude toward the court's decision indecisive. It might have been interpreted as a somewhat sympathetic reaction on the part of Stiles. He might be decrying the embarrassment brought on Lopez and Elizer by the judges in dealing with their application seriatim with the cases of an unsavory trio of criminals. However, Stiles writes on and makes a telling comment: "But this I remark, that Providence seems to make every thing to work for the mortification of the Jews, and to prevent their incorporation into any nation; that thus they may continue a distinct people."[11]

Stiles reveals his commitment to the classical Christian stance: For their rejection of Jesus long ago, the Jews suffer divine punishment. They have been and shall continue to be, because of their ancient obdurateness, a people apart, unassimilable. In writing of the court's "mortifying sentence" handed down in the company of three felons—a thief, an arsonist, and a forger, and Stiles's emphasis of "mortification of the Jews," undoubtedly the image in this preacher's mind is that of Jesus crucified in the motley company of convicted thieves. Here before his very eyes does Stiles see a divine meting out of measure for measure.

And as if theologizing about the Jews' circumstances were not enough, Stiles moves on to editorializing as he concludes his very comprehensive report of the Lopez-Elizer case:

Tho' the Naturalization Act passed by Parliament a few years ago [1753], yet it produced such a natural disgust towards the Hebrews, that the Jews themselves joyned in petition to Parliament to repeal the Act, and it was thereupon repealed for Britain. And tho' it was continued by way of permission in the Plantations upon seven years' residence, yet the tumult in new York in procuring the taking place of their Naturalization there, and the opposition it has met with in Rhode Island, forbodes that the Jews will never become incorporated with the People of America any more than in Europe, Asia, and Africa.[12]

What Stiles may have had to say when Aaron Lopez and Isaac Elizer were soon thereafter granted their naturalization, the first in Massachusetts and the other in New York, is not known. But Stiles was not thereby deterred from further keeping a close eye on Jews and in particular on Aaron Lopez, who was emerging as a very successful sea merchant in the Atlantic and Caribbean trade. In the decade since his naturalization struggle, he had come up rapidly as a financial equal with his fellow merchant-fleet owners of Newport.

The prospering Newporters, and among them Aaron Lopez, had not been at all enthusiastic about the nonimportation movement that had been under way in the American colonies since the unpopular Townshend Acts of 1767. Newport's sea merchants had lagged behind those of Boston, New York, and Philadelphia in the measures taken against the importing of British goods. But it was Lopez alone whom Ezra Stiles singled out for condemnation as being the laggard. Stiles criticized Lopez in his *Literary Diary* on August 25, 1772:

In the late Combinations of the American Merchants against Importation and against the exorbitant Fees of the Customhouses—some Merchants kept themselves from the Combinations. Mr. Aaron Lopez, a Jew Merchant in this Town is one. For this the Collector &c. shew him all Lenity and favor. He has about twenty Sail of Vessels, and his Captains are all exempted from Swearing at the Customhouse, and make their entries &c. without Oath. But the Oath is strictly exacted of all who were concerned with the Non-Importation Agreement. . . . Favor and Partiality!

It was not now "mortification of the Jews" that preoccupied Stiles. It was "Favor and Partiality" being shown to Lopez by the British authorities—with which anti-Tory sentiment of Stiles one might not quarrel,

though he himself had arrived at that outlook slowly and with caution.[13]
But his singling out of "a Jew Merchant, in this town" is clearly an indication of Stiles's bias. There was, after all, a roster of local sea merchants and, collectively, they were, all of them, playing the game of the
British. *Their* interests lay with importation from abroad rather than
with boycott.

That Stiles was focusing rather selectively on Jews at this stage is
further evidenced by other of his *Literary Diary* comments, in the early
1770s. In an entry of May 31, 1770, Stiles reports that Newport merchants had held a meeting on May 30. They had decided, in the face of
strong boycott threats against them from Boston and Philadelphia, that
they would, henceforth, more vigorously adhere to the nonimportation
of British goods. Concerning this most recent development Stiles comments: "An Instance, that five or six Jews & three or 4 Tories may draw
down Vengeance upon a Country." To Stiles, the Jews were obviously a
special class of culprits unto themselves. Otherwise he might have
placed the blame for Newport's current confrontation with Boston and
Philadelphia on nine or ten Tories and left it at that.[14]

Several months later, in August 1770, Stiles picked up a bit of intelligence that went well beyond the "six Jews and three or 4 Tories"
charge. If anything, it presaged an Elders of Zion canard of the future.
Stiles derived this sinister information from Captain William A. Peck,
who had just arrived from London. Reports Stiles in his *Literary Diary*
entry of August 23, 1770: ". . . he tells me there is a secret *Intelligence
office* in London in ——— street where the Jews live It has subsisted
about four years & has thirty clerks: it is supported by the Ministry: &
has settled a correspondence in all of America—has four Correspond[ts] in
Boston & two in Newport, one of which is Mr. Geo Rome Mercht: to
each of whom the Ministry exhibit Stipends." Now Stiles comes to
Peck's major point about this spy operation: "As it appears in London,
it is intirely a Jew Affair—a Jewish Compting House, & is unknown in
London." How had Captain Peck come upon this extraordinary secret?
Stiles reports: "Capt. Peck sailed to London in a Vessel of the Jews & by
this fell into the hands of the Jews there, decried with sundry, and not
being strong for American rights, they used to open before him; in company he heard one Mr Clark, I think, speak of their *secret Intelligence
office* & upon Peck's questioning, &c. he colored up and diverted the
Discourse." In summary of Peck's report, Stiles notes: "Capt. Peck says,
that the office boasted of having Intelligence of every Occurrence of any
consequence in America." So there it was. In London there existed a
cabal of Jews with international connections, whose attention nothing
escaped and to whom "every Occurrence" was known.

For the time being, Ezra Stiles tucked away this nugget of information about Jewish intrigue on behalf of the British government. Two years later he had the opportunity to check it out. Stiles was that kind of diligent researcher in all of his sundry interests, of which he had many. In 1772, Stiles's close friend and parishioner, Henry Marchant, had become the agent in London for the Rhode Island Colony. Stiles now wrote to Marchant to ascertain the veracity of Captain Peck's report. In due course, Stiles received a reply, and he entered Marchant's evaluation of the charge in his *Literary Diary* entry of April 11, 1772: "I think you must be mistaken about the ministerial Jew-store, 30 Clerks employed &c. if you mean literally so. They [the Government] have Intelligence from secret Quarters undoubtedly, but with such a Staff of Officers, Dependants, and growling Expectants, there can be no great Occasion of a particular Set of Men for that Purpose. . . ." The tale proved to be a product of Captain Peck's fertile imagination.

Stiles made no further mention of a Jewish cabal. But once more he did allude to their presumable collaboration with the British. As in the instance of Captain Peck's story, Stiles again took note of a piece of hearsay. It was in March 1777, in the midst of the war. Stiles had fled with his family from Newport to temporary refuge in Dighton, Massachusetts. Someone brought him news of Newport's critical situation under the British siege. There was hunger, illness, and general disarray in that formerly pleasant town. Stiles wrote in his *Literary Diary* on March 20, 1777: "It is very sickly both in the Army & among the Inhab. of Newport. Lords dy before last five of the Inhab. were buried."

And he added: "The Jews are very officious at Informing against the Inhabitants—who are one & another frequently taken up & put in Gaol. . . . So that the Inhab. are cautious & fearful of one another. . . ." He had again succumbed to rumor, even as he had previously to the Captain Peck report. And what he now had selectively overlooked, consciously or otherwise, was the fact that the majority of Newport's Jewish families had also fled in a variety of directions to avoid the British siege of that strategic town. The few Jewish families who had remained behind might very well be Loyalists, but that they were informers against their longtime neighbors was hardly conceivable. Ezra Stiles had let his bias run away with him one more time.

Stiles must have been disabused of his suspicions as the war years unfolded. For nowhere in his *Literary Diary*, after 1777, is there again to be found any allusion to conspiracy or disloyalty on the part of the Jews. Stiles must have come to know, for little escaped his endlessly curious mind, that the majority of the Jews in the colonies had identified with the revolution.

In 1778 Stiles assumed the presidency of Yale College. From his earlier years he had known about New Haven's single Jewish family, the Pintos.[15] Now, on his return to New Haven, he found the three Pinto brothers to be ardent Whigs. One of them, Solomon, was in the Connecticut Seventh Line Regiment through all the war, having been taken prisoner, released, and returned to battle. Abraham and William Pinto joined in the resistance to the British invasion of New Haven in 1779. William Pinto, a Yale alumnus, noted for his exquisite penmanship, had transcribed the Declaration of Independence and presented it to Yale. Stiles was certainly aware of the patriotism of the Pinto family. He came also to know of the Jews who had fled to the various towns in southern Connecticut when the British occupied New York. With one of these, Joseph Simson, Stiles made contact. He had learned of that aged Jew's Hebrew erudition. After visiting Simson in his home at Wilton, Connecticut, Stiles described him, on January 18, 1782, as being "a Refugee from N. York." The sight of this patriarchal Jew who had, in his eighties, chosen to leave New York, his home of nearly seventy years, must have moved the Yale president. Simson was widely known as "a very warm Whig" and a good conversationalist.[16] Certainly Simson's political views must have been conveyed to Stiles.

It was 1782, and twenty years had passed since Ezra Stiles had pronounced his judgment on the Lopez-Elizer naturalization case. Ten years had gone by since Stiles had attributed British favoritism to Lopez for the reason that he did not honor the nonimportation agreements. In the years immediately preceding the Revolutionary War, and in the war's early years, Stiles had suspected the Jews of possibly conspiring with the British and identified them as Tories. But, as already intimated, a change in his attitude to the Jews would appear to have been in process since his return to New Haven. How far that process had gone may be found in the fact that Stiles, in his capacity as Yale president, was actively negotiating with Aaron Lopez a project which, in Stiles's words, "would be honourable to your Nation [the Jews] as well as ornamental to this University." What Stiles was proposing, in a letter dated May 31, 1781, was his wish to have Lopez present a gift to Yale—a portrait of the late Rabbi Raphael Haim Isaac Carigal.[17]

When Ezra Stiles was still a Congregationalist minister in Newport, he had sought out the several rabbis who had visited there at different times. He was much taken with these men and very especially with Rabbi Carigal, who spent five months, from March through July 1773, as guest of the Newport Jewish community. In the vigorously searching manner characteristic of Stiles, he engaged Rabbi Carigal in a wide-ranging exploration of Jewish sources. Together, they touched on theological issues of the Bible, the Talmud, and the Kaballah. For Ezra Stiles, the many dialogues with the rabbi during that spring and summer were extraordinarily fruitful. For Carigal, it was a wholly new experience, the opportunity to share with a Christian erudite in matters Hebraic. When Rabbi Carigal left Newport for Barbados, Stiles confessed that he "parted with him with great reluctance and should ever retain an affection for him." Stiles continued in correspondence with Carigal until 1777, when, in May of that year, the rabbi died at Bridgetown. How genuine and lasting was the affection in which Stiles held Carigal became further manifest in the 1781 negotiations between Stiles, president of Yale, and Lopez, the philanthropist, now living in Leicester, Massachusetts. Rabbi Carigal and the other rabbis who had come to Newport had their impact on Ezra Stiles. He paid his warm tribute to all of them, in his first major address, at Yale's commencement exercises of 1781.[18] "I have been taught personally at the mouths of the Masters of Wisdom," Stiles proudly declaimed, "at mouths of five Rabbis, Hochams of names & Eminence." Stiles proposed to the Yale faculty and students that the wisdom of Israel conveyed by the Talmud, the Targums, the Zohar, Maimonides, and the Bible commentators was the "kind of Learning worthy to be sought after and transplanted into the Colleges of America." As testimony to the high esteem in which he held the Jewish "Masters of Wisdom," he wanted one of them, if only in the portrait of Rabbi Carigal, to be present at Yale.

Now, in 1782, the news of Aaron Lopez's sudden death reached Stiles and it evoked a profound reaction, perhaps the strongest to be found anywhere in his *Literary Diary*. Not only would Stiles appear to have set aside his earlier biases, but he actually paid tribute to Lopez in a manner uncharacteristic of him. His encomium of Aaron Lopez was grandiloquent! There was only one regret expressed. In his *Literary Diary* entry for June 8, 1782 Stiles wrote:

On 28th of May died the amiable, benevolent, most hospitable & very respectable Gentleman *Mr. Aaron Lopez* Merchant, who retirᵍ from Newpᵗ Rhd. Island in these Times resided from 1775 to his Death at Leicester in Massachusetts. He was a Jew by nation, came from Spain or Portugal about 1754 & settled at Rhd. Isld. He was a Merchant of the first Eminence; from Honor & Extent of Commerce probably surpassed by no Merchᵗ in America. He did Business with the greatest Ease & Clearness—always carried about with him a Sweetness of Behav. a calm Urbanity an agreeable & unaffected Politeness of manners. Without a single Enemy & the most universally beloved by an extensive Acquaintance of any man I ever knew. His Beneficence to his Famʸ Connexions, to his Nation & to all of the World is almost without Parallel. He was my intimate Friend & Acquaintance!

Now there came Stiles's one regret: "Oh! how often I wished that sincere pious & candid mind could have perceived the Evidences of Xty, perceived the Truth as it is in Jesus Christ, known that JESUS was the MESSIAH predicted by Moses & the Prophets!" Stiles held out the hope that Lopez, along with others whom he esteemed, would yet be united in Christian brotherhood:

The amiable & excellent Characters of a *Lopez*, of a *Manasseh Ben Israel*, of a *Socrates*, & of a *Ganganelli*,[19] would almost persuade us to hope that their Excellency was infused by Heaven, and that the virtuous & good of all Nations & religions, notwithstand⁸ their Delusions, may be bro't together in Paradise on the Xtian System finding Grace with the all benevolent & adorable Emmanuel who with his expiring breath & in his deepest agonies, prayed for those who knew not what they did.

Stiles remained firm, then, in his hope that the religious "Delusions" of those whom he considered in error, would be lifted. In the meanwhile, he was willing to concede that the illustrious Socrates, Menasseh ben Israel, the pope, and Aaron Lopez, though religiously misguided, were good, virtuous, even excellent.

But Stiles's *Literary Diary*, which he kept until close before his death, in 1795, reveals no more of the narrow anti-Jewish bias of his earlier years. If at all, two extensive entries made by Stiles were of an extraordinarily sympathetic nature insofar as Jews were concerned. The first of these was an open letter by Ben Solomon to Dr. Joseph Priestly. The second was Voltaire's *Sermon du Rabbin Akib*. That Stiles chose to copy them into his *Literary Diary* would be a reasonable indication that their messages had appeal for him, that he was on the side of their authors vis-à-vis the Jews.

Stiles's entry of January 4, 1788, consists of a lengthy open letter by Ben Solomon to Dr. Joseph Priestley,[20] scientist turned religionist, who "lately addressed the Jews to convert them." Ben Solomon, a champion of his people, ridicules Priestley's efforts to bring over the Jews to Christianity. "The Morality of the New Testament," argues Ben Solomon, "is partly taken from the Old and partly from the doctrine of the Essenes, as you find it described by Josephus." Since Judaism has already offered such good and complete doctrine, including that of Resurrection, what gain could there be for the Jews in converting to Christianity? Stiles had likely read the Ben Solomon polemic in one of the London journals which he read regularly, and the published response to Priestley had appealed to him. He therefore entered it into his *Literary Diary*.

The second entry, a far stronger critique of Christianity from the Jewish vantage point than that of Ben Solomon, was Voltaire's *Sermon du*

Rabbin Akib.[21] Stiles translated it from the French and recorded it February 17, 1790. In this sermon, Voltaire puts into the mouth of a Smyrna rabbi a powerful *j'accuse* against the Catholic church, in reaction to an *auto-da-fé* by the Portuguese Inquisition[22] at Lisbon in 1671. That Stiles was stirred by this work of Voltaire's is attested not merely by the fact of his having included it in his *Literary Diary* in its lengthy entirety, but also by the particular portions which he underlined. These had special meaning for Stiles. The points made in the underlined portions include: the frightful savagery of the church in murdering human beings for their convictions; the ungratefulness of Christianity and Islam to their mother religion, which gave them the ground of their being; the misreading of the dispersion as divine punishment for the crucifixion of Jesus, which, in fact, had been done by the Romans; the distortion of the Gospels by the Church in their representation of Jesus as God, when Jesus had spoken of himself only as the Son of God, the Son of man, and no more; that Jesus had not intended the establishment of a church institution with popes, cardinals, Dominicans, and inquisitors; that Jesus had urged the observance of the Law, and above all, the love of God and neighbor; and was it not therefore *Adonai's* will "that there be no longer on this little Globe, this least of thy Worlds, either Fanatics or Persecutors!" These were the sentiments of Voltaire that seemed to speak to Stiles's heart and mind, if we have judged correctly his underlining of them.

In a self-evaluation which Ezra Stiles did of himself in later life (ca. 1790), he wrote: "It has been a principle with me for thirty-five years past, to work and live in a decent, civil, and respectful communication with all; although in some of our sentiments in philosophy, religion, and politics, of diametrically opposite opinions. Hence, I can freely live, and converse in civil friendship, with Jews, Romanists, and all the sects of Protestants, and even with Deists."[23] That there were those who were critical of him for his civility and friendliness, Stiles was well aware, but he was willing to stand his ground. "I am," he wrote, "all along, blamed by bigots for this liberality, though, I think, none impeach me now of hypocrisy; because I most freely, fully, and plainly, give my sentiments on every thing in science, religion, and politics."[24]

Ezra Stiles kept an open mind through his lifetime, allowing knowledge and ideas to flow freely through it. And, although there was undoubtedly an ambivalence in his attitude to the Jews, he had not allowed the scales of judgment to tip over into a fixed, antipathetic stance on his part. His continuing study of the Hebraic sources, which extended throughout his lifetime, his intimate association with Newport Jews and their visiting rabbis, his very profound feelings for Rabbi Carigal in particular,[25] all of these had had their cumulatively positive effect upon him.

As far back as 1749, when he was a young man of twenty-two, Stiles had delivered a valedictory oration at Yale College, in which he apostrophized liberty: "'Tis Liberty, my friends, tis the cause of Liberty we assert—a Freedom from the Bias of vulgar Education, and the Violence of prejudicate Opinions—a Liberty suited to the Pursuit and Enquiries after truth—Natural and Moral."[26] For a certainty, Ezra Stiles had persisted in his pursuit and inquiry after the truth. His untiring search was well rewarded. He had freed himself substantially from bias and prejudicial notions.

Notes

1. Autobiographical Fragment, in *Memoirs of the Family of Stiles*, Stiles Papers, Beinecke Library, Yale University.
2. *Review of the Authors I read and admired during the Rise Height and Decline of my Scepticism, Dec. 12, 1768*. Stiles Papers.
3. In a Stiles *Miscellany volume* (Beinecke Library, Yale University), Stiles indicates that he had arrived at a conviction regarding the return of the Jews to Jerusalem as preliminary to the absolute redemption on the basis: (1) of discussions with Rabbi Moses Malchi, who visited Newport in 1759, from whom he "received great Lights . . . ," and (2) from his (Stiles's) careful study of Justin Martyr's *Dialogue with Tryphon* and Increase Mather's *Mystery of Israel's Salvation*. The dispersion and ultimate ingathering of the Jews were crucial to Stiles's thinking from 1762 and through the rest of his life.
4. Morris A. Gutstein, *The Story of the Jews of Newport: Two and a Half Centuries of Judaism, 1658–1908* (New York: Bloch Publishing Co., 1936).
5. A. Chiel, "Ezra Stiles, the Education of an Hebrician," *American Jewish Historical Quarterly [AJHQ]* 60 (March 1971): 235–41.
6. A. Chiel, "The Rabbis and Ezra Stiles," *AJHQ*, vol. 61 (June 1972), 294–312.
7. Franklin B. Dexter, ed., *The Literary Diary of Ezra Stiles*, 3 vols. (New York, 1901), 1:377. (hereafter referred to as *Literary Diary*.)
8. For full treatments of the Lopez-Elizer case, see: Abram Vossen Goodman, *American Overture, Jewish Rights in Colonial Times* (Philadelphia: Jewish Publication Society, 1947), chap. 4, and Stanley F. Chyet, *Lopez of Newport* (Detroit: Wayne State University Press, 1970), chap. 5.
9. Franklin B. Dexter, ed., *Extracts from the Itineraries and other Miscellanies of Ezra Stiles* (New Haven, 1916), 52–53.
10. Ibid.
11. Ibid.
12. Ibid.
13. For Stiles's political views, see Edmund S. Morgan, *The Gentle Pu-*

ritan: A Life of Ezra Stiles (New Haven: Yale University Press, 1962), particularly chaps. 15 and 17.

14. That there were Tories among the Jews is a fact. But Jews reflected politically in their communities the split that existed in the communities at large. "Families everywhere were divided," writes Samuel Eliot Morrison. "Almost every leading American—Adams, Otis, Lee, Washington, Franklin, Jefferson, Randolph, and Rutledge—had Loyalist kinsmen" (S. E. Morison, *The Oxford History of the American People* [New York, 1965], 236). See also: Cecil Roth, "Some Jewish Loyalists in the War of American Independence," *Publications of the American Jewish Historical Society* 38 (December 1948): 81–107.

15. *Itineraries*, 1:283–84.

16. "The New York Jew, from the Diary of the Hon. Arthur Lee," *American Jewish Archives* (June 1954), 105–6.

17. For fuller treatment, see the author's "The Mystery of the Rabbi's Lost Portrait," *Judaism* 22 (Fall 1973).

18. *An Oration upon the Hebrew Literature*, Stiles Papers.

19. Lorenzo Ganganelli, who was Pope Clement XIV and pontiff during the 1770s.

20. Ben Solomon may have been a pseudonym for David Levi, the London Hebraist and polemicist, Dr. Joseph Priestley had published his *Letters to the Jews* in his effort to missionize them. David Levi responded in his *Letters to Dr. Priestley* (1787–89).

21. *Oeuvres complètes de Voltaire, Mélanges III* (Paris: Garnier Frères, 1879), 24:277–87. That Voltaire was hardly a philo-Semite is open knowledge. What then had prompted him to write his *Sermon*? His dislike for the Church surpassed even his antipathy to the Jews. In the *Sermon* he was *using* a rabbinic spokesman through whom to lash Christianity. It was a bit of clever Voltairean ventriloquy.

22. Aaron Lopez, Stiles's friend, had fled from the Portuguese Inquisition, as had others who settled in Newport during the years that Stiles had been minister there. Stiles may have found particular poignancy in Voltaire's *Sermon* for this reason, too.

23. Abiel Holmes, *The Life of Ezra Stiles* (Boston, 1798).

24. Ibid.

25. Lee M. Friedman, *Rabbi Haim Isaac Carigal* (Boston, 1940) and the author's "The Mystery of the Rabbi's Lost Portrait," *Judaism* 22 (Fall 1973).

26. Valedictory Oration, June 15, 1749, Stiles Papers.

Four

The Colonial American Jewish Community and the Hebrew Language

Portrait of Rabbi Haim Isaac Carigal of Hebron (1773), one of the rabbis with whom Ezra Stiles studied Hebrew and discussed the Bible, Talmud, and Kabbalah.

Leo Hershkowitz

New Amsterdam's Twenty-Three Jews—Myth or Reality?

There are several intriguing questions involving the first years of Jewish contact with New Netherland. In the mid-seventeenth century there was a Jewish community in the Dutch possession in Recife, Brazil. When the Portuguese reconquered Recife, the Jews, fearing the Inquisition, fled. In early September, 1654, twenty-three Jews, "big and little" arrived in New Amsterdam. But who were the twenty-three and why is there never any mention of children during the first five decades of "settlement." Further, by 1664 when the Dutch colony surrendered to the British only two Jews can be specifically identified as being in New York. What of the rest? Where did they go? Asser Levy, one of these two, is the only one of the first Jewish arrivals who remained in the province and in fact died there. Only three Jews are known to have died before 1690 in New York—Levy, his wife Miriam, and Benjamin Bueno de Mesquita.

There is no record of births in this Jewish "community." It surely can be suggested, therefore, that 1654 as a date denoting the beginning of Jewish settlement in New York seems somewhat optimistic and misleading. Were the first fifty years of Jewish experience years of establishment, or really a time of testing, at best providing a point of contact for a future, more permanent society? How far and how deep did their commitment go? Were these few so-called "Pilgrims" seeking to build homes and sink roots into the soil? Were they anxious to establish a viable community? What follows is a short reexamination of some old references and some new, unpublished material, basically from the Gemeente Archief, Amsterdam, in an effort to shed light into some dark corners of past history and to provide answers to some queries and, in turn, to raise others.

Domine Johannes Megapolensis, writing from New Amsterdam on March 18, 1655, informed the Classis of Amsterdam that "God has led Domine Johannes Polhemius from Brazil over the Caribbean Islands to this place—. Last summer some Jews came here from Holland, in order to trade. Afterwards some Jews poor and healthy also came here in the same ship with D. Polhemius—."[1] Obviously, there were two separate immigrant groups in 1654—one from Holland and the other from Brazil which arrived with Domine Polhemius. Earlier on September 7, 1654, Solomon Pieterson, one of the first group, testified before the Court of Burgomasters and Schepens in a matter relating to a debt owed by several Jews to Jacques de la Motthe, master of the *St. Catherine* or *St. Charles.* (Samuel Oppenheim was of the opinion that it was the *St. Charles,* Arnold Wiznitzer was sure it was *St. Catherine.*) The vessel brought Jews from Cape St. Anthony, probably Cuba, after they left Brazil, seemingly via Jamaica. Pieterson said that "twenty-three souls, big and little" had reached New Amsterdam; unfortunately, however, he provided no specific census. With a good deal of imaginative arithmetic that figure can be reached. But it cannot be done using historic evidence.[2]

About two weeks earlier the ship *Peartree* had arrived in New Amsterdam on or about August 22, 1654, following a voyage from Holland. On board were at least two Jews—Jacob Barsimon and very likely Solomon Pieterson, but Megapolennis does not write of two Jews, but rather that "some Jews came from Holland" just as he says "some Jews" came from Brazil. One implication is surely that there could be more than two Jews on the *Peartree.* If so, who could they have been? And again, who were these twenty-three? Are the answers related?

From the testimony taken before New Amsterdam's municipal court on or soon after September 7, four individuals were named as owing de la Motthe for freight and passage—Abraham and David Israel, Judicq (Judith) de Mereda, and Moses Ambrosius. These, the "greatest" and "principal" debtors, were clearly on the *St. Catherine* or *St. Charles* and they can sensibly be traced through extant congregation lists to Brazil. Abraham Israel was likely Abraham Israel de Pisa, and David Israel likely David Israel Faro. Perhaps the latter was the David Israel who stated while in Amsterdam in January 1658, just before going to Barbados, that he, together with Abraham Querido de Jonge, while in Brazil had, on July 18, 1641, purchased ten "negerslaven" from the Dutch West India Company.[3] Beyond the four mentioned debtors who else can be added? One would surely appear to be Ricke Nunes, but *not* necessarily Asser Levy. On September 14, 1654, Levy brought Nunes to court and asked repayment of money advanced to her at "Gamonike," probably Jamaica. Nunes acknowledged some of the money had been lent to her husband—

not further identified but possibly Mosseh Nunes (was he one of the twenty-three?). She claimed other money due her for the repayment of freight on Levy's behalf. Then, on October 19, 1654, Nunes, represented by Pieterson, sued Levy again for freight paid for his goods brought from the West Indies. Levy claimed he was unable to pay as his property had been sold at public vendue seemingly to help pay de la Motthe. Earlier, on October 5, 1654, Jan Martyn from Harfleur, maybe a sailor on the *St. Catherine*, represented other crew members in filing a suit against Levy for 106 florins still remaining due for freight. This would appear to be the same sum asked by Nunes, and Levy used the same argument with respect to the Martyn claim as in the Nunes suit.[4] In none of his testimony is it clear that Levy had actually been in "Gamonike" let alone Brazil. Money lent to Nunes may not have been personally given by Levy and in none of these suits is fare or passage mentioned. Freight *and* passage figure in the other de la Motthe actions. Further there is no Asser Levy on any published Brazilian congregational list. Benjamin Levy appears on these records but that he may have had a son Asser is unsupported by any evidence.[5] That Levy was on the *Peartree* seems a more plausible argument.

In 1655, seven other Jewish names are to be found in New Amsterdam. None is directly connected with the *St. Catherine*. It is difficult to know whether in fact they were part of the "twenty-three souls," or whether they arrived with the *Peartree* or on some other ship. That all of the seven would have been in Brazil is evident. They are on congregation lists, but there is nothing to show that they came on the *St. Catherine*. They more likely left Recife in early 1654, at the time of surrender to the Portuguese, and sailed to Holland as did so many other Netherlanders, and then came to New Amsterdam.[6]

In 1656, two other names appear, two more the following year, two in 1658–1659, two in 1660, and one each in 1661, 1662, 1666, and 1670. In the 1680s there are eight more. Some are on congregational lists, a number are not. Which of these came on the *St. Catherine* or *Peartree*, which on other ships? As of now this is not known.[7] But there are at least doubts about the origins of some of these early "Pilgrims," more correctly visitors, including, as noted, Asser Levy. If Levy was not on the *St. Catherine* and not from Brazil then was he on the *Peartree*? Where did he really come from? Why was he the only one of the first contact group to remain to live and die in New York? A brief look at Levy's career is in order, partly because he was the only successful member of the early group—a "Pilgrim" in the true sense. Levy married Miriam, sometimes known as Maria or even Mary, but where and when is not known. The event was not recorded in the Amsterdam archives; Jews were not required to do so prior to 1695. Miriam died sometime in 1688 in New York, as mentioned. She was the sister of Judith Israel, who died in Amsterdam by 1692, and whose daughter Hannah Israel was by that year the wife of Gomes Uldricx. Was Miriam Levy born Miriam Israel? Were these Dutch Israels the same as the Sephardic families in Brazil? This appears very doubtful. Important information comes from testimony mentioning the Israel family, given in 1692 by one Asser or Ansel Levy, then 39 years old, who was living in Vloyenburgh, the Jewish quarter of Amsterdam, and by Lambert Benedictus, aged 29, the stepson of Hannah Israel, from Düsseldorf, both identified as High German Jews, Ashkenazim. Seemingly, *this* Asser Levy could be the half brother of the New Netherland Levy who married his widow, Miriam Levy, in New York on January 1, 1685. He signed his name in Hebrew as Ansel Samuel. In New York he was also known in court records as Ansel Samuel Levy or also David Levy. He apparently moved back to Amsterdam after 1685, probably after his wife's death in 1688.[8]

In April 1650 in Amsterdam an Abraham Israel, a merchant, then thirty-six years old is also mentioned as a High German Jew, and in October 1653 in another record his father is given as Isaac Israel. In 1661, Abraham, now forty-seven, still in Amsterdam, is again mentioned in a business transaction.[9] These Israels in Amsterdam had not been in Brazil. Though at this point there is no more specific evidence, it would seem a good chance that Miriam Levy and these Ashkenazic Israels were related. It would appear much less certain that the Sephardic Levys, or de Pizas were related to Miriam or to either Asser Levy.

This becomes even less likely in light of other evidence. Levy is sometime referred to as Asser Levy van Swellem. On occasion Levy wrote his name that way.[10] On May 24, 1660, while in Amsterdam on a business trip following a voyage from New Amsterdam (Jacob Barsimon was there also about the same time), Levy stated that he was about to leave for Germany. It seems plausible he meant to go to Schwelm, a city in Westphalia west of Düsseldorf. The earlier mentioned Benedictus was from Düsseldorf. Levy had some close connection with that part of Germany. Probably he had been there before. Then, intriguingly, Levy, in the May 1660 document (one which involved Levy in a business relationship with two other Ashkenazic Jews, Alexander Pollack and Jacob Gomprich), signed his name in Hebrew—at this point the only example known, which translates as "attested to by Asser, the son of master and teacher, Rabbi and teacher Judah Leib of Blessed memory who is of Vilna." The signature is in a well schooled hand indicating a formal knowledge of the language. Asser Levy was, then, an Ashkenazic Jew, who appears to have been born in or was from Vilna, then Poland, and could very well have been a refugee fleeing the indescribable horrors of the Chimielnicki Cossack pogroms of 1648–58. Interestingly, Levy is sometimes referred to as Asser Levy Wilde or Vanderwilde; his sister Rachel married David Valentine Vanderwilde, who was the brother of Simon Valentine, the "pretended heir" of Asser. These Vanderwilde or Wilde references may be corruptions of Vilna; a Dutch clerk hearing Asser Levy saying Vilna wrote what, to him, was a more understandable Wilde. It would appear that Ashkenazic Asser Levy was not the son of Benjamin Levy, had not been in Brazil, and more than likely arrived in New Amsterdam *not* on the *St. Catherine* but on the *Peartree*.[11]

Those on the *Peartree* came to New Amsterdam by choice not chance, not by an unlucky storm or any other misadventure. Can the same be said of the other seven 1655 individuals who seem to have no relationship with the *Peartree* or *St. Catherine*? Jews arrived in New Amsterdam soon after September 1654. On March 1, 1655, Cornelis van Tienhoven, schout or sheriff, brought Abraham de Lucena, who probably arrived with his wife, to court charging that de Lucena left his store open during "the Sermon," supposedly Sunday, and sold goods retail. The schout demanded withdrawal of trade privileges and a heavy fine of 600 florins. He reminded the court that Director General Stuyvesant and his council had resolved that "Jews who came last year from the West Indies and now from Fatherland must depart forthwith." Clearly over time, between September 1654 and March 1655, other Jews had arrived from Holland.[12] On May 5, 1655, William Tomassen, skipper of the ship *Great Christopher*, sued David de Ferera, Abraham de Lucena, and Salvador d'Andrada for the payment of freight for goods shipped from Amsterdam to New Netherland. While this does not indicate that he brought the defendants with him, it remains a possibility. Surely other Jews could have been aboard the *Great Christopher*. In any event that voyage was not made by chance.[13]

By 1655, then, a number of others had arrived in New Amsterdam, not directly from Brazil, including, in addition to those mentioned, Joseph d'Acosta and Jacob Cohen Henriques. These individuals had been in Brazil, but by early 1654 had left for Holland, and not to the West Indies on the *St. Catherine*. A brief evaluation of some of the group is worthwhile.

D'Acosta, who spent several years in New Netherland, was an important though temporary figure in the community. In 1657 he was official translator of Spanish, probably Portuguese, into Dutch, and in the following years he translated Hebrew into Dutch. He was involved in a number of suits, including one in 1658 in which he was represented by Asser Levy. He left the province shortly during or shortly after 1660.[14]

The earliest document so far discovered regarding d'Acosta is one dated October 18, 1645, and here he is identified as being twenty years old and a Portuguese living in Amsterdam.[15] In February 1652, d'Acosta, still in Amsterdam, was appointed to represent the activities of two Portuguese merchants in settling their accounts with various persons connected to Lisbon, Pernambuco, and Bahia. Seemingly around this time he went to Brazil and apparently left for Holland at the time of the January 1654 surrender.[16] In Amsterdam, on March 22, 1655, a company was formed to trade between Amsterdam and New Netherland. Major investors included Gillis Verbrugge and Co., who were involved in New Netherland trade as early as the 1640s, one-quarter part; Mordohay Abendana, one-quarter part; and David Cardozo Davillar, one-sixteenth part. Three others held remaining shares. Verbrugge and Abendana, the principal investors, authorized d'Acosta, a shareholder in the West India Company and about to leave for New Amsterdam, to be their agent in New Netherland. He was to receive 9 percent of the trade in New Netherland for a four-year period.[17] This contract was signed by d'Acosta on the same date. He was still in Amsterdam on April 7, 1655, when some of the terms of the agreement were altered. Shortly after this, d'Acosta sailed for New Amsterdam. In December 1655, he leased a house in New Amsterdam, possibly now 27 Pearl Street, for one year from July 1, 1656, to July 1657.[18] Just how the affairs of this trading company prospered is not known, as of now, nor is the role played by d'Acosta as their agent. However, there is little question that d'Acosta came to New Netherland by design and not by the winds of fortune. At the end of four years he left for the Netherlands and did not return.

Sometime later d'Acosta went to Germany, for in November 1673, while once again in Amsterdam, he requested as "d'Acosta from Hamburg" some 275,000 guilders as reparations from the West India Company for losses incurred in Brazil as a result of the Portuguese conquest. This is of course a huge sum, perhaps inflated in preparation for future negotiation. It is not known whether he recovered his claim.[19]

As mentioned, d'Acosta left New Amsterdam at the end of his contract. Almost all the others, except Levy, left, too, for various reasons. Jacob Cohen Henriques, also in the frontier city by December 1655, encountered a great many difficulties, enough to guarantee a short stay. In December 1655 he and Salvador d'Andrada had to post a bond on suspicion of local authorities that their importation of eleven carts of tobacco might have been smuggled aboard the ship *New Amsterdam*. Were they passengers in this ship? In February 1656 he had a bitter fight over a canoe which Cohen said was his but the defendant claimed was bought from Indians. It was a long drawn out affair with the end not clearly determined in the record.[20] On April 11, 1657, Cohen was refused permission to bake bread behind closed doors. No other bakers were allowed to do so either. Why closed doors?[21]

In April 1658 Cohen was accused of selling liquor without a permit. He was fined and must have left shortly after as there are no further references to him. He, like most of the others, does not return.[22] Cohen's stay in New Amsterdam, as well as those of many others, was not under the happiest of circumstances.

Abraham de Lucena, after his March 1, 1655 summons by schout Cornelis van Tienhoven, next was involved in a suit in April 1655, involving a payment for tobacco. He lost the case, and in May of that year he, David Ferera, and Salvador d'Andrada were made to pay freight for a shipment of goods on board the *Great Christopher*. De Lucena's claim that two pipes of brandy were missing when the ship landed was not allowed.[23] In March 1656 he lost a case that involved costs of a lot of dry and "salted" or wet hides. De Lucena wanted to pay different rates for each sort of hide.[24] On June 15, 1660, de Lucena and his wife both appeared in court; she had called the defendant a rogue, and he in turn had called her a whore. Each retracted their statements. But it was not a happy affair. De Lucena seems then to have left the city soon after. On November 7, 1662, again appeared before the burgomasters and Schepens after he had been ordered to pay three beavers for his burgher right; de Lucena refused, saying he did no business in the city and had only stopped off on his way to Holland. If he were going to remain, he said, he would pay. Had de Lucena gone in 1660 to the West Indies after leaving New Amsterdam? The burgomaster excused him "this time." He did not remain and probably saved himself three beavers.

Jacob Barsimon, who was in New Amsterdam from 1654 to early 1660, was probably helped on his way out of the city when on April 3, 1656, he brought Isaac Israel to court, charging that Israel had struck him in the face while both were in de Lucena's cellar. The incident surely quickened Barsimon's exit. He returned to Amsterdam by 1660.[25]

David Ferera's sojourn was shorter than most, with the exception of the original five *St. Catherine* members. As mentioned, Ferera was first involved in the *Great Christopher* case of May 5, 1655. Beginning on July 13, 1656, he was defendant in a very bitter suit in which he was accused of the theft of a chest of clothes from bailiff Dirck van Schelluyne's house. The chest had been placed on consignment with the bailiff as a result of an earlier suit involving the merchandise. Ferera was asked to return the clothes, which, despite the van Schelluyne's warnings and protests, Ferera had taken by cart "making use moreover, of many words in his tongue," an action which the bailiff said, "tends to the great disrespect and prejudice of your Honors—." In anger, the court seized beaver skins placed as security by Ferera while the suit was being settled and ordered "that the said Jew shall be publicly whipped at a stake and banished forth from this Province of New Netherland." In the meantime he was to be kept in close confinement. Joseph d'Acosta was Ferera's interpreter. It would appear Ferera might have spoken and cursed in Portuguese, surely not in Hebrew. D'Acosta managed by July 26, 1656, to have the penalty reduced to no whipping and a fine of 170 guilders. D'Acosta was one of three arbitrators assigned by the court.[26] Ferera must have departed for friendlier shores shortly after for he does not again appear in the city.

Salvador d'Andrada is first on record on May 5, 1655, also as part of the *Great Christopher* case; then, on December 17, 1655, he petitioned to be allowed to buy a house located at the corner of what are now Broad and Stone Streets, which was being offered at public auction. The owner, Teunis Craay, was willing to sell to d'Andrada but asked if the director and council would not first wish to purchase, using their right of preemption. D'Andrada did not gain ownership. Interest in such purchases was also indicated by Cohen Henriques, de Lucena, and d'Acosta when they petitioned for the right to trade and acquire real estate. Their petitions were granted on April 21, 1657.[27] D'Andrada also had other problems. On November 8, 1655, Cornelis van Tienhoven, the schout, brought d'Andrada to court, charging that the defendant had in his possession a small silver cup that had been originally stolen from Jan Rutgersen. Rutgersen said d'Andrada offered to return the cup if he, Rutgersen, would pay one half the cost of his purchase of it. When this was refused d'Andrada quietly returned the stolen property and lost whatever sum he had supposedly paid.

It was not a profitable experience, especially coming as it did at a time when many in New Amsterdam were "voluntarily" taxed to pay the expenses of the construction of a protective wall, later Wall Street. On October 11, 1655, five Jews, all placed together in the tax list—Abraham de Lucena, Joseph d'Acosta, David Ferera, Jacob Cohen, and d'Andrada— were made to pay "voluntarily" 100 florins each. Stuyvesant paid 150 florins. Several others, absent ship captains, also paid similar amounts, but only about a dozen other non-Jews paid 100 florins, while some 250 others were taxed for six to twenty florins on average. This seemingly one-sided and heavy tax, and threats of others in the future, was cause enough for Jews to make a quick retreat from the province. Interestingly, Asser Levy was asked to pay a minimum of six florins. Was this a result of a favored status? Anyway, Levy remained in New Amsterdam and

New York. Jacob Barsimon, however, who also paid six florins, left by 1660.

Elias Silva was not taxed but was probably not in New Amsterdam at the time, he didn't stay long enough for any such distinction. He first appears in the city on March 27, 1656, when Jan Ferritsen, a brewer, brought suit against "Elias Silva, Jew," on the complaint that he had "detained his negress or slave and had carnal conversation with her." The accused appeared with Jacob Cohen, who was probably interpreter. The case was resumed the following April 24, but without resolution; the matter disappears and so does Silva.[28]

At the time of the surrender of the province early in September 1664, English officials asked for an oath of allegiance from the inhabitants of New York. The oath was taken from October 21 through October 26, 1664, by several hundred individuals—only two mentioned were Jewish, Asser Levy and Jacob Israel. It is possible the listed Jacob Leunizin is Jacob Lucena. Jacob Leunizin and Asser Levy were the only Jews among the burghers of April 1665, though there were two other Jews in the province in 1664: Abraham Israel de Pisa and his son, not identified, were witnesses in a suit in New Amsterdam on July 17, 1664. De Pisa, the "gold finding Jew," was in Jamaica in 1663, but where he was between 1654 and 1663 and after July 1664 is not yet known. As for other Jews, perhaps individuals such as Moses de Lucena, interpreter and butcher in 1657–60, Isaac Mesa, 1657, Manuel Roiz Lucena 1658–59, Joseph Frances, 1660, David Machero, 1662, might have witnessed the surrender. But by that date, September 1664, the first "visitors" were surely gone and there exists no firm evidence as to the last-mentioned "minor" figures, later arrivals, remaining at the time of the Dutch capitulation. In the November 1676 tax list, there are four Jews—Asser Levy, Moses the Jew [Lucena], "Jacob Israel ye Jew," and Isaac Continho and Company; except for Levy, the careers of the others are largely unknown. Benjamin Bueno de Mesquita was in New Amsterdam in 1661. He died in New York in 1683, but nothing is mentioned as to where he was in between those dates. There is little if anything to show whether Mesquita was, like Levy, a full-time resident in the province.[29]

Asser Levy was of all the early arrivals a special instance—a real "Pilgrim." He remained while others left. He was successful while others were indifferently so. He was widely accepted and had considerable influence, surely more than the others. He more clearly integrated himself within the host society. His inventory, the only one extant for a Jewish inhabitant, reveals a person of means and position. Why Levy was so unique, why he remained, are questions that may never be fully answered. Perhaps he was more accommodating or more accepting. Scandal such as theft, sexual misadventure, or disregard of law are rarely if ever connected with him. He was Ashkenazic, most of the others Sephardic. Is there an answer in this? For whatever reason, his was a stay that was written indelibly in the pages of early New York history.

There are some evident conclusions to be drawn from the story of early "Pilgrims," a term that, again, is not particularly descriptive or accurate for the Jewish experience. Unlike the Cape Cod colonists, except for Levy the first Jewish arrivals, whether from Holland or Brazil, did not settle in New Amsterdam. Even though through their efforts and that of their coreligionists in the Netherlands they obtained such basic citizenship rights as trade, residency, and a burial ground, most did not remain long enough to fully use these rights. Further, Bradford's colonists basically sought religious freedom, while trade motivated Jewish interest. Though Jews sought permission to have a synagogue, this was denied by the Dutch, and the subject was not raised again until 1728. This early experience produced less a settlement than a point of contact and a very tenuous one at that. The few who were here, including only three women, or four if we add Asser Levy's wife, seem seldom to have had families. There is no mention of children except for a reference to Abraham de Pisa's son. It is very difficult to make up the names of the twenty-three "big and little" souls described by Solomon Pieterson. There were hardly enough Jews in any given year to have a *minyan,* surely one of the major reasons a synagogue was never built, and, as far as is known, no congregation was permanent until 1730.[30] It is difficult on the basis of any historical evidence to date Sheareth Israel to 1654. That its present congregation does so is more an act of faith than of substance.

In sum, most early Jews, many of whom had been in Brazil, came to the Dutch colony from Holland. They were an extension of the Jewish-Dutch business community. Their interests here were commercial and their stay very contentious. The balance sheet of profits and losses has as yet not been compiled, but it would seem the experience was in general not an economically successful one. Almost nothing is now known of the place of birth of most of them, nor of their place of death, and little is known of what took place in between. We have no physical descriptions except for Ansel Levy's and d'Acosta's age. This small band had travelled from distant regions, including Brazil, Holland, London, and Germany. Asser Levy would seem to have journeyed from Vilna, Poland. An Eastern European connection for others seems evident as well. Perhaps it was Ashkenazic Jews, especially those of the early eighteenth century—Moses Levy, Jacob Franks, and Nathan Simson—who, with

Asser Levy, were chiefly responsible for permanent settlement. These, perhaps, were the principal founding fathers.

Hebrew plays an important part in our knowledge about these few. Asser Levy's signature might prove primary in opening new opportunities for research and in re-evaluating the careers of the early travellers. Both Asser Levys wrote Hebrew. D'Acosta was a translator of Hebrew. Others surely had familiarity with the language, though for Ashkenazis, like Levy Yiddish would be used more commonly.

Finally, if there is a basic conclusion to be drawn it is that there remains a great deal of work to be done not only in the Gemeente Archief but in other Dutch repositories such as those in The Hague. Levy and d'Acosta were at one point or another in Germany, in Hamburg, in Schwelm, maybe Düsseldorf. What were they doing there? Obviously a search of existing German archives should be considered. What records are in Vilna? Is there anything remaining that could identify Judah Leib? Were the various Israels in Amsterdam, including Miriam Levy, from Vilna? Questions are almost endless and surely answers for the most part unobtainable, but not entirely so. This depends on how much effort is made.

The voyage started in 1654 continues today and surely will continue into the future. History is never etched in stone. It is or should be constantly reevaluated and reinterpreted. This is especially true for this early Jewish experience. Its history merits this attention. Asser Levy, Joseph d'Acosta, and their contemporaries deserve no less.

Notes

1. The best translation of this letter is in Samuel Oppenheim, *The Early History of the Jews of New York* (New York, 1909), 73. See also Edward T. Corwin, ed., *Ecclesiastical Records State of New York* (Albany, 1901) 1:334–35. It is possible that Jacob Lucena was in New Amsterdam in 1654 (Joseph R. Rosenbloom, *A Biographical Dictionary of Early American Jews* [University of Kentucky, 1960], 101).

2. Berthold Fernow, ed., *Records of New Amsterdam* (New York, 1897), 1:240 (hereafter *R.N.A.*). Professor Jacob Marcus thinks it probable that there were among the twenty-three "four married males, six adult widowed women and thirteen children of various ages" (Jacob R. Marcus, *The Colonial American Jew 1492–1776* [Detroit, 1970] 1:210).

3. Gemeente Archief Notarial Archives, Amsterdam (hereafter G.A.A.), 2859/1; Arnold Wiznitzer, "The Exodus from Brazil and Arrival in New Amsterdam of the Jewish Pilgraims Fathers, 1654," *Publications of the American Jewish Historical Society* 44 (1954): 90; Oppenheim, 63.

4. Fernow, 240, 249.

5. Jacob R. Marcus, *The Colonial American Jew* (Ft. Wayne, Indiana,

1970) 1:216; Arnold Wiznitzer, *The Record of the Earliest Jewish Community in the New World* (New York, 1954), 42.

6. The seven are Abraham de Lucena, Jacob Cohen Henriquez, Salvador d'Andrada, Joseph d'Acosta, Isaac Israel, David de Ferera, and Benjamin Cardozo. Mevrouw Lucena appeared in a court suit of 1660. She could have been with her husband in 1655. These can be found in congregation rolls (Wiznitzer, 50–52). His theory of the "Jewish Exodus" seems accurate (ibid., 85, R.N.A. 3:174.

7. The names are Elias Silva and Moses de Silva, 1656, Moses de Lucena and Isaac Mesa, 1657; Manuel Roiz Lucena, 1658–59; Joseph Francis, Mevrouw Abraham de Lucena, 1660; Benjamin Buena de Mesquita, 1661; David Machero, 1662; Rabba Couty, 1666; Jacob Lumbrozo, 1670?; Joseph Buena de Mesquita, Asser Levy, David and Simon Valentine Vanderwilde, Jacob Israel, David Abendana, Joshua Servateyn, Asser Michaels in the 1680s. This list is taken from Earl A. Grollman, "Dictionary of American Jewish Biography in the Seventeenth Century," *American Jewish Archives* 3 (1950): 3–10; Rosenbloom, and Samuel Oppenheim, 28. For the Roiz Lucena reference, see G.A.A. 2998/241. For another list of early Jews, see David De Sola Pool, *Old Faith in the New World* (New York, 1955), 468.

8. G.A.A. 3121/619; *New York Marriages Previous to 1784* (Baltimore, 1968), 577; *Levi v. Vanderwilde*, Chancery Papers, 40A-D, American Jewish Historical Society.

9. G.A.A. 1092/100; 2436/1032; 3002/157. In the last reference Abraham Israel is mentioned with several Sephardic Jews in a business transaction.

10. Jonathan Pearson, ed., *Early Records of the City and County of Albany and Colony of Rensselaerswyck* (Albany, 1918), 3:518; 4:11.

11. G.A.A. 2443/761; 1133/144. Thanks are due Dr. Nathan M. Kaganoff for the translation and evaluation of the Hebrew script. For Barsimon, see G.A.A. 2487. See also Leo Hershkowitz, "Another Abigail Frank Letter and a Genealogical Note," *American Jewish Historical Society Quarterly* 59 (1970): 227; see fn. 8, re *Levi v. Vanderwilde*.

12. *R.N.A.* 1:290.

13. *R.N.A.* 1:313. Oppenheim thought d'Andrada, de Ferera, and de Lucena had arrived in New Amsterdam about the end of February, with Joseph d'Acosta and Joseph Cohen Henriquez arriving later (Oppenheim, 52).

14. Oppenheim, 60, 61; *R.N.A.* 2:141–47; 3:57.

15. G.A.A. 1077/592.

16. G.A.A. 15571B/1541.

17. G.A.A. 1112/244; Oppenheim, 56. E. B. O'Callaghan, *Documents Relative to the Colonial History of the State of New York* (Albany, 1849) 1:432, 457.

18. G.A.A. 1113/32; 1116/1321; 1119/79. The lease is dated December 6, 1655, and is signed by d'Acosta and Isaac Israel (Arnold Van Laer, *New York Historical Manuscripts, Dutch* [Baltimore, 1974], 3:437–38).

19. G.A.A. 3109/181. See also *Maandblad van Het Geneologisch-heraldieck genootschap "De Nederlandsche Leeuw"* (s'Gravenhage, Nederlands, 1887), no. 8. It would appear d'Acosta's claim was first filed on February 28, 1663. For d'Acosta's house see Oppenheim, 67.

20. G.A.A. 2:67, 74, 83.

21. Van Laer, 3:438–39; *R.N.A.* 7:154.

22. *R.N.A.* 2:374–75.

23. Ibid., 1:290–91, 306, 313.

24. Ibid., 2:66–67.

25. Ibid., 2:80, 81, 165; 3:174.

26. Ibid., 2:120, 122, 124, 130, 136, 140–41, 145, 147.

27. E. B. O'Callaghan, ed., *Calendar of Historical Manuscripts in the Office of the Secretary of State* (Albany, 1865), 156–57.

28. Ibid., 184.

29. *R.N.A.* 2:76, 90; Oppenheim, 67–68. Interestingly, Jacob Lucena who was in New York and Connecticut around 1670 through 1678 was tried in Hartford for "lascivious dalliance and wanton carriage and proffers to several women." Asser Levy managed to have the fine reduced (Grollman, 9). For the list of Jews taxed, see *R.N.A.* 1:240, 371; and for Manuel Roiz Lucena, see G.A.A. 2998/241. For lists of oath of allegiance and burgers see O'Callaghan, *Documents Relative* 3:74–76; 5:222, 224. If Jacob Lucena is Leunizen, who is Pieter Lurenzen? (Ibid., 1:225). For the 1676 tax list see *Minutes of the Common Counsel of the City of New York* (New York, 1905), 1:29, 34, 36, 37. For de Pisa see *R.N.A.* 5:96; Oppenheim, 63.

30. Nathan Simson kept congregational records for 1720–21, but there is a question as to whether these were of Shearith Israel. Marcus accepts Shearith Israel. (Jacob R. Marcus, *The Colonial American Jew 1492–1776* [Detroit, 1970], 3:1180). The Simson papers of the early eighteenth century, in the Public Record Office, London, are a mine of information about not only his business records but those of other members of the Jewish and non-Jewish community. They contain a large number of letters in Yiddish. The whole collection should be edited and certainly more widely used. For the Asser Levy inventory see Leo Hershkowitz, "Asser Levy and the Inventories of Early New York Jews," *American Jewish Historical Society Quarterly* 80 (1990): 21–55.

Nathan M. Kaganoff

Hebrew and Liturgical Exercises
in the Colonial Period

Conventional wisdom has it that the level of Jewish education, and especially the knowledge and reading of Hebrew among the Jews in colonial America, was very low. Hyman B. Grinstein in his classic study *The Rise of the Jewish Community of New York* states that "except for Gershom Mendes Seixas and a few others, men trained in New York were grossly ignorant even of the pronunciation of Hebrew. . . . The printing of Isaac Pinto's English translation of the Prayer Book in New York in 1761 and 1766 indicates that even at that early date many Jews were unfamiliar in the Hebrew and were obliged, therefore, to use a translation to understand the prayers."[1] I wish here to provide some background and offer a different interpretation for these two very unusual publishing events that occurred in the New York Jewish community in the decade before the Revolutionary War.

In 1761 there appeared in New York City a Jewish prayer book in English translation under the title *Evening Service of Rosh Hashanah and Kippur or the Beginning of the Year and the Day of Atonement.* The printer was W. Weyman of Broad Street, New York. The name of the translator is nowhere given and to this date there is no documented proof of who he was—although there is consensus among almost all historians about his identity.[2] This 1761 publication is the first appearance anywhere of a published translation of any portion of the Jewish liturgy into English for use in the synagogue. The question has been raised—why should such a volume have appeared in New York, which contained a Jewish community numbering in the hundreds, rather than in London, which had some ten thousand Jews?

The latest statement on the subject is that of Abraham J. Karp in his 1975 publication *Beginnings: Early American Judaica.* His reasoning follows that of Grinstein and points to the ignorance of Hebrew of the New York Jewish community. To quote, "London Jewry at this time had no pressing need for an English translation of the Hebrew prayer book and, therefore, none was forthcoming. Because of its size, the London community was able to support schools whose function was to prepare the young for worship in Hebrew. However, in the Colonies a different situation prevailed . . . clearly, here was another instance of necessity dictating innovative procedure. . . ."[3]

In 1766, five years after the publication of the first prayer book, a second volume of English translation appeared in New York, under the title *Prayers for Shabbat, Rosh-hashanah and Kippur*. This time the translator's name is given—Isaac Pinto—with an introduction explaining the reason for its publication.[4] Almost all scholars identify the anonymous translator of the 1761 edition as also being Isaac Pinto.[5] Why should he have withheld his name in 1761 and identified himself in 1766? Many theories have been suggested to explain this but, whatever the reason, there is little doubt that Isaac Pinto was the translator of both. Each translation is of a fairly high calibre and it would seem somewhat difficult to imagine that the minuscule Jewish community of New York contained two such Hebraic scholars. The publication of these two translations has been used as the main source for the statement that colonial Jewry was ignorant of Hebrew. It will be demonstrated here that this may be a faulty conclusion.

A good part of Jewish ritual observance involves the use of Hebrew. As far as we know all the Jews in colonial America, certainly those in the large cities, and probably even those in isolated areas, for the most part identified as Jews. How did they participate in the various practices of Jewish life? What does this tell us about their knowledge of Hebrew?

Jacob R. Marcus has published a very detailed three-volume study, *The Colonial American Jew*, which documents and describes every aspect of American Jewish life in the seventeenth and eighteenth centuries. Marcus sums it up as follows:

The fate and development of "Jewishness" on American soil cannot be grasped unless one has some notion of the nature and scope of Jewish culture as it was then known and cultivated in Europe. Jewish culture meant . . . a knowledge of the Jewish way of life and thought, a familiarity with Jewish worship, with the ritual, observances, practices and holidays of Judaism . . . it involved the knowledge of the Hebrew and Aramaic languages. It would seem that the typical Colonial Jew could at least read Hebrew, and quite a number appeared to have been capable of translating many parts of the Prayerbook and the Pentateuch. The professional functionaries and a limited number of laymen could consult the standard legal works in rabbinic Hebrew and an exceptional few were genuinely at home in Hebrew sources.[6]

Marcus's assessment can be easily verified by the extant documents or other primary sources that have survived for this 150-year period of American history. It should be remembered that there was only one Jewish denomination in existence at this time—what is today labeled Orthodoxy. Reform had not yet made an appearance. This does not mean that every Jew in colonial America was the seventeenth-century equivalent of a twentieth-century Satmarer hasid of Williamsburg or Borough Park, Brooklyn. Many, indeed, wandered from the path of true observance, as there was no communal pressure to conform. But these are Jews who nonetheless wanted to participate in Jewish life and in those matters that require the use of Hebrew, and there is more than enough proof that they could fully participate, though at what level of practice or observance is not clear.

Of course the most pervasive Jewish observance requiring a knowledge of Hebrew is that of prayer—whether on a daily basis or on the Sabbath, Holy Days, or special occasions. Enough copies of prayer books for every possible religious occasion have survived from colonial American Jews to indicate that almost everyone had some prayer book in his possession. Presumably they could also read well enough the Hebrew it contained, though in many instances they may have understood very little of its contents.

Of the various religious observances or rites of passage, a number would also require some ability to write and read Hebrew. Since in these instances, unlike the prayer book, the event was highly personal, there would be a need for a greater knowledge of Hebrew than mere recitation. These would include the bar mitzvah ceremony, weddings, divorces, and the decisions or actions of rabbinic courts. There are also some ceremonies and religious practices (for instance, tombstone inscription) which, while not requiring the use of Hebrew, often employ it nonetheless, and these can help to reveal how much Hebrew the colonial Jew actually possessed.

Circumcision, even though it requires recitation of Hebrew blessings to accompany the ceremony, is not included here because every Jewish community in colonial America had within its group a competent mohel (circumcizer) and whatever Hebrew was needed was provided by the mohel himself. Rarely did a Jewish child have to wait longer than the ritually required eighth day to be introduced into the "Covenant of Abraham." In the small towns, however, individuals had to wait the arrival of a mohel, and there are several instances of some children not being ritually initiated until their fifth or eighth year of age.

Oddly enough, although there were certainly a substantial number of young boys who would have become bar mitzvah at the traditional age of thirteen, there are no recorded descriptions of the preparation a boy would have made to learn the Pentateuchal or prophetic portion he must read in the synagogue service on his bar mitzvah Sabbath. Nor is there any text of an address delivered by a bar mitzvah boy until well into the nineteenth century. Considering what bar mitzvah celebrations have developed into in contemporary American Jewish life, it seems almost beyond belief that the observance of the ceremony cannot be dated to the very founding of the American Jewish community.[7]

A large number of marriages took place in colonial America. The wedding ceremony requires the preparation of a marriage contract (ketubah) written in Aramaic in which the bridegroom obligates himself to provide support for his wife in the event of divorce or his demise. The ketubah at this period was almost always handwritten and it required the ability not only to write the prescribed Aramaic text but to adapt it to the circumstances at hand—the names of the bride and groom, the place and date, supplementary obligations made by the groom and, if a dowry was brought by the wife, in what manner it should be disposed of when the marriage ended. The Sephardic custom is for the groom also to sign the ketubah in addition to the two witnesses and the officiating clergyman. Many such ketubot have survived and in all instances seem to have been competently prepared. Mr. Joseph Jesurun Pinto, the hazzan of Shearith Israel in New York and no relation to our translator, Isaac Pinto, apparently had a blank ketubah prepared for him in Europe prior to his arrival in the New World in the 1750s, which he used for guidance in writing the ketubot he prepared.[8]

Although many of the grooms were Ashkenazy, the Sephardic custom prevailed in America and provides us with quite a bit of information about the level of Hebrew knowledge of some very prominent colonial figures. Some signed the ketubah in English. Haym Salomon's signature on his ketubah—the only extant Hebrew version of his name—is very stilted and forced, and looks as if it were written by a child.[9]

As noted before, what is at issue here is the ability to read or write Hebrew, and not textual understanding or religious observance. We have extant the record book of Reverend Jacob Raphael Cohen, who served as hazzan of Congregation Mikveh Israel in Philadelphia and of Shearith Israel in New York. Among other things that it contains are meticulously listed records of circumcisions, marriages, and deaths covering the period 1776 to 1812. Among the marriages recorded is that of Manuel Noah with Zipporah Phillips, daughter of the Philadelphia merchant Jonas Phillips. Zipporah and Manuel later became the parents of the very prominent nineteenth-century American Jew Mordecai Manuel Noah. The ketubah records a dowry of £1000 sterling, by far the largest of any dowry in the record book.[10] Manuel, who seems to have been somewhat of a "schlimazel," a person plagued by bad luck, entered the world of business and went bankrupt a year after his marriage. Deeply in debt, he left home. Zipporah, his stranded wife, apparently could not endure the strain and died in 1792 at age 28.[11] It is not our job to look for any skeletons in the Noah or Phillips closets. Mordecai Manuel Noah, the son, has recently been the subject of a doctoral dissertation at Yale, a full-scale biography, and many articles. According to the record book of Reverend Cohen, one of the witnesses on the ketubah for his parents' marriage was Jonas Phillips, the bride's father, which would have made the marriage invalid according to Jewish law.[12]

Turning to the matter of divorce, no bills of divorce (gittin) seem to have survived from colonial times even though we know that several took place. It would be fascinating to see one, since the laws involving divorce are much more complex than those pertaining to marriage, and the preparation of a bill of divorce (get) requires both a rabbinic court and a broader knowledge of Jewish law.

We know of at least one instance of the establishment of a rabbinic court of arbitration, set up by Haym Salomon to settle an estate in 1784. Detailed accounts of the proceedings are found in a letter preserved at the Jewish Theological Seminary in New York. The letter is signed by Haym Salomon but was written by a Joseph Carpeles of Prague, who had recently arrived in the United States. The letter reveals an intimate knowledge of rabbinic Hebrew although it does contain an occasional spelling error. It seems that there were enough resident or visiting Jewish scholars in the larger cities to provide all services that involved the use of the Hebrew language.[13]

The one other source mentioned earlier that would shed light on the Hebrew erudition of colonial American Jews is the inscriptions placed on tombstones. The number of extant tombstones utilizing Hebrew is very impressive. One may of course argue that many of the Hebrew phrases are traditional and are repeatedly used; still, in all the colonial Jewish cemeteries there are several original inscriptions that reflect the writer's intimate acquaintance with Hebrew. One may still argue that these inscriptions may have been composed many years later after the death of the decedent or may have been prepared in Europe so that we cannot actually deduce the Hebrew competency of the period. But the fact that most eighteenth century tombstones contain some Hebrew reflects at the very least some emotional attachment to the language.[14]

Another method that can be utilized to provide us with information on the Hebrew competence of individuals during the colonial time is an examination of the Hebrew signatures when such have survived. Within the past year, two such signatures have been discovered. One is that of Asser Levy, the prominent seventeenth-century New York Jew. Dr. Leo Hershkowitz discovered the signature in Amsterdam, written by an individual with a very sophisticated exposure to Hebrew. The other recently discovered Hebrew signature, together with an extensive citation, is that of Aaron Levy, the eighteenth-century Philadelphian and western Pennsylvania land speculator for whom Aaronsburgh, Pennsylvania, is named. Aaron Levy had the habit of placing the Hebrew letters *aleph* and *lamed* in the loop under his name, but until recently we were only acquainted with his English signature. The American Jewish Historical Society has recently acquired a volume that Aaron Levy owned in which there is a Hebrew inscription indicating that he originated in Lissa or Lezno, Poland, not Amsterdam as has been previously thought, and his writing is also of a highly sophisticated nature.[15]

In conclusion, it is possible to offer what seems a more accurate interpretation of the circumstances surrounding the two volumes of liturgical translation that appeared in New York in 1761 and 1766. First of all, there seems little doubt that both volumes were written by the same individual. But in the arguments presented by other historians, no one has noted the following: The first volume contains a translation of the evening prayers only. The second volume contains the translation of all prayers recited on weekdays and the Sabbath and all Holy Days but for the daytime services only. The evening service is completely ignored. It seems obvious that the two volumes were meant to be utilized together.

Second, on page twenty of the 1766 volume, there is an interesting footnote provided by Pinto in his translation of "Hannoten," the Prayer for the King, which reads as follows: "In the Colonies, after the king and royal family, the governor and magistrates are added."[16] This would indicate that the volume was not only intended for American Jews but for English-speaking Jews throughout the world. Pinto may only have been testing the market in 1761. There was no English translation of a prayer book as yet available. That the first English translation appeared in New York, rather than in London, may only have been a coincidence because Pinto happened to be in New York. He was a Jewish scholar, "well versed in several of the foreign languages."[17]

The fact that an English translation was made does not necessarily reflect on the level of Hebrew education of the community. We live today at a time when knowledge of Hebrew is probably greater among Jews than it has been for two millennia. Hebrew has been revived as a living language and a large number of American Jews have intimate contact with Israel. And yet, the phenomenal success of the numerous Art Scroll editions of the various Jewish prayer books with English translations reveals a situation that might not have changed in over two hundred years. Ability to read Hebrew and knowledge of the language are not the same. When Isaac Pinto prepared his English translation, there were already available Spanish and Yiddish translations. Pinto may have sensed that the growing number of Jewish communities in the British colonies in the West Indies, in Great Britain itself, and in North America would provide a market for an English translation as well.[18]

Notes

1. Hyman B. Grinstein, *The Rise of the Jewish Community of New York, 1654–1860* (Philadelphia, 1945), 226.

2. A. S. W. Rosenbach, *An American Jewish Bibliography* (Baltimore, 1926), no. 41; Abraham J. Karp, *Beginnings: Early American Judaica* (Philadelphia, 1975), 5–6.

3. Ibid., 4.

4. Rosenbach, no. 46.

5. Karp, 5; Jacob R. Marcus, *The Colonial American Jew* (Detroit, 1970), 968–69.

6. Marcus, 1069.

7. Ibid., 988–89; the first recorded and published bar mitzvah address is that of Jacob Appel delivered in Baltimore, December 17, 1864.

8. Marcus, 991.

9. Haym Salomon Papers (P-41), American Jewish Historical Society Library.

10. Alan D. Corré and Malcolm H. Stern, "The Record Book of the Reverend Jacob Raphael Cohen," in *American Jewish Historical Quarterly* 59 (September 1969): 44.

11. Jonathan D. Sarna, *Jacksonian Jew* (New York, 1981), 2.

12. Corré and Stern, 44.

13. Hyman B. Grinstein, "A Haym Salomon Letter to Rabbi David Tevele Schiff, London, 1784," in *Publications of the American Jewish Historical Society* 34 (1937): 107–16.

14. Marcus, 1078–80.

15. *American Jewish History* 79 (Summer 1990).

16. *Prayers for Shabbath, Rosh-Hashanah and Kippur . . .* (New York, 1766), 20.

17. Karp, 8–9.

18. Ibid., 4.

Jacob Kabakoff

The Use of Hebrew by American Jews During the Colonial Period

Because of their limited numbers and their preoccupation with the problems of adjustment and acculturation, American Jews could but pay scant attention to cultural endeavor during the colonial period. It is not until the East European immigration that we witness the development of an American Hebrew press and literature. American Jews had practically no connection with the development of Hebrew study in the colleges during the colonial period. The use of Hebrew was confined mainly to religious purposes and we have but rare examples of its employment for secular purposes.

From the few Hebrew documents of the early period that have come down to us, the lack of acquaintance of the Sephardic Jews with Hebrew is more than apparent. Isaac Rivkind in his study entitled "Early American Hebrew documents" was led to reflect sadly: "It took fully 200 years from the arrival of the Jews in North America before the pangs of Hebraic culture produced a Hebrew book in the full sense of the term."[1] He had in mind, of course, the first scholarly Hebrew book printed in America, *Avnei Yehoshua*, by Rabbi Joshua Falk, which was published in New York in 1860. In the introduction to his book, which is a commentary on the ethics of the Fathers, Rabbi Falk recounted his difficulties in getting it published.

Among the early American Hebrew documents that Rivkind described were a New York Tosephet Ketubah (supplementary marriage document) of 1718, which was termed perhaps the first extant American document in Hebrew; a receipt for a Torah scroll sent from Congregation Shearith Israel to the Jews of Reading, Pennsylvania, which is dated 1761; and a Shehitah certificate issued in 1782 to Solomon Etting in Lancaster and signed by Bernard Gratz and Aaron Levy, of Philadelphia.

Hebrew was used not only as the language of prayer and of religious documents, such as ketubot and gittin, but also of tombstone inscriptions. Such inscriptions are found in the Jewish cemeteries of New York, Newport, and Charleston. In his volume *Portraits Etched in Stone: Early Jewish Settlers 1682–1831*,[2] David de Sola Pool reproduced the inscriptions on the tombstones of the members of Congregation Shearith Israel. Hebrew was used on almost all the stones. In the case of Samuel Levy, who died in 1719, there is a double acrostic based on his name Shmuel Zanvil. The Hebrew inscription for Miriam Lopez de Fonseca, who died in 1732, invokes the memory of Miriam the prophetess. Isaac Adolphus, who died in 1774, is the subject of another acrostic based on his name Avraham Yitzhak. Isaac Pinto, who was a good Hebraist and the translator of prayer books, is called *ha-ish ha-gadol be-doro*, a man great in his generation.

A further example of the use of Hebrew verse for religious purposes is the tombstone of the Reverend Moses Cohen, who died in Charleston, South Carolina, on April 19, 1762. At the request of Professor Jacob R. Marcus, I had occasion to deal with the laudatory verses inscribed on this tombstone.[3] Apparently, Reverend Cohen, who had come from London to Charleston, where he made a living as a shopkeeper, also served Charleston's first Jewish congregation, founded in 1749, as its first "rabbi" on a volunteer basis.

At the top of the tombstone appears an elaborate carving of two hands outstretched in priestly benediction, indicating the priestly descent of the deceased. Above the carving are the Hebrew words *keter kehunah*, or priestly crown. The Hebrew inscription characterizes Moses Cohen as an "accomplished scholar" and "an eminent man of riches." The first line of the verses begins with the Hebrew name *Moshe* and the initials of *ha-kohen* appear as an acrostic in the following lines. The Hebrew verses are rendered also in English. It is to be noted that the stonecutter was obviously not well versed in Hebrew. In one place he substituted a *kaf* for a *beth*; in another, he used a *resh* instead of a *daleth*. He omitted letters from two words, as in the case of the name of the angel Michael which appears without an *aleph*.

There are a number of examples of original Hebrew prayers which were composed to mark special occasions and events. Jacob Marcus has noted the Hebrew prayer composed in Newport by Hazzan Isaac Touro for Thanksgiving Day in 1765.[4] On that occasion Newport Jews assembled in their synagogue to listen to this prayer, which was then published in translation in the *Newport Mercury*.

Another example was the *Form of Prayer* composed by Joseph Jessurun Pinto, a leader of Congregation Shearith Israel from 1759–66, as a "General Thanksgiving for the Reducing of Canada to His Majesty's Dominions" on October 23, 1760. The English translation, which appeared the same year, contains the note: "N.B. The foregoing prayer may be seen in Hebrew, at the Composer's Lodgings," indicating, as George A. Kohut has pointed out, that "apparently Hebrew scholarship was a curiosity in New York City in 1760."[5]

A Hebrew prayer written for the inauguration of George Washington in 1789 in which the name of Washington appears as an acrostic is found at the National Museum of American Jewish History. It has been reproduced in Maxwell Whiteman's pamphlet *American Jewish Life and the Constitution*.[6] The prayer invokes God's blessing not only on Washington but also on the vice president, the senators, and the representatives of the United States. It ends with a prayer for the security of Judah and Israel and the redemption of Zion.

An outstanding example of an original Hebrew prayer composed for synagogue use in 1784 is the one that was published by Raphael Mahler from the Shearith Israel documents in the Lyons Collection.[7] The author of this prayer, which was offered following the American Revolution and the reconstitution of the Jewish community of New York, was Rabbi Hendel Johanon Von Oettingen, a Dutch Jew of German extraction. It expresses thanksgiving for peace and singles out Governor Clinton and General Washington for special approbation. It vouchsafes unto them the blessings of the kings and heroes of Israel and concludes with the hope for Jewish redemption and the restoration of Zion. The prayer is interesting for both its content and its style and is marred only by a few slight errors.

While Hebrew remained the language of prayer, the need soon became evident for an English translation of the Siddur. In 1761 there appeared an English version of the Sephardic ritual for the evening services of the High Holy Days, which is attributed to Isaac Pinto. Five years later Pinto issued a complementary volume containing a translation of the morning and afternoon services for Sabbath, Rosh Hashanah, and Yom Kippur. Apparently Pinto was moved to undertake his translation because he felt the prayers were not being understood. In his preface he professed a high regard for the Hebrew language and expressed the conviction that "it will again be reestablished in Israel." At the same time he added that it "Being imperfectly understood by many, by some, not at all, it has been necessary to translate our prayers in the language of the Country wherein it hath pleased the divine Providence to appoint our Lot."

It appears, then, that the greater majority of the worshippers at this time were not well versed in Hebrew and that men like Isaac Pinto were the exception. Thus, when the wealthy Isaac Hart of Newport received a Hebrew letter from Hebron he had to ask Ezra Stiles, the Christian Hebraist, to translate it for him. Or when Haym Salomon was led to address a Hebrew letter to Rabbi David Tevele Schiff of London in 1784 concerning a certain inheritance, he asked Joseph, the son of Wolf Karpeles of Prague, to write it for him.[8]

There are but few instances of the use of Hebrew by Jews for secular purposes. It appears that a Hebrew diary was kept by Benjamin Sheftall, who settled in Savannah, Georgia, in 1733. Originally from Bavaria, Sheftall arrived with a group of Portuguese Jews and his diary of events contains important data on the history of the Jews in the southern colonies. That he translated his diary into English at the request of his son Levi is sufficient indication that the family did not continue the chain of Hebrew knowledge. Extracts from this diary were first published in the *Occident* by Mordecai Sheftall, Benjamin's grandson.[9]

The outstanding example of the secular use of Hebrew was Sampson Simson's Hebrew oration delivered on June 21, 1800, when he graduated from Columbia College. The Hebrew text of the oration was published by Isidore S. Meyers in two separate versions. The first version[10] contains an introductory note by Gershom Mendes Seixas indicating that he was asked to compose a Hebrew oration for Simson, who had studied Hebrew at Columbia and was its first Jewish graduate. The second version, entitled "Some Historical Traits of the Jews from Their First Settlement in North America,"[11] contains a brief overview of the Jewish experience in America and closes with a prayer for the government. Written in square characters, it has some errors in grammar and punctuation.

The American-born Seixas, who was elected hazzan of Shearith Israel in 1768 at the age of 22, had no formal Hebrew training. Yet he achieved some facility in Hebrew and was asked to compose Hebrew tombstone inscriptions. The Lyons Papers contain Hebrew verses written in honor of his second marriage (November 1, 1786), which incorporate acrostics of the names of the bridegroom Gershom and his bride Hannah. These verses have been published both by Isaac Rivkind[12] and Jonathan Sarna.[13]

There is also a record of a Hebrew correspondence with the Jews of Cochin, India. Solomon Simson, father of Sampson Simson, had commercial relations with the Orient. In 1787, he received a Hebrew letter from leaders of the Jewish community of Cochin and was in communication with them. Some years later, in 1794, he endeavored, together with Alexander Hirsch, to contact the Jews of China. It is thought that their Hebrew letter was written by Hirsch.[14] Hebrew served also as a bond between American Jews and Palestine as a result of the repeated visits of *meshulahim* or emissaries from the Holy Land. The most important of these emissaries was Rabbi Haim Isaac Carigal, who was in touch with Ezra Stiles. Rabbi Carigal showed him the letter he received from Isaac Pinto, the translator of the prayer book, who had asked him about some Arabic words in the biblical commentary of Abraham Ibn Ezra.[15]

The educational goals of the early American Jews were minimal. They sought to transmit to their children the rudiments of Jewish knowledge, including the mechanical reading of Hebrew, bar mitzvah preparation, and some knowledge of the Humash in translation. At Congregation Shearith Israel private teachers were employed at first and some had to be brought from Jamaica or England. There is, for example, a record of Benjamin Elias, a shohet who had served as a Hebrew teacher at the congregation prior to 1728, when he was pensioned. Various functionaries, who served in the position of hazzan, engaged also in Hebrew teaching as part of their duties.

In 1731 Shearith Israel established the first Hebrew school with its own building under the name Yeshibat Minchat Arav. Its curriculum was limited to the study of Hebrew, which was pursued for three or more hours daily. By 1755, secular subjects, including Spanish, English reading, and mathematics, were introduced. The school lasted until the time of the Revolution, when the Jews of New York left the city.

Ezra Stiles, who recorded in his diary his impressions of his visits to the Newport synagogue, described two occasions when youngsters participated in the services, indicating that they had attained fluency in Hebrew reading. In his entry of January 12, 1770, he reported that he had heard the son of the deceased Moses Lopez lead the evening service in the presence of Hazzan Isaac Touro. Since that date fell on a Friday, we may assume that he led the Kabbalat Shabbat service. Stiles' entry for May 28, 1773, which fell on Shavuot, records that he had heard Jacob Rodrigues Rivera's young son, who was eight or nine years of age, read the first chapter of Ezekiel, the haftarah for the holiday. These references indicate that the Hebrew schooling of the children of the members of the Newport congregation enabled them to acquire synagogue skills.

In his comprehensive history of colonial Jewry Jacob Marcus has assiduously collected the available data about the sprinkling of learned men who had Hebrew knowledge. Among them were some who owned Hebrew books and some who had contacts with non-Jews who were interested in Hebrew learning. The most learned Jew was Manuel Josephson, who died in 1796. Josephson is said to have owned the best library of rabbinic texts in colonial times and was well versed in rabbinic Hebrew.[16] He sat together with Joseph Simson and Jacob Franks as a member of the Shearith Israel congregational bet din. All three men were of German origin. With the coming of increased numbers of German Jews who joined Shearith Israel, the minutes of the congregation contain more Hebrew phrases and usages, some of which are not without error. Joseph Simson was considered an excellent Hebraist and is reported to have had a fine manuscript of the Bible. Stiles relates that he called on him because of his reputation as a scholar.

As indicated, colonial American Jews, with few exceptions, had but a meagre knowledge of Hebrew. Still they clung to it as the language of prayer and religious instruction, demonstrating thereby that the Hebrew language was a necessary instrument for maintaining their identity. That Jewish leaders were concerned with the role of the Hebrew during the coming decades is clear from Mordecai Manuel Noah's admonition in his discourse delivered at the consecration of the Mill Street building of Shearith Israel in 1818. In that discourse he declared that "with the loss of the Hebrew language may be added the downfall of the house of Israel." Fortunately, by the 1840s and 50s the field gradually opened up for religious functionaries who came here for the most part from Germany and brought with them Hebrew knowledge. It was due to the efforts of these pioneer spiritual leaders that the vineyard of Hebrew was not left entirely unattended and that the foundations were laid for future development.

Notes

1. *Publications of the American Jewish Historical Society* (hereafter *PAJHS*), 34 (1935): 53.

2. David de Sola Pool, *Portraits Etched in Stone: Early Jewish Settlers 1682–1831* (New York: Columbia University Press, 1952).

3. See my "The Tombstone of the Reverend Moses Cohen," *American Jewish Archives* 27 (April 1965): 77–79.

4. *The Colonial American Jew 1492–1776* (Detroit: Wayne State University Press, 1970), 2:973.

5. "Early Jewish Literature in America," *PAJHS* 3 (1895): 122.

6. Philadelphia: Congregation Mikveh Israel and the National Museum of American Jewish History, 1987, 4.

7. "American Jewry and the Idea of the Return to Zion in the Period of the American Revolution" (in Hebrew), *Zion* 25 (1950): 122–24.

8. Hyman B. Grinstein, "A Haym Salomon Letter to Rabbi David Tevele Schiff, London, 1784," *PAJHS* 34 (1937): 107–11.

9. "Early Settlement of the Israelites in Savannah," *The Occident* 1 (November 1843).

10. "Sampson Simson's Hebrew Oration, 1800," *PAJHS* 37 (1947): 430–31.

11. *PAJHS* 46 (1956): 51–58. The text has been published in S. Goldman, "Two American Hebrew Orations, 1799 and 1800," *Hebrew Annual Review* 13 (1991).

12. "The Correct Date of Gershom Mendes Seixas' Second Marriage," *PAJHS* 35 (1939): 309–10.

13. "Early American Hebrew Poetry," *American Jewish History* 69 (March 1980): 389.

14. Hyman B. Grinstein, *The Rise of the Jewish Community of New York 1654–1860* (Philadelphia: The Jewish Publication Society, 1945), 416–18.

15. Pool, *Portraits Etched in Stone*, biography of Isaac Pinto, 261.

16. It is noteworthy that while Josephson specified in his will that his books in Western languages be sold at auction, he asked that his Hebrew books be sent back to his brother in Germany, indicating thereby that he did not have much hope for the future of rabbinic learning in America. See Jacob R. Marcus, *The Colonial American Jew: 1492–1776* (Detroit: Wayne State University Press, 1970), 2:1076; Arthur Hertzberg, *The Jews in America: Four Centuries of an Uneasy Encounter* (New York: Simon and Schuster, 1989), 53.

Five

Colonial American
Hebraists

תעשה את משפט:
יכון כל חכם את עלילותיו בקו נכון ישר
יחפצו הנבלים הלוך בארחות נדרות אומרם
כי דרך בהן: יאמר כל אמש עשה את
משפט אם לא נתן הוא את ההבנית:
ומי נאז הכון חועה בלב מחקדשה כו
יאוהה קוב נבליות בשכויי אשר חועה:
לכן לא יחזה בה ימראוחו בה ימיהחהפכ
מיאונו: אבל לעשיותנו את משפט
נתנגאה בטעם יבדע יצלפנו את
חשבונינו ואת המגנוחינו ושטמנו
את משאון: האמיז או לאל האמיז את
כל נאמר הואל רע: עשה לאחרים כמו
תצבא לעשותם לך, הלזו חק הלזו
משפט כל עליות אשר מאשיר את חבר:
יהן עם עדי עד את דברה, אבל הולכים
רבים על את אפיהם הרבה מן בינוח
יהם, ומולדים המיאויי חיוה על כל מחים
במעשיהם הרבה מן מולך רעם עליהם:
סוף דבר הכל נשמע. אה האלהים ירא
ואת מצוחיו שמור כי זה כל האדם:

Dartmouth, July 16th 1794. Jacob Patch

The Dartmouth Hebrew Oration of Jacob Patch (July 16, 1799).

Shalom Goldman

Biblical Hebrew in Colonial America: The Case of Dartmouth

That the Puritans were avid students of the Hebrew language has long been recognized and documented.[1] Their interest in "that most ancient language and Holy tongue in which the Law and Oracles of God were write"[2] led to the inclusion of Hebrew in the curricula of the early American colleges. The curricula of the ten schools founded before the American Revolution were centered on mastering theological treatises, the art of rhetoric, and the learned languages. These last included Greek, Latin, and often Hebrew and Aramaic.[3] Dartmouth, founded in the decade before the Revolution, gave Hebrew a special place of prominence. This was evident in the structure of the curriculum, the appointment of faculty, and the acquisition of Hebraica for the college library.

At Harvard, where the first two presidents were scholars of Hebrew, all freshmen had to study the language.[4] As early as 1653, the students complained about this requirement. Michael Wigglesworth, author of *Day of Doom* and a figure who has been described as "the embodiment of repulsive joylessness,"[5] was the instructor in Hebrew. He wrote in his diary in 1653: "Aug. 29. My pupils all came to me this day to desire they might cease learning Hebrew: I withstood it with all the reason I could, yet all will not satisfy them. Thus I am requited for love; and thus little fruit of all my prayers and tears for their good." A little later he is heard contemplating resignation, in part because of "my pupils froward [sic] negligence in the Hebrew."[6]

Judah Monis, a converted Jew, taught Hebrew at Harvard from 1722–61.[7] His Jewish origins are variously described as Italian, Algerian, or Moroccan. In an extended essay G. F. Moore made a strong case for Monis being a member of a "Portuguese Marano family which had emigrated from the Peninsula (and settled in Italy) in the sixteenth Century." His conversion to Christianity, on the urgings of his teachers, has been often described. His career as both student and instructor at Harvard was not a distinguished one—his students often complained about the quality of his teaching. Monis's *A Grammar of The Hebrew Tongue* (Boston, 1735), the first to be published in the colonies, was riddled with inaccuracies and inconsistencies.[8]

Monis's grammar was used at a number of New England colleges, including Dartmouth, but because of its faults it was eventually replaced by Israel Lyons's *The Scholar's Instructor: or Hebrew Grammar*. Lyons was an English Hebraist who taught at Cambridge University and his grammar was both more accurate and more practical than its predecessor: "The method of this grammar is simpler, and was probably introduced because of its greater practical utility."[9]

Yale, founded in 1701, offered Hebrew in its early years. The founders of the Collegiate School, from which Yale developed, stated that students would spend their first year in "practice of tongues," especially Hebrew. Yale was later to become a center of interest in Hebrew under its president Ezra Stiles, who assumed leadership of the college in 1777. Stiles's study of the language deepened to include readings in rabbinic and kabbalistic literature; these endeavors led to his establishing friendships with six European and Palestinian rabbis.[10]

A number of Yale graduates founded Dartmouth in 1769. The college evolved from the Moor school for American Indians in Lebanon, Connecticut. Founded by Eleazar Wheelock, a Yale graduate and one of the itinerant preachers of the Great Awakening of the 1740s, the school's stated purpose was the education and conversion of the Indians.[11] Wheelock's most promising pupil, Samson Occom of New York's Mohegan tribe, was a diligent student of Hebrew. Occom methodically worked his way through Monis's *Grammar* and went on to read biblical texts in Hebrew and Aramaic.

No doubt inspired by the millenarian concerns of the Great Awakening, Occom struggled to find an American interpretation of the prophecies of Daniel chapter 8—a text which has provided material for centuries of eschatological speculation.[12] On the pages bound in the back of his copy of Monis's *Grammar*, Occom jotted down "Some new thoughts as to Prophetic Numbers." Writing in 1767, he predicted that the Second Coming would occur in 1843. These scriptural citations, along with the numerical calculations by which he arrived at that date, cover three closely written pages, now preserved in the Dartmouth Library Special Collections.

In the early 1760s Wheelock sent Occom to England, hoping to impress his English colleagues with his success with the Indian tribes. "An Indian minister in England might get a bundle of money for the school," wrote Wheelock in his journal. During his two-and-a-half year sojourn, Occom preached between three and four hundred sermons—displaying his erudition in matters biblical, including Hebrew grammar and syntax. While in London, Occom acquired some Hebraica—a Hebrew Bible printed in Amsterdam, with a lexicon and concordance (these items remain in the college's original library collection). A portrait of Occom, painted during his sojourn in London, shows him reading a large Bible.[13]

The considerable sum of money raised on Occom's trip—a total of £11,000—enabled Wheelock to purchase the land and found the college. In 1769 Dartmouth was established at Hanover, New Hampshire. Its founders no longer stated as their aim the education and conversion of the Indians; rather they reviewed the new institution as "primarily a college for those who would go out among the Indians as roving missionaries."[14]

The curriculum was modelled on that of Yale; and "here too Hebrew was obligatory for all students for a long time."[15] The school day began and ended with readings from the Bible. Amused, we read that "the college assembled in the chapel at five, or in the winter, as early as the President could see to read the Bible."[16]

Dartmouth's first group of students was joined in its third year by John Smith of Byfield, Massachusetts. A brilliant student of Greek and Latin, Smith was preparing for Yale at the Dummer Academy, but was persuaded to join the first Dartmouth class as a junior. During his first year he advanced quickly in the study of Hebrew and Aramaic (the "Chaldee" of the Puritans). We are told that Smith "was so proficient in Hebrew that he read through the Hebrew Bible, and most of it twice, during his junior year."[17]

As a senior, he began to write grammars for both biblical languages. The manuscripts of these works found in the Dartmouth Special Collections demonstrate Smith's remarkable ability to organize and classify the linguistic material. Neither the manuscripts nor the final publication (which was not to appear until thirty years later, in 1803) presents the system of Hebrew vowels. The work is titled *A Hebrew Grammar Without Points*—hearkening back to the arguments that raged among Christian Hebraists as to the antiquity and utility of the vowel points. More than a century earlier Cotton Mather (at age eighteen) defended the proposition that the Hebrew vowel points were of divine origin: "Puncta Hebraica sunt originis divinae." To buttress his opposition to the teaching of the vowels, Smith closes his Hebrew grammar with a long quote on the topic from the Englishman Charles Wilson's *Elements of Hebrew Grammar* (London, 1782):

This method of using marks for vowels was adopted by a few of Jewish critics, called Masorityes, who flourished after the commencement of the Christian era.

These men bestowed much pains upon the text of the Old Testament, particularly that portion of it which was named the law. Their labor indeed did not penetrate very deep. They afford us little or no assistance in the investigation of the sense of the scriptures.[18]

This quote speaks to an attitude toward the Masoretes that was prevalent among the Puritans. As George Foot Moore noted more than a century ago, "The bigger the ignorance of these gentlemen, the more they looked down their noses at anything *masoretic.*"[19]

Smith was appointed a tutor upon graduation, but shortly afterwards he moved to West Hartford, Connecticut to become the local pastor. In 1777 he was called back to Dartmouth and appointed "Professor of English, Latin, Greek, Hebrew, and Chaldee." In addition, he regularly gave the sermons at the local Congregational church. Classroom instruction consisted of translation exercises; students would have to "turn-out" passages from one learned language to another. Professor Smith's efforts did not gain him popularity. There were complaints about both his teaching and his preaching. A colleague, remembering him in a history of Dartmouth that was compiled in the 1850s, said of him: "Professor Smith was an amiable man, but of formal manners, a critical book scholar, but an artificial teacher. He preached with little animation or force in his composition or delivery."[20] A more succinct and biting comment came from one of Smith's students, Judah Dana (class of 1795). "He was the best linguist in New England but did not know beans about anything else."[21]

The grammar that Smith wrote as a student was printed in Boston in 1803. The expense was considerable, as Hebrew type was rare and difficult to set. Unfortunately, the Aramaic section was left out, probably because of the added expense that its printing would have entailed. The work differed considerably from Judah Monis's book. Its grammatical sections were more accurate, as was its system of transliteration (though it was far from perfect). Too, it did not contain any translations of Christian texts (Monis's grammar closed with Hebrew translations of the Lord's Prayer and the Nicene Creed). College records show that Dartmouth's original order for one hundred copies had to be scaled down because of unexpected expense. The printer's estimate of forty cents per copy rose to seventy-five cents by the time of publication. Only sixty copies were purchased.[22]

During Smith's tenure, seven of the college's commencement speeches were given in Hebrew. This was in addition to the regularly delivered orations in Greek and Latin. No doubt all of these were composed under Smith's supervision. One hopes that Smith's students' speeches were received in more kindly fashion than were his own, which were characterized by a contemporary as "ponderous and periodic."[23]

Smith taught at Dartmouth for thirty-six years. His early demise in 1809, caused by tuberculosis, left the Hebrew chair empty. Although a professor of Greek and Latin was appointed in 1811, the Hebrew Professorship position was left unfilled. A Mr. Horowitz, about whom little else is known, was employed on a part-time basis to teach Hebrew and French. Approximately thirty students and instructors enrolled in his classes, but it is unclear how many students enrolled to study Hebrew and not French.

The college archives reveal nothing more of Hebrew instruction until 1825, when we read that Benjamin Hale, a professor at the Medical School, taught Hebrew for two seasons. "Not perhaps," he said, "much to the profit of my classes but because I happen to be fresher in the study than any college officer."[24] This leavening influence of the medical faculty is of interest; it presaged a shift in the previously inflexible curriculum of the college, which, along with the curricula of other New England colleges, has been called "as rigid and inexorable as fate."[25] With this shift, more emphasis was placed on the natural sciences and on the literature and languages that formed the core of the humanist tradition.

At the annual meeting of the Dartmouth trustees, it was voted "That the President be requested to correspond with other colleges; and, if he thinks best, with the Theological Seminary at Andover, on the expediency of introducing Hebrew, as a language to be studied in colleges."[26] The trustees' zeal for encouraging the study of Hebrew on a widespread basis did not bear fruit at Dartmouth. Despite the inclusion of the Hebrew language among the subjects enumerated in the 1828 Laws of the College, the professorship in Hebrew was not reestablished. The centrality of the "learned languages" in American education had diminished. While Greek and Latin were still taught, their importance had diminished as well.[27] At Harvard, Hebrew ceased to be an obligatory subject in 1787. "As a result, the number of students [of Hebrew] was so minute that the Professor of Oriental languages had been assigned the teaching of English grammar and rhetoric."[28] At Yale, where the study of the language flourished during the presidency of Ezra Stiles, it was no longer required after 1789. Upon granting his students' request that the obligation to study Hebrew be lifted, Stiles wrote in his diary: "From my first Accession to the Presidency 1777 to 1790 I have obliged all the Freshmen to study Hebrew. This has proved very disagreeable to a number of the Students. This term I have determined to instruct only those who offer themselves voluntarily."[29] But Stiles was not completely disappointed in his students. He goes on to record in his diary that: "Accordingly, of 39 Freshmen, 22 have asked for Instruction in Hebrew, and thus accordingly I teach at IV p.m. Mondays, Wednesdays, Fridays."

Jeremiah Mason, a student of Stiles, was to remember later that Stiles emphasized the practical aspect of learning Hebrew. "He said that one of the psalms he tried to teach us would be the first we should hear sung in heaven, and that he should be ashamed that any of his pupils should be entirely ignorant of that holy language."[30]

Upon granting his students' request that the obligation to study Hebrew be lifted, Stiles confided to his diary that he feared for their souls— for they would not understand the Psalms when they were admitted to the Heavenly court.

Though the decline of Hebrew at Dartmouth was not mourned in such grand theological terms, its absence was felt. Throughout the nineteenth century we find sporadic attempts to revive its study. Study of New Testament Greek did continue at the college, as did the study of the Hebrew Bible in English translation. Dartmouth students knew their Bible, and this long tradition of study informed the development of *The Dartmouth Bible*, edited in the 1940s and published in a number of editions between 1950 and 1960.[31] Professor Smith's stated aim, "to facilitate the study of the scriptures in the original," was not to be fulfilled until the 1980s with the reestablishment of the Hebrew Professorship in the Asian Studies Program.

Notes

1. For an early survey see David de Sola Pool, "Hebrew Learning Among the Puritans of New England Prior to 1700," *Publications of the American Jewish Historical Society* 20 (1911): 39–82. Later reviews of the literature may be found in Cyrus Adler, "Hebrew and Cognate Learning in America," *Lectures, Selected Papers, Addresses* (Philadelphia, 1933), 277ff; Robert H. Pfeiffer, "The Teaching of Hebrew in Colonial America," *Jewish Quarterly Review* 45 (1955): 363–73; Salo W. Baron, "From Colonial Mansion to Skyscraper: An Emerging Pattern of Hebraic Studies," *Steeled by Adversity: Essays and Addresses on American Jewish Life* (Philadelphia, 1971), 106–26; David Rudavsky, "Letoledot ha-limudim haivrim" in *Bitzaron* (1972), 349–

55; and in Eisig Silberschlag, "reishita verishonuta shel ha-ivrit ba-amerika," M. Zohari, ed., *Hebrew Thought in America* (Tel Aviv, 1972), 1:15–40.

2. Gov. William Bradford of the Plymouth Colony, quoted in Isidore S. Meyer, *The Hebrew Exercises of Governor William Bradford* (Plymouth, Mass., 1973), 9.

3. Leon Huhner, "Jews in Connection with the Colleges of the Thirteen Original States Prior to 1800," in *Publications of the American Jewish Historical Society* 19 (1910): 101.

4. Isidore S. Meyer, "Hebrew at Harvard (1636–1760): A Resume of the Information in Recent Publications," *Publications of the American Jewish Historical Society* 35 (1939): 145; Samuel Eliot Morison, in *The Puritan Pranaos; Studies in the Intellectual Life of New England in the Seventeenth Century* (New York, 1936), 18, n. 5.

5. Thomas Johnson and Perry Miller, *The Puritans* (New York, 1938), 548.

6. Quoted from Wigglesworth's diaries: George F. Moore, "Alttestamentliche Studien in Amerika," *Zeitschrift für alttestamentliche Wissenschaft* 3 (1888): 7.

7. George A. Kohut, "Judah Monis, M.A., The First Instructor in Hebrew at Harvard University (1683–1764)," *The American Journal of Semitic Languages* 14 (1898); and Meyer, "Hebrew at Harvard."

8. On Monis as a teacher, see remarks by his student and successor, Stephen Sewall (in manuscript), cited in *American Jewish Archives* 6 (January 1954). For evaluations of Monis's *Grammar*, see Kohut, 225. On his ancestry see George F. Moore, "Judah Monis," *Proceedings of the Massachusetts Historical Society* 52 (1919): 285. For a recent survey of Monis's life and career, see M. Klein, "A Jew at Harvard in the Eighteenth Century," *Proceedings of the Massachusetts Historical Society* 97 (1986): 135.

9. Kohut, "Judah Monis," 223.

10. Stiles's meditations on Hebrew and the Jews are sprinkled throughout his diary, Franklin B. Dexter, ed., *The Literary Diary of Ezra Stiles* (New York, 1901), 3 vols. Many of these citations have been collected and commented on in George A. Kohut, *Ezra Stiles and the Jews* (New York, 1902).

11. On the founding of Dartmouth College against the background of the Great Awakening, see Frederick Chase, *A History of Dartmouth College and the Town of Hanover, New Hampshire (to 1815)* (Brattleboro, Vt., 1913–1928) 2 vols., ed. John K. Lord; Ralph N. Hill, ed., *The College on the Hill: A Dartmouth Chronicle* (Hanover, N.H., 1964).

12. On eschatological speculation in early New England, see Harry S. Stout, *The New England Soul* (New York, 1986), 102–103.

13. Hill, 28.

14. Ibid.

15. Moore, "Judah Monis," 9.

16. Hill, 249.

17. Chase, 630.

18. John J. Smith, *A Hebrew Grammar Without Points* (Boston, 1803).

19. Moore, "Judah Monis," 13.

20. Quoted in Chase, 631.

21. Quoted in Hill, 254.

22. Dartmouth College Archives.

23. Hill, 122. The 1799 oration has been published in S. Goldman, "Two American Hebrew Orations: 1799 and 1800," *Hebrew Annual Review* 13 (1991).

24. John K. Lord, *A History of Dartmouth College, 1815–1909* (Concord, N.H., 1913), 255.

25. Hill, 248.

26. Dartmouth College Archives.

27. Moore, "Judah Monis," 11.

28. Ibid.

29. Stiles, *Diary* 3:397.

30. Ibid., 306.

31. Roy B. Chamberlin and Herman Feldman, eds., *The Dartmouth Bible* (Boston, 1961).

Matthew I. Wiencke

Classical and Hebraic Models of Moral Instruction at Dartmouth College, 1770–1800

Introduction

All who have written on Dartmouth College in the colonial era agree that the history of the infant school is the history of its founder and first president, Eleazar Wheelock (1711–79).[1] His concept of curriculum included much more than a catalogue of courses—indeed, such an approach to learning did not exist in his day; he was concerned, rather, with the whole of the environment of learning, with the design and governance of the college, with self-governance and self examination, and with the moral purposes of instruction. All these considerations have roots in the generation preceding the actual founding of the school and its establishment on the Hanover plain in the fall of 1770.

We must touch briefly on two external events that took place during this period. The first is the religious movement known as the First Great Awakening, which traces its origin to sermons preached by Jonathan Edwards in Northampton in the years 1740, 1741, and 1742, and its influence upon the young Wheelock. The second is the Indian Wars and the plight of the native peoples. Wheelock's perception of the causes and roots of the conflict, which laid waste the towns and settlements on the frontiers, is surprising. While they were in progress, he wrote these often quoted words: "And there is good Reason to think, that if one half which has been, for so many Years past expended in building Forts, manning and supplying them, had been prudently laid out in supporting faithful missionaries and School-Masters among them, the instructed and civilized Party would have been a far better Defense than all our expensive Fortresses and prevented the laying waste so many Towns and villages."[2]

Wheelock was among the first to recognize the neglect of the Indians, which neglect he described as "a partaking in the Public guilt of our Land and Nation." He speaks of his contemporaries' "want of Charity," calling them "criminally deaf and blind to the Intimations and of the Favour and Displeasure of God"; and he charges that, because of such neglect, God has permitted "such depredations on our Frontiers, inhuman butchery and captivity of our People." (1 [1763]: 10–14)

He understood only too well the plight of the Indians, robbed of their lands, "removing further into the wilderness," and under threat of extinction. To reach, to help them before they passed from the earth was his design. He strove to bring them the blessings of literacy and to win them over to agriculture as the means of survival. He deplored the depredations made upon them by the English, "making merchandise of the souls of the Savages"; and he called the "Avarice and other Vices of the Traders" (8 [1771]: 477), the "greatest outward Impediment to [the Indians'] endeavours" (8 [1772]: 476–77). In this he reflected a widely held belief, as expressed by a contemporary who remarked "how the Indians do not migrate and form distinct colonies: they die away, or disappear from the places where they are" (Memoirs, 173–74).[3] If the Indians were not won over to agriculture, they would disappear.

Actually, what Wheelock proposed was a radical scheme: to take the Indian youths directly from their tribal habitat into a school organized around an English way of life. The beginnings were simple, starting with two Indian boys of the Delaware nation, fourteen and eleven years of age, whom Wheelock took under instruction in December of 1754. In two years, it is reported, these two "became well acquainted with the English language, writing and common arithmetic, and acquired considerable knowledge of the Latin and Greek" (Memoirs, 23). Wheelock's interest in the native peoples was profound. In a remarkable letter to the sachems and chiefs of the six nations, he opened with the words, "I have you upon my heart ever since I was a boy" (Memoirs, 259).

On these modest beginnings the Indian Charity School was founded in Lebanon, Connecticut. Its fame spread, and support flowed into it from both sides of the Atlantic, from persons of every station in life. As the school grew in numbers, there was added a tutor, Bezaleel Woodward, who opened a "collegiate" department with a faculty of one. We must pass over the efforts of the school's benefactors to secure a charter for a college to be called Dartmouth, yet to be established, and the removal to Hanover in western New Hampshire. Having selected the site, Wheelock set out ahead, in the summer of 1770, the thirty charity students, including three Indians, and their tutor, followed on foot, a distance of 170 miles.

The Founder's Design and Commitment to Providence

The charity school and the college were devoted to a single purpose, or Design as Wheelock everywhere called it. The pursuit of this Design, or Great Design, was his total object. Throughout his letters and the *Narratives*, which are the accounts of his daily struggles, debts, quarrels, the ceaseless task of clearing land, putting up housing, farming, settling disputes, gathering a congregation, preaching—all in addition to, and intermingled with, the care of the students, to "cloathe, board, and educate" them—throughout all of this, there is one constant and recurring theme, the guiding hand of Providence. It has been dismissed or obscured in the older biographies and histories of the college; yet it is unmistakable in all that he wrote, evident on every page of his prose narratives.

The roots of the Design are to be found in the preamble to the Narrative for 1766, written in the third person, probably not in Wheelock's own hand, where we read of Wheelock's "Sense . . . of the Obligation the Descendents of the ancient *New Englanders* still lie under to keep in View the avowed Design of their Forefathers original Emigration" (3 [1766]: 85; reprinted in 4 [1767]: 133). May we not hear in these words an echo of the Mayflower Compact and the hope of establishing a theocracy upon these shores? The thought recurs in a recommendatory letter signed by twenty-five Connecticut pastors in support of Wheelock's labors, that "the wide extended wilderness of America, may blossom as the rose; habitations of cruelty become dwelling places of righteousness" (*Memoirs*, 179). As the school's reputation grew, Wheelock remarked "in what an important Point of Light this Design is already viewed" (3 [1766]: 88). For Wheelock the reliance upon Providence was biblically based and, like the Exodus of Israel, defined in the metaphor of a journey, eventually into the wilderness, with God revealing the way step by step. To keep pace with Providence was his initial concern. The testimonies and contributions in support of the school were "Tokens of a Divine Hand in Favour of it . . . plain Intimations of the Divine Will concerning it." In Wheelock's own words, "I thought it a Duty, notwithstanding all Discouragements, to pursue the Design, and endeavor to keep Pace with the Providence of God in Favour of it" (1 [1763]: 37). As to this measured progress, he wrote two years later, "we have endeavored to go no faster in the Affair, than to observe its openings, and follow the plainest dictates of Providence in every step that has been taken . . . And if the Cause be God's, and the Course we steer is right, it is safe enough" (2 [1765]: 76). It was a measured, considered pace in which he feared "zeal without Motive," exertions beyond what is required (5 [1769]: 210). Even in his search for the location of the infant college and school, once that move was decided upon, it was put to the same test. In a letter of 5 July 1768, Wheelock wrote, "God has seen fit to keep me in the dark with respect to the Place where to fix the School" (to Robert Keen, 5 [1768]: 263); but this waiting upon Providence did not prevent his laying plans for a thorough investigation of the sites offered on the east bank of the Connecticut River. In one of the longest ascriptions to Providence, in the sixth narrative, covering the years 1768 to 1771 and the removal to the Hanover plain—an eloquent, periodic sentence—he concluded, "And I have partly learnt, that there is nothing more remaining for me to do, than in the capacity of a servant, to follow him without fear, wherever he does, by word, or providence, point out my way for me" (6 [1771]: 346). But his was not a blind faith. He modified the preceding statement in the same narrative by saying "I have invariably followed the plainest dictate of reason, scripture and providence in every step I have taken" (6 [1771]: 360).

Two years later, in 1773, at a point when he reported that a number of Indians, sensing the oncoming of hostilities, were withdrawn from the school, and support was cut off from England—a year which the biographies describe as the depth of his personal disillusionment—Wheelock's confidence and hope were never stronger. He was convinced that "the Plan is the Cause of God; . . . certainly his Hand has been conspicuous, in the Beginning, Rise and Progress of it, through so many dark Scenes"; and that "these Things are not the Result and Product of the Wisdom, Sagacity, or Prudence of the wise Politicks of the Age" but through human agents God has "made Choice of an Instrument every way unequal to it" (8 [1773]: 475, and see the parallel in 9 [1775]: 539).

In the view of his contemporaries, the working of Providence was no more than "creation continued" (Memoirs, 112). To John Thornton, an English patron, Wheelock wrote, "The storm that is raised against me don't, can't dismay me, while I believe the cause is God's, and see him prospering it among the floods, see him evidently sitting upon them." To this Thornton replied, "Every rod has a voice; and whether the Almighty plans to warn, correct, or edify us, we happily know, that love is at the bottom."[4]

Wheelock was his own keenest judge of the prospects of success or failure of the Design. He entertained, from the beginning, the prospect of failure, not because of want of effort and means, but from the withholding of divine blessing. His most poignant reckoning of the cost appears in the very first narrative, written in 1762: "And if one half of the Indian Boys thus educated should prove good and useful Men, there will be no Reason to regret our Toil and Expence for the whole. And if God shall deny his Blessing on our Endeavours, as to the general Design, it may be these particular Youth may reap eternal Advantage by what we do for them; and if but one in ten does so, we shall have no Cause to think much of the Expence. And if a Blessing be denied to all, 'we shall notwithstanding be unto God a sweet Savour of Christ in them that perish'" (1 [1763]: 28–29).

It is a passage that evokes the cry of Abraham to God, bargaining for the righteous souls in Sodom; of Esther preparing to go before the king, resolved in her immortal words, "And if I perish, I perish"; of Paul to the Philippians on the threshold of Macedonia and Europe.

Wheelock daily lived with this Design, and modelled and shaped the school to its unfolding. The ultimate course lay hidden in the knowledge of God, revealed to him in times of crisis, altered with changing circumstances. The words fate, fortune, chance, even probability, are absent from his vocabulary. During the Revolutionary War the sources of income from England were cut off; in fact, the trust funds were exhausted as well as contributions from the settled colonies. The number of Indian scholars declined. It has been called his moment of disillusionment; but it does not reflect clearly the narrative for 1773, when in despair his hope shone brightest. He sensed a change in the Design, and lay plans to train missionaries and teachers to carry education and the benefits of religion to the new settlements springing up in the Connecticut Valley and in the Indian country.

The school and college from the beginning were multinational and multilingual. There could be heard daily the Indian tongues—the languages of the Mohawk, Oneida, Mohegan, and, beyond the six nations, those of the Huron—alongside the English of the English youths (never called Americans), who, preparing to go out as teachers, set to work to learn the Indian tongues directly from the native students—we would say today by the Rassias method of one-on-one language instruction. Latin, Greek, and Hebrew, as well as English, were taught as living languages, to be read and spoken; the mastery of grammar was the mere preliminary. One native scholar as Wheelock described "uncommonly promising, of the Huron Tribe, who is Master of the French and Mohawk as well as Huron languages" and "of a manly, sprightly, and enterprizing Genius" (9 [1775]: 539). Shortly after his arrival at the college, in company with another Huron, there appeared a Canadian, one Verruiel, a refugee from Quebec. His father, a Lieutenant-Colonel of the Militia, had been reduced to poverty after the fall of Quebec. The son, who had been sent to a school in France, was called home. Fending for himself and making his way "through the woods from Canada to Connecticut," he came within thirty-five miles of Hanover when he first heard of the college. He spoke no English, but could communicate with the tutors in Latin. Wheelock took him on. As for the young Hurons, "they soon began to read and write English (which an Indian may do before he can discourse in that Tongue), and as they could speak French well, I ordered Joseph Verruiel . . . to teach them to read the French Bible" (8 [1773]: 450).

The School of the Prophets *and* the Prophetic Model

To provide both native and English teachers to carry the rudiments of learning and the civilizing arts to the six nations, and to prepare ministers to the new towns now organizing in the upper Connecticut, were Wheelock's dual purpose. Both the founder and his contemporaries spoke of the college as the "school of the prophets," deliberately choosing the prophetic, rather than the apostolic model. It was best expressed, long afterwards, by a contemporary, David McClure, in his *Memoirs of Wheelock*. To encourage his flock and his pupils, McClure wrote of Wheelock, "he derived support from the example of the prophet Elisha (2 Kings 6:1–7) who founded a college or *school of the prophets* in the wilderness of Jordan, by divine direction, for the preservation and diffusion of true religion, and in circumstances bearing considerable analogy to his" (*Memoirs*, 57).

The metaphor appears frequently in Wheelock's prayers. In 1771 on the occasion of his gathering "the church in this college, and school," he entreated the people's "entire devotedness of body and soul, and all endowments of both, without reserve to God, for time and eternity," praying that never "an evil heart of unbelief in or departing from God, nor any root of bitterness . . . spring up in this seminary to obstruct the growth and progress of true religion in this school of the prophets, to the latest posterity" (6 [1771]: 370–71; and see also 6 [1771]: 374, 378, "in the spirit and power of Elias," and the prayer in 8 [1773]: 464–65).

In the narrative of 1775 he concluded the reports on his native teachers in these words, "If God shall graciously make these Youths the subjects of his special Grace, and furnish them with all necessary Knowledge . . . may we not hope that their united Force will be terrible against the Kingdom of Darkness, in the Wilderness" (9 [1775]: 539).

The school and college clearly embodied a *kerygmatic* mission, one of proclamation. Public speaking, or declamation, was integral to the training from the beginning. Classes consisted of oral recitations before the tutors. The undergraduates were required to write and deliver weekly declamations in the chapel, by class; the seniors, on the first Wednesday of the month, before the entire college. These weekly declamations measured the students' progress in learning, the requirements of oral delivery being far greater than in any comparable period in the history of the college. In a general sense, what was required was the profession of reasoned knowledge. The statistics show that in the first fifty years of the college, from 1770 to 1820, ninety percent of the graduates entered the professions of law, ministry, teaching, and medicine, generally in that order, law and ministry close competitors for first place. H. D. Foster, in "Webster and Choate in College," the source for these statistics, interpreted this phenomenon as follows: "In a college where nine out of ten . . . were to follow the learned professions, the emphasis on literary expression, philosophy, theology, and principles of law was admirably adapted to a world keenly interested in those subjects" (Foster, 514).[5] The first three of these professions were largely devoted to public speaking, oral persuasion, and recitation, the training to be articulate in oral and written expression stemming from the prophetic model. "Vox clamantis in deserto," the "Voice of one crying in the wilderness"—the voice speaking through the prophet Isaiah—was the motto Wheelock himself chose for the infant college.[6]

The picture of the college and its efforts in its first decade thus is one of radii extending to the supporting network of the coastal towns and the lower Connecticut, and west and northward into the wilderness where schools to teach literacy were being founded—the whole of this activity multiethnic and multilingual, Wheelock himself at the hub and center. He seldom travelled, rarely left the college, but, through emissaries and a voluminous correspondence, nurtured his young protégés and begged support for them, and administered the college and school under a form of government which was uniformly described as paternal.

The Paternal Model of Government

The word patriarch occurs very seldom in the sources; rather, the Indian nations called Wheelock "Father," or the "Great Father," as was their custom.[7] The trustees, in one of their first acts (22 October 1770), "resolved that the college as well as the school should continue under parental government till they should find occasion to alter it," adding, "But if God shall please graciously to continue the same influence upon the minds of the students, as there has hitherto been, there will never be need of any other form of government to the end of time" (6 [1771] 372).

The college and school constituted a family, in 1770 numbering about seventy persons, including children, youths, and adults. Over all of their common endeavors, Wheelock presided as a father, directing the clearing of land, farming, teaching, preaching, molding the lives of the students. The parental governance was of the biblical model, encompassing both the rod of discipline under the law and the heart overflowing with love and reconciliation. The *Narratives* reveal Wheelock as a keen judge of character, his descriptions of individual students, English and Native, ring true, a single phrase revealing a real and believable person. A tradition persists that he was a stern taskmaster, demanded unquestioned obedience, and ruled with a rod of iron. I find little to support this view; on the contrary, the scale inclines heavily to the opposite, grace rather than law, and kindness; in modern terms, caring and concern, and attention to practical needs. For example, during the blockade, when there was no cloth to be had, he and his household used their own linens to make clothing for the charity students; and he begged donations of cast-off garments from his benefactors in the settled towns. Of his governance, I have not found a single adverse record in the testimony of his students and contemporaries.

It must be remembered that Wheelock was in his fifty-ninth year at the founding of the college, and in five year's time his health was in decline. What he accomplished was effected within that short interval. Indeed, he is described in the *Memoirs* as "like a venerable patriarch, surrounded by his affectionate family and pupils;" or, as one of his tutors remembered him, in the first year of the college, "standing in the open air, at the head of his numerous family, presenting to God their morning and evening prayers." His exercise of discipline was swift and decisive. Governor Wentworth, inquiring of Wheelock about a disturbance at the college, hoped for a reply, "with that warmth and earnestness, that must and ought to flow from the bosom of a parent, tenderly watching over the most important interests of a child."[8] Wheelock's reply was quick to inform the governor of the cause. The disturbance had occurred during one of his rare absences from the school—a "formidable combination of profaneness, licentiousness and intemperance," on account of which he had to dismiss a number of students. But such occurrences were rare. He cherished his time spent with the students. "It is quite a refreshment," he wrote to Thornton in the late fall of 1774, "to meet them at prayers, as soon as it is light in the morning, and read and expound a chapter to them before prayer, when there is nothing but silence, gravity, and attention: and again at the edge of the evening to sing a psalm, and ask them questions, and discourse with them about half an hour, on some important point in divinity."[9] His treatment of the students was long remembered, as we read in a letter from a former student, then a pastor in Farmington, written in 1804, in which he said, in part, "I gratefully remember that he treated me with the tenderness and familiarity of a parent toward a child" (*Memoirs*, 166). The name of Wheelock was known and revered among the Indian nations, hundreds of miles distant in the wilderness, whose greetings were directed "to the great Minister, and common Father," and to his son Ralph as "Flesh of their Great Father" (5 [1769]: 223, 225, 239, 254). In the letter quoted above, Pitkin recalled of Wheelock that "his sermons were from a heart warmed by divine grace, and animated by divine love." Another early graduate, Asa Burton of the class of 1777, of whom we shall hear more presently, long after recalled his frequent visits to the president. After a long absence from the college because of illness and an epidemic of fever in which his mother, his sister, and his brother next to him in age all perished, he turned in his distress to President Wheelock, "for I consider him a father to me, and as I had no hope, I expected he might give me those instructions, which would at last prove saving to my soul."[10] We will return to these conversations presently.

These testimonials, however selective—we have no others to the contrary—reveal the true character of Wheelock, who is described as "of an open and frank disposition" and "affectionate in his reconciliation" on occasions of discipline (*Memoirs*, 110, 111). His advice and his chastisements were marked by appeals to the reason; with respect to beliefs, he was careful to avoid coercion whatsoever, but relied rather upon persuasion, reasoned argument, and example.

Taken together, all of these recollections agree with Wheelock's written expression, the clarity of statement, "great plainness of speech," that mark his literary style. (see *Memoirs*, 165). Were his parental governance tyrannical, dictatorial, self-serving, we should expect to see the signs of it in his writing. Nothing of this sort is discernible. He is reported to have said, "I abhor religion without manners." There is little that is coercive in his writing. His sentences, however crafted on classical and biblical models, read as idiomatic English, the words often used in their root meanings, the whole conveying reason and warmth. His perceptive oversight was consistent with the parental style of governance. During his presidency we hear of no written code or regulations for the college, beyond the stated hours for morning and evening prayers, recitations, and declamations. The moral code, so to speak, was assumed, formed by the mores of civilized society and the religion of the time. Its administration, in the parent-child relationship, followed the biblical, indeed Hebraic model of the Puritan household.

The parental, biblical model helps to explain the daily routine. In both the charity school during the Lebanon years and in the college, the day began with prayers at dawn, five o'clock in the summer, spring and fall, six in the winter. These consisted, in the morning, of recitation or singing of the Psalms, Scripture and benediction for the assembled college and school, which now numbered around one hundred persons, in the unheated chapel which stood near the site of the present Thornton Hall. Prayers were followed with the first recitation of the day, except on Monday, then breakfast. The day ended with prayers at sunset, Monday through Saturday. On Sundays, there were two services, morning and early afternoon. Morning prayers and recitation before breakfast continued until 1859; morning prayers were held in the unheated chapel as late as 1871, and congregational singing was introduced at the unanimous request of the graduating seniors. It is an exaggeration to say that the college in the early years resembled "a penal institution."[11] Morning and evening prayers were the rule of every Puritan household; and every hour of daylight was put to use, whether in learning, in farming, or in the trades.

Indeed, the school was not governed by the students, rather, a far weightier responsibility was laid upon them, or upon the most earnest and perceptive among them, that of self-governance and examination of conscience. It is here that we see the Puritan ethic in its clearest light. The object of these reasoned, spiritual exercises was to bring one's life under the obedience and understanding of the divine commands.

Self-Examination, Contrition, Law, and Grace

The inner life of the school and college in the Wheelock era was fed by seasons of special enlightenment and awakening of the spirit. Examination of conscience was the objective of the Puritan ethic, not self-punishment or self-degradation. In no other aspect have Puritan theology and morality been so misunderstood and subject to greater caricature than in this. There is needed a fresh reading of the Wheelock *Narratives*, of the sermons of the period, and above all, of Jonathan Edwards's *Freedom of the Will*, which last, together with Locke, *On Human Understanding*, was read in the senior year at Dartmouth for upwards of fifty years. It is difficult to assess exactly Wheelock's relation to the First Great Awakening, which was without question the strongest impulse in his early ministry. He was swept up in it, and because of it he won a reputation for preaching; and it made him both friends and enemies. It kindled and awakened those latent qualities which were to shape his entire life. In speaking of religious conversion he observed that those who have not "'known the Terrors of the Lord' . . . such were never under the governing influence of a real Sense of the Truth, Reality, Greatness and Importance of eternal Things" (1 [1763]: 27–28). His understanding of religion was never far from the "experimental," what we might call the experiential.

It is to the experiential effects, bred of self-examination, contrition, and the profound experience of forgiveness, law, and grace, that we now turn. Space does not permit a detailed exposition; rather, I cite two exemplary anecdotes in the lives of Wheelock's students and protégés, who were the primary beneficiaries of his spiritual understanding and practice. The young Asa Burton has been mentioned earlier. His family, among the first settlers of Norwich, Vermont, entertained in their house a succession of ministers, one of whom inspired Asa to seek a "learned education." At age sixteen he prepared himself for entrance to Dartmouth College by memorizing a Latin grammar and walking to Hanover daily to recite before Professor Smith. He was admitted by President Wheelock, but shortly thereafter was obliged to withdraw because of calamities that befell his family and his own illness. When he returned in mid-January of 1774 he found that his class had read through Matthew, Mark, and Luke in the Greek Testament, and were beginning John. He settled in for the winter, cooking his own victuals, which he brought from home. "I associated with no one," he recalled, "recited daily, conversed with no one but my roommates and a sophomore, and Dr. Wheelock." Earlier he had passed through periods of warmth and hopes alternating with despair, "my heart" he wrote, "appeared to me very wicked and hard and stupid beyond description. It seemed to me, that I had no feeling, and justly deserved eternal death." During the time of sickness, he was "constantly exercised with a sense of my own sinfulness and fears of death." Dr. Wheelock was of help to him, observing that "some persons might be Christians, yet not know it." From this oracular saying followed much self-examination. "And from that time to the present day," wrote the young Burton, "I have entertained a hope that I am a child of God; whether well founded or not has always been a matter of doubt to me." It should be added that what further relieved his mind was his meeting a young lady at his brother Elisha's, whose name was Mercy and who later became his first wife.[12] His doubts of whether he was a child of God reflect, of course, the Puritan doctrine of election, and the lifelong question, "Am I one of the elect, the chosen of God?"

A second example is the life story of one of Wheelock's Indian protégés, a Mohegan who took the name of Joseph Johnson. He entered the charity school, then at Lebanon, Connecticut, in his seventh year, proceeded rapidly in his studies, and by age fifteen or sixteen, proficient in English, was ready to return to his nation as a teacher. There he opened a school. All went well, as his letters to Wheelock attest, but after a while he could not resist the enticements of strong drink and licentious living. He struggled, pouring out his heart to Wheelock in letters that, to us, read like the Penitential Psalms:

... to return to you whom I have so greatly grieved, I dare not; I am ashamed, and Conscience strips one to the very heart; I am Sorry; my Spirits cast down. Methinks I feel in some Measure the down Cast Spirits of Cain when He received the curse; but no Equal to his; tho my Crimes are more than Equal, the thought of your School haunts my Mind dayly, and to turn my face that way I dare not ... but what Course to take, I know that God is Everywhire, and is Acquainted with Actions past, and will punish without Mercy those that Be Disobedient to his Laws and Commandments.

He goes on to speak of the mercy of God, "though I have Openly Rebelled against Him." And if this mentor should turn a deaf ear, "would this be the Event, I must in silence depart, and weep with a Bitter cry as Esau when he lost his blessing."[13]

His contrition and resolve to lead a better life, followed by lapses and backsliding, present a picture of a young man, little more than an adolescent, who has lost every shred of self-confidence, chastising himself, seeing nothing but ruin. He abandoned his school. The reports of him are alarming; Wheelock gave up on him, pronounced him totally lost. He is next heard of in Providence, Rhode Island, where he went to sea on a whaling vessel. For three years there is silence. Then, on returning to Providence, he experienced a spiritual renewal; his life was changed. He returned to his nation, not as a teacher but as an arbiter. During the war he succeeded in keeping the Oneidas neutral, and for that he was commended by the Continental Congress, eventually in a personal letter by George Washington (the holograph is in the Dartmouth College Archives). He died at the age of twenty-four.

In the moral direction and guidance of those in his charge, Wheelock himself was orthodox in his theology and church polity, though he differed from President Stiles at Yale and was viciously attacked by a prominent divine in Boston. Of his undergraduate years at Yale, in the class of 1733, we know to date very little beyond a significant award: in his senior year he was the first recipient, jointly with a classmate, of the Berkeley Foundation prize in Greek. His contemporaries, including the critical President Stiles, attest to his classical and biblical learning. We can say with confidence that he never abandoned it; indeed, it formed the lucid and persuasive style, the reason and warmth, the sweetness and conviction of the *Narratives*.

Classical and Biblical Models in the Dartmouth Curriculum

The Latin and Greek authors and the Hebrew Bible were the core curriculum in the freshman, sophomore, and junior years, to which were added logic, the rudiments of natural philosophy, that is, the physical sciences, including astronomy; mathematics, through algebra, trigonometry, and conic sections; and the principles of surveying. In the senior year the scholars advanced to philosophy and metaphysics, specifically in the reading of two major works of which we have clear record, Locke's *Essay On Human Understanding* and Edwards's *Freedom of the Will*. From 1796 on there is mention of Paley's *Moral and Political Philosophy*, and lectures in medicine with the coming of Nathan Smith, professor of Chemistry and Anatomy. A knowledge of English grammar, Virgil, Cicero, *Select Orations*, and Greek New Testament were made the requirements of admission as early as 1796.[14] While there is occasional reference to the difficulty of Greek, early facility in Latin is assumed. One learned Latin grammar as a child along with reading and writing English, by the simple expedient of copying out the forms and memorizing them, as quickly as possible, in order to get on with reading. From the early years Wheelock reported the Indian students reading Virgil and Tully; from all indications they were scarcely into their teens. Daniel Webster, class of 1801, who read the Latin classics throughout his life, was reported as saying, "Latin should be learned for the sake of the good things which are in Latin. It is folly to learn a language and then make no use of it." And as an undergraduate he noted "three or four hours devoted to a lesson."[15]

Professor Smith compiled his own grammar, *The New Hampshire Latin Grammar*, published in 1802, but in use for some twenty years prior. It bore the imprimatur of President Wheelock as the grammar for students in Dartmouth College. The pace with which one was to master the grammar, all the conjugations, moods, and tenses, all the declensions, synoptically, and at a glance, is formidable—a procedure which in current pedagogy is sometimes described as a "new approach to language proficiency." But it is the moral *exempla* that are cited to illustrate syntax that are of interest to this study. The English examples are taken from the Bible, Milton, Addison, and Pope. For example, the use of commas to set off words in a series is illustrated in these lines from Pope:

Gods partial, changeful, passionate, unjust;
Whose attributes were rage, revenge, and lust.

What impressionable mind would ever forget the use of the comma in the light of such a paradigm? It is followed by a passages from Judges (14:18): "What is sweeter than honey? what is stronger than a lion?" to illustrate two interrogation points in a single sentence.[16]

To illustrate the relative *qui*, we have in the Latin Vulgate, "God will punish the wicked, who transgress his commands" and "God, who created all things, is to be worshipped." Further examples to illustrate agreement of noun and verb include "Cicero and Cato were wise" and "I and my brother read Terence." To illustrate the use of the genitive case after substantive nouns, the examples are: "The fear of the Lord is the beginning of wisdom" and "Riches, the incentives of vice, are dug out of the earth." Elsewhere we meet such Ciceronian tenets as "non nobis solum nati sumus," "we are not born for ourselves only," to illustrate the use of the dative. For verbs governing the ablative we are offered *Fruere Deo*, translated "Enjoy God." In a footnote, students are reminded: "Amor Dei, the *love of God*, may either mean the love of God toward us, or our love toward Him." (Nothing is said about subjective and objective genitive, as if the point is more a spiritual than a grammatical one.) "But often the substantive can only be taken either in an active, or in a passive sense; thus *Timor Dei* always implies *Deus timetur*" (that is, "God is to be feared"). And finally the student's attention is called to "adulescens eximia spe, summae virtutis," "a youth of least hope, but of greatest courage."[17]

Epilogue

It can be said, in conclusion, that all of the aspects briefly examined here have relevance to education today, some unchanged, others in a different guise. All have lingered in the Dartmouth tradition, none wholly extinguished.[18] Those who rewrote the life of Wheelock and the early history of the college for their generation, that of the 1930s—the last full-length studies—could not have foreseen in what ways Wheelock's Design is being fulfilled in the present era. World War II, Korea, Vietnam, the civil rights movement have intervened to change profoundly the makeup and direction of Dartmouth. Once again the college is multiethnic, multilingual in ways not unlike those envisioned by the founder. In Wheelock's presidency the percentage of native to the total number of students in the school and college hovered around twenty percent, roughly twenty out of the one hundred in the best years; that proportion of minority to the total number of students was not to be reached again for nearly two and a quarter centuries, until the class of 1994. Parental

governance is now transmuted into caring and nurture, no longer patriarchal, in the form of the close relation between students and faculty,
so sought after in a residential college. The school of the prophets is
today in need of a new metaphor to express a mission to meet the dearth
of teachers in languages and in the humanities projected in the 1990s,
and to address the want of literacy in our land. Self-examination and self-
reflection are today the foundations for rehabilitation of lives more des-
perately fragmented than those of the young Asa Burton or the tormented Mohegan, Joseph Johnson. As for Providence and Design, in the
long history and tradition of the college these are no less binding than
in Wheelock's day, nor is the outcome ultimately in our hands. For Jonathan Edwards, the implications were both moral and universal. In the
conclusion to his masterpiece on the *Freedom of the Will,* he wrote,
"Hereby it becomes manifest, that God's moral government over mankind, his treating them as moral agents, making them objects of his
commands, councils, calls, warnings, expostulations, promises, threat-
enings, rewards and punishments, is not inconsistent with a determining disposal of all events, of every kind, throughout the universe, in his
providence."[19]

The appeal to the Dartmouth seniors, in the first half-century of the
college's history, was as to moral agents, given freedom to act, to respond, to receive, to reject, in ways not inconsistent with the working
of a larger Design, under God's Providence, in an ordered universe.

Notes

1. I wish to acknowledge the generous assistance of Mr. Kenneth C. Kra-
mer, Archivist of Dartmouth College, and the staff of the Treasure Room,
Baker Library, in making available source materials for this essay.

2. *Wheelock Narrative* (Boston, London, Hartford, 1763–75; Rochester
Reprint, facsimile edition, n.d.), 9 vols., 1 (1763): 11. Subsequent references
to the *Narratives* are given in the text by volume, date, and page.

3. David McClure, D. D., S.H.S., and Elijah Parish, D.D., *Memoirs of the
Reverend Eleazar Wheelock, D.D. Founder and President of Dartmouth
College and Moor's Charity School; with a summary history of the college
and school. To which are added copious extracts from Dr. Wheelock's Cor-
respondence.* (Newburyport, 1811), 173–74. Subsequent references to the
Memoirs are given in the text.

These astute observations stand in marked contrast to the usual motives
ascribed to Wheelock in his mission to "Christianize" the native peoples.
James McCallum, for example, expressed a commonly held view in *The Letters of Eleazar Wheelock's Indians* (Hanover: Dartmouth College Publications, 1932), where he writes of the "tragedy of coercing the savages to
studies for which he had little aptitude and no use—to Latin, Greek, and
Hebrew; to a religion, the Calvinism of the eighteenth century, from which

he too often took not much more than the introversions, and to the white man's civilization from which he was prone to borrow the vices" (11).

While there is truth in these words, McCallum generalized upon a widely held sociological viewpoint. The evidence yields a more qualified account. Two modifying points need citing. Wheelock's most celebrated and influential protégé, Samson Occom, though neither a student of the charity school nor, later, of Dartmouth College, came to Wheelock's door of his own volition. Others of the native sons were sent to the school by their chieftain fathers, some of them traversing hundreds of miles on foot to acquire what benefit they could from their English teachers. Others were recruited by their peers from among Wheelock's native students; but it would be inaccurate to say they were "coerced."

As one reads the journal of David Maccluer [sic] and Levi Frisbee, writing of a missionary journey to the Delaware nation in the western reaches of Pennsylvania, it becomes clear that the mission was a failure, when their *king*, as he was called, after listening for two days to the appeal of the missionaries, returned their answer on the third day, and declined the continued presence of the missionaries in their midst, believing that "the Great Being did not intend the religion of the White People should be their's, that if he had intended it, he would have let them know it long ago." And in a later colloquy on the fourth Sabbath of their sojourn, after a sermon expounding the doctrine of sin, "one of the Council objected, that he did not know whether it was best for them to receive the *English Religion*, 'for the White People, says he, who are acquainted with, and who say they are Christians, are worse than the worst of us, and we had rather be what we are, than such as they are.'" To which the writer added in the very next sentence, "This Objection, I thought, had Weight in it" (8 [1773]: 503, 511). The episode ended with the entry of the next day, when the council "thanks the missionaries for coming, appreciates the opportunity to hear them, sends love to those who have sent them." On the Friday following, "there being no change of heart . . . [we] set out to visit settlements west of the Appalachians." The journal closes with the rather mild observation, "Hearing nothing in the mean Time, from the *Indians*, to encourage us to make a second Attempt, we set out for *New England* where we at last arrived, having experienced much of the divine Goodness through the whole Journey" (8 [1773]: 514).

Wheelock's Puritan conviction was pervasive throughout all his undertakings, that is, the leading of Providence and the free operation of the Spirit. These were fundamental to Puritan theology, even in the doctrine of the elect. The motive underlying the *narratives*, as his earliest biographers recognized, was love, not coercion. That his mission failed according to his lights, and that the college in Wheelock's last years and under his successor gradually shifted its course, would not be the ultimate tragedy, but, in Wheelock's own terms, the manifestation of the working of Providence in a new light.

Peter Bien, Professor of English at Dartmouth College, observes of this passage, "Wheelock's sense of 'public guilt' is amazing. His remedy, namely to turn the Indians into English gentlemen, is perhaps not so amazing, yet understandable given his beliefs. George Fox, the founder of Quakerism, was better in that he went to the Indians themselves as to noble philosophers, and sat at their feet. In other words, he understood that they possessed an advanced culture of their own." [Private communication to the author, 14 August 1990].

4. *Memoirs*, 287–88. The original letters, to John Thornton (6 May 1772, Hanover, #772306) and from John Thornton (14 Sept. 1772, Brighton, #772514) are to be found in *A Guide to the Microfilm Edition of the Papers of Eleazar Wheelock. The Early Archives of Dartmouth College . . . in the Library of Dartmouth College and Moor's Indian Charity School*, with an Introduction by Edward Connery Lathem, Librarian of the College (Hanover: Dartmouth College Library, 1971).

5. Herbert Darling Foster, '85, "Webster and Choate in College: Dartmouth under the Curriculum of 1796–1819," *The Dartmouth Alumni Magazine* (April–May 1927), 514. Daniel Webster's testimony and Foster's evaluation of the classical/philosophical curriculum of Dartmouth in the early decades of its history belie the criticism of Leon Burr Richardson (*History of Dartmouth College* [Hanover: Dartmouth College Publications, 1932], vol. 1) that "once admitted to the institution, the student found the curriculum of the college to be as rigid and inexorable as fate . . . as fixed as the rock of ages." Further, "the requirements of scholastic attainment do not appear to have been high . . . it is more likely the standards were such as to make few demands even on the lowest stratum of the student body." These evaluations are anachronistic and apparently without foundation. They contradict the evidence of such scholars as Ezra Burton, Daniel Webster, and later, Rufus Choate. Webster continued to read the Latin classics, especially the historians, throughout his political career; the rhetoric of Cicero underlay the power of his oratory. As their recollections attest, these and other early students at the college devoted day and night to study. While the college enrolled students at all levels of learning, the requirements in languages alone were such as rather few entering students today could meet. Comparisons between the late eighteenth- and late twentieth-century college curricula are invidious at best: the single valid conclusion is that the intellectual level of the college was and remained high in both its infancy and its maturity.

Richardson underestimated the eighteenth-century emphasis upon Greek, Latin, and Hebrew as the acknowledged source of wisdom and learning, and upon such contemporary works as Locke's *Essay on Human Understanding* and Edwards's *On the Freedom of the Will*, both read in the senior year, as works deemed acceptable to the Puritan mind in the fields of philosophy and systematic theology. Their appeal and how keenly they were argued can be documented here and there in the comment and recollections of early Dartmouth students. How thoroughly Locke and Edwards were understood is another matter. In the case of Asa Burton, class of 1777, the study of these two alone planted the seeds of a lifelong obsession with philosophy.

6. The Latin motto on the Dartmouth College seal has led to much misunderstanding. Wheelock used the text in the Latin Vulgate (Matt. 3:3), which follows the Greek, φςνη βοςντοσ εν τη εϙημς. The genitive singular, *clamantis*, of the present participle, *clamans*, is properly translated "of one crying." The parallel form occurs in the Greek. The Hebrew, however (Isa. 40:3), to which this passage refers, is קוֹל קוֹרֵא כמדבר, literally, "a voice crying." The Hebrew is ambiguous, mysterious, a "voice sounding in the

wilderness." The variance lies in the Vulgate (Greek) and Hebrew versions of Scripture, not in a misunderstanding on Wheelock's part, who would have been familiar with both texts. The motto on the seal is properly translated, "A voice of one crying in the wilderness," and signifies the source in Hebrew prophecy. It should be added that, *in deserto*, Γϰ. εν τη εϱημς, means "in an uninhabited place," for which "wilderness" is today an apt, if symbolic, equivalent.

7. The divine name on the Dartmouth College seal, *El-Shaddai*, in the Hebrew scriptures, is that of the God of the patriarchs, Abraham, Isaac, and Jacob. Cf. Gen. 17:1, 28:3, 35:11; Ex. 6:3.

8. *Memoirs*, 310. From Governor Wentworth 19 February 1774. Portsmouth. The holograph is not listed in Lathem, and is apparently lost.

9. *Memoirs*, 320. To John Thornton 10 Nov. 1774, Dartmouth College, Lathem 774610.1.

10. *The Life of Asa Burton Written by Himself*, ed. Charles Lathem, Jr. (Thetford, Vt.: The First Congregational Church, 1973), 16. Excerpts from MSS in the Vassar and Yale libraries, including the *Life* and MS additions made by Asa Burton in 1820, 1824, and 1825.

11. Richardson, 249. Richardson's exaggeration can hardly be meant seriously. Without doubt the day's routine in the Dartmouth of Wheelock was Spartan in the extreme as judged by today's standards; but aside from the food, there is little complaint in the contemporary accounts. Buildings devoted to divine worship were seldom heated, unprofaned by stoves or chimneys; the working day was ordered, in both the New England academy and populace at large, by the available daylight. As late as 1871, the college chapel in the old Dartmouth Hall was unheated. An appeal by the seniors in the *Aegis* in the Spring of that year reads, "And the idea that troubles us is that over three hundred students, every one of whom has been known to sing in cases of emergency, should attend Chapel seven times a week, the Church twice, and yet need a choir of from six to ten to sing a hymn for them at morning prayers. . . . We ask not now a modern Chapel; we ask not voluntary attendance; we ask not to have it warmed in winter; we ask not even easy seats; we do ask hymn-books." (*The Aegis*, 14:45–46). The fall issue reports, "We have congregational singing in chapel, and gas in prospect." Apparently as yet no heating. (15:54.)

12. Burton, 14–16.

13. McCallum, 136–37, 139. From Joseph Johnson, 28 Dec. 1768, Providence. Lathem #768678.2. A selection of the letters of Joseph Johnson to President Wheelock, together with a first-person narrative of his spiritual awakening, but not written in his own hand, is reproduced in McCallum, 123–45, with a brief introduction. Though McCallum offered them as "interesting examples of the heart searching and religious enthusiasm of the time," the letters are the far more revealing struggle of a young man, not more than a late adolescent, of profound spiritual capacity, his self-confidence totally undermined, against guilt and inadequacy; and of his seeking relief in pouring out his soul to his spiritual mentor. McCallum seemed not to hear the cry *de profundis* which rises from this letter—today so much more clearly recognized in the familiar struggle with alcohol and drugs. By the time Joseph began a spiritual rehabilitation, it was too late, his health undermined and beyond recovery. The story of his life, though redeemed in his latter services to the cause of peace, is tragic and heartrending.

14. McClure notes that the senior class "read metaphysics, theology, natural and political law," and that "the study of the Hebrew and other Oriental languages [e.g., Chaldee, or Aramaic] as also the French language is recommended to the students" (*Memoirs* 154).

There is further record that at a "meeting of the President and other executive officers of the college held Dec. 26th, 1804," the following action was taken: "RESOLVED, that no person shall be admitted a member of the Freshman Class in this college, for the year 1806, unless he be found, on examination, thoroughly to understand the whole of the Greek New Testament, Cicero's select Orations, Virgil's Æneid and Georgicks and the fundamental rules of Arithmetick." There follows the specific curriculum of study for each of the four years (*The Repository*, 19 Oct. 1805, Dartmouth College Archives).

15. Foster, 606.

16. *The New Hampshire Latin Grammar, comprehending all the necessary rules in orthography, etymology, syntax, and prosody; with explanatory and critical notes, and an appendix by John Smith, A.M., Professor of the Learned Languages, at Dartmouth College* (Boston, 1802), 12.

17. Ibid.; 65–86 passim.

18. Peter Bien, in the communication to the author noted above, offers the following criticism: "True, we once more are multi-lingual and multi-ethnic. True, we are still struggling with literacy. But where is Wheelock's unifying vision? Where is the 'providential' aspect of 'fragmented lives'? How many teachers believe in the moral purposes of instruction or, even if they do believe in it, are willing to proclaim this belief openly? In all these ways, the Dartmouth that I know seems eons distant from the Founder's hopes and accomplishments."

19. Jonathan Edwards, *The Freedom of the Will*, The Work of Jonathan Edwards, vol. 1, ed. Paul Ramsey (New Haven: Yale University Press, 1957), 431.

Thomas J. Siegel

Professor Stephen Sewall and the Transformation of Hebrew at Harvard

Historians have traditionally presented the story of the study of Hebrew at Harvard as the decline of the subject from its promising introduction into the curriculum in the college's first years to its ultimate banishment from the required courses in the late eighteenth century. Most of the earlier accounts begin with an examination of the importance of Hebrew to the New England Puritans and of the hopes of Henry Dunster, Harvard's first president, to nurture in the students a love for his favorite subject. Unfortunately, the students, for the most part, did not share Dunster's zeal, and as a result the study of Hebrew began an almost immediate decline, which continued through the colonial period, broken only by the occasional moments of renewed interest that occurred when the college hired its first Hebrew instructor in 1722 or when it installed its first Hebrew professor in 1765. Finally, in 1785, Hebrew was made an "elective," a sure sign that it had lost its status as one of the more important subjects.

Though many of the details of this story are well documented in the earlier accounts, I would propose a somewhat different conclusion. Rather than telling the story as one of extended decline, I would argue that the study of Hebrew went through a transformation during the mid-eighteenth century, at about the same time that the philosophical assumption that served as the foundation for all of the college's curriculum was changing. That is, the seventeenth-century Puritan belief that all knowledge was interconnected and could be taught by a single tutor using Ramean deductive logic was being challenged and transformed by the more modern concept that individual subjects should be examined independently and should be taught by specialists using the empirical method. This transformation with regard to the study of Hebrew can be seen in the different goals contemplated and the different methods used by its two eighteenth-century instructors. Judah Monis was appointed instructor because he was thought to possess rabbinical knowledge of the Old Testament, and after his conversion to Protestantism provided evidence of Harvard's ongoing role in God's glorious plan for New England. Trained in the traditional methods, Monis tutored, using recitations—that is, memorization and repetition—to teach the rules of the language. In later years, Stephen Sewall was elected professor because he was one of the best scholars of his generation, an expert in several subjects, but most especially oriental languages. Trained in the modern methods, Sewall lectured, encouraging his students to examine the language and history of the Hebrew Bible as they would the sources of human knowledge or the natural laws of the heavens. Furthermore, in his lectures, Sewall engaged the students in the academic debates of his day, providing the sources and the contexts for later study. Ultimately, these differences do not signal a decline in the study of Hebrew. Rather they reveal the more remarkable reconceptualization of the philosophical goals and pedagogical methods that had occurred in nearly all the courses at Harvard College during the eighteenth century.

The study of Hebrew at Harvard in the seventeenth century was one part of the legacy that the founders brought with them from their Puritan colleges at Cambridge and Oxford. For many of the first generation of ministers and magistrates, Hebrew was one of the three "learned" languages and considered perhaps the most important of the three for two significant reasons. First, knowledge of Hebrew provided the Puritan scholar with the possibility of removing from God's first revelation the layers of confused interpretation that had been added by medieval scholars. Though New England was a somewhat isolated community after the great migration in the 1630s, it was never cut off from the intellectual trends in England that formed and guided its belief in the truth of Scripture. Second, through the study of the Hebrew Bible in the original language the New England Puritans gained a powerful reinforcement for their typological analysis of their own important role in God's teleological plan.

Almost from the beginning, however, the tutors had difficulty convincing the students that the study of Hebrew was as important as that of Latin and Greek.[1] Part of the problem may have been that the students already had some knowledge of Latin and Greek upon entering college and that most of the texts used were in those other languages. The only Hebrew text used by the undergraduates beyond the several grammars was the Hebrew Bible, and then it was generally used for translation practice only.[2] The study of Hebrew, therefore, was perceived as an extraneous means rather than as a significant end. Rarely after the first decades was the language studied by the undergraduates for its intrinsic beauty or its rhetorical power. Nevertheless, it remained part of the required curriculum.

Later in the century, several graduate students did show an interest in the subject; in their commencement quaestiones, these students declaimed on several of the topics that had occupied the study of the Christian scholars during the seventeenth century. Cotton Mather, later one of the leading ministers of his generation in Boston, and Gurdon Saltonstall, later the governor of Connecticut and one of the founders of Yale, both defended, for their masters' quaestiones in 1681 and 1687 respectively, the affirmative side of the question of the divine origin of vowel points. Stephen Mix argued the affirmative side of the question of whether the present Hebrew letters were the original ones.[3] But, despite these examples, there was no general revival of the subject, in large part because its popularity depended on the variable skills of the tutors and on the changeable interests of the students. During the first two decades of the eighteenth century, the turnover in the tutorial staff and the reforms in other subjects, especially logic and astronomy, meant that Hebrew would not get the same kind of attention that it had during the previous century under Dunster and Charles Chauncy.

At just that time, however, the Harvard Corporation was approached by Judah Monis, a rabbinically trained scholar recently arrived from New York, who offered the college a new Hebrew grammar that he had prepared and by implication his services for instructing the students. At first, the corporation ignored Monis's offer.[4] But after the tutors turned to him for help in training themselves in Hebrew, a few of the college governors recognized the advantages to the college if they hired a full-time Hebrew instructor. The Reverend Benjamin Colman, a member of the Harvard Corporation, was at that moment trying to increase the size of the faculty by adding a number of independent scholars, and he had just received word that Thomas Hollis, a wealthy benefactor in England, was planning to endow a chair in Divinity, giving Harvard its first professorship. Given Monis's talents and his reputation, which had been enhanced by his conversion to Protestantism in a public ceremony in Cambridge in March 1722, Colman tried to convince the Board of Overseers to hire Monis not just as an instructor but as the first Hebrew professor.[5]

In April 1722, the overseers demurred and the corporation went ahead and hired Monis simply as an instructor. In the rules for his position, it was established that Monis would teach Hebrew to all the undergraduates, except the freshmen, four days a week and that he would use the accepted tutorial method: copying the grammar, reciting it, construing, parsing, translating, composing, and reading with points.[6] In 1734, following the trend toward having the students use printed texts rather than copied manuscripts, the corporation recommended and then later supervised the publication of one thousand copies of Monis's grammar, which he was permitted to sell to the students.[7]

Monis's tenure at Harvard was never a completely happy one. First, he was constantly plagued by financial problems that were not of his own making.[8] Second, Monis had to deal with the general suspicion toward him expressed by some members of the college and the New England community.[9] Though he had the encouragement of the corporation,[10] Monis did not have the support of all the faculty,[11] or of the students, who increasingly took out their general frustrations about the tutorial method by viciously ridiculing him.[12] By the end of his tenure, Monis's teaching schedule was reduced to roughly one day a week.[13] Most historians have argued that the reason for this reduction has to do with the students' attitude toward Monis or toward the subject he taught. There is, however, another explanation.

During the eighteenth century, Harvard's curriculum went through an important change. The simple explanation of this change is that the curriculum grounded in seventeenth-century Puritanism was replaced by one based upon the ideas of the eighteenth-century Enlightenment. But this explanation is too linear and fails to take into account how the changing goals and methods used in the study of all subjects, but especially Hebrew, reflected the college's desire to balance its adherence to orthodoxy with its excitement for the new.

For their theory of education with regard both to content and to method, the founders of Harvard and their immediate successors, drawing upon English and European sources, followed the essential idea that the whole body of knowledge could, if properly organized, be reconnected into a circle, called "encyclopedia." They also believed that this circle could be taught by a single master to a whole class of students if the students were correctly trained in the well-established methods of scholarship. Briefly stated, the tradition of "encyclopedia" was based on the accepted truth that after the Fall of man, the precise correspondence between God's perfect idea of creation and man's understanding of that idea had become obscured. It was the goal of Christian scholars to find the way back to that true correspondence. The quest, using the proper method of deductive logic—"dictum de omni et nullo"—began with the contemplation of knowledge revealed in God's visible creations. Initially, this meant the two Testaments, but after the Renaissance it also included the natural world. The final step in the process should be man's recreation of God's creation, however imperfect that must necessarily be.[14]

What made the manifestations of God's revelations difficult for man to comprehend and the recreation of them difficult for man to demonstrate was the fact that fallen man could no longer conceive of knowledge in the way that God could. For God, all knowledge and all creation were part of a single, simple idea. For man, since the Fall, knowledge was divided into diverse subjects, having no easily discernible connections. To see it as a whole, that unattainable but necessary goal, required the proper ordering of knowledge and the proper method, along with supreme diligence. Therefore the tutors required the students to learn the traditional schema and methods, trusting that eventually the students would be able to understand the body of accepted knowledge. In this context, the study of Hebrew was essential for the true scholar, not because Hebrew was one of the subjects in the circle, but rather because it was important to study the original documents—since God's truths were contained in the several revelations in their original forms—to be able to judge the true axioms from the false.

The dominance of this view of knowledge and method was of course challenged during the late seventeenth century by the works of John Locke, Isaac Newton, and others. But at Harvard, the Puritan tradition lived on in the curriculum longer than it did among the leading thinkers of the day. At first, Locke's work was rejected at Harvard because his emphasis on sensations as the source of knowledge and his rejection of innate ideas was seen as a threat to the accepted idea of man's ability to judge the truth of any proposition without relying on the vagaries of human sense experience. But during the middle decades of the eighteenth century, Locke's ideas concerning knowledge and method were gradually incorporated into the curriculum through the use of mediating texts, written by dissenting scholars such as the Reverend Isaac Watts. The works of Newton were more readily accepted at the college, because, by the late seventeenth century, most New England Puritan scholars had accepted the study of the natural world as an integral part of the study of God's creation. Nevertheless, the college officials were still careful to warn that an overemphasis on natural truth could lead to errors.[15]

A major consequence of the eventual acceptance of Locke and Newton was the reorientation of the educational system toward individual subjects and academic specialists. The older idea of the circle and the tutorial method was not completely discarded, but it was no longer the main pedagogical focus. Rather the search for new knowledge and the use of specialists was preferred, and the modern approach was finally recognized by the college governing bodies in reforms that were proposed in the 1750s. At Harvard, the additions to the teaching staff after 1720 foreshadowed this change in the overall approach to education; the faculty expanded from a group of three tutors to a collection of four tutors (each one still responsible for a class), two Hollis professors (in Divinity and in Natural Philosophy), and an instructor in Hebrew. The professors' lectures, especially those by the natural philosophy professor, were more popular by far than the tutors' recitations or the instructor's classes.[16]

Within this changing educational environment we can now better explain the problems faced by Judah Monis in his attempt to use traditional methods for the instruction of Hebrew. By the 1750s, his classes must have seemed like a relic of some ancient time. When he retired in 1760, both the college reformers and the students were probably relieved. In October 1761, the corporation chose as Monis's successor Stephen Sewall, who, though a recent graduate, was already known as a specialist in languages. Sewall began immediately to devise ways to improve the basic teaching method. Drawing upon sources from the library (or available by purchase from Boston bookseller Jeremiah Condy), Sewall prepared a new Hebrew grammar for his students' use.[17]

Soon after Sewall's appointment, the reformers pressed forward with their other plans to alter the college's mode of formal instruction from a tutorial system based upon generalist tutors to one based upon specialist professors. One part of this plan included the establishment of endowed chairs in important subjects.[18] With regard to the study of Hebrew, the reformers were lucky to have already found a donor, Thomas Hancock, a Boston merchant, who had revealed his interest in creating a chair in the oriental languages by leaving a substantial legacy in his will. In October 1764, three months after Hancock died, Sewall was elevated to the new position, the first chair in Hebrew among the several American colleges.

The teaching requirements for the Hancock professorship in Hebrew and other Oriental Languages followed those established for the two previous professorships.[19] The professor was expected to deliver a course of "public" lectures on the history and on the genius and idiom of Hebrew, Chaldee, and other oriental languages. Also, he was expected to hold "private" lectures, for which the students were charged an extra fee; the format for these lectures probably resembled the regular tutorial work in Hebrew. Finally, the professor was expected to set aside two or three hours a week to instruct privately those students who wanted to go beyond the normal undergraduate course to learn the other oriental languages in depth. The key feature of the professor's program was his "public" lectures on the scholarly importance of the Hebrew language; these "new" lectures were to be attended by all the students.

In June 1765, Sewall was installed as the first Hancock professor of Hebrew in a public ceremony.[20] In December, Sewall delivered his first of seventy-two lectures. In general, he delivered a lecture every other Monday during the school year, though the full series of his seventy-two lectures was not completed even over a four-year course. Rather, Sewall delivered his last lecture in the series in 1774, more than eight years after he began. He did begin again in the fall of 1769, and in 1773, 1777, and 1781, weaving his few new lectures in with the older ones.[21]

The scope of the series was broad. From the first, Sewall made it clear that he would touch upon the key debate which engaged the Christian Hebraic scholars in England at the time.[22] Among those issues was the question of the history of the original language and letters, with special mention of the significances of the Israelites' dispersion after the tower of Babel was built, and of their return from the Babylonian captivity.[23] Sewall also argued against the divine origin of vowel points, employing an extensive "historical" analysis to pinpoint the time of their man-made origin.[24] In other lectures, he explained the value of Benjamin Kennicott's collation of the manuscript Hebrew Bibles, which was in the process of being completed in England in the 1760s.[25] And Sewall spent a great deal of time on the historical and grammatical genius of Hebrew as well as Chaldee, Syriac, Samaritan, Ethiopic, Arabic, and Persic.[26] Beyond these essential topics, Sewall also digressed occasionally to cover other aspects of the study of Hebrew and the Old Testament. For example, he delivered several lectures explaining and then refuting John Hutchinson's literal reading of the Hebrew Bible;[27] and he gave one lecture on the various theories concerning the rules of Hebrew poetry, thereby extending his coverage beyond philology and history to include belles-lettres.[28] In his later lectures, Sewall dealt with other issues, including an extended discussion of the origin of the Book of Job,[29] the Mosaic practice of circumcision—refuting the arguments of Voltaire,[30] the location of Sodom and Gomorrah, and the general importance of the Shechinah (the tabernacling of God with man).[31]

Given this range of material in Sewall's lectures, we can discern the new meaning that the study of Hebrew came to have at Harvard in the late 1760s. Having studied under Monis, Sewall understood well the problem of trying to teach Hebrew using solely the traditional recitation method. As a consequence, Sewall attempted to establish a new, more modern approach more in agreement with that used in the other "subjects" at the college—particularly the lectures in the sciences by Professor John Winthrop and the readings in history and politics that the students were doing on their own.[32] In his very first lecture, Sewall gave us a clue of how things had changed by the mid-eighteenth century. Of course, there were religious reasons for learning Hebrew, but, he argued, "setting aside the consideration of the oriental languages in point of religion, and viewing them merely as languages, they will afford exercise for the acutest parts, and give pleasure to the most curious." There are, he admitted, two reasons why students had avoided studying Hebrew in the recent past. They thought that it was too difficult and that it was a "dry, [and] unentertaining study, fit only for men of dull and plodding genius, who want abilities to excel in politer and more valuable knowledge." The truth of the matter, however, Sewall argued, is that freed from "useless incumbrances of points and accents," it is "a language not only easy but delightful," and one that opened the reader to other oriental languages as well as Greek and Latin. It was Sewall's intention therefore to strip away the medieval schema and rabbinical practices that had prevented the students from seeing the Hebrew language in what he thought was its purest, most natural light.[33]

In order to win students over to his new approach, Sewall had to convince them that the study of this learned language could be modern and scientific, with laws comparable to those found in Newtonian science, and explanations of the causes of events comparable to those found in the best histories. During his many lectures, he continually commented on the need to use the most accurate interpretation of a particular passage of Scripture or the most precise meaning of a particular word, which always happened to correspond to the verifiable and empirical truth, equal in every case with "common sense," the rational theory that had come to dominate the study of logic and metaphysics at Harvard in the 1760s. For any given issue, Sewall was careful to lay out the several possible arguments, trying to make clear that a fair accounting of other points of view was a prerequisite of modern scholarship. Then he answered each of these arguments, point by point, leading to his own explanation, derived from a wealth of scholarly works, but always argued using his own combination of logic and history.

An example of Sewall's approach will make clear his desire and his method to modernize the study of Hebrew. In the first lectures, Sewall made his main point, that the original language had to have been the "simplest" because it was the language that had come from God and had not yet been corrupted by human experience.[34] Having established that point, Sewall could later refer back to it when he came to discuss the controversy over which of the various known languages and letters fit most closely the designation of the original language. For Sewall and the Christian Hebraists that he followed, the first language was ancient Hebrew, but not the present day Hebrew. He argued that the Hebrew of the Christian era was actually derived from Chaldee and that the true original language passed from the ancient Hebrew through Samaritan to Phoenician to Greek to Latin. Having planted the idea that "simplicity" was a prerequisite of the true original language, he could then argue that the original Hebrew letter *bet* had only one sound, as it did in Phoenician and Greek, not the two possible sounds, *bet* or *vet*, it had in modern Hebrew, depending on whether or not it had a *dagesh* (a point in the middle of a Hebrew consonant that denotes the strengthening of that letter). According to Sewall, this corruption of the original language was a later addition of the "Jewish Grammarians," as he called them. (And that is the nicest name that he called them.) Sewall told his students that God would not have made the original language so complicated that a letter could have two sounds.[35] Sewall used the same argument with regard to the vowel points. Because these points complicated and even distorted the true meaning of words in the original texts, they could not be of divine origin. Instead, he argued, following the beliefs of modern Christian scholars, that the soundless consonants in Hebrew—*aleph*, etc.—were intended to have sounds and therefore made the vowel points unnecessary.[36]

Of course, not all of Sewall's lectures were philological disputations. Instead, he understood the need to appeal to the students' other interests, particularly natural science and history; he spent several lectures discussing the importance of not supposing that all Old Testament accounts of miracles should be accepted as literal truth when the phenomena could be accounted for on natural principles. Yet Sewall did not intend to substitute natural explanations for theological ones in every case. He also argued quite seriously that when examining certain passages of Scripture natural principles should not be manipulated to deny the true possibility of an act of Providence.[37] Here was a combination of the modern and the orthodox.

At the heart of this line of discourse was perhaps a new version of the older Puritan notion that man should study the collected fragments of divine truth, whatever their location and circumstance, in order to discover the correct recreation of God's simple, perfect idea. Yet true to his own time also, Sewall's theories always required a rational and empirical explanation. In his lectures, Sewall argued that scholars had to learn not only the ancient language of the Old Testament precisely as it was given to the people of Israel, but also, because of human corruptions, the languages derived from that first language, the manners and customs of the peoples who lived near the first chosen people, the geography and natural history of the Holy Land of the Jews, and the laws of nature, ultimately in order to discover the "design of providence in the several dispensations, in which the Deity hath been pleased to correspond with the human race."[38]

Sewall was successful in his first years in encouraging some of the students to study Hebrew.[39] Over time, however, even though his "public" lectures were quite popular, his efforts did not lead to a broad and sustained revival of the subject. Of course, getting all the students to learn Hebrew was neither his nor the college's primary goal anymore. The idea that each student should learn all the subjects had given way to specialization even among the students. Nevertheless, the college officials continued to consider Hebrew as one of the three learned languages. And in 1783 Hebrew orations were included with the other learned languages in the general examination plan, during which students earned gold medals by voluntarily demonstrating their expertise in the several subjects.

At about this time, Professor Sewall's health began to fail. After the death of his wife and several unsuccessful attempts to deal with his problem with alcoholism, Sewall's coursework began to suffer, and in 1785 he was removed from his professorship.[40] The corporation quickly elected a successor, Eliphalet Pearson, but also made two significant changes in the statutes of the professorship. Given the burden the extra fee for attending the professor's "private" lectures placed on some parents in hard economic times, the corporation voted to let students out of those lectures if they produced a "certificate" from their parents. And, because of the lighter load, Pearson was told to add the teaching of English grammar to his other duties.[41] From a seventeenth-century perspective, it might seem that the study of Hebrew at Harvard, no longer a requirement, had become less important. But, given the larger changes taking place with regard to the whole conception of the curriculum, we can now understand that the study of Hebrew had been transformed and modernized by the addition of the professor's "public" lectures, joining Divinity, Natural Philosophy, and the Medical Sciences as the most specialized and most respected courses in Harvard's late eighteenth-century version of the circle of knowledge.

Notes

1. The first record we have of the students' displeasure came as early as 1653, when one of the tutors, Michael Wigglesworth, complained that the students did not want to study the holy language. John L. Sibley and Clifford K. Shipton, *Biographical Sketches of Those Who Attended Harvard College* (Cambridge, Mass., 1873–1973), 17 vols., covering the classes of 1642–1771, 1:265–66.

2. The extant records reveal that the students probably used Wilhelm Schickard's *Horologium Hebraeum*, John Udall's *The Key to the Holy Tongue*, and the several works by the elder and the younger Johannes Buxdorfs. See Samuel Eliot Morison, *Harvard College in the Seventeenth-Century* (Cambridge, Mass., 1936), 203–204; and Robert H. Pfeiffer, "The Teaching of Hebrew in Colonial America," *Jewish Quarterly Review* 45 (1954–55): 366–67.

3. Pfeiffer, 367–69.

4. See Milton M. Klein, "A Jew at Harvard in the 18th Century," *Proceedings of the Massachusetts Historical Society* 97 (1985): 138–40.

5. Colman announced his hopes in a preface he wrote to a series of three lectures published by Monis on the "truth" of the second dispensation, written with the intention of revealing Monis's broad knowledge of Protestant theology. See George Foot Moore, "Judah Monis," *Proceedings of the Massachusetts Historical Society* 52 (May 1919): 293–94, for a discussion of Colman's hint to the Board of Overseers. For a discussion of the ideas in Monis's three essays and the help that he probably received in their preparation from Colman and Increase Mather, see Moore, 302–306; and Klein, 140–41.

A second value in Monis's conversion had to do with the Protestant reading of the history of the work of redemption. According to the seventeenth-century Puritan reading of that history that was passed on to the eighteenth-century New Englanders, the conclusion of the history of God's work of redemption would begin with the conversion of the Jews to Christianity. Word of Monis's conversion was announced in newspapers in New England, and was the topic of many letters between New England Puritans and their correspondents in England and Scotland. Not all Harvard officials or friends of the college in America and in Great Britain were convinced of Monis's sincerity. See Klein, 140.

6. See Moore, 295–96. Later that year, the overseers approved the appointment, though they advised the corporation to renew the appointment on a yearly basis. Monis accepted the appointment, though he was concerned about the salary offered him. Later, he successfully petitioned the corporation for an addition.

According to Moore, the overseers passed all of the several rules except the law that granted the Hebrew instructor the same disciplinary powers as the tutors. Moore writes that this was because they did not trust Monis. A more correct explanation has to do with the overseers not wanting to lower the authority of the tutors to the level of the instructor. At the time, the governing boards were locked in a controversy over the right of the tutors to have places on the corporation. Several of the overseers supported the tutors and therefore had other motives for acting as they did on the grant of power to Monis. See Thomas Jay Siegel, "Governance and Curriculum at Harvard College in the Eighteenth Century" (Ph.D. diss., Harvard University, 1990), chap. 1.

7. See Moore, 298. At the same time, several other members of the faculty were preparing and publishing a version of William Brattle's *Compendium Logicae*, the catechetical text in the logic recitations.

As to the pedagogical value of Monis's grammar, George Foot Moore has written that the text was not easy for beginners, starting "with close-packed pages enumerating and classifying the various functions of the so-called 'servile' letters in word-formation, inflection, and syntax," but Moore also notes that Monis was aware of the problem and appended a maxim that beginners "should not perplex themselves about any Rule that at first view seems difficult. . . ." See Moore, 298.

8. In 1730, the town of Cambridge assessed a tax upon his salary. Because this tax was contrary to the college charter, the corporation supported Monis and the tax was eventually dropped. Later during the economic hard times in the 1740s, he had trouble keeping up with the inflationary effects on his salary, and once again he had to fend off the efforts of Cambridge to tax him. This time, the town tried to tax Monis and Professor John Winthrop because they were faculty members who were not specifically named in the charter. Once again, the corporation supported the rights of the members of the college faculty. See Siegel, "Governance and Curriculum at Harvard College in the Eighteenth Century," chap. 2.

9. For a discussion of the community's attitude, see Klein, 142 and 143.

10. In particular, Colman maintained his friendship, as did Tutor Henry Flynt, who aided Monis's efforts to continue his studies in the New Testament and Protestant theology by lending Monis quite a few works from his personal library. See Edward Thomas Dunn, "The Diary of Henry Flynt," Mss. typescript in two vols., Harvard University Archives.

11. Many of the younger tutors and professors, some of whom he had once taught, bickered with him over discipline cases and over classroom use.

12. See Sibley, 7:643. Three contemporary opinions give some sense of the attitude toward Monis and his methods by the end of his tenure. Stephen Sewall, who was a student of Monis, wrote of his predecessor in a letter to President Samuel Johnson of King's College in New York, "I was taught the rudiments of Hebrew by Mr. Monis. But, as he understood but little of grammar, I must confess, while I attended his instructions and studied his grammar only, I never could discover any 'form or comeliness' in the language." Edward Wigglesworth, Jr., a student of Monis in the 1740s and later the successor to his father as the Hollis professor of Divinity, wrote to his friend, Sewall, soon after Monis's death in 1764, wondering if perhaps an "insolent letter," written by Sewall to Monis, might not have contributed to the latter's death. Wigglesworth concludes his letter with a comment about the future home of Monis: "I would hope he is gone to Abraham's Bosom, as he used to term it. If he is, his death is not a loss to himself. His friends are certainly freed from a very troublesome guest." For both letters, see *American Jewish Archives* (1954), 58–59 and 61.

Finally, Thaddeus Mason Harris, though not a student at the college while Monis was teaching, nevertheless had collected enough contemporary opinions about Monis to offer the following remarks concerning the instructor's teaching style: "He was appointed to teach a language, which though he perfectly understood himself, as a grammarian and philologist, he was not happy in enabling others to understand. He retained, moreover, a great fondness for rabbinical lore, and his criticisms were so abstruse, and his conversation and manners so uncourteous that he did not conciliate the respect of his pupils, and attendance on his teaching was deemed a disgusting requisition." See the prefatory comments in the Mss. Sewall lectures, Papers of Stephen Sewall, Harvard University Archives.

13. See Benjamin A. Peirce, *A History of Harvard University from its*

Foundation, in the Year 1636, to the Period of the American Revolution (Cambridge, Mass., 1833), 233; and Lee M. Friedman, "Judah Monis, First Instructor in Hebrew at Harvard University," *Publications of the American Jewish Historical Society* 22 (1914): 17.

14. See Elizabeth Flower and Murray G. Murphey, *The History of American Philosophy* (New York, 1977), 21–40; Norman Fiering, "President Samuel Johnson and the Circle of Knowledge," *WMQ*, 3d ser., 28 (1971): 199–236; Wilbur Samuel Howell, *Eighteenth-Century British Logic and Rhetoric* (Princeton, N.J., 1971), 259; and Perry Miller, *The New England Mind: The Seventeenth Century* (Cambridge, Mass., 1939), 154–80.

15. See Arthur Kaledin, "The Mind of John Leverett" (Ph.D. diss., Harvard University, 1965).

16. The trend toward independence was evident in other subjects as well. A quick glance at the commencement theses for the years from 1730 to 1760 reveals the strong student interest in subjects—some new, others old and redefined—that focus on nature and natural truths. For example, see the theses in ethics and politics, in mathematics, and in rhetoric (Harvard University, Commencement theses and quaestiones, Harvard University Archives).

17. Stephen Sewall, *An Hebrew Grammar, collected chiefly from those of Mr. Israel Lyons, Teacher of Hebrew in the University of Cambridge; and the Rev. Richard Grey, D.D., Rector of Hinton, in Northamptonshire, to which is subjoined a Praxis, taken from the Sacred Classics, and containing a Specimen of the whole Hebrew Language: with a Sketch of the Hebrew Poetry, as retrieved by Bishop Hare* (Boston, Mass., 1763). Sewall bought an "Arabic Psalter," "the Westminster Hebrew Grammar," and "Lyon's Hebrew Grammar" from Condy (see Jeremiah Condy Accountbook, American Antiquarian Society).

During the fall of 1762, Sewall took the following works out of the college library: Johannes Buxtorf, *Lexicon Hebraicum et Chaldaicum* (1607); Castelli E., *Biblia Polyglotta complectentia textus originales Hebraicos cum Pentat. Samarit: Chaldaicos Graecos versionumque antiquarium quicquid comparari poterat* (1657); John Michael Dilherrus, *Eclogae Sacrae Novi Testamenti, cum Manuali Lexici Syriaci* (1638); Thomas Erpenius, *Grammatica Arabica* (1613); John Guyse, *The Practical Expositor; or, an Exposition of the New Testament, in the form of a Paraphrase* (1739–52); *The Hebrew Bible*; Daniel Whitby, *Paraphrase and Commentary on the New Testament; with a Chronological Index and Alphabetical Table of the Places* (1703–09); Johannes Buxtorf, *Thesaurus Grammaticus Linguae Hebraecae* (1609); John Leusden, *Onomasticum Sacrum* (1665); Samuel Bochart, *Geographia Sacra* (1646); Lewis Capellus, *Critica Sacra* (1650); and Johannnes Cocceius, *Lexicon et Commentarius Sermonis Hebraici et Chaldaici* (1669). See Harvard University, Library, Student Charging Records, Harvard University Archives. Given the depth of his readings, one may speculate that he was already preparing a series of lectures by 1762.

In a letter to Grey in September 1764 asking for his support in replacing the volumes of Hebraic studies lost in the fire that had destroyed almost all of the library collection, Sewall remarked that the corporation had decided to use Lyons's work "in the room of a very bad one, which had been used here before." The corporation had ordered that Lyons's work be republished in Boston, but "that such alterations & additions should be made in it, as their Hebrew instructor should think fit." Sewall had just then received Grey's work, a new and easy method of learning Hebrew without vowel points, and found that he "was agreeably surprised to find a language, hitherto generally esteemed jejune, rough & uncouth, restored almost to its primitive beauty & uniformity. It appeared to be so well adapted to remove the common prejudices against the Hebrew language, & to render the learning of it easy & pleasant, that I determined to transcribe as much of it into Mr. Lyons', as our proposed brevity would permit." The published version of the grammar included the vowel points, though Sewall acknowledged the rules he established for using the points to "fail in many instances." Sewall also mentioned his hope that "the revival of Oriental literature in Europe . . . in time will forward its cultivation in America, when the writings of those gentlemen, who have thrown so much light upon it, shall become more generally known here." This last prayer begins the paragraph in which Sewall made his pitch for Grey to send copies of his works to the new library. A copy of the letter exists in manuscript form in the Harvard Archives' copy of Sewall's grammar. It also has been published in Lee M. Friedman, *Publications of the American Jewish Historical Society* (1949), 147–49.

18. A second part of the reformers' plan was to alter the teaching responsibilities of the tutors, so that they would be responsible for a subject (or a group of related subjects) for the whole school rather than for all subjects for a single class. (The four tutors were responsible for Latin; Greek, Logic, Ethics, and Metaphysics; and Mathematics, Natural Philosophy, Geography, and Astronomy, respectively.) Finally, the reformers also appointed a French instructor, who would teach those students who wanted training in that modern language. See Siegel, "Governance and Curriculum at Harvard College in the 18th Century," chap. 5.

19. See Harvard University, Corporation, College Books, 1–6: minutes and other records, 1636–1893 [hereafter Corporation Records], 4 June 1765, Harvard University Archives.

20. Stephen Sewall was born in York, in the district of Maine, in 1734, the youngest of ten children. His father was a tanner by trade, and young Stephen was apprenticed to a joiner at an early age to raise the funds necessary for his education. After completing his academic preparation with a local minister, Sewall entered Harvard at the age of 23, quite a bit older than the average student in his class (16). During his college years, Sewall developed an interest in many subjects—the classics, rhetoric, history, and the sciences. But his favorite subject was oriental languages.

Soon after taking his bachelor's degree in 1761, Sewall was appointed to fill the vacant Hebrew instructorship. The position as it was funded at the time, however, did not provide a sufficient stipend, so Sewall spent his free time serving as the schoolmaster in Cambridge, the college librarian, and later the college butler. Then, in May 1763, the Board of Overseers voted to increase his teaching responsibilities at the college to include instruction for a part of one of the classes in the other learned languages, thereby helping out the tutors, who were overburdened by a recent increase in enrollment. At the request of the corporation, Sewall prepared a plan for the promotion of classical learning at the college. The plan was well received and generally implemented by the various governing boards. See "Stephen Sewall," *Sibley* 15:107–114.

21. Though the overall series was seventy-two lectures, the main body of material was covered in the first forty-five lectures, and he always completed those same lectures before he began the series over again. In his notebook, Sewall listed the dates that he delivered the lecture at the end of each lecture. See Stephen Sewall Papers, Harvard University Archives.

22. Sewall used the college library after it was reopened in 1766 extensively for the preparation of his lectures. See Student Charging Records, Harvard University Archives. Between 1766 and 1774, he took the following books out of the Library: Samuel Bochart, *Geographia Sacra* (1646); William Massey, *The Origin and Progress of Letters* (1763); Samuel Shuckford, *The Sacred and Profane History of the World, connected from the creation of the world to the dissolution of the Assyrian empire at the death of Sardanapalus, and to the declension of the kingdoms of Judah and Israel, under the reigns of Ahaz and Pekah* (1728); Charles Schaaf, *Novum Testamentum Syriacum, cum Versione Latina* (1708); William Warburton, *The Divine Legation of Moses demonstrated, on the Pronciples of a Religious Deist, from omissions of the Doctrine of a Future State of Rewards and Punishments in the Jewish Dispensation* (1737–38); Castelli, *S.S. Biblia Polyglotta complectentia textus originales Hebraicos cum Pentat. Samarit: Chaldaicos Graecos versionumque antiquarium quicquid comparari poterat* (1657); Lewish Capellus, *Critica Sacra* (1650); Benjamin Kennicott, *The State of the Printed Hebrew Text of the Old Testament Considered* (1753–60); Thomas Heath, *an Essay towards a new English Version of Job, from the Original Hebrew* (1756); Albert Schultens, *Liber Jobi cum nova versione et Commentario perpetuo* (1737); John Taylor, *The Hebrew Concordance, adapted to the English Bible* (1754); Humphrey Hody, *De Bibliorum Textibus Originalibus, Versionibus Graecis et Latin Vulgata libri* (1705); Samuel Pike, *Philosophia Sacra; or the Principles of Natural Philosophy, extracted from Divine Revelation* (1753); Robert Lowth, *Praelectiones de Sacra Poesi Hebraeorum* (1753); Thomas Erpenius, *Grammatica Arabica* (1613); Francis Masclef, *A Hebrew Grammar, according to the New Method, in which the points are discarded* (1716); George Otho, *Paleastra Linguarum: hoc est, capita prima quatuor Geneseos, Chadaice, Syriace, Samaritice, Arabice, Aethiopice, Persice* (1702); Moses Lowman, *a Paraphrase and Notes on the Revelation of St. John* (1737); James Macknight, *Harmony of the Four Gospels* (1756); Leonard Chappelow, *A Commentary on the Book of Job, in which are inserted, the Hebrew Text and English Translation* (1752); Lawrence Holden, *A Paraphrase on the books of Job, Psalms, Proverbs, and Ecclesiastes* (1764); James Macknight, *The Truth of the Gospel History* (1763); Edward Wells, *Sacred Geography; being a Geographical and Historical Account of Places mentioned in the Holy Scriptures* (1711–12); Hadrian Reland, *Palestina ex Monumentis veteribus illustrata, et Chartis geographicis accuratioribus adornata* (1714); George Campbell, *Dissertation on Miracles; containing an Examination of the principles advanced by David Hume* (1762); Henry Maundrell, *Journey from Aleppo to Jerusalem at Easter* (1703); Robert Clayton, *The Chronology of the Hebrew Bible vindicated* (1747); David Durell, *The Hebrew Text of the Parallel Prophecies of Jacob and Moses, relating to the Twelve Tribes* (1764); Thomas Erpenius, *Rudimenta Linguae Arabicae* (1620); Hugh Farmer, *A Dissertation on Miracles; designed to shew that they are arguments of a divine interposition, and ab-*

solute proof of the mission of a Prophet (1771); Edward Harwood, *A New Introduction to the Study and Knowledge of the New Testament* (1767); David Durell, *Critical Remarks on the Book of Job, Proverbs, Psalms, Ecclesiastes, and Canticles* (1772); Moses Lowman, *A Rationale of the Ritual of the Hebrew Worship* (1748); William Worthington, *An Essay on the Redemption of Man* (1743); John Taylor, *A Paraphrase and Notes on the Epistle to the Romans: to which is prefixed, a Key to the Apostolic Writings, or an Essay to explain the Gospel Scheme, and the principal Words, and Phrases the Apostles have used in describing it* (1745); Simon Patrick, *Commentary on the Historical Books of the Old Testament* (1727); Isaac Newton, *Observations on the Prophecies of Daniel, and the Apocalypse of St. John* (1733). These books are listed in the order that Sewall took them out.

23. See Sewall Lectures 1–11, Papers of Stephen Sewall, Harvard University Archives.

24. See Sewall Lectures 12–13.

25. See Sewall Lectures 15–16. Kennicott's project took over a decade, during which he searched all the libraries in England and many in Europe for Hebrew texts as well as other texts including the Samaritan Pentateuch. See "Benjamin Kennicott," *Dictionary of National Biography* (hereafter *DNB*) 11:10–12. Sewall greatly admired Kennicott and his work and he sent Kennicott several letters of personal support. See Benjamin Kennicott to Stephen Sewall, 14 May 1771 (received 26 August 1771), in the first volume of the Sewall lectures, Papers of Stephen Sewall, Harvard University Archives. In one letter, Sewall, joined by several of the Harvard tutors, sent Kennicott financial support (£1.1 each) for his projects. See Stephen Sewall to Benjamin Kennicott, 27 August 1771, Sewall Folder in the Wigglesworth Family Papers, Massachusetts Historical Society.

26. On Hebrew, see Sewall Lectures 19–22; on Chaldee, see Sewall Lectures 27–30; on Syriac, see Sewall Lectures 31–32; on Samaritan, see Sewall Lectures 24–35; on Ethiopic, see Sewall Lecture 36; on Arabic, see Sewall Lectures 38–39; and on Persic, see Sewall Lecture 43.

27. See Sewall Lectures 23–27.

28. See Sewall Lectures 44–45. Sewall began with an account of the rules according to Bishop Frances Hare. He had included a brief version of them in his grammar in 1763, in part on the recommendation in Richard Grey's introduction. Then he discussed Robert Lowth's refutation of Hare's rules, which Lowth had published in 1766. Sewall accepted Lowth's explanation, though he still applauded Hare's efforts. For information about Hare and Lowth, see "Frances Hare," *DNB* 7:1249; and "Robert Lowth," *DNB* 12:214. Sewall concluded the lecture with a discussion of the theory of John (?) Robertson on the poetry in the book of Job. "His hypothesis I confess appears to me founded upon more rational principles than any other I have seen; though I cannot say it gives entire satisfaction." Sewall Lectures 43.

29. See Sewall Lectures 54–58.

30. See Sewall Lectures 68–69.

31. See Sewall Lectures 64–67 and 71–72, respectively. Sewall later developed these last two lectures into pamphlets, which he published in the 1790s after he had retired from his professorship. *The Scripture Account of Shechinah* (1794); *The Scripture History Relating to the Overthrow of*

Sodom & Gomorrah, and to the Origin of the Salt Sea or Lake of Sodom (1796).

32. For a discussion of the students' formal and informal readings, see Siegel, "Governance and Curriculum at Harvard College in the Eighteenth Century," chaps. 6–8.

Sewall himself was something of an amateur scientist. "In October, 1780, he accompanied Professor [of Natural Philosophy] Samuel Williams on an expedition to observe the solar eclipse from a site behind the British lines at Penobscot. He had a real interest in science, and in 1782 he communicated to the American Academy of Arts and Sciences a paper on 'magnetical observations.' He also served the Academy as vice-treasurer and keeper of the cabinet." See *Sibley* 15:112.

33. See Sewall Lectures 1, 5–6.

34. In his first lecture, Sewall touched upon the scholarly debate concerning whether Adam innately had the knowledge of language, or gained that knowledge as he experienced life. Sewall concluded the discussion by explaining that "the truth, I imagine, lies, as it generally does, between the two extremes. In determining this point, we are not to attribute to the first man any other powers than what we now find belonging to his descendants; though we may suppose him to have possessed them in a much higher degree than they do, in their present lapsed state. Again we shall take for granted, that man was designed to enjoy all that rational happiness which his nature is capable of.

"In the first place, if no other powers are assigned to Adam, than what we now find among his posterity, we have then authority of one of the greatest masters of reason, Mr. Locke, to pronounce that the first man had no innate ideas, much less an innate language, which in the order of nature must be posterior to them. But,

"In the next place, if innocent man was designed, as the benignity of the Creator obliges us to believe he was, to enjoy all the rational happiness he was susceptible of, he must have had a language very soon after his creation; sooner than he could have possibly framed one by the mere exercise of his own powers. For the highest happiness of man consists in holding a correspondence with the Deity in acts of religious homage, & an amicable intercourse with his fellow creatures: Neither of which can in such a being as man, however they may in unembodied spirits, subsist without a language.

"Therefore I am inclined to believe, that the first language of man was derived from the immediate impressions of the Deity; so far only I mean, as to answer the purposes of his creation, till, from the hints now given, & by the exercise of his own powers, he should be able to make additions to his language as circumstances required. So far & no farther, I suppose language was given by divine inspiration." See Sewall Lectures 1, 11–13.

In the second lecture, Sewall argued that "simplicity . . . is the most essential property of the first language." See Sewall Lecture 2.

35. See Sewall Lecture 10. This lecture also revealed Sewall's anti-Semitism, especially in his criticism of Jewish scholars. "But considering that the Jews, even as early as the days of our Savior, had, through their traditions made void the divine law, it is not strange, that, from a like fanciful humour of innovation, they should have (destroyed the beautiful—[this was crossed out]) equally depraved their alphabet too."

36. See Sewall Lectures 11–12.

37. He made this point in lectures 33 and 42. In lecture 42, he used the example of the drying of the Red Sea. After disproving all of the natural explanations, he argued that the parting of the sea was a miracle. Then he showed how the feeding of Elijah in the desert could have been explained by natural phenomena.

38. See Sewall Lecture 33.

39. In 1771, nine of the fifteen thesis titles in the Grammaticae section of the commencement sheet were related to the Hebrew language. Several examples from 1771 include: (gram6) Verbs of the Hebrew language, which do not have a present tense, correspond more closely to nature than those of occidental languages; (gram7) Number and person pertain only to substantives. Ergo, (gram8) Number and person are attributed improperly to verbs; (gram12) Hebrew punctuation often permits certain letters to fall away from vowels. Ergo (gram13) Vowel punctuation has brought a great deal of harm to the Hebrew language; (gram14) From the Hebrew style in the Book of Job it is manifest how it was written around the time of Moses; (gram15) Knowledge of the character and idiom of the Hebrew language aids greatly in the understanding of the Old Testament.

A few of the thesis titles in later years were also drawn from Sewall's lectures. In 1778: (gram11) Hebrew is the simplest of all languages. From this it is inferred that (gram12) the Hebraic was the original language; in 1779: (gram10) One and the same language was used in Abraham's lifetime. From this it is inferred that (gram11) the confusion of languages was not the cause but a consequence of diaspora; and in 1783: (gram7) The holy Scriptures cannot be understood theologically unless they are first understood grammatically.

These thesis titles were translated from the Latin for me by Bruce Venarde.

40. See *Sibley* 15:112–14; and the Corporation Records, 23 September 1785, Harvard University Archives.

One kind friend attributed Sewall's health problems to another source: "A person, whose nerves are in a perpetual tremor from a long and laborious prying into the ramifications and import of words in Latin, Greek, Hebrew, Syriac, Arabick, Chaldee, Samaritan, Ethiopick, and Persick, may, to the careless observer, seem like one under the influence of inebriety." See *Sibley* 15:114.

41. See the Corporation Records, 4 June 1765, and 27 September and 4 October 1785, Harvard University Archives.

Notes on Contributors

ARTHUR A. CHIEL was a rabbi in Connecticut. He was author of *The Jews of Manitoba: A Social History* and editor of *Perspectives on Jews and Judaism: Essays in Honor of Wolfe Kelman.*

LOUIS FELDMAN, Professor of Classics, Yeshiva University, is author of *Josephus and Modern Scholarship, 1937–1980* (1984); *Josephus: A Supplementary Bibliography* (1986); and *Jew and Gentile in the Ancient World: Attitudes and Interactions from Alexander to Justinian* (1993). He is the co-editor, with G. Hata, of *Josephan Studies*, 4 vols. (in Japanese); *Josephus, Judaism, and Christianity* (1987), and *Josephus, the Bible, and History* (1989).

SHALOM GOLDMAN, Assistant Professor of Hebrew Studies, Dartmouth College, is writing a history of the study of the Hebrew language in America.

CYRUS GORDON, Professor Emeritus, Hebrew and Near Eastern Languages, New York University, is author of *The Ancient Near East* and *The Common Background of Greek and Hebrew Civilizations.*

LEO HERSHKOWITZ, Professor of History, Queens College, is author of *Wills of Early New York Jews: 1704–1793* and editor of *The Friedman Collection of American Jewish Colonial Correspondence: Letters of the Franks Family, 1733–1748.*

ARTHUR HERTZBERG, Professor Emeritus, Department of Religion, Dartmouth College, and Visiting Professor of the Humanities, New York University, is author of *The Jews in America: 400 Years of an Uneasy Encounter* (1989).

JACOB KABAKOFF, Professor Emeritus, Hebrew Studies, Lehman College of the City University of New York, has written extensively on Hebrew literature for English and Hebrew publications in Israel and America and has served as editor of the *Jewish Book Annual* since 1977. His books include: *Master of Hope: Selected Writings of Naphtali Herzl Imber* and the Hebrew volumes *Naphtali Herz Imber Baal Hatikvah, Shoharim ve-Ne'emanim* and *Halutze ha-Sifrut ha-Ivrit ba-Amerikah.*

NATHAN M. KAGANOFF, Librarian, American Jewish Historical Society, was editor of *Solidarity and Kinship: Essays on American Zionism* and editor of *Guide to America—Holy-Land Studies: 1620–1848.*

BARBARA KREIGER, Senior Lecturer, English Department, Dartmouth College, is author of *Living Waters: Myth, History and Politics of the Dead Sea* and has written introductions to new editions of *Baghdad Sketches*, by Freya Stark, and *Eothen*, by Alexander Kinglake. She is currently working on a book about American travellers to Palestine in the nineteenth century.

RICHARD H. POPKIN, Professor of Philosophy, University of California, Santa Barbara, is author of *The History of Scepticism from Erasmus to Spinoza* and editor of *The Philosophy of the Sixteenth and Seventeenth Centuries.*

THOMAS J. SIEGEL, Instructor in History and Literature at Harvard University, is the author of a forthcoming study of the Harvard curriculum in the seventeenth century.

KTZIAH SPANIER, Lecturer in Bible and Hebrew Studies, The New School for Social Research, is the editor of a forthcoming anthology of texts on women in the Bible and the Ancient Near East.

CHARLES STINSON, Associate Professor of Religion, Dartmouth College, has written on theology, law, and ethics.

GRANT UNDERWOOD, Director of the LDS Institute of Religion, Pomona, California, and author of a number of articles on comparative religion, was a Research Fellow at the American Jewish Archives.

MATTHEW I. WIENCKE, Professor Emeritus, Department of Classics, Dartmouth College, is the author of several articles on Greek art and Latin literature.

Index

UNIVERSITY PRESS OF NEW ENGLAND

publishes books under its own imprint and is the publisher for Brandeis University Press, Brown University Press, University of Connecticut, Dartmouth College, Middlebury College Press, University of New Hampshire, University of Rhode Island, Tufts University, University of Vermont, and Wesleyan University Press.

LIBRARY OF CONGRESS CATALOGING-IN-PUBLICATION DATA

Hebrew and the Bible in America : the first two centuries / edited by
    Shalom Goldman.
        p.   cm. — (Brandeis series in American Jewish history,
    culture, and life)
        Includes bibliographical references and index.
        ISBN 0–87451–617–X
        1. Hebraists, Christian—United States.   2. Hebrew language—
    Study and teaching—United States—History.   3. Ten lost tribes of
    Israel.   I. Goldman, Shalom.   II. Series.
    PJ4533.H43   1993
    492.4'097309032—dc20   92–56903